MW00989875

McGRAW-HILL

Language Arts

6-Trait Writing

Study Guide and Practice

GRADE 4

McGraw-Hill School Division
New York Farmington

6-Trait Writing

Study Guide and Practice

Here are six key tools that help make your writing clearer.

- Ideas and Content
- Organization
- Sentence Fluency
- Voice
- Word Choice
- Conventions

Ideas and Content

Is your writing clear and detailed?

Your **ideas** are the heart of your writing. They can also be called the main idea or theme, and must be clearly presented. Your writing should include **details** that keep the reader's attention and show what is really important about your topic.

- You need to know a lot about your topic. Be sure to do your research.
- Does your writing have interesting details that surprise the reader and make your piece fun to read?
- Be sure to *show* what is happening ("The flood water quickly began to rise from my ankles to above my knees.") rather than *telling* what happened ("The flood happened fast.")
- When brainstorming, be sure that the topic is small enough so your writing will be focused and clear. ("The History of Sailing" is a very big topic. You might narrow the topic to "Life on a Clipper Ship.")

Read John's **explanatory letter** below. Decide if you think his ideas are clear and if the details are well-chosen.

Dear Sue,

You said that a puffer fish is a weird pet. That may be true, but so what! We love Puffy and had good reasons for choosing him.

My family has always liked unusual pets. When I was little, I loved watching Amanda, our pig, pushing a bowling ball around the front lawn. Now, our new apartment is too tiny. We needed something unusual, but small.

The clerk at the pet store suggested fish or snakes. My mom is afraid of snakes so fish seemed like a better idea. ~~Snakes shed their skin several times a year.~~ Puffy is exciting to watch, because he can inflate to twice his normal size. The first time he did this, my sister laughed. ~~My little sister always liked Puffy.~~ We just had to bring him home with us.

Everyone has their own reason for liking particular pets. We think Puffy is the perfect pet for us.

Your friend,

John

The writer is clear about why he is writing this letter.

This surprising detail makes the reader want to know more.

This fact does not relate to the main idea.

John shows us how his sister feels.

- How can you tell if you have chosen a good topic to write about?
- What other details could John include that would make his ideas clear?

Writing

Organization

Is your writing well planned and easy to follow?

Organization is the **plan** or **pattern** you choose to put your ideas and details in order. Your plan may be to compare and contrast, state opinions and support them with facts, provide a time sequence, or any other clear pattern. The plan you choose depends on how you are going to explore your topic and how the details will help make your topic clear.

TIPS FOR BETTER WRITING

- Your beginning, or lead, should grab the reader's attention and give a hint about what is coming.
- All of your details add a little more information to your main idea or story. There is no extra information.
- The transitions from sentence to sentence and paragraph to paragraph create bridges from one idea to the next.
- Make sure to give the reader information in the right amounts at the right times. If you give too little information, the reader will get bored, and if you give too much, the reader might feel overwhelmed.
- Your ending makes a strong point.

Well-organized writing makes the reader want to know what will be coming up next. Rita wrote a **personal narrative**. Read it and see what you think of its organization.

I had that nightmare again! I dreamed I was a giant, juicy, red cherry.

I always loved cherries. They used to be one of my favorite foods in the world. ~~Cherries are grown all along the east coast of the United States~~. One day, my father came home with a huge bowl of freshly picked cherries, and I was as happy as could be.

The next morning, before my father left for work, he warned me not to eat too many cherries, but I could not help myself. I ate cherry after cherry after cherry. My whole face was covered in cherry juice, but I did not stop eating.

After about thirty minutes, I started to feel sick. I shouted for help. My mother came rushing in from the other room. She saw that I was sick and became worried. She took me to the car and drove me to the hospital.

The doctor gave me some medicine and told me that everything was going to be fine. I haven't eaten cherries in four years!

But I still have that dream.

This opening grabs the reader's attention.

This sentence does not relate to the main idea.

The paragraphs flow smoothly and use transitional words.

The ending leaves the reader something to think about.

- **How do you choose what beginning to use when writing?**
- **Why do you think Rita mentioned the dream again at the end?**

Sentence Fluency

Do you like the way your writing sounds when it is read aloud?

When you write, your sentences need to make sense, and they should sound like they fit together when read aloud.

- Check that your writing is easy to read aloud. It should sound natural and have an easy flow.
- Rewrite sentences that are hard to read aloud. Cut any words that seem to be extra.
- Use a variety of simple and complex sentences.
- Vary the beginnings of your sentences.
- Use words that show how your ideas connect.

Writing

As you read Alex's **persuasive essay**, ask yourself if it moves easily from sentence to sentence. Also, notice if the sentence structures vary.

I think that I should be allowed to go to music camp for the summer. ~~I have been playing the trumpet for two years now and I want to improve by September so I can be part of the school's marching band and be in the parade in January.~~ I have been playing the trumpet for two years now. I want to improve by September so I can march with the school band. Music camp would be a perfect place for me to get better.

Also, music camp does not cost much, and I can learn a lot of new things. If I went to music camp, I would work very hard and be very serious about my work. I would meet many other kids who are interested in music. If I had friends who were interested in music, I would have people to practice with.

On the other hand, my parents don't think that I need music camp if I just practiced more. This is not true, though. The music teachers at camp are excellent, and can teach me things I have never tried before.

The main reason I should go to music camp is that I am serious about becoming a better trumpet player. I will practice hard, and the camp is definitely worth the money.

This sentence is long and confusing.

The writing is easy to read. It flows well.

Transitional words and phrases help connect sentences, paragraphs, and ideas.

It is good to use a variety of simple and complex sentences.

- **What steps would you go through to improve sentence fluency in something you have written?**
- **Read Alex's essay out loud. Note any sentences which are difficult to read or do not sound natural. How would you rewrite these sentences?**

Writing

Voice

Does your personality shine through your writing?

Your paper should sound different from the way anyone else writes. When people read your paper, they should feel that you are talking right to them. When you really care about what you are writing, your personal stamp can be seen all the way through.

- Write about what you know and what you really care about.
- Be sure to write directly to the reader or audience.
- Don't be afraid to say what you really think.
- Write so the reader will feel just what you feel.

Good writers write about things they are excited to share. Look at Cress's **narrative**, and see how much she enjoys telling this story.

NASA Secrets Revealed

My friend Mike was seven years old when he shocked his class with some exciting news. Our teacher had asked the class to give presentations on a topic of our choice. Now, Mike was a real know-it-all. He was very interested in science fiction, so he decided to do a presentation on NASA.

The day came for Mike's presentation, and he had researched his topic very well. He spoke as though he knew everything there was to know about NASA. The class loved it.

After he finished, the teacher asked the students if they had any questions, and several raised their hands. Finally, the teacher raised her hand and said, "Mike, I have a question. What does NASA stand for?" Mike looked the teacher straight in the eye and mysteriously answered, "Nobody knows."

The entire class began to laugh. The teacher simply said, "NASA stands for National Aeronautics and Space Administration. Please take your seat, Mike."

The writer is writing to the audience.

In a narrative, don't be afraid to say what you feel.

The writer knows these events well because she was there.

The reader can get a good feel for what is going on.

- **What things make each individual's writing sound different?**
- **How might Cress write the story differently if she didn't know Mike very well?**

Word Choice

Do you choose words that create a picture in the reader's mind?

Good **word choices** paint clear pictures in the reader's mind. They also help move the reader to feel and think the way you do. This doesn't mean you use a big vocabulary to impress the reader, but you use just the right word in the right place.

- Use very specific nouns that clearly name a person, place, or thing. (The word *sneakers*, *loafers*, *high-heels*, or *sandals* is clearer than just the word *shoes*.)
- Choosing vivid verbs shows the reader exactly what the action is. (The word *sprinted*, *dashed*, or *darted* is a better choice than the word *ran*.)
- Good use of adjectives is more than just a descriptive list. Adjectives should tell the reader exactly how something looks, sounds, feels, tastes, or smells.
- Adverbs can make your verbs come alive. (Did the man *read* the newspaper *intently*, *breezily*, *angrily*, or *casually*?)
- Try to paint pictures so vivid they stick in the reader's mind.
- Cut or revise sentences or phrases that seem flowery.
- Look for words that you repeat over and over again, and try to choose different words.

Read this draft of Sal's **expository composition** to see where he can improve his word choice.

Writing

Being a good teacher is one of the hardest jobs in the world. A good teacher has many different ~~things~~ tasks to do. This is often difficult and tiring.

Choose the most specific noun you can. (Tasks is a better choice here than things.)

The main job of a teacher is, of course, to instruct the class. A teacher has to present many difficult subjects and help a large class to understand them.

This can be difficult by itself, but a teacher must also deal with bad behavior in a classroom. Sometimes students act selfishly and disturb the class. ~~The students yell, bother other classes, make trouble, fight, and throw things.~~ The students act out of line. The teacher has to settle the class down and begin again.

The same idea can be said in fewer words.

Another difficult job the teacher has is grading exams and papers. A teacher sometimes has over thirty students and must grade ~~an exam from each one of them.~~ a mountain of exams. Teachers sometimes ~~work~~ labor long hours over papers.

Use words to paint pictures that will stick in the reader's mind.

Choose exciting verbs. (Labor is more interesting than work.)

So what makes a good teacher? A good teacher is willing to work very hard so students will get a good education. A good teacher cares about children and their future.

- **What words do you use most often when writing? Where can you go to find words to replace overused words?**
- **Sal uses the word *difficult* many times. What other words might he use instead?**

Conventions

Did you revise and proofread your writing carefully?

Here's an easy way for you to remember what to look for when you are proofreading your work: **CUPPS**. That stands for **C**apitalization, **U**sage, **P**unctuation, **P**aragraphs, and **S**pelling. These are the five conventions that need to be correct for your writing to be clear.

- For help with rules for capitalization, see Handbook pages 547–551.
- Usage means the rules of English language. For help with rules for usage, see Troubleshooter pages 512–524 and Handbook pages 526–543.
- The rules for punctuation can be found in the Handbook pages 552–556.
- Check that your paragraphs develop only one main idea.
- For help with spelling rules and strategies, see Handbook pages 582–585.

Everyone makes mistakes, so it is important to set aside time to proofread your work. Read Tran's **comparative essay** to find where he can correct errors.

Although the golden retriever and the Labrador retriever are alike in many ways, they also have a number of differences. Both retrievers are good-tempered, excellent companions, and kind with children. Retrievers ~~don't~~ never act badly around elderly people either. They need plenty of ~~exercize~~ exercise, and can be kept groomed by simply brushing their coats.

The main difference between the dogs is their appearance The golden retriever can be light gold, dark gold, or cream colored. The labrador is one color all over—black, yellow, or liver/chocolate. The Labrador has a short, thick coat of hair with no waves or feathering, unlike the golden, which has a flat or wavy coat with good feathering. Labradors make great pets since they are not aggressive.

Labradors have fine temperaments, so they are easily trainable. Today they are often used in police work. The golden is also used as a guide dog for the blind.

Check usage.

Check spelling.

Check punctuation.

Check capitalization.

This sentence does not belong here. Paragraphs should stick to only one main idea.

- **What advice would you give someone who has trouble proofreading?**
- **What books could Tran use to help him check the five conventions of CUPPS?**

Use the checklist to help you with your writing.

PREWRITE

Ideas and Content

- ❑ Do I know what I want to say?
- ❑ Do I know a lot about this topic? Do I need to do more research?
- ❑ Have I listed details that will make my ideas come alive?

Organization

- ❑ Do I have a clear plan or pattern for my writing?
- ❑ Do all the details in my plan connect to an idea or theme?

Voice

- ❑ Am I really interested in the topic?

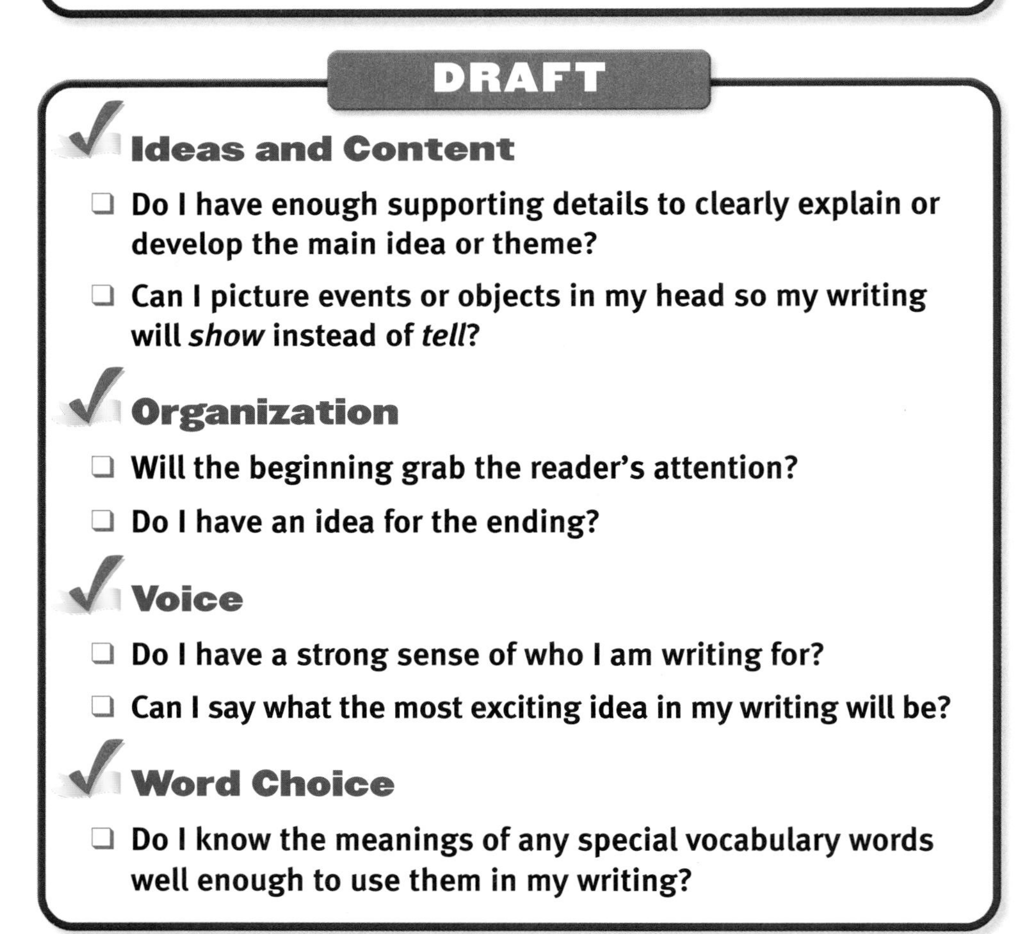

DRAFT

Ideas and Content

- ❑ Do I have enough supporting details to clearly explain or develop the main idea or theme?
- ❑ Can I picture events or objects in my head so my writing will *show* instead of *tell*?

Organization

- ❑ Will the beginning grab the reader's attention?
- ❑ Do I have an idea for the ending?

Voice

- ❑ Do I have a strong sense of who I am writing for?
- ❑ Can I say what the most exciting idea in my writing will be?

Word Choice

- ❑ Do I know the meanings of any special vocabulary words well enough to use them in my writing?

Writing

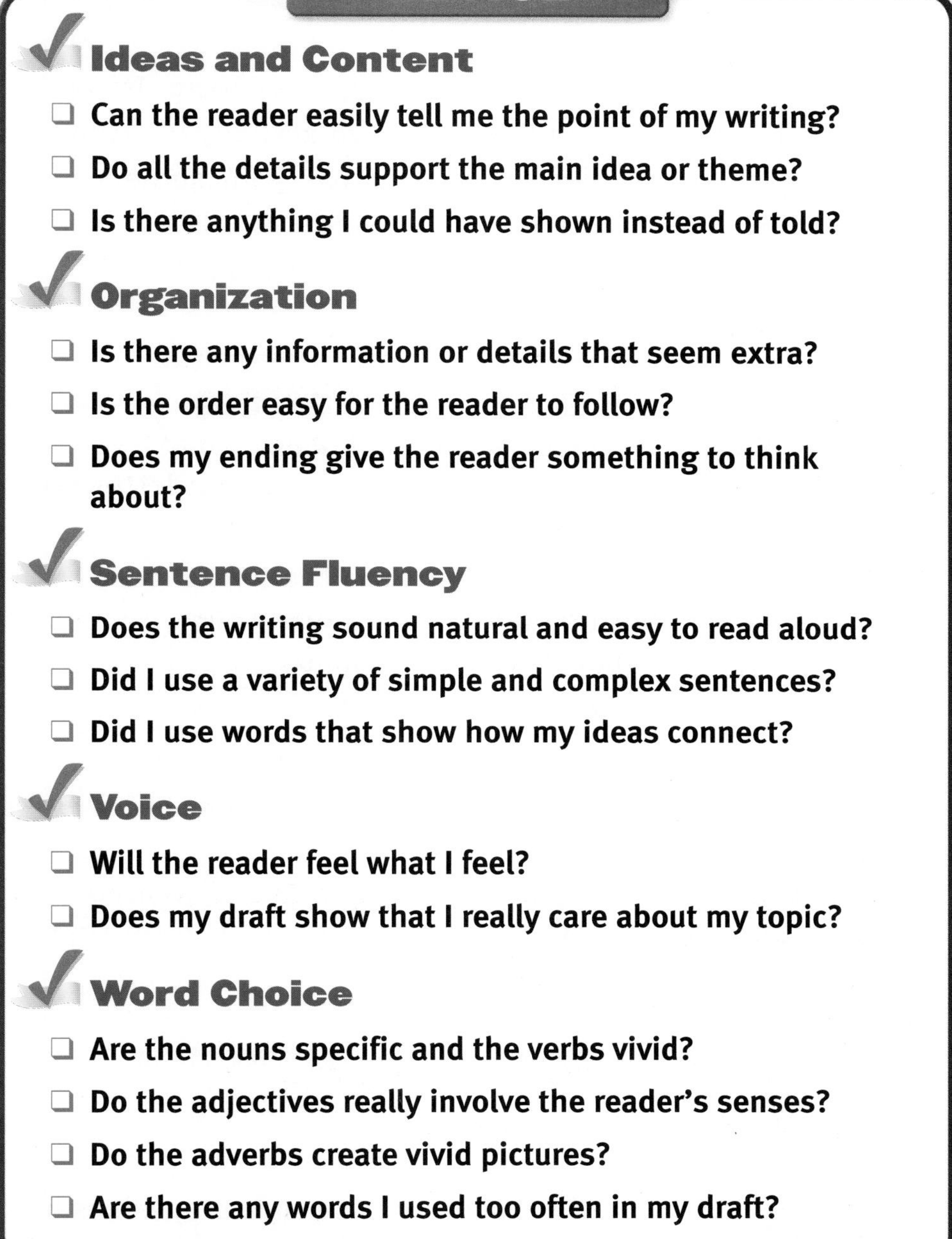

REVISE

Ideas and Content

- ❑ Can the reader easily tell me the point of my writing?
- ❑ Do all the details support the main idea or theme?
- ❑ Is there anything I could have shown instead of told?

Organization

- ❑ Is there any information or details that seem extra?
- ❑ Is the order easy for the reader to follow?
- ❑ Does my ending give the reader something to think about?

Sentence Fluency

- ❑ Does the writing sound natural and easy to read aloud?
- ❑ Did I use a variety of simple and complex sentences?
- ❑ Did I use words that show how my ideas connect?

Voice

- ❑ Will the reader feel what I feel?
- ❑ Does my draft show that I really care about my topic?

Word Choice

- ❑ Are the nouns specific and the verbs vivid?
- ❑ Do the adjectives really involve the reader's senses?
- ❑ Do the adverbs create vivid pictures?
- ❑ Are there any words I used too often in my draft?

PROOFREAD

Conventions

- ❑ Have I checked my writing for correct **CUPPS**?

Presentation

Are you sharing your writing in the best way you can?

Presentation is **how you share your writing**. It can be almost as important as what you have actually written. If your presentation is clear and attractive, your audience will want to pay attention to your words. If it is not, your audience may be distracted from your message.

- If your piece is handwritten, make sure your lettering and punctuation marks are easily readable.
- If you used a computer, make sure the font is easy to read and the margins and spacing are correct.
- Before reading aloud, practice to make sure that you do not stumble over words.
- For any presentation, consider using charts, graphs, pictures, headings, or other visual elements that might help make your meaning clear.
- Think about what other forms this piece of writing may take. Could it be a photo essay, a play, a postcard, or something else?

- **When might you use slide projections in your presentation? How would it help make what you are saying clear?**
- **What is your favorite form to write in? Why?**

Macmillan / McGraw-Hill Edition

McGRAW-HILL

Language Arts

The 6 Trait Writing rubric materials in this work use the Six Trait Writing criteria, as defined by the Northwest Regional Educational Laboratory. For more information, visit its website at www.nwrel.org.

Contributor

Time Magazine

Macmillan/McGraw-Hill

A Division of The ***McGraw-Hill*** *Companies*

Macmillan/McGraw-Hill
Two Penn Plaza
New York, NY 10121

Printed in the United States of America

ISBN 0-02-244653-2 / 4

4 5 6 7 8 9 (027/043) 05 04 03 02 01

Macmillan / McGraw-Hill Edition

McGRAW-HILL Language Arts

AUTHORS

Jan E. Hasbrouck

Donna Lubcker

Sharon O'Neal

William H. Teale

Josefina V. Tinajero

Karen D. Wood

Macmillan
McGraw-Hill

New York Farmington

Sentences and Personal Narrative

Theme: *Moments to Share*

Grammar

Spiral Review Every Day

Sentences

Build Skills

Writing

Personal Narrative

Review and Assess

UNIT 2 Nouns and Writing That Compares

Theme: Reaching Out

Grammar  Spiral Review Every Day

Nouns

Writing

Writing That Compares

Review and Assess

Verbs and Persuasive Writing

Theme: Speak Out

Grammar

Spiral Review Every Day

Verbs

Build Skills

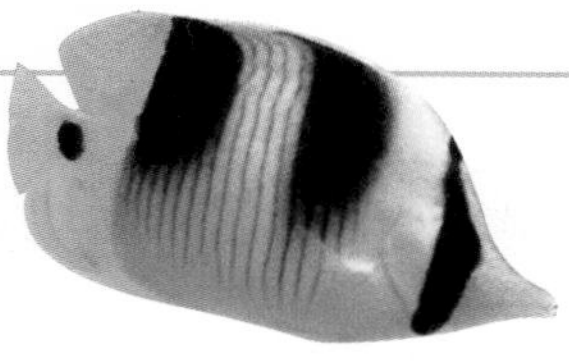

Writing

Persuasive Writing

Review and Assess

Adjectives and Explanatory Writing

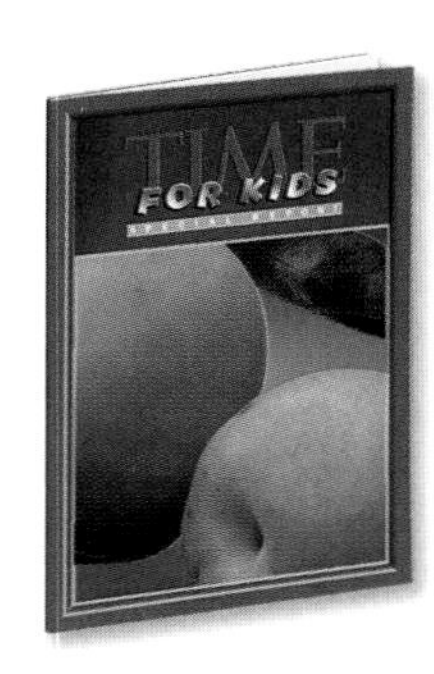

Theme: Find Out More

Spiral Review Every Day

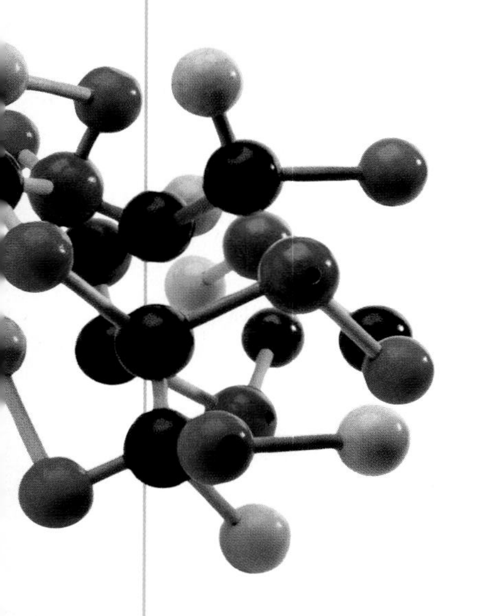

Adjectives

Writing

Explanatory Writing

Review and Assess

Pronouns and Story Writing

Theme: Plan Ahead

Grammar

Spiral Review Every Day

Pronouns

Writing

Story Writing

Review and Assess

Adverbs, Prepositions, and Expository Writing

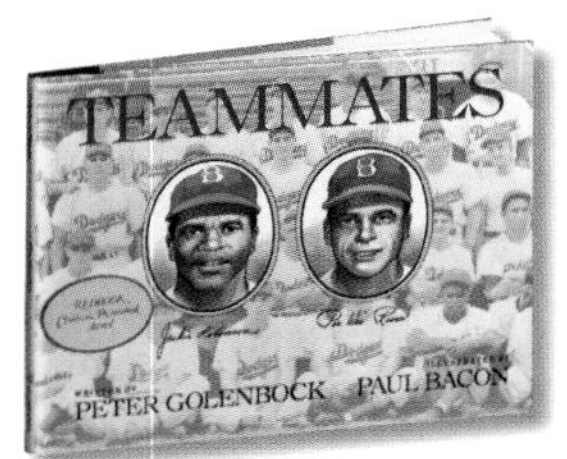

Theme: Choose Wisely

Grammar

Spiral Review Every Day

Adverbs and Prepositions

Writing

Expository Writing

Review and Assess

Theme Moments to Share

UNIT 1

Sentences and Personal Narrative

In this unit you will learn about kinds of sentences. You will also learn how to write a personal narrative. A personal narrative is a true story about someone's experience.

Science Link *Read about the unforgettable experience of Richard and Jonah Sobol. They traveled together to Prince Edward Island to observe and record the lives of baby harp seals.*

As soon as we stepped out of the helicopter, we could hear the soft cries of hungry newborn pups. These were the only sounds that drifted through the stillness of this frozen landscape. It was springtime but the air was very cold—five degrees below zero. The wind bit into our skin. As we walked toward the seals, the snow swished and swirled under our clunky survival boots. We were careful to avoid the smooth round holes in the ice—bobbing holes—that the mother seals dive in and out of to return to the water to feed on small shrimp or fish, or just to swim.

SEAL JOURNEY
By Richard and Jonah Sobol Photographs by Richard Sobol

from ***Seal Journey*** by Richard and Jonah Sobol

Thinking Like a Writer

Personal Narrative In a personal narrative, the author writes about a true experience. Reread the passage.

- From whose point of view is the passage told?

Sentences The author used long and short sentences to write his personal narrative. Read each sentence again.

QUICK WRITE What kind of sentences are they?

Grammar

Sentences

RULES

A **sentence** is a group of words that expresses a complete thought.

Ann and Lisa found an old photo album in the attic.

Someone had put the album in a box with some old books.

A **sentence fragment** is a group of words that does not express a complete thought.

Looked through the album.

All the black-and-white photographs.

Sentences

Write how you can tell whether a group of words is a complete sentence or a sentence fragment.

To be a complete sentence, a group of words must name the person or thing you are talking about. It must also tell what happens.

Who	What Happens
Ann and Lisa	found an album.
Someone	had put the album in a box.

Guided Practice

Tell whether each group of words is a sentence or sentence fragment.

EXAMPLE: The girls asked their grandmother about the old album.
Sentence

1. Turned to the first page of the old album.
2. Ann pointed to the girl with the curly hair.
3. Photos of Grandmother as a girl.
4. Wondered about life in the old days.
5. Many pictures were in the album.

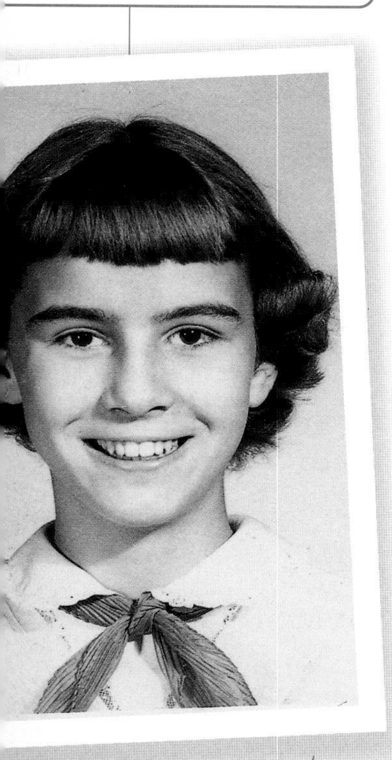

REVIEW THE RULES

- A sentence is a group of words that expresses a complete thought.
- A sentence fragment is a group of words that does not express a complete thought.

More Practice

A. For each group of words, write *sentence* or *fragment*.

6. Learned about the past from the old photo album.
7. Children enjoyed playing many kinds of games.
8. Played hopscotch.
9. Clothing styles have changed since the 1950s.
10. No computer games at the time.

Handbook page 526

B. For each pair, write the group of words that is a sentence. Then read the other words. Add your own words to make a sentence. Write the new sentence.

11. The old car in this photo. Cars seemed longer then.
12. A photo of the family. The girls giggled at the swimsuits.
13. Bought a television in 1955. People listened to the radio.
14. Children had many things to do. Rode bikes.
15. The county fair. Grandmother won a blue ribbon.

C. **Spiral Review** **Write the paragraph. Make complete sentences by adding a word or words in each blank.**

(**16.**____) saw many photographs of Grandmother as a girl. She and her brother (**17.**____). (**18.**____) had a lot of fun. Every summer, the children (**19.**____). Their parents (**20.**____).

Extra Practice, page 74.

Writing Activity A Note

Imagine you are sending a photo of yourself to your relatives. Write a note to them about the photo. Give details that will help them know your feelings when the photo was taken.

APPLY GRAMMAR: Use complete sentences in your note. Begin each sentence with a capital letter.

Grammar

Declarative and Interrogative Sentences

RULES

A declarative sentence makes a statement.

The Mississippi River is the longest river in the United States.

An interrogative sentence asks a question.

Do you know how long the Mississippi River is?

Sentences
How do you decide whether a sentence is declarative or interrogative? Write your ideas in your journal.

Every sentence begins with a *capital letter*. A declarative sentence ends with a *period*. An interrogative sentence ends with a *question mark*.

A Declarative Sentence	An Interrogative Sentence
tells something	asks something
ends with a period (.)	ends with a question mark (?)

Guided Practice

Tell which sentences are declarative and which are interrogative.

EXAMPLE: Have you ever traveled along the Mississippi River? *Interrogative*

1. The Mississippi River flows for more than 2,300 miles.
2. Where does the Mississippi River begin?
3. The river's source can be found on a map.
4. Do you see Lake Itasca in northwestern Minnesota?
5. The Mississippi River flows to the Gulf of Mexico.

REVIEW THE RULES

- A declarative sentence makes a statement. It ends with a period.
- An interrogative sentence asks a question. It ends with a question mark.

Grammar

More Practice

A. Write each sentence. Write *declarative* or *interrogative* to tell what kind of sentence it is.

6. People sometimes call the Mississippi River "Old Man River."
7. Did you know that *Mississippi* means "big river"?
8. The Mississippi River begins as a small, clear stream.
9. Near Cairo, Illinois, the river is about 4,500 feet wide.
10. Is "Old Man River" muddy near the Gulf of Mexico?

B. Write each sentence correctly.

11. which American author wrote about the Mississippi River
12. *life on the Mississippi* was written by Mark Twain
13. what animals live in and around the Mississippi River
14. the river supports many kinds of fish and rodents
15. does pollution threaten the wildlife of the Mississippi

Handbook page 526

C. Spiral Review **If the group of words is a sentence, rewrite it correctly, adding capital letters and punctuation. If it is not a sentence, write *sentence fragment*.**

16. have you seen the Mississippi River
17. dams and levees help protect cities from floods
18. has flooded many times
19. which other rivers flow into the Mississippi
20. the Mississippi River on a map

Extra Practice, page 75.

Writing Activity A Journal Entry

Imagine you are walking along a quiet, unexplored stream. Write your thoughts in your journal. Use colorful, precise words.
APPLY GRAMMAR: Include declarative and interrogative sentences. Use correct end punctuation.

Grammar

Imperative and Exclamatory Sentences

RULES

An **imperative sentence** tells or asks someone to do something.

Please help your father load up the wagon.

An **exclamatory sentence** shows strong feeling.

What an exciting day this is!

Sentences

Write in your journal how you can tell whether a sentence is imperative or exclamatory.

An imperative sentence ends with a *period*. An exclamatory sentence ends with an *exclamation mark*.

An Imperative Sentence	An Exclamatory Sentence
tells someone to do something	shows strong feeling
ends with a period (.)	ends with an exclamation mark (!)

Guided Practice

Tell which sentences are imperative and which are exclamatory.

EXAMPLE: Grease the wheels of the wagon.
Imperative

1. Help hitch the oxen team to the wagon.
2. Don't forget to load the flour, yeast, and cornmeal.
3. I can hardly believe it's finally time to go!
4. What an incredible journey this will be!
5. Please check the wagon one last time.
6. Watch the baby, please.
7. Feed the oxen.
8. How strong the oxen are!
9. It's surprising how much a horse eats!
10. Ask Father to stop the wagon.

REVIEW THE RULES

- An imperative sentence tells or asks someone to do something. It ends with a period.
- An exclamatory sentence shows strong feeling. It ends with an exclamation mark.

Grammar

More Practice

A. Write each sentence. Write *imperative* or *exclamatory* next to it.

11. What a strange looking animal the buffalo is!

12. Don't get too close to the oxen.

13. How bumpy and dusty this trail is!

14. How tired we are from walking all day!

15. Please ask the children to go to sleep.

B. Write each sentence correctly.

16. what a terrible storm that was last night

17. oh no, the wagon wheels are stuck in the mud

18. please gather sage for a fire

19. pass me a piece of fried bread, please

20. how hot and windy it is on the prairie

C. Spiral Review **Write each group of words. Write *declarative*, *interrogative*, *imperative*, *exclamatory*, or *fragment* next to it.**

21. How brave the pioneers were!

22. They faced incredible hardships.

23. Could you face a pioneer's hardships?

24. Traveled in a covered wagon for six months.

25. Check out library books today for your report.

Handbook page 526

Extra Practice, page 76.

Writing Activity A Postcard

Imagine you are traveling across country in a camper. Write a postcard to a friend. Be sure to choose just the right words.
APPLY GRAMMAR: Include imperative and exclamatory sentences in your message. Use correct capitalization and punctuation.

Combining Sentences: Compound Sentences

RULES

A conjunction is a word that joins words or groups of words.

A compound sentence contains two sentences joined by a comma (,) and the conjunction *and*, *or*, or *but*.

> *Greg found a bat in the attic, and it startled him.*
>
> *The bat had been asleep, but now it was flying around.*
>
> *Greg had to open the window, or the bat could not escape.*

Sentences

How do you know when a sentence is a compound sentence? Write your ideas in your journal.

When you want to show how the ideas in two separate sentences are related, you can combine them. Use a comma and a conjunction to join the two sentences. *And* means "in addition." *But* shows a contrast. *Or* shows a choice.

> *Bats fly like birds. + They are really mammals. =*
>
> *Bats fly like birds, but they are really mammals.*

Guided Practice

Join each pair of sentences by using the conjunction given.

EXAMPLE: A bat is a mammal. It can fly. (but)
A bat is a mammal, but it can fly.

1. A brown bat may live in a barn. It may prefer a cave. (or)
2. Their bodies are furry. Their wings are leathery. (but)
3. Bats have poor eyesight. They hear very well. (but)
4. Frogs eat bugs. Bats do, too. (and)
5. Kelly likes bats. She may study them. (and)

REVIEW THE RULES

- A compound sentence contains two sentences joined by a comma and the conjunction *and*, *or*, or *but*.

Grammar

More Practice

A. Join each sentence pair, using the conjunction provided. Write your compound sentences.

6. Some people fear bats. Others like them. (but)
7. Bats sleep during the day. They hunt at night. (and)
8. You could wear a bat costume. You could be a lion. (or)
9. Bats eat beetles. They also eat flies. (and)
10. I saw many bats. Some were unusual. (and)

Handbook
page 527

B. Write each pair of sentences as a compound sentence. Add a comma and a conjunction where needed.

11. Bats make high sounds. People cannot hear them.
12. The sounds bounce off objects. Bats hear these sounds.
13. Bats can locate objects. They can identify them, too.
14. Thousands of bats fly around at night. They never collide.
15. Observe bats one evening. You may be surprised.

C. Spiral Review Write each sentence pair as a compound sentence, using *and*, *or*, or *but*. Write *declarative*, *interrogative*, *imperative*, or *exclamatory* after each.

16. Is Luis afraid of bats? Does he like them?
17. Some bats have huge ears. Others have small ones.
18. We saw bats asleep. We saw them fly.
19. Does a fruit bat eat bananas? Does it eat bugs?
20. How amazing bats are! What great hunters they are!

Extra Practice, page 77.

Writing Activity A Paragraph

Write a paragraph to tell how you feel about bats. Include details that give reasons for your feelings.

APPLY GRAMMAR: Include at least one or two compound sentences in your paragraph. Circle the commas and conjunctions you use.

Grammar

Sentence Punctuation

RULES

Every sentence begins with a capital letter. Declarative and imperative sentences end with periods.

Jim plays the guitar. *Please play for us.*

An interrogative sentence ends with a question mark.

Do you practice every day?

An exclamatory sentence ends with an exclamation mark.

How well he plays!

A comma belongs before the conjunction *and*, *or*, or *but* in a compound sentence.

Jim plays folk music, but he prefers classical music.

Sentences

In your journal, write how you decide which punctuation marks to use in the sentences you write.

Remember to use the correct end punctuation mark.

Declarative ⟶ *period*

Interrogative ⟶ *question mark*

Imperative ⟶ *period*

Exclamatory ⟶ *exclamation mark*

Guided Practice

Name the words that should be capitalized, and give the punctuation marks that belong in the sentences.

EXAMPLE: listen to the song Jim is playing
Listen; period

1. what a wonderful song Jim is playing
2. do you know the title of the piece
3. "country" is the title and Jase Everett wrote it
4. let's hear the song again
5. how great it would be to play a musical instrument

REVIEW THE RULES

- Every sentence must begin with a capital letter and end with the correct punctuation mark.
- A comma belongs before the conjunction *and*, *or*, or *but* in a compound sentence.

Grammar

Handbook
pages 547, 552

More Practice

A. Write each sentence correctly.

6. the banjo is a stringed instrument
7. does the banjo have strings like the guitar
8. most banjos have five strings but some have four
9. try strumming the strings of a banjo
10. how different the banjo sounds from the guitar

B. Write each sentence correctly. Then label the sentence *declarative*, *interrogative*, *imperative*, or *exclamatory*.

11. look at the banjo
12. what an interesting instrument it is
13. the banjo has a round body
14. it's like a small drum with a long neck
15. was the banjo first used in jazz bands

C. Spiral Review Write each group of words. If it is a sentence fragment, write *fragment*. If it is a sentence, label it *declarative*, *interrogative*, *imperative*, or *exclamatory*.

16. the talented banjo player
17. have you ever played the banjo before
18. taught me how to play
19. watch me as I play
20. how well you play the banjo

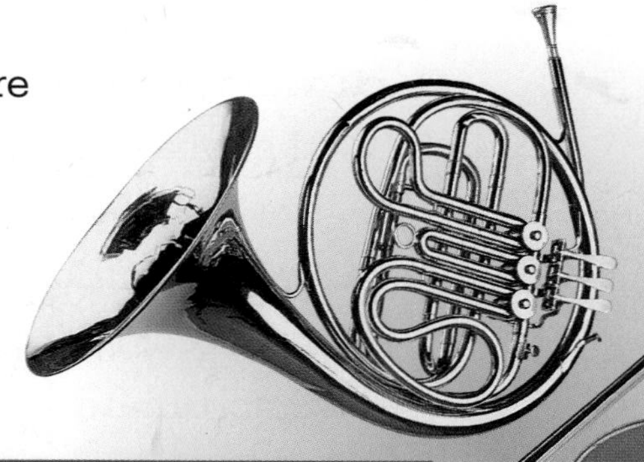

Extra Practice, page 78.

Writing Activity A Plan

Write the steps you would take to learn how to play a particular musical instrument. Organize your ideas logically.

APPLY MECHANICS AND USAGE: Use correct capitalization and punctuation in your sentences.

Music Link

Mixed Review

REVIEW THE RULES

- A sentence is a group of words that expresses a complete thought.
- Every sentence begins with a capital letter.
- A sentence fragment does not express a complete thought.
- A declarative sentence makes a statement. It ends with a period.
- An interrogative sentence asks a question. It ends with a question mark.
- An imperative sentence tells or asks someone to do something. It ends with a period.
- An exclamatory sentence shows strong feeling. It ends with an exclamation mark.
- A compound sentence is made up of two sentences joined by a comma (,) and the conjunction *and*, *or*, or *but*.

Sentences
Think about how each type of sentence is used. Then write four different kinds of sentences of your own. Check them for correct punctuation.

Practice

A. Write each sentence correctly. Add capital letters and end punctuation. Write *declarative*, *interrogative*, *imperative*, or *exclamatory* next to each to tell the kind of sentence it is.

1. what wonderful weather we've had this week
2. the weather has been sunny and mild every day
3. how I hope the weekend will be nice
4. are you curious about tomorrow's weather
5. meteorologists predict the weather
6. unfortunately, predicting the weather is difficult
7. will it rain tomorrow, or will it be sunny
8. listen to the radio for a weather report
9. please check the thermometer for the temperature
10. was the weather forecast correct

B. Write each pair of sentences as one sentence. Use a comma and *and*, *but*, or *or* to combine the sentences.

11. The weekend was finally here. We could hardly wait.

12. We could go on a picnic. We could go camping.

13. Dad turned on the television. We listened to the weather report together.

14. The forecaster called for sunshine. He mentioned a small chance of showers.

15. The next morning was a little cloudy. We decided to go anyway.

C. Challenge **Rewrite the following paragraph. Add missing commas, capital letters, and end punctuation.**

16–25. Weather forecasters are often correct but sometimes their forecasts are not accurate. at times they call for rain and then it's sunny instead Many people observe nature to predict the weather how do farmers know if it's going to rain They can watch the clouds or they can observe insects. For example, flies swarm before a storm and high clouds are signs of sunny weather. How interesting it can be to watch the weather

Grammar REVIEW

Handbook
pages
526–527, 547, 552

Writing Activity A Weather Report

Imagine you are a weather reporter. Write about today's weather. Then include a forecast for tomorrow's weather. Choose words that vividly describe the weather conditions.

APPLY MECHANICS AND USAGE: For each sentence you write, draw a line under the capital letter at the beginning and circle the punctuation marks.

Grammar

Complete Subjects and Complete Predicates

RULES

The subject part of a sentence tells whom or what the sentence is about. The complete subject is all the words in the subject part.

All the children gathered around Grandfather.

The predicate part of a sentence tells what the subject does or is. The complete predicate is all the words in the predicate part.

Grandfather is a great storyteller.

Sentences

Write how you can identify the complete subject and the complete predicate in a sentence.

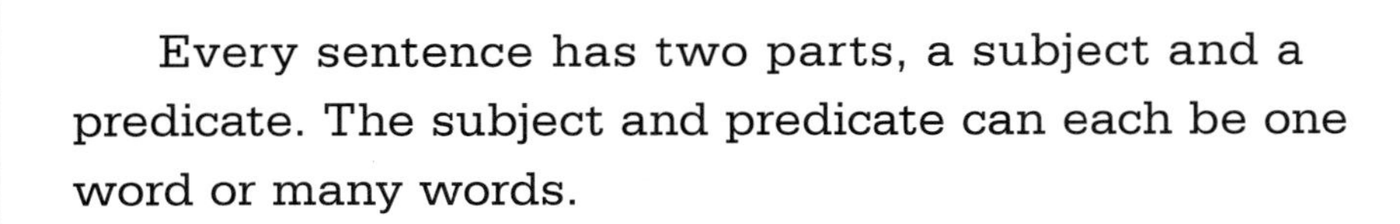

Every sentence has two parts, a subject and a predicate. The subject and predicate can each be one word or many words.

Complete Subject	Complete Predicate
Grandfather	begins.
Our grandfather	begins to tell his story.

Guided Practice

Tell whether each underlined sentence part is a complete subject or a complete predicate.

EXAMPLE: Grandfather's stories are always interesting.
Complete subject

1. Some of Grandfather's stories teach lessons about nature.
2. My younger sister likes Grandfather's animal stories best.
3. My favorite story is "How Turtle Flew South for the Winter."
4. Grandfather learned many stories from his grandmother.
5. Our whole family enjoys hearing Grandfather's stories.

REVIEW THE RULES

- The **complete subject** is all the words that tell whom or what the sentence is about.
- The **complete predicate** is all the words that tell what the subject does or is.

More Practice

A. Write *complete subject* or *complete predicate* to tell which part of the sentence is underlined.

6. Our family's ancestors once lived on the Great Plains.

7. Our people hunted buffalo.

8. Every part of the buffalo had an important use.

9. Our ancestors made clothing and tepees from the skins.

10. The buffalo hair was used for clothing.

B. Write each sentence. Draw a line between the complete subject and the complete predicate.

11. My ancestors belonged to the Blackfoot nation.

12. The Blackfoot nation was just one Plains tribe.

13. Grandfather told us about the origin of the name "Blackfoot."

14. Blackfoot ancestors crossed a burned prairie.

15. Their moccasins turned black from the ashes.

C. Spiral Review Add words to make each of the following a complete sentence. Use proper punctuation and capitalization.

16. the Blackfoot people

17. huge herds of buffalo

18. hunted the buffalo for its meat, skin, and hair

19. was a useful animal

20. also hunted other animals

Extra Practice, page 79.

Handbook
page 528

Writing Activity A Story

Choose a favorite story about your family and write it down. Make sure that your sentences flow.

APPLY GRAMMAR: Make sure each sentence has a complete subject and a complete predicate. Draw a line between the two parts.

Grammar

Simple Subjects

RULES

The simple subject is the main word in the complete subject.

My family visited colonial Williamsburg in Virginia.

You know that every sentence has two parts—a subject and a predicate. The complete subject is all the words in the subject part of a sentence. The simple subject tells exactly who or what the sentence is about. The simple subject in each sentence below is underlined.

Complete Subject	Complete Predicate
Many people	live in Austin.
This city in Texas	is a fun place to visit.

Sentences

Write how you can tell the difference between a complete subject and a simple subject.

Guided Practice

The complete subject in each sentence is underlined. Name the simple subject.

EXAMPLE: English settlers established Williamsburg in 1633.
Simple subject: settlers

1. Many visitors come to Williamsburg each year.
2. We started our tour on Duke of Gloucester Street.
3. Beautiful old homes line this main street.
4. The capitol building stands at the end of the street.
5. A guide in a colonial dress took us through some homes.

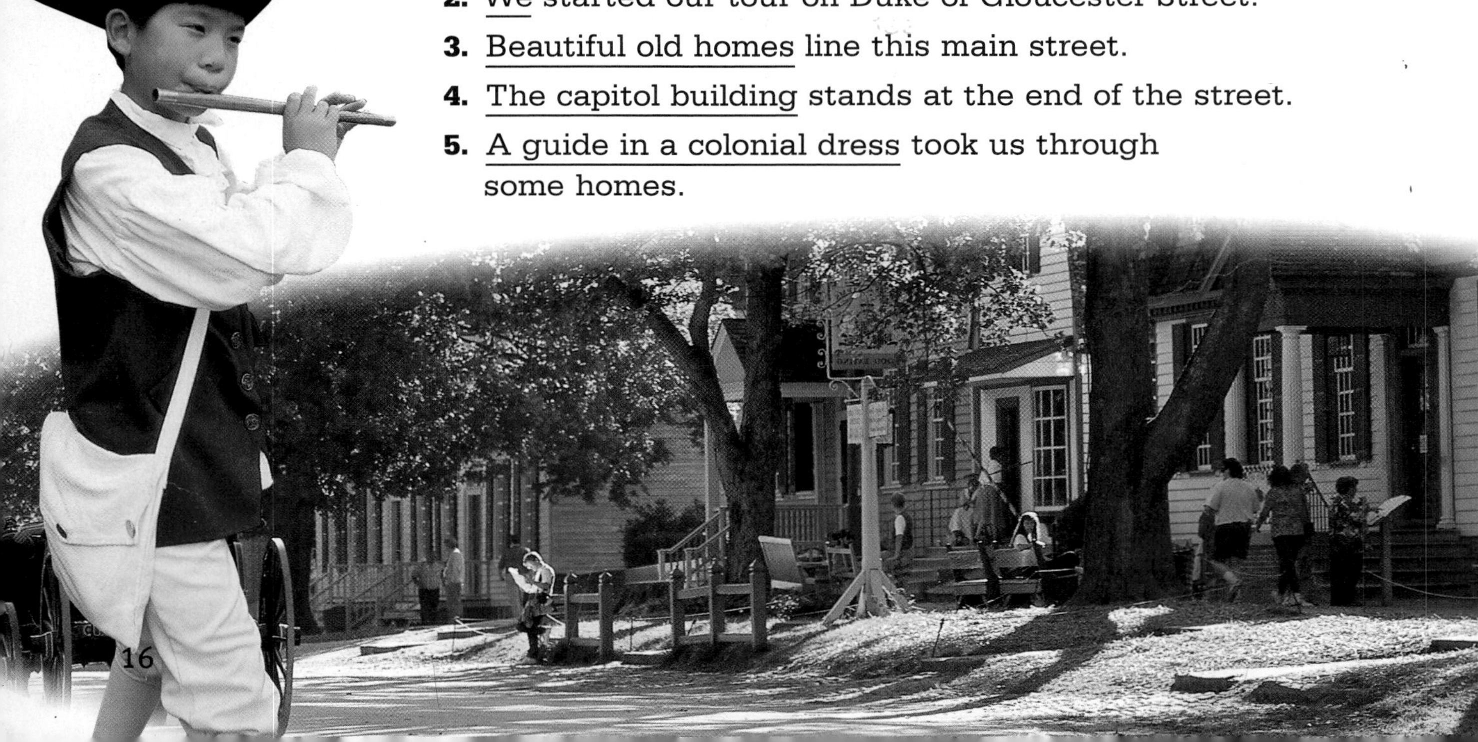

REVIEW THE RULES

The simple subject tells exactly who or what the sentence is about.

More Practice

A. The complete subject in each sentence is underlined. Write the sentence. Circle the simple subject.

6. Our tour guide took us to some of the shops after lunch.
7. The wig shop had wigs for women and men.
8. We saw a loom in a weaver's shop.
9. The bootmaker made shoes with square toes.
10. The candle-dipping demonstration thrilled us all.

Handbook page 528

B. Write each sentence. Draw a line under the complete subject. Circle the simple subject.

11. Colonial children played marbles, tag, and hopscotch.
12. Our guide showed us how to play a game called "bowls."
13. A fife and drum band marched across the field.
14. My mother photographed the glass maker.
15. We had such a great time at Williamsburg!

C. Spiral Review Write the paragraph. Correct each sentence by adding capital letters and end punctuation. Then underline each simple subject.

16–25. Williamsburg is a restored colonial city My family visited this city english settlers went there in the 1600s They established the settlement on land between two rivers. many famous Americans walked on the streets of Williamsburg, Virginia

Extra Practice, page 80.

Writing Activity Write a Diary Entry

Imagine that you live in Williamsburg during colonial times. Write a diary entry to tell something about your life. Your entry should show your personality.

APPLY GRAMMAR: Circle the simple subject of each sentence.

Social Studies Link

Grammar

Simple Predicates

RULES

The simple predicate is the main word in the complete predicate.

We visited the Colorado and Mojave Deserts.

As you know, a sentence has two parts—a subject and a predicate. The complete predicate is all the words in the predicate part of a sentence. The simple predicate tells exactly what the subject does or is. The simple predicate in each sentence below is underlined.

Sentences
Write how to tell the difference between a complete predicate and a simple predicate.

Complete Subject	Complete Predicate
Both deserts	lie in southern California.
I	noticed many animals in the desert.

Guided Practice

The complete predicate in each sentence is underlined. Name the simple predicate.

EXAMPLE: The desert contains a lot of wildlife.
simple predicate: contains

1. We saw two coyotes during a field trip.
2. They trotted alongside the bus for a few feet.
3. We looked for bighorn sheep during the hike.
4. I drew a picture of a roadrunner.
5. Hummingbirds fluttered around the flowers.

REVIEW THE RULES

The simple predicate tells exactly what the subject does or is.

Grammar

More Practice

A. The complete predicate in each sentence is underlined. Write the sentence. Circle the simple predicate.

6. Spring rains provide water for plants and animals.
7. The desert blooms for a few weeks in the spring.
8. Visitors from all over come for the spring flowers.
9. We made our trip at the end of the spring.
10. Our hike to an oasis took more than two hours.

B. Write each sentence. Draw a line under the complete predicate. Circle the simple predicate.

11. My hikers' club went to the Mojave Desert.
12. We drove to Joshua Tree National Monument.
13. I climbed boulders with our group leader.
14. My best friend brought her camera.
15. The group camped in the park.

Handbook page 528

C. Spiral Review Write each sentence correctly. Draw a line between the complete subject and the complete predicate. Circle the simple subject and the simple predicate.

16. the desert is not far from Los Angeles
17. many boulders in the Mojave Desert are great for climbing
18. people come from all over to climb the rocks
19. we drank a lot of water on the hike
20. the sizzling summer sun is very hot

Extra Practice, page 81.

Writing Activity A Photo Caption

Write a photo caption describing one of your favorite places. Write several sentences telling how you feel about the place.

APPLY GRAMMAR: In each sentence in your caption, underline the complete predicate and circle the simple predicate.

Grammar

Combining Sentences: Compound Subjects

RULES

A compound subject contains two or more simple subjects that have the same predicate.

Jenna and Patrick ***cleaned up the vacant lot.***

If two sentences have the same predicate, you can combine them by forming a compound subject. Use the conjunction *and* or *or* to join together the parts of a compound subject.

The children ***worked hard.*** / *The parents* ***worked hard.*** → *The children and parents* ***worked hard.***

Sentences

How can you tell if a sentence has a compound subject? Write your thoughts in your journal.

Guided Practice

In each sentence pair, name the simple subjects. Then name a conjunction you could use to join them.

EXAMPLE: Jenna will call the neighbors. Patrick will call the neighbors.
Jenna, Patrick, or

1. My sister told a story. My mother told a story.
2. Old tires were all over the lot. Old newspapers were all over the lot.
3. A neighborhood garden would be better than a vacant lot. A playground would be better than a vacant lot.
4. Good friends helped clean up the lot. Good neighbors helped clean up the lot.
5. Cassie will mow the grass. Chad will mow the grass.

REVIEW THE RULES

- A compound subject contains two or more simple subjects that have the same predicate.

More Practice

A. Underline the simple subjects. Then write a conjunction you could use to join them.

6. Jenna enjoyed working. Patrick enjoyed working.
7. Every neighbor came to their meeting. Every merchant came to their meeting.
8. The children were concerned about the trash. The parents were concerned about the trash.
9. Mrs. James had good ideas. Her husband had good ideas.
10. Tim called the trash haulers. Mike called the trash haulers.

B. Combine each pair of sentences by creating a compound subject. Write the new sentence.

11. Mr. Lee picked up bottles. Brad picked up bottles.
12. Jenna removed the tires. Patrick removed the tires.
13. The children picked up litter. The parents picked up litter.
14. The truck filled quickly. The dumpster filled quickly.
15. The friends were tired. The neighbors were tired.

C. Spiral Review **Complete each sentence with a simple subject or the correct end punctuation.**

(**16.** ______) worked in the neighborhood garden. Mr. Johns and his (**17.** ______) donated a bench. The store owner delivered a bird feeder (**18.** ______) Children and (**19.** ______) took turns watering the flowers. Have you ever worked in a garden (**20.** ______)

Extra Practice, page 82.

Writing Activity A Paragraph

Write a paragraph about something you've done to make your neighborhood, home, or school a better place. Be sure to describe the events in the order in which they happened.
APPLY GRAMMAR: Include compound subjects in some of your sentences. Circle the two simple subjects.

Handbook
page 529

Combining Sentences: Compound Predicates

RULES

A compound predicate contains two or more simple predicates that have the same subject.

Jan's grandfather showed and discussed pictures of a garage sale.

Jan phoned or e-mailed her friends about having their own garage sale.

Sentences

How do you know if a sentence has a compound predicate? Write your answer in your journal.

If two sentences have the same subject, you can combine them by forming a compound predicate. Use the word *and*, *or*, or *but* to join the two parts of a compound predicate.

Jan planned a garage sale.
Jan organized a garage sale. → *Jan planned and organized a garage sale.*

Guided Practice

In each sentence pair, name the simple predicates. Then name a conjunction you could use to join them.

EXAMPLE: Jan asked her parents to help. Jan persuaded her parents to help.
asked, persuaded, and

1. Mr. Lim cleared the garage. Mr. Lim swept the garage.
2. Angela worked quickly. Angela did a good job.
3. Alex washed the old card tables. Alex set up the old card tables.
4. Mrs. Lim sorted the toys. Mrs. Lim arranged the toys.
5. Children painted signs. Children drew signs.

REVIEW THE RULES

- A compound predicate contains two or more simple predicates.

Grammar

More Practice

A. Write each sentence pair. Underline the simple predicates. Then write a conjunction you could use to join them.

6. Ray baked cookies. Ray served cookies.
7. Children boxed the jewelry. Children priced the jewelry.
8. Megan sorted books. Megan displayed books.
9. Jim spoke quietly. Jim explained points clearly.
10. Matt dusted furniture. Matt polished furniture.

B. Combine each pair of sentences. Use *and*, *but*, or *or* to join the two predicates.

11. All of Jan's friends came early. All of Jan's friends helped out.
12. Jack repaired tables. Jack just painted tables.
13. People arrived slowly. People bought many things.
14. Iris collected the money. Iris counted the money.
15. The total surprised us. The total pleased us.

Handbook page 529

C. Spiral Review Combine sentence pairs by forming a compound subject, compound predicate, or compound sentence. Use commas where needed as you write each sentence.

16. The day came quickly. The day went quickly.
17. Jan gave a donation to the animal shelter. Her friends gave a donation to the animal shelter.
18. The shelter needed money. The owner thanked everyone.
19. Some animals were sick. Now a vet could help them.
20. The children worked hard. The children enjoyed helping the animals.

Extra Practice, page 83.

Writing Activity A Conversation

Write a conversation between Jan and the owner of the animal shelter. Write from each person's point of view.

APPLY GRAMMAR: Include compound predicates in some of your sentences. Draw one line under each simple predicate.

Grammar

Correcting Run-on Sentences

RULES

A run-on sentence contains two or more sentences that should stand alone or be connected as a compound sentence.

Some living things are very tiny you need a microscope to see them.

You can correct a run-on sentence by rewriting each complete thought as a separate sentence.

Some living things are very tiny. You need a microscope to see them.

You can also correct a run-on sentence by rewriting it as a compound sentence. Use a comma and *and*, *but*, or *or* to separate the two parts.

Some living things are very tiny, and you need a microscope to see them.

Remember to begin every sentence with a capital letter and use the correct end punctuation.

Sentences

In your journal, write how you can recognize a run-on sentence. Then write how you can correct it.

Guided Practice

Tell whether each sentence is a run-on sentence or a correct sentence. If it is a run-on sentence, name the two sentences it contains.

EXAMPLE: *Run-on sentence.* A microscope magnifies things it makes them look bigger.
A microscope magnifies things. It makes them look bigger.

1. There are many kinds of microscopic animals.
2. Some tiny animals live in water others live on land.
3. Thousands of small animals can live in a drop of water.
4. There are tiny animals in the sea whales eat them.
5. Look at a puddle think of the millions of animals in it.

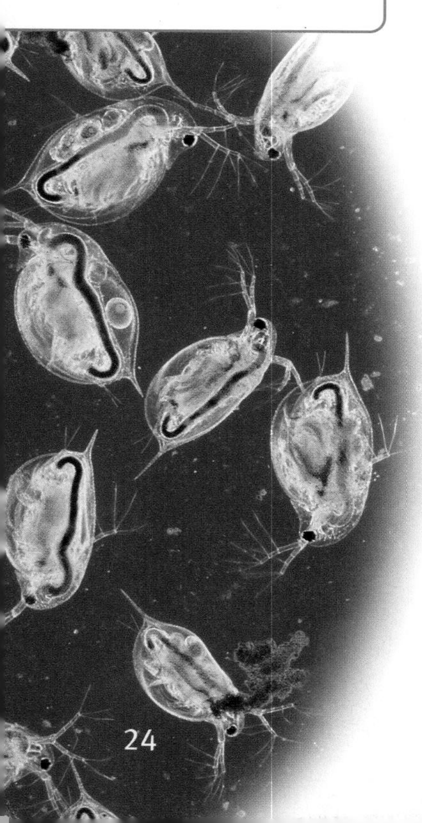

REVIEW THE RULES

- A run-on sentence joins two or more sentences that should stand alone or be connected as a compound sentence.

More Practice

A. Write each sentence. If the sentence is a run-on, write it as two separate sentences. If it is not a run-on, write *correct*.

6. You can study tiny water life with a microscope.
7. Ann walked to the pond her brother followed her.
8. The children put water, plants, and mud in a jar.
9. Lee covered the jar with plastic Ann put it on a shelf.
10. The children hoped life would grow they waited two days.

B. Rewrite each run-on sentence as a compound sentence.

11. Ann got the microscope Lee found the slides.
12. The children got the water they put a drop on a slide.
13. Ann put the slide on the microscope Lee looked at it.
14. Ann was surprised she was not as shocked as Lee.
15. Did the children see plants did they see animals?

Handbook
pages 526–529

C. Spiral Review Correct each run-on sentence. Combine each pair of sentences into one sentence. You can make compound subjects, compound predicates, or compound sentences.

16. Ann and Lee did an experiment they gathered leaves.
17. Lee put dried leaves in a jar. Lee added tap water.
18. Ann labeled the jar she did not cover it.
19. Ann waited two days. Lee waited two days.
20. Lee prepared a slide for Ann she observed tiny plants.

Extra Practice, pages 84-85.

Writing Activity A Descriptive Paragraph

Write about a large or small life form you have seen in any body of water, such as a river, lake, or puddle. Use descriptive words. **APPLY MECHANICS AND USAGE:** Check for run-on sentences. Correct them by writing two sentences or a compound sentence.

Grammar REVIEW

Mixed Review

REVIEW THE RULES

- The complete subject includes all the words in the subject.
- The complete predicate includes all the words in the predicate.
- The simple subject is the main word in the complete subject.
- The simple predicate is the main word in the complete predicate.
- A compound subject contains two or more simple subjects that have the same predicate.
- A compound predicate contains two or more simple predicates that have the same subject.
- A run-on sentence contains two or more sentences that should stand alone or be connected as a compound sentence.

Sentences

Write one example of each of the following: a sentence with a compound subject, a sentence with a compound predicate, and a compound sentence.

Practice

A. Write each sentence. Draw a line between the complete subject and the complete predicate. Then circle the simple subject and the simple predicate.

1. Children attended one-room schools in early America.
2. The teacher taught all grade levels of children.
3. Most students ranged in age from five to sixteen.
4. Early American schoolhouses were red.
5. Red paint was the cheapest paint color available.
6. Classrooms were small and dark.
7. Students went to school with their brothers and sisters.
8. Each teacher was very important.
9. The students used chalkboards or "slates."
10. Every child memorized the lessons.

Grammar REVIEW

B. Write each sentence pair as one sentence by forming a compound subject or a compound predicate. Correct each run-on sentence by forming a compound sentence.

11. Children read books aloud. Teachers read books aloud.

12. Children stood. Children recited their lessons.

13. They made their own ink. They used their own ink.

14. Mothers crushed berries. Children crushed berries.

15. Pioneers hammered nut shells for ink. Pioneers boiled nut shells for ink.

16. Roots made good inks. Bark made good inks.

17. Pencils didn't exist yet. Ballpoint pens didn't exist yet.

18. Students found twigs. They carved them to a point.

19. Children used the stems of feathers as writing tools they wrote with twigs.

20. Students faced many difficulties they were good learners.

Handbook
pages 528–529

C. Challenge Rewrite the paragraph. Correct run-on sentences. Combine simple subjects or predicates. When you are finished, you will have five sentences.

21–25. A quill is the hollow stem of a feather quills were once used for pens. Crow feathers made good pens. Turkey feathers also made good pens. Birds lost their old feathers in spring and fall those were the best times for getting a good quill.

Writing Activity A Diary Entry

Imagine that you have gone back in time to a one-room schoolhouse. Write a diary entry that tells about a typical day. Keep your tone friendly, but be informative.

APPLY GRAMMAR: In each sentence in your diary entry, draw one line under the complete subject and two lines under the complete predicate.

Social Studies Link

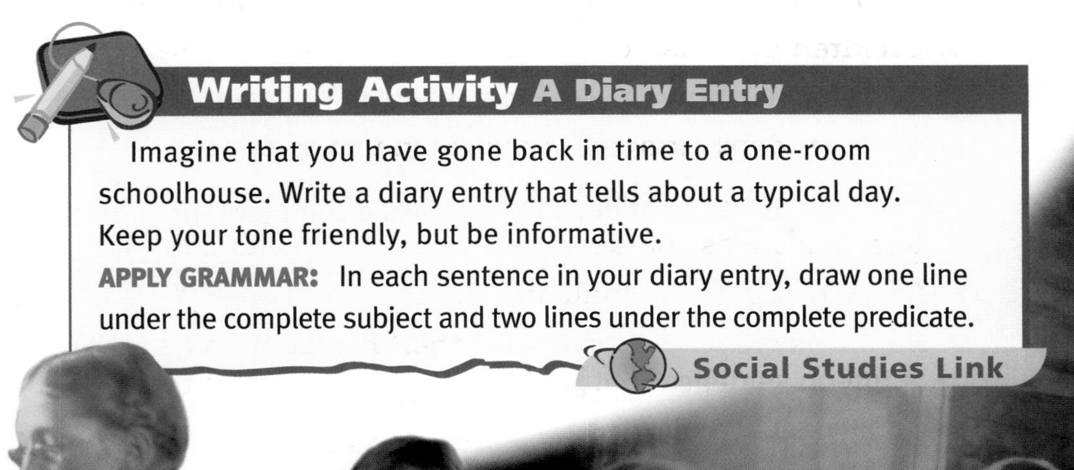

Grammar
COMMON ERRORS

Common Errors with Sentence Fragments and Run-on Sentences

Sometimes writers make the mistake of writing sentence fragments and run-on sentences instead of complete sentences. This chart shows examples of these two errors. Look at how each example is corrected.

Common Errors	Examples	Corrected Sentences
The fragment does not have a predicate.	Many animals.	Many animals live in the rain forest.
The fragment does not have a subject.	Run from tree to tree.	The monkeys run from tree to tree.
Two sentences are joined with only a comma.	I watch a colorful bird, it is building a nest.	I watch a colorful bird. It is building a nest.
Two sentences are joined with no punctuation.	Monkeys are cute birds are prettier.	Monkeys are cute, but birds are prettier.

Sentences

How are sentence fragments and run-on sentences alike and different? Write your answer in your journal.

SENTENCES

Every sentence has two parts: a subject and a predicate. A sentence must express a complete thought.

- A sentence fragment does not express a complete thought.
- You can often correct a sentence fragment by adding a subject or a predicate.
- A run-on sentence contains two or more sentences that should stand alone.
- Correct a run-on sentence by rewriting it as two sentences or be combined as a compound sentence.
- Remember Every sentence begins with a capital letter and ends with a punctuation mark.

Practice

A. Write each group of words. Write *F* if it is a fragment, *R* if it is a run-on sentence, or *S* if it is a complete sentence.

1. A rain forest is always green many plants grow there.
2. Three-fourths of all plants and animals.
3. The tall trees block the blue sky.
4. The rain forest is very wet, it gets more than 80 inches of rain each year.
5. Thirty million different kinds of insects.

B. Rewrite each run-on sentence as two separate sentences or as a compound sentence. Use correct punctuation.

6. A rain forest has many tall trees some trees can be 200 feet tall.
7. Some rain forest plants are used for medicines one medicine is for headaches.
8. Have you ever sprinkled cinnamon on toast, cinnamon comes from the rain forest.
9. People all over the world eat chocolate, chocolate comes from trees in the rain forest.
10. Bananas come from the rain forest, mangoes grow there, too.

C. Correct each sentence fragment by adding a subject or a predicate. Use the correct punctuation.

11. Grow in the tropical rain forest.
12. The damp rain forest.
13. Climb trees in the rain forest.
14. Live in the rain forest.
15. The temperature in the rain forest.

Grammar Troubleshooter, pages 506–509.

Handbook
pages 526–527

Writing Activity A Diary Entry

Is your favorite type of place the forest, the beach, or the city? Write a diary entry telling about your favorite place. Explain how the place makes you feel.

APPLY GRAMMAR: Correct all sentence fragments and run-on sentences in your diary entry. Make sure that every sentence begins with a capital letter and ends with the proper punctuation mark.

Mechanics and Spelling

Directions

Read the passage and decide which type of mistake, if any, appears in each underlined section. Choose the letter for your answer. If there is no error, choose "No mistake."

Sample

Ice skating is a challenging sport. A serious skater must have talent, determination, and skill. These athletes usually practice <u>every day? People who</u> **(1)** compete often have a trainer to help them.

The Olympic competition is probably the most difficult test for any <u>skater. it takes years</u> **(2)** to develop a style for competition. Skaters learn creative <u>dances on the ice, but they</u> **(3)** must also learn exact movements that are scored at the competition.

Only use a question mark at the end of a question.

Every sentence should begin with a capital letter.

A comma should be placed before the conjunction in a compound sentence.

1 **A** Spelling
B Capitalization
C Punctuation
D No mistake

2 **F** Spelling
G Capitalization
H Punctuation
J No mistake

3 **A** Spelling
B Capitalization
C Punctuation
D No mistake

Test Tip
When you come to a new section in a test, read the directions carefully.

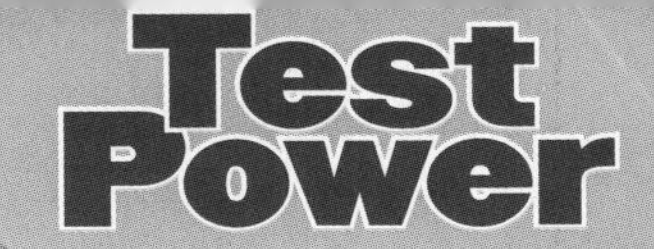

Grammar and Usage

Directions

Read the passage and choose the word or group of words that belongs in each space. Choose the letter for your answer.

Sample

Bascomb Beach is a special place. __(1)__ beauty attracts many visitors. There are steep cliffs and huge white boulders. From Dover Hill, you can see the __(2)__ views in the whole state. For true seashore lovers, there are plenty of things to do. My little sister and brother love to float in the clean, shallow water and dive into the waves. When the tide goes out, I collect shells. At sunset, my mom and dad __(3)__ to walk along the shore. I think that's __(4)__ favorite thing of all.

Possessive pronouns do not have apostrophes.

Use most or the -est form of an adjective when comparing more than two things.

Be sure to match compound subjects with the right verb form.

Remember: Some words that sound alike don't have the same meaning.

1 **A** It's
B Its'
C It
D Its

2 **F** more clearer
G most clearest
H clearer
J clearest

3 **A** liking
B like
C has liked
D likes

4 **F** their
G they're
H there
J they are

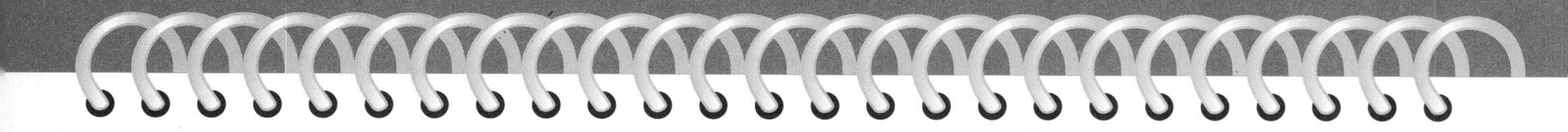

TIME FOR KIDS Writer's Notebook

RESEARCH

RESEARCH

When I'm researching a topic, I want to keep my facts straight. That's why I take notes and make a list of the main points as I read. Then I write a couple of sentences that describe each main point in more detail. Good **note-taking** helps me write my report more easily.

COMPOSITION SKILLS

WRITING WELL

A good story has the **main idea** right up front. I state my most important thought first. After all, I want my readers to understand what I'm writing about!

VOCABULARY SKILLS

USING WORDS

Words like first, next, and finally are called **time-order words**. They tell about the order in which things happen in a story. Time-order words help my readers keep track of the events I'm writing about. What time-order words can you think of?

Read Now!

Read the following photo essay about Jackie Robinson. As you read, take notes on the main points that are included in this essay.

TIME FOR KIDS
PHOTO ESSAY

Remembering Jackie

In 1947, Jackie Robinson became the first black player in the modern major leagues.

Thanks, Jackie!

Before 1947, there were no black players in the major leagues. Then Jackie Robinson came along.

On April 15, 1947, Jack Roosevelt Robinson stepped up to the plate for the Brooklyn Dodgers. Robinson did not get a hit that day. But through his courage, he forever changed the way Americans viewed baseball—and one another. Robinson had broken the color barrier in the major leagues.

Back in 1947, the U.S. was a land of cruel racial divisions. In baseball, black and white people could not play on the same teams. But Branch Rickey, president of the Dodgers, believed that blacks should play alongside whites. He signed Robinson to play ball.

Rickey made Robinson promise that he would not respond in anger when insulted. "Mr. Rickey, do you want a ballplayer who's afraid to fight back?" Robinson asked. "I want a player with guts," said Rickey, "the guts not to fight back."

It was a tough promise to keep. At first, Robinson received hate mail. Some pitchers even aimed at his head. But Robinson behaved with courage and dignity. Finally, Robinson, and other black players who followed him, were accepted.

White Sox outfielder Albert Belle believes that all players should be grateful for Robinson's courage. "It takes a big man to be the first in anything."

UPI/Corbis-Bettmann

After playing with the minor league Montreal Royals, Robinson joined the Dodgers.

National Baseball Hall of Fame

interNET CONNECTION Go to www.mhschool.com/language-arts for more information on the topic.

Jackie Robinson fought for civil rights. Here he urges people to hire African Americans.

Robinson greets fans during spring training. People came out in huge numbers to see Robinson play.

AP/Wideworld

UPI/Corbis-Bettman

The Negro Leagues

Because of discrimination, African Americans were forced to form their own teams. So they organized the Negro Leagues. The players were great showmen and athletes. Here, the Black Yankees get ready to take the field in 1942.

Write Now!

Jackie Robinson made an important promise and kept that promise. Think about a promise you've made and write to tell about it.

Note-Taking and Summarizing

Note-taking is a way to organize and remember important information. Your notes should include just enough words to help you recall main ideas and the important details that support each main idea. Notes can help you **summarize** the information in just a few sentences.

Here is an article about cattle ranching and the notes that a student used to write a summary.

Ranching Cattle ranching focuses on feeding cows and raising calves. Ranchers start their year in the fall. First, they prepare for winter by buying or harvesting a hay crop and such grains as barley, corn, oats, or sorghum. When winter comes and snow covers the ground, the cattle cannot find food by themselves. The ranchers then carry food in trucks or helicopters and spread it on the ground for cattle to eat.

During spring and summer, the herd grazes on the range. The cattle eat grass very early in the morning. During the middle of the day, they rest in the shade. Then in the late afternoon, most of the cattle go to a place where they can drink water. They then return to the field to graze until dusk.

The topic of the notes should be identified.

Notes include the main idea and important details.

Notes need not be in complete sentences.

Note Card

Cattle Ranching

–focus on feeding cows and raising calves.
–fall: ranchers gather food for winter
–winter: scatter food by truck or helicopter
–spring and summer: herd grazes on range

The main idea is always included in a summary.

A good summary includes all the important details that support the main idea.

A summary uses complete sentences.

Summary Card

Cattle Ranching

Cattle ranching is all about feeding cows and raising calves all year. Ranchers gather food in the fall to prepare for winter. To feed the cattle in winter, ranchers scatter food by truck or helicopter. The herd grazes on the range during spring and summer.

Read the following article and think about the notes you would take to help you remember important facts.

Sheep ranching involves producing two crops—lambs and wool. Most of the activity on the ranch happens in the spring. That is when new lambs are usually born. It is also the time for shearing the sheep's wool and selling it. When fall comes, the lambs are shipped to feeders or stockyards.

*inter*NET CONNECTION

Go to: www.mhschool.com/language-arts for more information on the topic.

Practice

A. Write *main idea* or *detail* to identify each note.

1. busy spring
2. sheep ranching—produces lambs and wool
3. lambs shipped to stockyards
4. wool sheared and sold in spring
5. new lambs born

B. Write your answer to each question.

6. In addition to important details, what should be included in your notes?
7. Do you need to write complete sentences on a note card or on a summary card?
8. Which would you prepare first, a note card or a summary card?
9. Is note-taking more important for reports or for writing that entertains?
10. Would you write a summary in your own words or copy sentences word for word from your source?

Writing Activity A Paragraph

Find an article about a farm or ranch. Take notes as you read the article. Then use your notes to write a paragraph that summarizes important information about the farm.

Vocabulary: Time-Order Words

DEFINITION

A time-order word tells when events happen and in what order. Sometimes a group of words is used to tell time order.

first	last	now
next	as soon as	before
then	finally	one day
later	this morning	tomorrow
after	yesterday	a long time ago

Time-Order Words

How can using time-order words make your writing clearer? In your journal, explain when you might use time-order words and phrases.

Look at the highlighted words in the paragraph below. How do these words help you know the order of events?

Last Saturday, I went to the art museum with my grandmother. First, we looked at paintings of mountains and lakes. Then, we walked through the room with all the portraits. After a quick lunch in the cafeteria, we toured the statues in the garden. Before we left, I bought a postcard to send to my cousin.

Practice

A. Write the sentences. Underline the time-order words.

1. Tomorrow, I will add photos to my new scrapbook.
2. I looked through all my photographs last night.
3. The photos made me remember things from a long time ago.
4. Later, I will sort through my postcards and souvenirs.
5. I will show this book to my grandchildren one day.

B. Choose a word or words from the Word Bank to complete each sentence. Write the complete sentence.

before	**last year**	**after**	**next**	**then**
first	**long ago**	**tomorrow**	**soon**	**yesterday**

6. ______, my aunt sent me a diary.
7. I write in it every night ______ I go to bed.
8. ______, I describe what happened during the day.
9. ______, I tell about my feelings and thoughts.
10. My diary will be full ______, and I will need a new one.

C. Grammar Link Write these sentences in the correct order. Punctuate each sentence correctly.

11. Second, pick out your favorite photographs ___
12. Do you want to learn how to make a scrapbook ___
13. First, find a book with heavy pages ___
14. What a great scrapbook you have now ___
15. Finally, paste down your photos and souvenirs ___

Writing Activity A Diary Entry

Write a diary entry about a special day or event in your life. Tell how you felt and what made the day so important. Include at least three time-order words or phrases in your writing.

APPLY GRAMMAR: Make sure each sentence has a complete subject and a complete predicate.

Composition: Main Idea

A writer usually states the main idea of a paragraph in a topic sentence. Other sentences in the same paragraph work together to develop this idea.

GUIDELINES

- The main idea tells what a piece of writing is about.
- The main idea is usually stated in a topic sentence.
- Supporting details help to develop or clarify the main idea.
- Take out any detail sentence that does not have anything important to say about the main idea.
- Put the main idea and the supporting details in the most sensible order.
- Use words like *next*, *first*, or *finally* to connect ideas.
- In a paragraph, all sentences should work together to develop one main idea.

Main Idea

Why is it important for a piece of writing to have a main idea? Write a brief explanation in your journal.

Read this paragraph about a personal experience. Notice that the writer states the main idea and uses supporting details to develop that idea and make it clearer.

The topic sentence states the main idea of the paragraph.

A supporting detail helps to develop or clarify the main idea.

A transition word helps to connect one idea to another idea.

I will never forget the day I found twenty dollars on the sidewalk. The money did not seem to belong to anyone, so I picked it up. First, I told my brother about my good luck. He happily showed me the cost of repairing his bicycle, which I had broken. When my mom heard the good news, she gladly told me to buy my sister's birthday gift. Then when my friends learned about it, they all reminded me that I owe them a pizza treat. Next time I find money, I think I will leave it there.

Practice

A. Write *detail* or *not a detail* to identify if each sentence supports the main idea in the box.

Main Idea: My last birthday was wonderful.

1. My friends surprised me with a party.
2. It was a sunny day in the city.
3. Everybody signed a funny birthday card.
4. I had been practicing soccer that afternoon.
5. I found a very special present on my bed.

B. Write a sentence that states the main idea of each of the following topics.

6. An Unforgettable Day
7. My Greatest Game Ever
8. My Cat's First Kittens
9. Moving to a New Home
10. The First Time I Met My Best Friend

C. Grammar Link **Change each main idea sentence to form a different type of sentence, such as declarative, interrogative, imperative, or exclamatory.**

11. Will I ever forget the first time I wore glasses?
12. Aunt Lisa is a wonderful relative.
13. Visit your grandparents often.
14. Winning a contest is not always an exciting event.
15. What fun shopping can be!

Writing Activity A Paragraph

Write a paragraph about an unforgettable experience. Make sure all the sentences in the paragraph work together to develop one main idea.

APPLY GRAMMAR: Be sure each sentence you write has a subject and a predicate. Draw a line under each subject and circle each predicate.

Better Sentences

Directions

Read the passage. Some sections are underlined. The underlined sections may be one of the following:

- **Incomplete sentences**
- **Run-on sentences**
- **Correctly written sentences that should be combined**
- **Correctly written sentences that do not need to be rewritten**

Choose the best way to write each underlined section. If the underlined section needs no change, choose "No mistake."

A sentence fragment does not express a complete thought.

A run-on sentence contains two or more sentences that are incorrectly joined together.

Sample

Fossils are plants or animals that turn to stone. After they die. (1) This happens when something is buried in mud or in lava from a volcano. Some fossils are imprints of leaves other fossils preserve bones. (2) Hardened tree sap can contain whole insects or small animals.

1 **A** Fossils are plants. Or animals that turn to stone after they die.

B Fossils are plants or animals that turn to stone, and after they die.

C Fossils are plants or animals that turn to stone after they die.

D No mistake

2 **F** Some fossils are imprints of leaves, other fossils preserve bones.

G Some fossils are imprints of leaves. Other fossils preserve bones.

H Some fossils are imprints of leaves, or preserve bones.

J No mistake

Test Tip
Read all the answer choices before making your selection.

Vocabulary and Comprehension

Directions

Read the passage. Then read each question that follows the passage. Decide which is the best answer to each question. Choose the letter for that answer.

Sample

"Wait, Jessie!" Mom warned when she saw me at the door. "You can come in, but those stay outside." I hadn't noticed that my shoes were dripping wet.

I took off my shoes and put them on the front steps to dry. "I'm ready to come in!" I said.

"Not until you take those off," Mom said, pointing at the floor. I was shocked! My socks had made a puddle on the floor!

I quickly pulled off my socks and stuffed them into the wet shoes. "Can I please come in now, Mom?" I asked.

"Eventually, you can," she said. "First, put these on." She smiled and gave me a pair of warm, dry socks.

Time-order words can help you understand when story events take place.

1 How does Jessie feel when she sees her wet socks?

A happy

B proud

C sad

D surprised

2 In this passage, the word *eventually* means—

F never

G maybe

H before long

J tomorrow

Seeing Like a Writer

A picture can give you a writing idea. Imagine you are in one of the pictures. Look at the details. How would you feel?

A Boy Fishing Along a Quiet Stream by José Gulio Souza Pinto

Writing from Pictures

1. Write a caption for each picture. Include declarative, interrogative, exclamatory, and imperative sentences.
2. Put yourself in one of the pictures on these pages. Write a title that tells what you're doing and how you feel.
3. Choose two pictures that contain something similar. Write a paragraph that describes what is the same about them.

   Apply Grammar: Include a compound sentence in your writing. Underline the conjunction in your compound sentence.

Personal Narrative

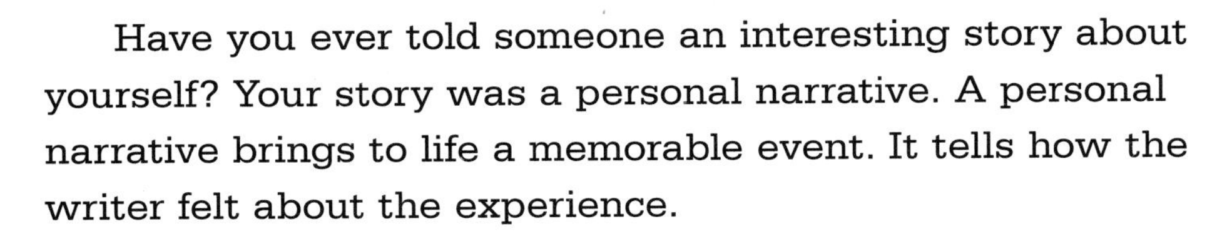

Have you ever told someone an interesting story about yourself? Your story was a personal narrative. A personal narrative brings to life a memorable event. It tells how the writer felt about the experience.

Purpose

Why do you think people write personal narratives? Write a brief explanation in your journal. Also tell why other people like to read them.

Learning from Writers

Read the following examples of personal narrative. What stories do the writers tell? Why do you think they wanted to share their experiences? As you read, look for phrases in each example that show the author's feelings.

A PLAY

When I was in the fifth grade, I was famous for a whole day, and all because of a play. The teacher had given me a big part, and I didn't want it. I liked to be in plays where I could be a part of a group, like being one of the talking trees, or dancing, or singing in the glee club. But having to talk by myself—*uh uh!*

I used to slide down in my chair and stare at my desk while the teacher was giving out the parts, so she wouldn't pay any attention to me, but this time it didn't work. She called on me anyway. I told her I didn't want to do it, but she said I had to. I guess she thought it would be good for me.

On the day of the play, I didn't make any mistakes. I remembered all of my lines. Only—nobody in the audience heard me. I couldn't make my voice come out loud.

For the rest of the day, I was famous. Children passing by my classroom door, children on the playground at lunchtime, kept pointing at me saying, "That's that girl! That's the one who didn't talk loud enough!"

—Eloise Greenfield, from *Childtimes*

Misty and Me

I'll never forget the day my cat Misty had kittens. Cats like to have a warm, private place to have their kittens. So my dad and I made a bed out of a large basket and an old baby blanket. We put it in my closet and left the door open a little. After that, we left to do an errand.

When we got back, we couldn't find Misty! I was very worried. I looked all over the house. Then I searched the garage, but she was nowhere to be found. I was in the yard when I spotted her. She just appeared from the woods behind our house. In her mouth she was carrying a tiny new kitten! She had had her kittens outside.

When I thought more about it, I wasn't too surprised. Misty had always been very independent!

—Jeff Andrews

PRACTICE AND APPLY

Thinking Like a Reader

1. Name, in the order they happened to the author, three events in "A Play."
2. How did the author of "Misty and Me" feel when he found that his cat was missing?

Thinking Like a Writer

3. How did the author let you know in what order the events in "A Play" took place?
4. What words did the author of "Misty and Me" use that help you understand how he felt?

5. **Reading Across Texts** Compare the endings of the two literature models. Do they contain any surprises?

Features of a Personal Narrative

DEFINITIONS AND FEATURES

A personal narrative is a form of writing that shares your personal experiences, including what you did and how you felt about your experiences. A good personal narrative:

- Tells a story from **personal experience.**
- Expresses the writer's feelings using the ***I* point of view.**
- Has an interesting **beginning, middle,** and **end.**
- Uses **time-order words** to show sequence of events.

Personal Experience

Reread "A Play" by Eloise Greenfield on page 46. Whom is the narrative about?

> For the rest of the day, I was famous.

The story is about the author. In a personal narrative, you write about something that happened to you.

I Point of View

When you write about yourself, you tell a story from your point of view, using the word *I*. You share your thoughts and feelings with the audience. Notice the *I* point of view in the sentence below. How do you think the author felt?

> The teacher had given me a big part, and I didn't want it.

When the author says "I didn't want it," you know she was unhappy about getting the part.

▶ Beginning, Middle, and End

Greenfield's personal narrative begins with the sentence below. How does she catch your attention?

> When I was in the fifth grade, I was famous for a whole day, and all because of a play.

This beginning may make you wonder how a play made Greenfield famous.

Now read the ending sentence from "A Play."

> "That's the one who didn't talk loud enough!"

A good ending is just as important as a good beginning. The ending might tell how the author felt or what you learned from your experience. A good ending finishes the personal narrative in a way that makes sense.

▶ Time-Order Words

To help your readers clearly understand your experience, you need to tell about events in a logical sequence, or order. Use time-order words and phrases, such as *first*, *the following day*, and *finally*.

> On the day of the play, I didn't make any mistakes.

What time-order phrase did the author use?

PRACTICE AND APPLY

Create a Features Chart

1. List the features of a good personal narrative.
2. Reread "Misty and Me" by Jeff Andrews on page 47.
3. Write one example of each feature in Jeff's writing.
4. Write what you liked about Jeff's personal narrative.

Features	Examples

Prewrite

A personal narrative is a true story about yourself. Writing a personal narrative gives you a good chance to share a story about your own experience.

Purpose and Audience

The purpose of writing a personal narrative is to express your thoughts and feelings about an experience. It is also to entertain your readers, or audience.

Before writing, you need to think about your audience. Who will be reading your personal narrative? Use language that is right for your audience.

Choose a Topic

Start by **brainstorming** a list of memorable experiences that have happened to you. Think about which topic would be most interesting for your readers.

After choosing your topic, **explore ideas** by making a list of events. Also list some of your thoughts and feelings about them. Later, you will organize these ideas.

Audience

How will your audience affect the way you plan and write your personal narrative? Write your ideas in your journal.

A Vacation Surprise

Ran into the water
Something amazing happened
Not too many people on beach or in water
Noticed something swimming toward me
Water was calm and clear
Got out of the water
Thought it was a shark
Saw that it was really a dolphin
It wasn't afraid of swimmers
The dolphin kept returning
A reporter interviewed me

PREWRITE
DRAFT
REVISE
PROOFREAD
PUBLISH

Organize • Sequence

The events in a personal narrative happen in a certain order, or sequence. To plan your narrative, you can use a sequence-of-events chart. Not all your ideas may be necessary in order to tell your story. What ideas from her list did this writer leave out of her chart?

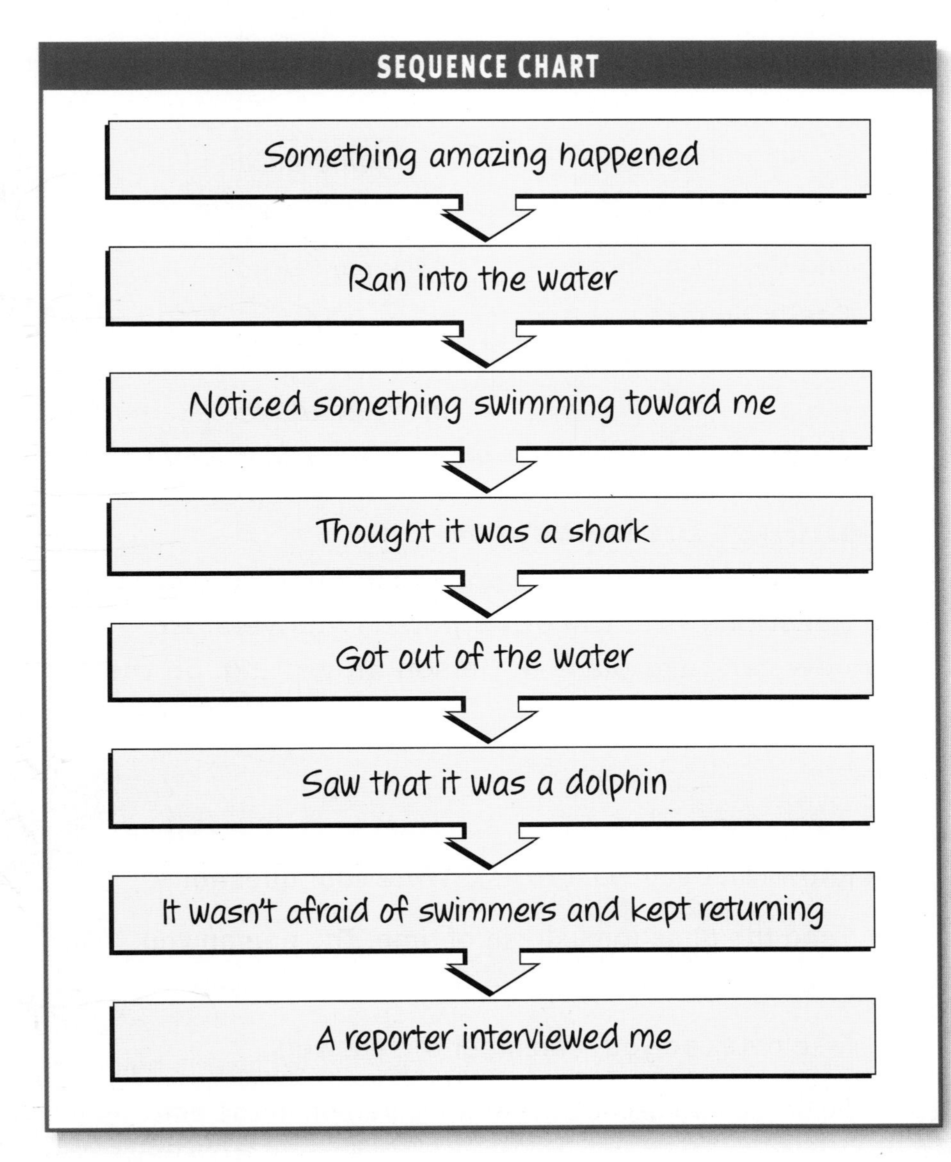

Checklist

Prewriting

- Have you listed your experiences?
- Have you thought about your purpose and audience?
- Have you chosen a topic and explored ideas about it?
- Are your ideas organized into a chart?
- Have you checked the order of events?
- Do you need to do any research?

PRACTICE AND APPLY

Plan Your Own Personal Narrative

1. Think about your purpose and audience.
2. Brainstorm ideas for a topic.
3. Choose a topic and explore ideas.
4. Organize your ideas.

Prewrite • Research and Inquiry

▶ Writer's Resources

You may have to do research to get more information for your personal narrative. First, make a list of questions. Then decide what resources you need in order to answer your questions.

What Else Do I Need to Know?	Where Can I Find the Information?
How long did the dolphin keep returning?	Check my journal.
What kind of dolphin was it?	E-mail the reporter who interviewed me.

▶ Conduct an Interview

An interview is really a conversation. One person asks questions, and the other person answers. An interview can take place in person, in writing, on the telephone, or by e-mail.

STRATEGIES FOR INTERVIEWING

- **Know what you want to ask. Write your questions.**
- **Send the questions ahead of time. The person you interview will have time to think about answers.**
- **Take notes so you remember the answers.**
- **Be polite and friendly. Thank the person at the end.**

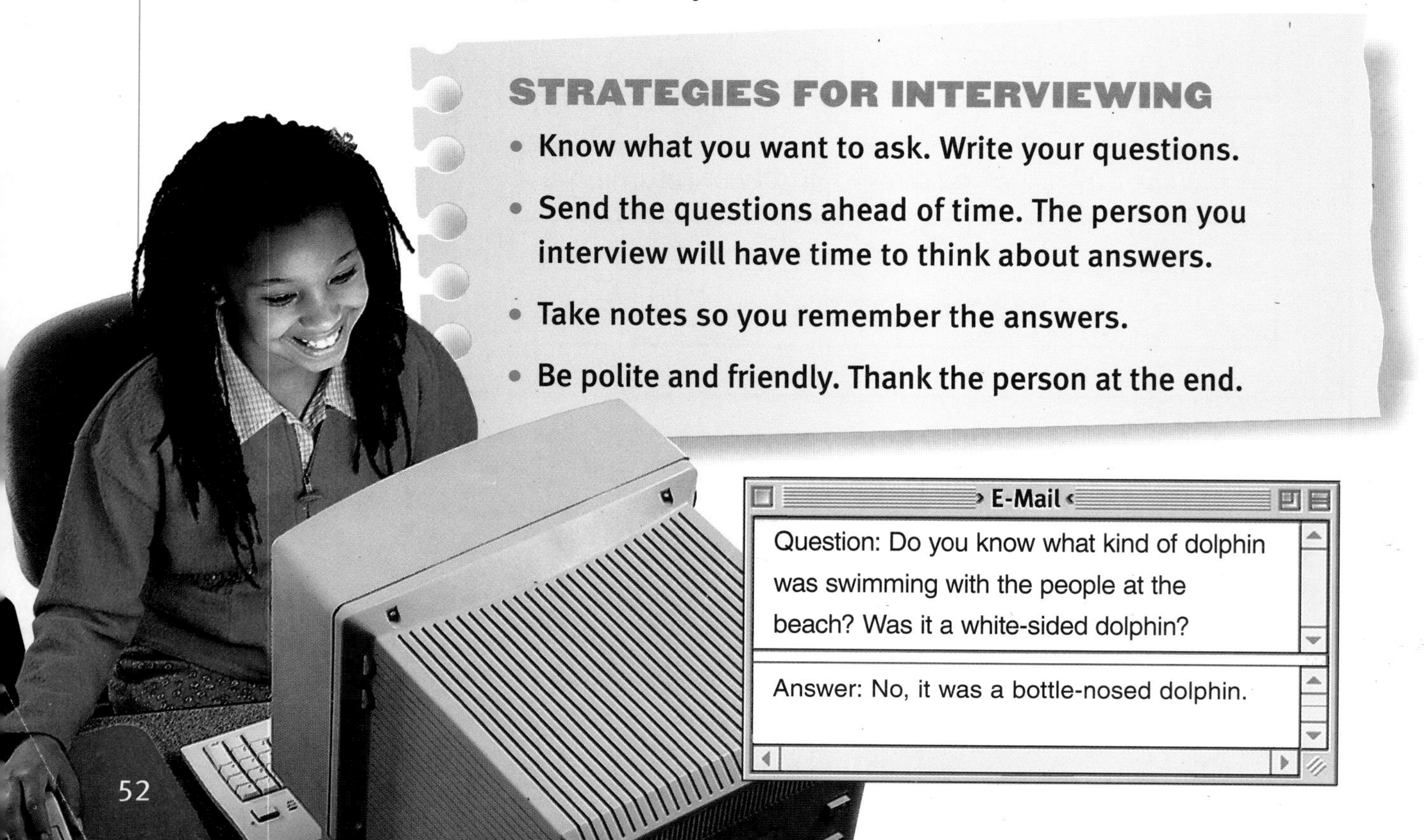

PREWRITE
DRAFT
REVISE
PROOFREAD
PUBLISH

▶ Study Personal Records

Photographs, journals, and souvenirs can be helpful sources of information. Look for specific details in photos or journal entries that will help you write clearly and specifically. Try to remember sensory details of color, sound, or smell. Using these details in your writing will make the event more real to your audience.

▶ Use Your Research

New information gathered from your research can go into your sequence-of-events chart. This writer learned something important from her interview with the newspaper reporter. How did she change her chart?

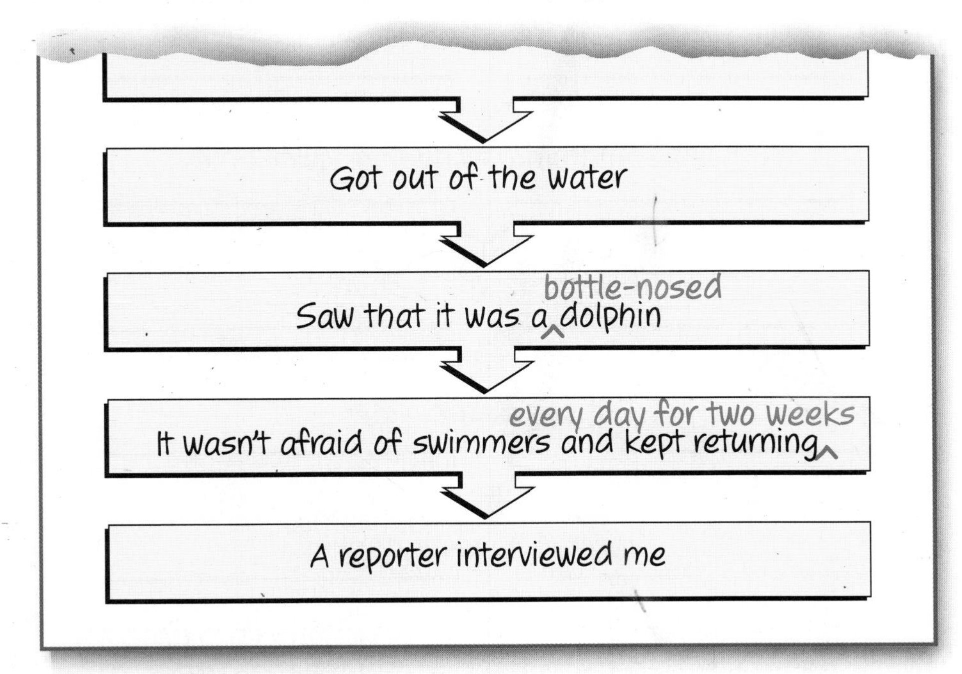

Handbook
page 564

Checklist ✓

Research and Inquiry

- Did you list your questions?
- Did you identify possible resources?
- Did you take notes?

PRACTICE AND APPLY

Review Your Plan

1. Look at your sequence-of-events chart.
2. List questions you have about your topic.
3. Identify the resources you will need to find answers to your questions.
4. Add new information you gather to your chart.

Writing PROCESS

Draft

Before you begin writing your personal narrative, review the chart you made. Think about making a paragraph for every main idea. Include the details that support each main idea.

Main idea for first paragraph: Something amazing happened.

SEQUENCE CHART

Something amazing happened

Ran into the water

Noticed something swimming toward me

Thought it was a shark

Got out of the water

Saw that it was a bottle-nosed dolphin

It wasn't afraid of swimmers and kept returning every day for two weeks

A reporter interviewed me

Main idea for second paragraph: Tell what happened.

Main idea for third paragraph: A reporter interviewed me.

Checklist

Drafting

- Does your narrative fit your purpose and audience?
- Have you used the word *I* to show that the events happened to you?
- Have you included your thoughts and feelings?
- Does your narrative have a clear beginning, middle, and end?
- Are the events in a logical order?
- Do you give details that will help readers feel as though they had been there?

Look at how this writer used the ideas in her chart to write a first draft. She elaborated on the story by adding details. She told about the feelings she had about the amazing event that happened.

DRAFT

I used to feel that nothing exciting would ever happen to me I don't feel that way anymore. While I was visiting my grandmother in Florida, something amazing finally happened. I will never forget that amazing vacation

It was the second day of our vacation. We got to the beach early. I dropped my stuff and ran into the water. I noticed something moving toward me. I thought it was a shark. I backed out of the water. I saw that it was a bottle-nosed dolphin. It wasn't afraid of the swimmers. In fact, it returned every day for two weeks.

A reporter heard about the dolphin. The reporter interviewed me. a picture appeared in the newspaper

Supporting details tell how the writer feels.

Main idea of first paragraph

Supporting details tell what happened.

Main idea of second paragraph

Practice and Apply

Draft Your Own Personal Narrative

1. Review your prewriting chart.
2. Write about your feelings.
3. Put events down in the order they happened.

TECHNOLOGY

Give your document a detailed name that you will remember. You may wish to include the word *draft* in the name.

Writing PROCESS

Revise

Elaborate

One way to improve your writing is to elaborate. When you elaborate, you add important ideas and details that might be missing from your writing. When you revise your personal narrative, you may need to tell more about your feelings.

The details that the writer added let the reader know how she feels.

> was afraid and qickly
> I thought it was a shark. I ^ backed out of the water.

The writer added the fact that she was with her grandmother at the beach to help the reader better understand her writing.

> My grandmother and I
> ^ ~~We~~ got to the beach early.

Word Choice

When you are writing, it is important to choose just the right words for your topic and audience.

In a personal narrative, you need to find words that will help you tell the story events in order.

> At first, was afraid and qickly
> ^ I thought it was a shark. I ^ backed out of the water.
> Then,
> ^ I saw that it was a bottle-nosed dolphin.

TIME-ORDER WORDS

first
next
then
later
this morning
yesterday
before
after
last
as soon as
finally
one day
tomorrow
a long time ago

Better Sentences

As you continue to revise your draft, check your sentences to make sure they fit together well. Read the sentences aloud. How do they sound? Have you included different types of sentences? Using compound subjects and compound predicates can help your sentences flow better.

Sometimes you can combine two short sentences to make one sentence that is longer and more interesting.

A reporter heard about the dolphin.

The reporter interviewed me.

A reporter heard about the dolphin and interviewed me.

Handbook
page 529

Practice and Apply

Revise Your Own Personal Narrative

1. Read your draft aloud to yourself or a partner.
2. Add details or information that will make your writing clearer and more interesting.
3. Tell more about your feelings.
4. Take out information that isn't necessary.
5. **Grammar** Should you combine any sentences in your personal narrative?

TECHNOLOGY

When you are making revisions, do a "save as" and add the date to your document name so that you can easily tell which is the most recent version of your writing.

Revise • Peer Conferencing

Take a break from your writing. Give your draft to your partner to read. Read your partner's writing. Someone else may have some fresh ideas or suggestions you haven't thought of yourself.

Good beginning!

This would make a good ending.

What did it look like?

Can you tell me more about the picture?

I used to feel that nothing exciting would ever happen to me I don't feel that way anymore. While I was visiting my grandmother in Florida, something amazing finally happened. I will never forget that amazing vacation

It was the second day of our vacation. We got to the beach early. I dropped my stuff and ran into the water. I noticed something moving toward me. I thought it was a shark. I backed out of the water. I saw that it was a bottle-nosed dolphin. It wasn't afraid of the swimmers. In fact, it returned every day for two weeks.

A reporter heard about the dolphin. The reporter interviewed me. a picture appeared in the newspaper

Conferencing for the Reader

- Are features of a personal narrative included in your partner's piece?
  - personal experience
  - *I* point of view
  - interesting beginning, middle, and end
  - sequence that makes sense
  - time-order words
- Make sure to tell your partner what's good about the piece, as well as what needs improvement.

When you revise your personal narrative you will want to think about the comments and suggestions your conferencing partner gave you. This writer made some changes based on her partner's ideas.

REVISE

Vacation Surprise

I used to feel that nothing exciting would ever happen to me I don't feel that way anymore. While I was visiting my grandmother in Florida, something amazing finally happened. I will never forget that amazing vacation

My grandmother and I
It was the second day of our vacation. ~~We~~ got to
bag and towel
the beach early. I dropped my ~~stuff~~ and ran into the
Suddenly huge At first,
water. I noticed something moving toward me. I
was afraid and qickly
thought it was a shark. I backed out of the water.
Then,
I saw that it was a bottle-nosed dolphin. It wasn't afraid of the swimmers. In fact, it returned every day for two weeks.

and
A reporter heard about the dolphin. ~~The reporter~~
of the dolphin and me
interviewed me. a picture appeared in the newspaper

PRACTICE AND APPLY

Plan Your Own Personal Narrative

1. Take notes from your partner's comments.
2. Use the notes to help make your draft better.
3. Add colorful and exact words that will create a clear picture in the reader's mind.
4. Add an interesting title.

Checklist ✓

Revising

- Does your story suit your purpose and audience?
- Do you need to elaborate on any part of your narrative?
- Have you described your feelings clearly?
- Did you use colorful, exact words?
- Did you write the events in the order in which they happened?
- Do the sentences flow smoothly when you read them aloud?
- Did you add a good title?

Writing PROCESS

Proofread

After you have revised your narrative, you will need to proofread it to find and correct any errors in mechanics, grammar and usage, and spelling.

STRATEGIES FOR PROOFREADING

- Reread your revised paper, each time looking for a different type of error. You'll have a better chance of catching all errors.
- Read each sentence for correct capitalization. Each sentence must begin with a capital letter.
- Reread for punctuation. Make sure each sentence ends correctly. Use a comma in a compound sentence.
- Reread aloud to check for run-on sentences. Be sure to correct them properly.

Spelling

The letter *q* is always followed by *u*, as in the word *quack*.

REVIEW THE RULES

GRAMMAR

- A run-on sentence contains two or more sentences that should stand alone. You can correct a run-on sentence by writing each sentence separately or by forming a compound sentence.

MECHANICS

- A sentence begins with a capital letter.
- A declarative sentence ends with a period.
- An interrogative sentence ends with a question mark.
- An imperative sentence ends with a period.
- An exclamatory sentence ends with an exclamation mark.
- A comma belongs before *and, or,* or *but* in a compound sentence.

Look at the proofreading corrections made on the draft below. What does the symbol ≡ mean? Why does the writer use that symbol?

PROOFREAD

Vacation Surprise

I used to feel that nothing exciting would ever happen to me [^ , but] I don't feel that way anymore. While I was visiting my grandmother in Florida, something amazing finally happened. I will never forget that amazing vacation! [circled and moved to end]

It was the second day of our vacation. ~~We~~ [^ My grandmother and I] got to the beach early. I dropped my ~~stuff~~ [^ bag and towel] and ran into the water. [^ Suddenly] I noticed something [^ huge] moving toward me. [^ At first,] I thought it was a shark. I [^ was afraid and ~~qickly~~ (sp) quickly] backed out of the water. [^ Then,] I saw that it was a bottle-nosed dolphin. It wasn't afraid of the swimmers. In fact, it returned every day for two weeks.

A reporter heard about the dolphin. ~~The reporter~~ [^ and] interviewed me. a [≡] picture [^ of the dolphin and me] appeared in the newspaper [⊙]

Practice and Apply

Proofread Your Own Personal Narrative

1. Correct spelling mistakes.
2. Include end punctuation for every sentence.
3. Correct run-on sentences.
4. Indent paragraphs.
5. Add a comma before *and*, *or*, or *but* in compound sentences.

PREWRITE

DRAFT

REVISE

PROOFREAD

PUBLISH

Checklist ✓

Proofreading

- Did you spell all the words correctly?
- Did you begin every sentence with a capital letter?
- Did you end each sentence with the correct end mark?
- Did you correct any run-on sentences?
- Did you indent each paragraph?
- Did you add commas where they belong?

PROOFREADING MARKS

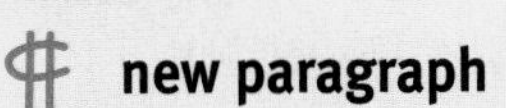

- ¶ new paragraph
- ^ add
- ℘ take out
- ≡ Make a capital letter.
- / Make a small letter.
- (sp) Check the spelling.
- ⊙ Add a period.

Publish

Before you publish, review your writing one last time. Using a checklist can help you focus your efforts.

Self-Check Personal Narrative

- ❑ **Who was my audience? Did I write in a way that will interest them?**
- ❑ **What was my purpose? Will the reader know how I felt?**
- ❑ **Did I use the *I* point of view to tell about a personal experience?**
- ❑ **Did I begin and end my narrative in an interesting way?**
- ❑ **Did I choose time-order words carefully to help make the sequence of events clear?**
- ❑ **Are my sentences varied? Do they fit together well?**
- ❑ **Did I begin and end all my sentences correctly?**
- ❑ **Did I combine sentences when I could to make my writing flow better?**
- ❑ **Did I correct any sentence fragments and run-on sentences?**

The writer used the checklist to review her narrative. Read "Vacation Surprise" and discuss the writer's published piece. Do you think it was ready to publish? Why do you think so?

Vacation Surprise

Jasmine Wright

I used to feel that nothing exciting would ever happen to me, but I don't feel that way anymore. While I was visiting my grandmother in Florida, something amazing finally happened.

It was the second day of our vacation. My grandmother and I got to the beach early. I dropped my bag and towel and ran into the water. Suddenly I noticed something huge moving toward me. At first, I thought it was a shark. I was afraid and quickly backed out of the water. Then, I saw that it was a bottle-nosed dolphin. It wasn't afraid of the swimmers. In fact, it returned every day for two weeks.

A reporter heard about the dolphin and interviewed me. A picture of the dolphin and me appeared in the newspaper. I will never forget that amazing vacation!

Handwriting

If you are not using a computer, take your time and use your best handwriting so that your final copy will be neat and legible for your readers.

Practice and Apply

Publish Your Own Personal Narrative

1. Check your revised draft one more time.
2. Make a neat final copy.
3. Add a border or decorative art.
4. Place your narrative in a scrapbook.
5. Add photos, drawings, or postcards to your scrapbook.

LISTENING
SPEAKING
VIEWING
REPRESENTING

Present Your Personal Narrative

To make a good presentation, you need to plan. There are things you can do to make sure your presentation is successful.

STEP 1

How to Tell Your Story

Strategies for Speaking As you prepare your personal narrative, remember that your purpose is to entertain your listeners.

- On note cards, write each main idea and a few details to help you remember your story.
- Tell your narrative in an interesting way.
- Make eye contact with your audience.
- Use gestures and expressions to communicate.

Listening Strategies

- Set a purpose. Are you listening for new information or for enjoyment?
- Try to picture in your mind what the speaker is describing.
- Don't interrupt the speaker. Jot down questions to ask later.
- Keep your eyes on the speaker. Let the speaker know you are paying attention.

Multimedia Ideas

You might want to play sound effects with your story. You can find sounds on the Internet or play a sound-effects recording. You can also tape-record the sounds yourself!

STEP 2

How to Show Your Story

Suggestions for Visuals Make your presentation clearer and more interesting by adding visuals.

- A large poster can help get across your ideas.
- If your audience needs to understand exactly where something happened, a diagram or map can help.
- Photographs and drawings can bring your audience into the story with you.

STEP 3

How to Share Your Story

Strategies for Rehearsing The more you practice, the more comfortable you'll feel on the day of your presentation.

- Practice in front of a mirror.
- Ask a friend to listen and make suggestions.
- Rehearse in front of family members. If you make a mistake, don't start over, just go on with your presentation.

Viewing Strategies

- **Look carefully at the materials the speaker displays.**
- **Visuals may contain information the speaker does not tell you directly.**
- **Read all the labels on the visuals.**

Practice and Apply

Present Your Own Personal Narrative

1. Make note cards with your most important ideas and details.
2. Choose maps, illustrations, or photographs to help your audience understand your personal narrative.
3. Practice saying your personal narrative out loud in front of a mirror.
4. Present your personal narrative, using your visuals.

Writing Tests

A writing test requires you to write a composition in response to a prompt. A writing prompt presents a situation and tells you what kind of writing to do. Look for key words and phrases in the prompt that tell you what you should write about and how you should present your ideas.

Stories can entertain or inform an audience. Does this story have more than one purpose?

This phrase tells you to use "I" and to write in the first person.

Look for words or phrases that name your audience.

Prompt

Celebrating a holiday with family or friends can be an unforgettable experience. Write a story about a special holiday celebration. Tell what happened and explain your feelings about the day.

How to Read a Prompt

Purpose Sometimes a piece of writing has more than one purpose. Read the prompt again. Look for important words that tell you the goal or goals of your writing. The sentence "Write a story about a special celebration" tells you that your purpose is to entertain and inform.

Audience Sometimes a prompt will tell you whom to write for. If it does not, think of your audience as your teacher.

Personal Narrative When you are asked to write a story about your own experiences, you are writing a personal narrative. The phrases "Tell what happened" and "explain your feelings" show you that you should write about your own experiences and emotions.

Test Tip

Check your composition for errors in capitalization, punctuation, and spelling.

How to Write to a Prompt

Here are some tips to remember when you respond to a prompt on a writing test.

Before Writing **Content/Ideas**	• Think about your writing purpose. • Keep your audience in mind. • Make a list of your ideas. • Stay focused on the assignment.
During Writing **Organization/ Paragraph Structure**	• Start with a good topic sentence. • Put your ideas in an order that makes sense. • When you are writing a personal narrative, use time-order words to connect ideas. • End with an interesting conclusion.
After Writing **Grammar/Usage**	• Proofread your writing. • Check that each sentence begins with a capital letter. • End all sentences with the correct punctuation. • Spell all words correctly.

Apply What You Learned

When you read a prompt on a writing test, look for words and phrases that tell you the purpose and the audience. Then think about the best way to organize your ideas.

Prompt

Making a new friend is a fun experience.

Write a story that tells how and when you made a new friend. Tell what happened and describe how you felt during and after the experience.

Unit 1 Review

Grammar and Writing Review

pages 2–3

Sentences

A. Write each group of words. Next to each group write *sentence* or *sentence fragment*.

1. Clara listened to my story.
2. Hiked through the Grand Canyon.
3. A book about flowers.
4. Takes pictures.
5. I will always remember this trip.

pages 4–7

Four Kinds of Sentences

B. Write each sentence. Then write whether the sentence is declarative, interrogative, imperative, or exclamatory.

6. My family planned a trip to the Grand Canyon.
7. What a vacation we had!
8. What did the canyon look like?
9. It was deep, wide, and colorful.
10. Read my story about it.

pages 8–9

Combining Sentences: Compound Sentences

C. Combine each pair of sentences into one compound sentence. Use a comma and the word *and, but,* or *or* to connect ideas. Write the new sentence.

11. I like to climb. My brother likes to hike.
12. Would we find a hiking trail? Would we have to make our own?
13. Our map showed the way to Treasure Cove. We took the wrong path.
14. The park ranger saw us. He gave us directions.
15. I wrote down the directions. I put my hiking journal in my pocket.
16. My journal fell out of my pocket. I did not notice that I had lost it.
17. We looked for my journal. We finally found it.

18. We could continue our hike. We could go home.
19. Some of us were tired. We completed the hike.
20. The mountain view was beautiful. We were very happy.

pages 10–11

Mechanics and Usage: Sentence Punctuation

D. Write each sentence correctly. Add capital letters, end punctuation, and commas where needed.

21. on the first day of school, I was nervous
22. would I make new friends or would I be alone
23. my classmates were friendly and funny
24. tell us about yourself
25. what an exciting year it will be

pages 14–15

Complete Subjects and Complete Predicates

E. Write each sentence. Draw one line under the complete subject and two lines under the complete predicate.

26. Danny spent last summer with his grandparents.
27. His grandfather told him many stories.
28. His older cousin visited his grandparents, too.
29. They looked at old photographs together.
30. The whole family learned a lot last summer.

pages 16–19

Simple Subjects and Simple Predicates

F. Write each sentence. Draw one line under the simple subject. Draw two lines under the simple predicate.

31. The old, rusty car needed repairs.
32. We waited near the garage.
33. A bus arrived a few minutes later.
34. We joined the tour group.
35. The guide knew a lot about the city.
36. We visited a science museum.
37. I saw several monuments.
38. My parents loved the large library in the city.
39. My younger sister played in the park.
40. She found a fountain for cooling off!

Unit 1 Review

pages 20–21

Combining Sentences: Compound Subjects

G. Combine each pair of sentences. Use the word *and* to make a compound subject. Write the new sentence.

41. The captain described the voyage. The sailor described the voyage.

42. The photographs of the trip were interesting. The maps of the trip were interesting.

43. Annette asked many questions. Steven also asked many questions.

44. Eric wanted to learn how to sail. Nina wanted to learn how to sail, too.

45. The students asked for a tour of the ship. The teachers also asked for a tour of the ship.

pages 22–23

Combining Sentences: Compound Predicates

H. Combine each pair of sentences. Use the word *and* to make a compound predicate. Write the new sentence.

46. Susan saw the high cliffs. Susan shouted excitedly.

47. The wind blew constantly. It whistled in our ears.

48. Our dog ran ahead. Our dog caught up with Susan.

49. Some hikers left the trail. They took pictures.

50. We noticed another trail. We opened our map.

pages 24–25

Mechanics and Usage: Correcting Run-on Sentences

I. Correct each run-on sentence by writing it as two sentences or by making it a compound sentence. Write the corrected sentence.

51. The photograph showed our house it was painted white.

52. A road was near the house it was really a path.

53. The path was covered with stones how bumpy it was!

54. We took the photograph to the library we spoke with the librarian.

55. She promised to find more information isn't history interesting?

Unit 1 Review

pages 38–39

Vocabulary: Time-Order Words

J. **Write these sentences in the correct order. Use the time-order words and phrases in the sentences as a guide.**

56. Finally, I reached the other side.

57. One morning, I decided to swim across the lake.

58. When I got tired, I did the backstroke or just floated.

59. Then, I did a brisk crawl to warm up.

60. First, I waded slowly into the cold water.

pages 40–41

Composition: Main Idea

K. **Write a sentence that states the main idea of each of the following topics.**

61. A Recent Surprise

62. A Day I Will Never Forget

63. My Favorite Subject

64. A Place I Would Like to Visit

65. Reaching My Goal

pages 50–65

Proofreading a Personal Narrative

L. **Write the following paragraph. Correct the ten mistakes in punctuation, capitalization, grammar, and spelling.**

For days, I had looked forward to our class camping trip. The wether had been hot all week and my friends and I packed lightweight clothing. Who could have guessed that the temperature would drop on the first day of our trip. Soon, we were freezing two of my friends had even forgotten to bring their sleepping bags. A third friend suddenly caught a cold next, the bag containing our food ripped. Then, I fell and tore my shirt. Could anything else go wrong. Finally, we decided to go home. we would go back next year and try again.

Project File

ACTIVITY 1 A Shape Poem

Poems help you express feelings. They let you say things about yourself through interesting words, sound, rhythm, and rhyme. Some poems even use shapes to get across the poet's feelings or message. Look at this shape poem. Think about how the poet uses a certain shape to express something that is important to him.

Title Tells the reader what the poem is about.

Shape Helps the reader see the meaning of the words.

Rhythm Gives the poem a steady beat.

Rhyme The rhyming words small and all create an interesting sound.

For more information, see Handbook page 586.

Write a Shape Poem As you think about something or someone that is special to you, picture a shape in your mind. This might be a room, a cat, a baseball, or some other simple shape that describes your topic. Write a shape poem about your special person or thing. Choose a shape that will go with the topic. Look at the model on page 72 to make sure you include all the parts of a shape poem.

ACTIVITY 2

A Journal Entry

Jackie Robinson showed courage and strength as he stepped up to the plate for the first time in a Dodgers' uniform. Do research to find out about Robinson's first game in the major leagues. Then imagine you are Jackie Robinson just before his big game.

A Daring Feat Write a journal entry to describe your thoughts and feelings about the important step you are about to take as Jackie Robinson. Be sure to use words such as *I, me,* and *my* to let readers know that you "are" Jackie Robinson.

Grammar

Extra Practice

Sentences

A. For each group of words, write *sentence* or *sentence fragment.*

1. Supplies for school at my desk.
2. I'm using my old backpack.
3. Mrs. Cheeves is a new teacher.
4. Gave me a blue writing folder.
5. Tomorrow we meet our writing buddies.
6. We will write stories together.
7. Our new teacher.
8. We'll tell her about school events.
9. Nathan and Fred will draw pictures.
10. Showed my photo album from home.

B. Write each group of words. Underline the sentences. Add words to correct sentence fragments.

11. Everyone wants a turn at the computers.
12. Wrote a story about camp.
13. Lisa and I swam often this summer.
14. The town pool closes this weekend.
15. This book about baseball.
16. Mark and his brother played in a summer league.
17. Byron wrote a funny story about their last game.
18. Mark wants to publish his story.
19. Typed it on the computer.
20. In his book, John.

C. For each pair, write the group of words that is a sentence. Then add words to correct the sentence fragment.

21. Early lunch this year. We eat at 11:15 A.M.
22. It's my turn in the author's chair. Your turn soon.
23. Reading time after lunch. This is my favorite activity.
24. Our buses in the driveway. The second bus is mine.
25. I'll see you tomorrow. My homework tonight.

Declarative and Interrogative Sentences

A. Read each sentence. Write *declarative* or *interrogative* to tell what kind of sentence it is.

1. My mother is an excellent gardener.
2. Every year I help her in the garden.
3. What kinds of flowers does she grow?
4. This year she tried something new.
5. Do you think we should grow vegetables?
6. Why don't you draw a picture of the garden?
7. I like tomatoes and green beans.
8. What vegetables do you like?
9. Zucchini is easy to grow.
10. What will we do with all these vegetables?

B. Write each sentence. Add the correct end punctuation. Write *declarative* or *interrogative* after it.

11. We prepared the soil in the spring
12. How big is the garden
13. My map shows the size of the garden
14. Half of the garden has vegetables
15. What kinds of vegetables did you plant
16. How often did you water the garden
17. It rained a lot this summer
18. Mother's roses didn't like all the rain
19. The vegetables were plentiful
20. Which vegetables did you pick first

C. Write each sentence correctly.

21. the neighbors appreciated the vegetables
22. would you like to taste some zucchini bread
23. did Grandmother love the tomatoes we gave her
24. it's my turn to weed the garden
25. are you going to plant the vegetables next year

Extra Practice

Imperative and Exclamatory Sentences

A. Read each sentence. Write *imperative* or *exclamatory* to tell what kind of sentence it is.

1. What fun it will be working with Mrs. Abramson today!
2. Help me unpack these bottles of paint.
3. Put everything on this cart.
4. Wash the paintbrushes carefully.
5. I've never seen so many beautiful colors!
6. Watch out for that glue.
7. What a colorful butterfly that is!
8. How easy it is to make a butterfly!
9. Tell me what color butterfly you want to paint.
10. This project is so exciting!

B. Write each sentence. Add the correct end punctuation. Write *imperative* or *exclamatory*.

11. Please visit my classroom
12. Look at this butterfly I made
13. How lucky we are to have a great art teacher
14. What a great helper you were
15. What a marvelous artist you are
16. Please go to your classroom now
17. Make sure that you get to class on time
18. What wonderful projects we do
19. How delicate the butterflies are
20. Don't worry about the glue

C. Write each sentence correctly.

21. ask Mrs. Abramson about the next project
22. tell us how to make the glass vase
23. what a great idea that is
24. please show me how to begin the project
25. what fun we will all have

Combining Sentences: Compound Sentences

A. Write each sentence. If it is a compound sentence, circle the conjunction that joins the two parts. If it is not a compound sentence, write *not compound*.

1. This summer, I helped my grandma paint her garage.
2. We went to the store, and Grandma bought the paint.
3. The paint matched the rest of the house.
4. It was a beautiful shade of yellow.
5. Grandma turned on the water, and I washed off the dirt.
6. The garage was clean, but it started to rain.
7. Did it rain for one day, or did it rain for two days?
8. Finally, the weather cleared, and we got back to work.
9. Grandma's neighbor helped us each day.
10. The three of us worked hard, but it still took a week.

B. Combine each pair of sentences. Use the conjunction given.

11. I like to paint. It was too hot to work. (but)
12. Did we need more helpers? Did we need water? (or)
13. Grandma made lemonade. Granddad made cookies. (and)
14. We had two accidents. No one got hurt. (but)
15. Mr. Bentley stepped into a paint bucket. He fell down. (and)
16. I wasn't paying attention. I hit Seth with the ladder. (and)
17. Seth was okay. He took a long break in the shade. (but)
18. Jed got him an ice pack. Mr. Lu got him some aspirin. (and)
19. We finished the garage. We decided to celebrate. (and)
20. First, we had pizza. Then, we had chocolate cake. (and)

C. Write each pair of sentences as a compound sentence.

21. Grandma wants to have a party. She hasn't planned it yet.
22. I decorated an empty paint can. Grandma put flowers in it.
23. My parents came to the party. They met Seth's family.
24. The garage looks like new. Now we want to paint the house.
25. Should we paint it? Should we call painters to do it?

Grammar

Extra Practice

Sentence Punctuation

A. Read each sentence. Write *declarative, interrogative, imperative,* or *exclamatory* to tell what kind of sentence it is. If the sentence is compound, write *compound*.

1. Black bears are found in many parts of North America.
2. They can weigh as much as 650 pounds.
3. What an amazing animal the black bear is!
4. Can a black bear climb trees very quickly?
5. Black bears rarely attack, but sometimes they do.
6. Hikers on the Appalachian Trail sometimes see them.
7. Do you know what to do if you see a black bear?
8. Make a lot of noise.
9. A camper in Yosemite National Park turned on a car alarm.
10. The bear was startled, and it ran into the woods.

B. Write each sentence correctly. Add capital letters, commas, and end punctuation where needed.

11. these bears will do just about anything to find food
12. don't leave food in your car or tent
13. black bears have torn off car doors to get food in ice chests
14. the parks have food lockers but you need to reserve them
15. does the black bear have any enemies
16. you can read about this but black bears are very unpredictable
17. bear cubs are cute but you shouldn't go near them
18. mother Bear is sure to be close by
19. how can you protect yourself from bears
20. hikers use food lockers or they hang their food bags in trees

C. Write each sentence. Add capital letters, commas, and the correct end punctuation. Then write *declarative*, *interrogative*, *imperative*, or *exclamatory* for each sentence.

21. grizzly bears are larger than black bears and they run fast
22. they have thick brown fur and they have sharp claws
23. what great fishers they are
24. how many salmon will they eat
25. remember never to run from a grizzly

Complete Subjects and Complete Predicates

A. Write *complete subject* or *complete predicate* to tell which part has been underlined in each sentence.

1. My great-grandfather came to America in 1915.
2. He sailed on a boat with two of his brothers.
3. The brothers cried at the sight of the Statue of Liberty.
4. The boat docked at Ellis Island.
5. Hundreds of people got off the boat.
6. Some cousins met the three brothers.
7. All three brothers were carpenters.
8. They found work quickly in New York City.
9. New York City was a very big place.
10. It was so different from their village in Italy.

B. Write each sentence. Draw one line under the complete subject and two lines under the complete predicate.

11. New York City had a lot of farmland in 1915.
12. Some farms were close to the city.
13. Big bridges linked parts of the city.
14. An underground subway system was designed.
15. A tunnel was built to connect some parts of town.
16. Immigrants made up half of the city's population.
17. New York City was the movie-making capital of the world.
18. New Yorkers enjoyed going to the theater, too.
19. My mother remembers many of her grandfather's stories.
20. I love the old stories about my family.

C. Add a complete subject or a complete predicate to each group of words. Write the new sentence.

21. ______ wants to take me to the Statue of Liberty.
22. ______ will take a boat from Manhattan.
23. The harbor ______.
24. ______ sailed into the same harbor.
25. I ______.

Grammar

Extra Practice

Simple Subjects

A. The complete subject is underlined in each sentence. Write the sentence. Circle the simple subject.

1. <u>The basketball season</u> starts next week.
2. <u>Our math teacher</u> is our coach again.
3. <u>Our T-shirts</u> are red.
4. <u>Eight other teams</u> have signed up.
5. <u>The schedule</u> looks very busy.
6. <u>My younger sister</u> decided to play.
7. <u>She</u> dribbles the ball very fast.
8. <u>Weekly practices</u> start on Monday.
9. <u>Our first game</u> is the following week.
10. <u>This team</u> wants to win.

B. Write each sentence. Underline the simple subject.

11. Ten children play on the red team.
12. The team picks a special name.
13. Our coach takes photographs.
14. The Red Dogs play their first game.
15. The other team plays well.
16. Both coaches give instructions.
17. Many parents come to the game.
18. The score is tied at halftime.
19. A few players look tired.
20. The next half goes quickly.

C. Write each sentence. Draw a line under the complete subject, and circle the simple subject.

21. Our team finally wins the game.
22. All our friends congratulate us.
23. The next practice is tomorrow.
24. My sister falls asleep in the car.
25. My eyelids feel heavy, too.

Simple Predicates

A. The complete predicate is underlined in each sentence. Write the sentence. Circle the simple predicate.

1. My pets require a lot of care.
2. I check their food and water after school.
3. The rabbit likes lettuce and carrots.
4. My hamsters nibble seeds.
5. Finn finishes his dog food in a hurry.
6. Smokey finds a drink in a puddle.
7. I feel very proud of my pets.
8. They look healthy and happy.
9. I take Finn for a walk.
10. Finn leads the way.

B. Write each sentence. Underline the simple predicate.

11. We see Mr. Diaz.
12. Mr. Diaz walks two dogs at once.
13. Finn says hello to his dog friends.
14. Mr. Diaz works as a guard at night.
15. His two dogs go to work with him.
16. We pass Jeanette on the way home.
17. Jeanette loves all kinds of animals.
18. Finn recognizes Jeanette right away.
19. He wags his tail happily.
20. Jeanette waves good-bye to us.

C. Write each sentence. Underline the complete predicate, and circle the simple predicate.

21. Finn makes so many people happy.
22. I took this picture of him last month.
23. Jeanette asked me for a copy of it.
24. Finn likes his walks with me.
25. He rushes home for a treat.

Extra Practice

Combining Sentences: Compound Subjects

A. Write each sentence. Underline the compound subject. Circle each simple subject.

1. My family and I visited Korea.
2. The girls and boys went to a special show.
3. Dancers and musicians formed a circle.
4. My sister and I clapped for them.
5. The actors and actresses began the first story.
6. Mother and Father remember the old stories.
7. Hand motions and music helped me understand.
8. Costumes and wooden masks were on all the actors.
9. The farmer and the old woman fool the rich man.
10. Visitors and Koreans enjoyed the show.

B. Write each sentence. Underline the simple subjects, and circle the conjunction used to join them.

11. Rice or soup is served with most Korean meals.
12. Spices and pickled vegetables taste good.
13. Chopsticks and spoons make eating a little hard.
14. Mother and Father don't mind sitting on the floor.
15. My back and legs hurt all the time!
16. These rice cakes and nuts taste delicious.
17. A boat ride and a hike sound great.
18. The lunches and the snacks are in the bag.
19. Uncle and Auntie stay at home.
20. My sister and I want to go back to Korea next year.

C. Combine each pair of sentences by creating a compound subject. Write the new sentence.

21. Korean letters are different. Korean words are different.
22. The boys count in Korean. The girls count in Korean.
23. Father came here long ago. Mother came here long ago.
24. The mountains are pretty in Korea. The rivers are pretty, too.
25. My uncles want us to visit. My aunts want us to visit.

Extra Practice

Combining Sentences: Compound Predicates

A. Write each sentence. Underline the complete predicate. Circle each simple predicate.

1. Mystery writers record and check every clue.
2. My story twists and turns.
3. A thief sneaks onto a boat and hides.
4. Then he starts the boat and goes for a ride.
5. Some detectives discuss and question every clue.
6. Then a bird on the boat squawks and opens its crate.
7. A rare parrot says good-bye and flies away.
8. The officers see and identify the bird.
9. The Coast Guard captures and arrests the thief.
10. My friends read and enjoy my story.

B. Write each sentence. Underline the simple predicates, and circle the conjunction used to join them.

11. Megan checked and searched for clues.
12. Then she listened and watched for an hour.
13. She heard and saw everything.
14. Two raccoons opened and climbed into the garbage can.
15. They threw and scattered trash.
16. Megan ran and called her dad.
17. He packed and returned home.
18. A veterinarian arrived and caught the animals.
19. He fed them and released them in the woods.
20. I wrote and edited this story myself.

C. Combine each pair of sentences. Use *and*, *but*, or *or* to join the two predicates.

21. This mystery begins well. This mystery ends well.
22. I write mysteries. I read science fiction.
23. Mom reads my story. Mom enjoys my story.
24. The ending surprised Mom. The ending scared Mom.
25. I rewrite this story. I illustrate this story.

Grammar

Extra Practice

Correcting Run-on Sentences

A. Write *run-on* if the sentence is a run-on. Write *correct* if the sentence is not a run-on.

1. Two cowboys came to town they were looking for gold.
2. They heard about some gold in this town.
3. You need a license to look for gold they didn't have one.
4. They traded their horses for the license.
5. They couldn't get to the gold mine without the horses.
6. That was easy to fix they walked up the trail.
7. One backpack was too heavy to carry up the mountains.
8. They threw away their pots and pans to lighten their load.
9. They were almost there they were a few miles from the gold mine.
10. The cowboy wanted his pans back he wanted to look for gold.
11. It is hard to cook without them, too.
12. Some cowboys made a campfire others scouted for water.
13. One cowboy made soup it was delicious.
14. Another cowboy made hot corn bread.
15. Coyotes howled nearby a cowboy shook in his sleeping bag.
16. Some other miners stopped by in the morning.
17. They told everyone about a town.
18. They explained that the next gold mine was many miles away.
19. The cowboys needed supplies they needed horses, too.
20. They would all travel together it would be an interesting trip.

B. Write each sentence. If the sentence is a run-on, write it as two separate sentences. If it is not a run-on sentence, write *correct*.

21. Chad bought three mules they looked very old and tired.
22. That was all he could afford.
23. Ben's mule is faster than Chad's Chad wanted to trade.
24. Ben agreed to trade he liked traveling slowly.
25. My cousin went with the group he had a horse.
26. He searched for gold he found some huge nuggets.
27. He brought the nuggets home to sell.
28. He used the money to buy a ranch.
29. I work on the ranch I help take care of the cattle.
30. I want to buy a ranch of my own someday.

C. Rewrite each run-on sentence as a compound sentence. If the sentence is not a run-on, write *correct*.

31. Next time, Cowboy Bob will come with us he will lead the way.
32. He'll help us find mules to ride.
33. My mule will be quick and careful.
34. Bob knows where the gold is he knows how to recover it.
35. Cowboy Bob is famous he is humble.
36. He will help everyone he will just watch.
37. I will bring my gold home my friends will be amazed.
38. My friends will be excited they will ask me many questions.
39. I will show them my photo album and postcards.
40. The trip was fun I hope to go back soon.

Theme

Reaching Out

UNIT 2

Nouns and Writing That Compares

In this unit you will learn about nouns. You will also learn how to produce a piece of writing that compares. Writing that compares tells how two things are similar and how they are different.

Math Link *In 1996, the National Basketball Association celebrated its 50th anniversary season. Read about how much basketball has changed over the years.*

Basketball is not the same game it was in 1946. Players, on average, are 3 inches taller now! Most players in 1946 were paid less than $5,000 a year. They had to take other jobs to support themselves. Now N.B.A. players can rest easy in the off-season. The average N.B.A. salary: $2.1 million. Big stars like Shaq and Michael Jordan make millions more.

N.B.A. games travel via satellite to TVs the world over. In Beijing, China, folks love the Chicago Bulls, whom they call the "Red Oxen." It's hard to believe that in 1962, when Wilt Chamberlain scored 100 points in a single game for the Philadelphia Warriors, there wasn't even one TV camera to film his amazing feat.

from "Basketball Flashback" from ***Time for Kids***

Thinking Like a Writer

Writing That Compares Writing that compares tells how two things are alike and different. Reread the passage.

- How was basketball different in 1946 from how it was in 1996? How is it the same?

Nouns The narrator describes several different people, places, and things. Read the sentences again.

QUICK WRITE What are some of the nouns used in the passage?

Grammar

Nouns

RULES

A noun is a word that names a person, place, or thing.

The boy is sad. The lot is dirty. The garbage is smelly.

A noun may appear in any part of a sentence.

The boys clean up the garbage in the lot.

A noun may name one or more than one person, place, or thing.

THINK AND WRITE

Nouns

In your journal, write how you can decide if a word is a noun.

	Nouns
Person	boy, child, neighbor, teachers
Place	lot, towns, store, city, park
Thing	garbage, bags, trees, flowers

Guided Practice

Read the sentences below. Tell whether each underlined noun names a person, place, or thing.

EXAMPLE: The two friends want a clean neighborhood.
friends: person; neighborhood, place

1. The boy and the girl clean the lot.
2. The friends pull up the weeds.
3. The teacher places paper in a bin.
4. My sister puts garbage in a bag.
5. The students need more helpers.
6. Did your brother clean up a vacant playground?
7. A huge truck hauled the trash.
8. Our city has several parks.
9. Parents and children raked the yard.
10. A gardener will plant flowers.

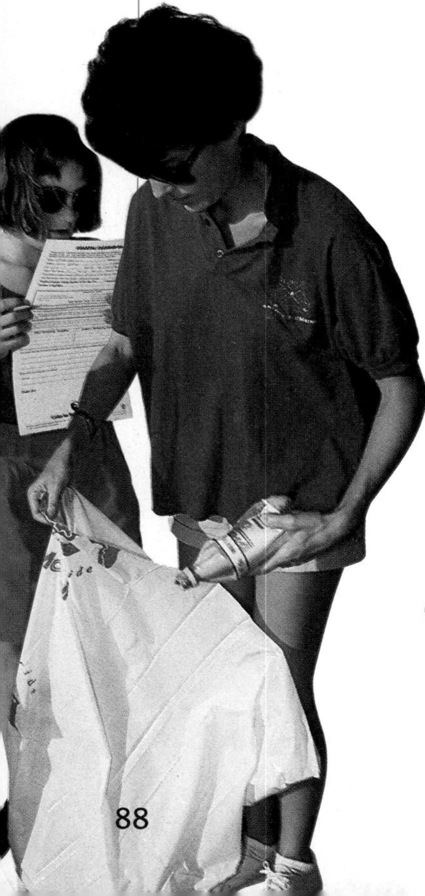

REVIEW THE RULES

- A noun names a person, place, or thing.

Grammar

More Practice

A. Write each underlined noun. Then write whether the noun names a person, place, or thing.

11. The girl makes a sign.
12. The volunteers bring gloves and tools.
13. The boy describes the problem.
14. Men, women, and children come from all over town.
15. The people want a clean neighborhood.

B. Write each noun. Write *person*, *place*, or *thing* after it to tell what kind of noun it is. Nouns are underlined.

16. The staff cuts the grass.
17. A teenager finds some broken toys.
18. Your father removes a rusty box.
19. My mother trims the bushes.
20. The neighbors clean up the litter.

Handbook
page 530

C. Spiral Review Write each sentence, adding the correct end punctuation. Draw a line between the complete subject and the complete predicate. Underline the nouns.

21. The yard is now clean
22. Some students built benches
23. A photographer took pictures of the lot
24. The neighbors plan a party
25. My relatives bring balloons

Extra Practice, page 158.

Writing Activity A Paragraph

Write a paragraph describing two neighborhoods in your community. Reread your paragraph to be sure the sentences flow smoothly and the ideas are easy to follow.

APPLY GRAMMAR: Include nouns that name people, places, and things in your sentences. Underline each noun that you use.

Grammar

Singular and Plural Nouns

RULES

A singular noun names one person, place, or thing.

The boy saw a bird at the beach.

A plural noun names more than one person, place, or thing.

The boys watched the birds eat on the dunes.

Add *-s* to form the plural of most nouns. Add *-es* to form the plural of nouns ending in *s*, *x*, *ch*, or *sh*.

Singular	Plural
boy	boys
bus	buses
box	boxes
dish	dishes
beach	beaches

Nouns

What clues do you look for to decide whether a noun is plural? Write your answer in your journal.

Guided Practice

Name the nouns in each sentence. Tell if the nouns are singular or plural.

EXAMPLE: The beach was beautiful.
beach, singular

1. The day started out quietly.
2. The beach was crowded with sunbathers.
3. The waves crashed on the shore.
4. Several boys played football.
5. California and Florida have wonderful beaches for tourists.

REVIEW THE RULES

- A **singular noun** names one person, place, or thing.
- A **plural noun** names more than one person, place, or thing.

More Practice

A. Write the nouns in each sentence. Write *singular* or *plural* beside each noun.

6. The sunbathers heard a loud, screeching sound.
7. My friends on the beach turned around.
8. A sea gull swooped down to get a cracker.
9. The bird was caught in some string.
10. Several adults helped the bird.

B. Write the plural form of each underlined noun.

11. The tangled bird was frightened.
12. The bird could not move an inch.
13. Could they use a box?
14. The man next to the bus had an idea.
15. He helped the bird and set it near a bush.

Handbook
page 530

C. Spiral Review Write each sentence, adding the correct end punctuation. Draw a line under singular nouns, and circle plural nouns. Then write *declarative*, *interrogative*, *exclamatory*, or *imperative* to tell what kind of sentence each is.

16. The sun set, and the bird flew away
17. The bird grabbed a bag of peaches
18. How did the helpers feel
19. Watch the bird fly away
20. How excited that sea gull must have been

Extra Practice, page 159.

Writing Activity A Bumper Sticker

Write a bumper sticker that tells how taking care of a helpless animal can be like taking care of a good friend. Be sure to use interesting words or phrases.

APPLY GRAMMAR: Circle singular and plural nouns.

Grammar

Nouns Ending with *y*

RULES

Nouns ending with *y* form plurals in two ways:

If a noun ends in a consonant + *y*, change the *y* to *i* and add *-es*.

family *families* *buddy* *buddies*

If a noun ends in a vowel + *y*: add *-s*.

boy *boys* *key* *keys*

Noun	Ending	Plural
country	consonant + *y*	countries
holiday	vowel + *y*	holidays

Nouns

Write a rule to help you decide if a noun ending in *y* needs a spelling change in the plural form.

Guided Practice

Tell the correct plural form of each noun.

EXAMPLE: puppy *puppies*

1. day
2. lady
3. baby
4. turkey
5. daisy
6. key
7. ferry
8. bay
9. kitty
10. Wednesday

REVIEW THE RULES

- When a noun ends in a consonant + *y*, change the *y* to *i* and add *-es* to make the noun plural.
- When a noun ends in a vowel + *y*, add *-s* to make the noun plural.

Grammar

Handbook
page 530

More Practice

A. Write the correct plural form of each noun.

11. birthday **12.** company **13.** fly **14.** lily **15.** subway

B. Rewrite each sentence. Write the plural form of the noun in parentheses ( ).

16. Lucia and Eliot saved all their (penny).

17. They spent the money on (cherry).

18. They bought the fruit for their (journey).

19. They were going to visit several (city).

20. They hoped to see (monkey) in the wild.

C. Spiral Review **Correct the run-on sentences by dividing them into two sentences. Add the correct punctuation and capitalization. Make the underlined nouns plural.**

21. Charlie helped Juan they fed the pony.

22. The cows finished their meals the donkey were next.

23. The baby were hungry the boys rushed to feed them.

24. All the berry were gone where did they go?

25. They had set down their tray the geese stole the food.

Extra Practice, page 160.

Writing Activity A Message

Imagine that you baby-sat for a neighbor's baby and her dog. Write a message to your neighbor to tell her how the job went. How was taking care of the baby different from caring for the dog? How are the two jobs the same? Make sure your writing flows smoothly.

APPLY GRAMMAR: Include the plural forms of nouns that end in *y*. Write the singular forms of the nouns in the margin.

More Plural Nouns

RULES

A few nouns have special plural forms.

The women and the men planned the event.

A few nouns have the same singular and plural forms.

There is one sheep. There are many sheep.

To form the plural of most nouns, add *-s* or *-es*. Nouns that have special plural forms and nouns that have the same singular and plural forms do not follow this rule.

Nouns

How can you remember the nouns that have special plural forms? Write your answer in your journal.

Singular	Plural	Singular	Plural
woman	women	foot	feet
man	men	tooth	teeth
child	children	goose	geese
mouse	mice	sheep	sheep
ox	oxen	moose	moose

Guided Practice

Read each sentence. Name the plural form of each word in parentheses ( ).

EXAMPLE: The sisters brushed their (tooth).
teeth

1. The (child) unfolded the blanket.
2. Two (woman) unpacked the basket.
3. The (man) served the food.
4. The girls watched the (goose) near the pond.
5. The boys took pictures of some (sheep).

REVIEW THE RULES

- Some nouns have special plural forms.
- A few nouns have the same singular and plural forms.

More Practice

A. Write each sentence. Use the plural form of each word in parentheses ( ).

6. The (sheep) fed near the pond.
7. The (woman) went fishing.
8. The boys told stories about four (moose).
9. Ryan saw a beaver with big (tooth).
10. Dad dipped his (foot) in the stream.

Handbook page 530

B. Write the sentences. Write the plural form of one of these nouns in each blank: *ox*, *goose*, *child*, *mouse*, *foot*.

11. The ______ went to the pond.
12. Caroline fed the ______.
13. Jan watched some ______ scurrying in the bushes.
14. Two ______ pulled the cart.
15. One catfish was two ______ long.

C. Spiral Review **Write each sentence. Draw a line between the complete subject and the complete predicate. Underline the simple subject. Circle the plural nouns that are formed in special ways.**

16. The white sheep reminded me of clouds.
17. The deer huddled under the trees.
18. Some mice ate our muffins.
19. The men loaded up the supplies.
20. We brushed our teeth after dinner.

Extra Practice, page 161.

Writing Activity Character Descriptions

Describe two members of a family. Tell how they are alike and different. Use interesting details to describe the people.
APPLY GRAMMAR: Circle plural nouns in your description.

Grammar

Common and Proper Nouns

RULES

A common noun names any person, place, or thing.

My brother went to the park last month.

A proper noun names a particular person, place, or thing.

John went to Oceanside Park last July.

Notice that a proper noun always begins with a capital letter. If a proper noun has more than one word, each important word begins with a capital letter.

Nouns

Write how you can tell whether a word is a common noun or a proper noun.

	Common Nouns	Proper Nouns
Person	brother	John
Place	park	Oceanside Park
Thing	day holiday	Sunday Thanksgiving

Guided Practice

Name the nouns in each sentence. Tell whether each is a common noun or a proper noun.

EXAMPLE: Ruby and Tom are neighbors.
Ruby, Tom: proper; neighbors: common

1. Bakersville just passed a new law.
2. Students will attend school in June, July, and August.
3. Two friends wrote a letter to Mayor Chen.
4. Ruby Gomez called the mayor on the phone.
5. Tom Peters went to a meeting at Reed High School.
6. The Fourth of July is a holiday.
7. The school is on Parker Road.
8. The city is hot in the summer.
9. Labor Day falls in the month of September.
10. Some parents spoke Spanish.

REVIEW THE RULES

- A common noun names any person, place, or thing.
- A proper noun names a particular person, place, or thing.

Grammar

More Practice

A. Write the nouns in each sentence. Then write *common* or *proper* next to each one to show what kind of noun it is.

11. There will be a rally next Tuesday.
12. People will go to City Hall with signs.
13. Ruby and Tom made posters.
14. The rally falls on Groundhog Day.
15. The citizens spoke with Mayor Chen.

B. Write each sentence correctly. Capitalize the proper nouns. Underline the common nouns.

16. terrence and lameca wrote a speech.
17. Students and parents gathered in washington park.
18. Some teachers took a bus to the park.
19. A reporter wrote an article for the bakersville times.
20. Mayor chen thought more about the law.

C. Spiral Review Combine each pair of sentences into one sentence. Draw one line under each common noun and capitalize each proper noun.

21. Lisa learned about the law. Al learned about the law.
22. Tom talked to mayor chen. Some teachers talked to mayor chen.
23. Students liked the principal. Students respected the principal.
24. Experts gave advice. Officials listened to opinions.
25. People worked together. People shared ideas on friday.

Handbook page 531

Extra Practice, page 162.

Writing Activity A Letter

Write a letter telling about a typical day in school and a typical day during the summer. Organize your ideas logically.
APPLY GRAMMAR: Draw a line under each proper noun. Circle each common noun.

Capitalization

RULES

Proper nouns, including names of **days**, **months**, and **holidays**, always begin with a **capital letter**.

Friday *August* *Fourth of July*

Family names that refer to specific people begin with a capital letter.

I asked Father for a ride to school. Mother rode, too.

Titles of respect that are part of a specific name begin with a capital letter.

President Lincoln *Miss Gertrude Martin*

The first word and all important words in the **title** of a book, song, poem, play, short story, or movie begin with a capital letter.

The Wind in the Willows

Nouns

Write how you know when to begin a noun with a capital letter.

If a proper noun has more than one word, each important word begins with a capital letter.

Guided Practice

Name the nouns that should begin with a capital letter.

EXAMPLE: We began school on a monday.
Monday

1. In september, a new student joined our class.
2. Our teacher, miss ping, introduced the girl.
3. She had lived in atlanta, georgia.
4. I read "the princess and the pea" to my sister.
5. On tuesday, mom will speak to the class.

REVIEW THE RULES

- Capitalize the names of specific persons, places, things, days, months, and holidays.
- Capitalize family names and titles of respect.
- Capitalize the first word and all important words in titles.

Grammar

More Practice

A. Write each sentence correctly. Add capital letters.

6. I introduced linda to my friend seth.

7. Seth is reading *just a dream* by chris van allsburg.

8. By thanksgiving, linda seemed very happy.

9. Every friday, miss lopez gives piano lessons.

10. Last week, mother played the piano, too.

Handbook
pages 548–551

B. Write each sentence. Fill in each blank with a proper noun that fits the description shown in parentheses ( ).

11. ______ started a club for new students. (a person)

12. The club meets every ______. (day of the week)

13. We celebrated ______ at one of the meetings. (a holiday)

14. Linda brought the movie ______. (title of movie)

15. The club's final meeting was held in ______. (month)

C. Spiral Review **Combine each pair of sentences using compound predicates. Underline each simple subject. Correct all capitalization errors.**

16. miss ward created the club. miss ward supervised the club.

17. Members suggest new ideas. Members discuss new ideas.

18. On thursday, we made signs. On thursday, we hung signs.

19. The members behaved seriously. The members were friendly.

20. The new club helped linda. The new club encouraged linda.

Extra Practice, page 163.

Writing Activity A Poster

Create a poster telling new students about school clubs. Use precise words to describe similarities and differences.

APPLY GRAMMAR: Draw a line under proper nouns.

Mixed Review

REVIEW THE RULES

- A noun names a person, place, or thing.
- A singular noun names one person, place, or thing, and a plural noun names more than one person, place, or thing.
- Add *-s* to form the plural of most nouns. Add *-es* to nouns ending in *s*, *x*, *ch*, or *sh*. When a noun ends in a consonant + *y*, change the *y* to *i* and add *-es*.
- A common noun names any person, place, or thing.
- A proper noun names a particular person, place, or thing and begins with a capital letter.
- Days, months, and holidays begin with a capital letter.
- Family names that refer to specific people and titles of respect that are part of a specific name begin with capital letters.
- The first word and all important words in the title of a book, song, poem, play, short story, or movie begin with a capital.

QUICK WRITE

Nouns

Write five sentences about what you see in your classroom. Use singular nouns, plural nouns, common nouns, and proper nouns.

Practice

A. Write each sentence. Draw one line under each singular noun. Then write the plural form of each noun you underlined.

1. The boy and girl went to the country.
2. The child took a bus to a farm.
3. A man pointed out a deer and a goose.
4. Each student learned about an animal.
5. A kitten crawled into a box.
6. The farmer chased the mouse.
7. The woman fed the ox.
8. Another friend sheared the sheep.
9. My brother fed the chicken.
10. Each helper picked a berry to add to the pie.

Grammar REVIEW

B. Write the sentences correctly. Use capital letters where they are needed.

11. The friends spent all of august on the farm.

12. They helped miss brown take care of her animals.

13. Each night rex read from his book *the boy farmer*.

14. On tuesdays, jan got milk from newport dairy.

15. Hannah wrote in her journal on thursdays.

16. Bill picked apples at green meadows orchard.

17. The group made pies for the fourth of july.

18. Last saturday, uncle ernie came for a visit.

19. The country adventure ended on labor day.

20. Maya learned that grandfather had been a farmer.

C. Challenge **Rewrite the paragraph correctly. Look for proper nouns that need to be capitalized and plural nouns that are not spelled correctly.**

21–30. The children left green meadows farm on friday afternoon. Farmer Brown gave them apples and berrys for their trip. Jack promised to return on memorial day. Jan read the book *becoming a farmer* all the way home. Rex and danny looked at the photographs they had taken of sheeps, deers, gooses, and oxes. What a fun way to learn about farming!

Handbook
pages 530–531, 548–551

Writing Activity A Magazine Article

Write a magazine article telling about life on a farm and life in the city. What can you do and see on a farm? What can you do and see in a city? Check your article carefully for mistakes in punctuation and capitalization.

APPLY GRAMMAR: Draw one line under each common noun and two lines under each proper noun.

Social Studies Link

Singular Possessive Nouns

RULES

A possessive noun is a noun that shows who or what owns or has something.

A singular possessive noun is a singular noun that shows ownership.

The boy's skateboard is yellow.

Add an *apostrophe* and *s* to a singular noun to make it possessive.

dog + ' + s = dog's

The dog's bowl is green.

Nouns

In your journal, write when you would use a possessive noun.

Guided Practice

Name another way to say each phrase. Use the possessive form of the underlined noun.

EXAMPLE: the business of my father
my father's business

1. the job of the boy
2. the desk of the secretary
3. the mail of the owner
4. the idea of the client
5. the office belonging to Jerry
6. the desk of Jan
7. a letter belonging to the teacher
8. the car of the salesman
9. the bookshelf of the man
10. the pen of the writer

REVIEW THE RULES

- Form a singular possessive noun by adding an apostrophe and an *s* (*'s*) to a singular noun.

Grammar

Handbook page 531

More Practice

A. Write each phrase in another way. Use the possessive form of the underlined noun.

11. a computer belonging to the boss
12. the papers belonging to my friend
13. the books belonging to my dad
14. the folders that belong to Brian
15. the backpack that Mrs. Everett owns

B. Write each sentence. Use the singular possessive form of the noun in parentheses ( ) to complete each sentence.

16. ______ delivery service was quite successful. (Lee)
17. ______ help was very important. (Sue)
18. Each ______ mail came on time. (person)
19. ______ package had to be delivered first. (David Woo)
20. The______ idea helped him earn money. (boy)

C. Spiral Review Write each sentence, adding the correct end punctuation. Replace the underlined words with a phrase containing a possessive noun. Write *interrogative* or *declarative* after each sentence.

21. Everyone knows about the job of my neighbor
22. What is the business of that boy
23. Sue worked on the team of Bob, too
24. Is that the bicycle belonging to Sue
25. The delivery of Carl got to his house on time

Extra Practice, page 164.

Writing Activity An Advertisement

Imagine that you own a company. Write an ad that tells why your company is better than other ones. Use vivid words.

APPLY GRAMMAR: Include possessive nouns and underline them.

Plural Possessive Nouns

RULES

A plural possessive noun is a plural noun that shows ownership.

The president spoke about the members' needs.

When a plural noun ends in *s*, add an *apostrophe* (') to form the plural possessive noun.

members + ' = members'

When a plural noun does not end in *s*, add an *apos-trophe* and *s* ('s) to form the plural possessive noun.

children + 's = children's

Nouns

How is a plural possessive noun different from a singular possessive noun? Write your ideas in your journal.

Guided Practice

Name another way to say each phrase. Use the possessive form of the underlined noun.

EXAMPLE: the announcement of the boys
the boys' announcement

1. the rules of the children
2. the discussion of the experts
3. the decision of the voters
4. the conference of the students
5. the members of the groups
6. the chairs of the secretaries
7. the ties of the gentlemen
8. the briefcases of the teachers
9. the keyboards of the computers
10. the seats of the guests

REVIEW THE RULES

- Add an apostrophe to a plural noun that ends in *s* to form the plural possessive. Add *'s* to a plural noun that does not end in *s*.

Grammar

More Practice

A. Rewrite each group of words. Use the possessive form of the underlined noun.

11. the speeches of the leaders

12. the ideas of the women

13. the rights of the children

14. the votes of the committees

15. the plans of the judges

Handbook
pages 531, 553

B. Write each sentence. Use the possessive form of the plural noun in parentheses ( ) to fill in each blank.

16. The students listened to the ______ plans. (candidates)

17. The ______ ideas were very clear. (citizens)

18. It was difficult to hear the ______ voices. (speakers)

19. The ______ reactions were exciting. (crowds)

20. The ______ choice will be known tomorrow. (voters)

C. Spiral Review **Rewrite each sentence. Replace the underlined words with a possessive noun. Underline the complete subject. Circle the simple subject.**

21. The comments of the men were very interesting.

22. The questions of the listeners were intelligent.

23. The cheers of my classmates were loud.

24. The opinions of my peers were finally heard.

25. The jobs of the new leaders will begin next week.

Extra Practice, page 165

Writing Activity A Speech

Write a speech describing the jobs of class president and president of the country. Make your sentences flow.

APPLY GRAMMAR: Include plural possessive nouns. Underline them.

Social Studies Link

Grammar

Combining Sentences: Nouns

RULES

You can combine sentences that have similar ideas by joining two nouns.

You can combine nouns in the subject.

Ann and Al saw the play.

You can combine nouns in the predicate.

They saw a comedy and a drama.

THINK AND WRITE

Nouns

How do you know when to combine sentences? Write your ideas in your journal.

Use the conjunction *and* or *or* to join together nouns in the subject or predicate. The word *and* shows that the ideas are linked. The word *or* shows a choice between ideas.

Peg wrote the play.
Jim wrote the play. → *Peg and Jim wrote the play.*

Does the story take place in Texas?
Does the story take place in Ohio? → *Does the story take place in Texas or Ohio?*

Guided Practice

Name the nouns that could be combined in the subject or predicate. Tell what word you would use to join them.

EXAMPLE: The Drama Club needs new members. The Art Club needs new members.
Drama Club, Art Club; and

1. Joy wanted to join a club. Jon wanted to a join club.
2. Ron joined the Drama Club. Sean joined Drama Club.
3. Sean may get the lead part. Joan may get the lead part.
4. Carol may sing jazz. Carol may sing opera.
5. The teacher addressed the students. The teacher addressed the parents.

REVIEW THE RULES

- You can combine sentences with similar ideas.
- Use the word *and* or *or* to join nouns in the subject or the predicate.

Grammar

Handbook
page 529

More Practice

A. Write each sentence. Underline the nouns that could be combined. Write the word you would use to join them.

6. Marc made the costumes. Marc made the scenery.
7. Joan sold shirts. Joan sold tickets.
8. Matt designed posters. Lana designed posters.
9. Did Max play the piano? Did Max play the drums?
10. Liz may say the first lines. Ed may say the first lines.

B. Combine the sentences by joining nouns with *and* or *or*.

11. Donna went to the play. Carl went to the play.
12. Did James see the play first? Did James see the game first?
13. Ron acted well. Joan acted well.
14. The actors shared their thoughts. The actors shared their ideas.
15. Nina got to the theater early. Pilar got to the theater early.

C. Spiral Review Combine each pair of sentences, using *and*, *or*, or *but*. Write *declarative* or *interrogative* after each sentence.

16. The actors were tired. They were happy.
17. Was the party at the school? Was the party in the park?
18. Did Sean order the cake? Did Joan order the cake?
19. The boys were excited. The girls were excited.
20. The director was pleased. She congratulated the cast.

Extra Practice, page 166.

Writing Activity A Review

Write a review of two plays or movies you have seen. Tell which one you liked better. Include interesting details.

APPLY GRAMMAR: Combine sentences with related ideas.

Grammar

Abbreviations

RULES

An abbreviation is the shortened form of a word. An abbreviation usually ends with a period.

Abbreviations are used for most titles of people before names.

Dr. Brent *Ms. Ping* *Mr. Barker* *Gov. Richards*

Abbreviations are also used for days and months.

Tues. *Fri.* *Feb.* *Dec.*

Titles	Mr.	a man	Dr.	Doctor
	Ms.	any woman	Sen.	Senator
	Mrs.	a married woman	Gov.	Governor
Days	Mon.	Monday	Thurs.	Thursday
	Wed.	Wednesday	Sat.	Saturday
Months	Jan.	January	Sept.	September
	Apr.	April	Oct.	October
	Aug.	August	Nov.	November

Nouns
How can you recognize an abbreviation? Write your ideas in your journal.

Guided Practice

Name the abbreviation for each underlined word.

EXAMPLE: Sunday evening
Sun.

1. Thursday at noon
2. Governor Bailey
3. last Sunday
4. Doctor Engel
5. January 1
6. Senator Berry
7. October 20
8. Mister Sheinman
9. next Saturday
10. in April

REVIEW THE RULES

- **Abbreviations** are used for **days**, **months**, and **titles**.

More Practice

A. Write the abbreviation for each underlined word.

11. Saturday morning
12. Monday, September 19
13. Senator Mendez
14. Wednesday evening
15. Doctor Parker

B. Write the groups of words, replacing the words in parentheses ( ) with abbreviations.

16. (a married woman) Gina Shea
17. (any woman) Roberta Tack
18. (Governor) Heiser
19. (Friday), (December) 12
20. the last (Wednesday) in (November)

C. Spiral Review Rewrite each group of words. Change each underlined word to an abbreviation. If the group of words is a sentence, add the correct punctuation. If it is not a sentence, write *fragment* after it.

21. Will Mister Kirby take his class to Washington
22. Airplane reservations on Thursday morning
23. Monday, January 3
24. The bus dropped us off at Senator Taylor's office
25. What a great speaker Doctor Howard was

Extra Practice, page 167.

Writing Activity A Letter

Write a letter describing what you did on two days. How were the days alike and different? Organize your ideas logically.

APPLY GRAMMAR: Underline words that could be abbreviated. Write the abbreviations at the end of your letter.

UESDAY WEDNESDAY THURSDAY F

Grammar

Handbook
pages 544–545

Grammar REVIEW

Mixed Review

REVIEW THE RULES

- A singular possessive noun is a singular noun that shows ownership.
- Add an apostrophe (') and *s* to a singular noun to make it possessive.
- A plural possessive noun is a plural noun that shows ownership.
- Add an apostrophe to a plural noun that ends in *s* to make it possessive.
- Add an apostrophe and *s* to a plural noun that does not end in *s* to make it possessive.
- You can combine sentences that have similar ideas by joining two nouns.
- An abbreviation is the shortened form of a word.

Nouns

Write five sentences. Use a possessive noun in each sentence. Underline singular possessive nouns and circle plural possessive nouns.

Practice

A. Rewrite each phrase using a possessive noun. Use abbreviations when possible.

1. the lessons of the teachers
2. the study hour of the class
3. the room belonging to Mister Meyer
4. the story time of the children
5. the uniforms belonging to the band
6. the birthday of Doctor McDonald
7. the lunches of the students
8. the ideas of the women
9. the report of the committee
10. the decision of Governor Todd

B. Combine each pair of sentences by joining nouns with *and* or *or*.

11. Carlos helps a student. Carlos helps a friend.

12. Carlos knew John. Meg knew John.

13. Is Beth taking music first? Is Beth taking art first?

14. Dan tutors in history. Dan tutors in science.

15. José enjoyed math. Meg enjoyed math.

16. Did Pam erase that math problem? Did John erase that math problem?

17. Did the club invite Governor Jones last? Did the club invite Senator Abrams last?

18. Is Marie the club president? Is Meg the club president?

19. Did David attend the drama club today? Did David attend the poetry club today?

20. The club held a picnic. The club held a contest.

C. Challenge Rewrite the paragraph. Correct the possessive nouns and abbreviations.

21–25. Some of mrs Bakers students want a class pet. On Monday, the class had a meeting. One students' opinion was heard at a time. The childrens' decision was final! The class is getting a new pet. Brians brother will donate a furry little hamster.

Handbook pages 531, 544–545, 553

Writing Activity A Paragraph

Write a paragraph about two of your favorite subjects or activities. How are they alike and different? Make sure the reader understands your feelings.

APPLY MECHANICS AND USAGE: Put apostrophes in the correct place when you form possessive nouns. Circle the apostrophes.

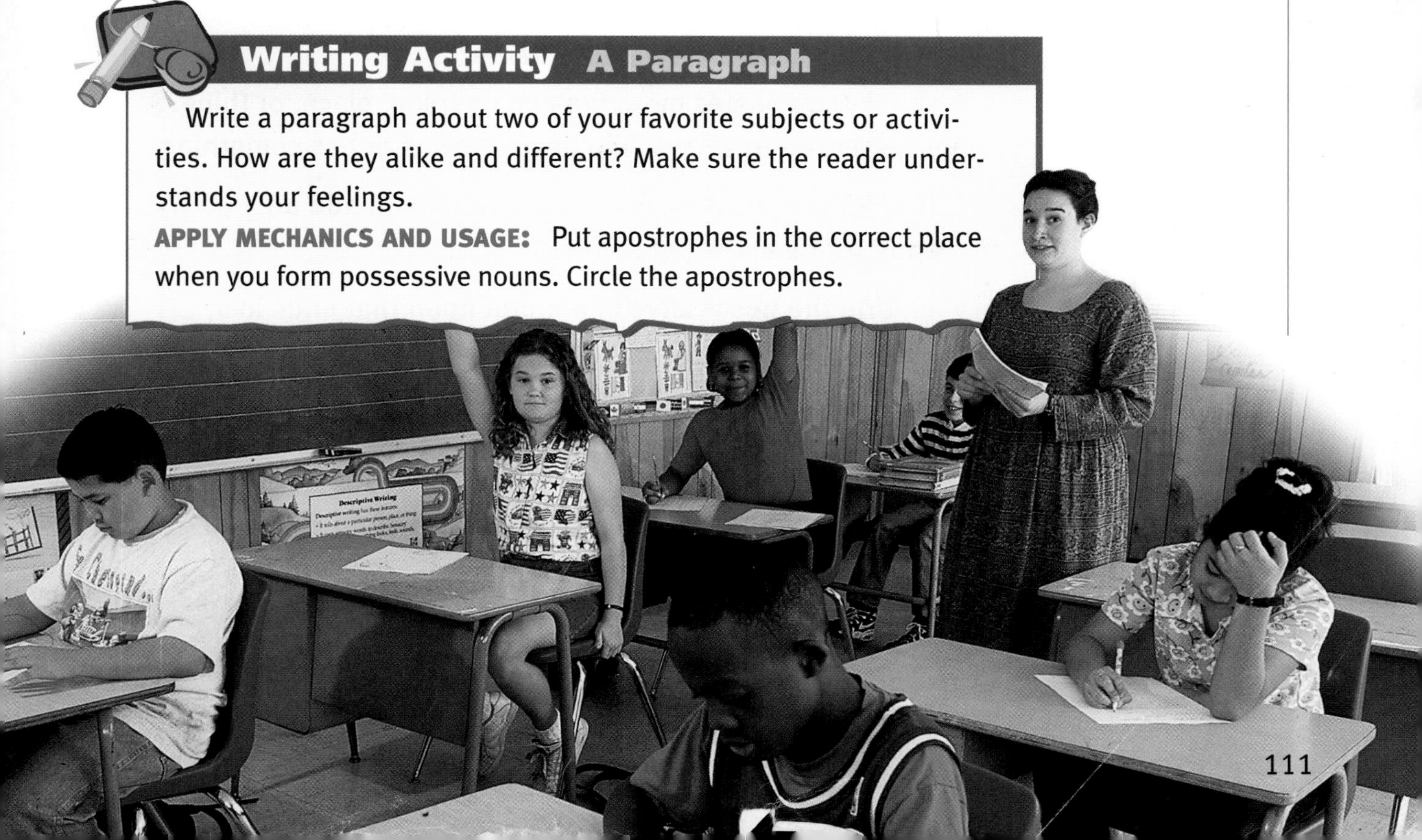

Common Errors with Plurals and Possessives

Writers sometimes make mistakes when they use two kinds of nouns: plural nouns and possessive nouns. This chart gives examples of mistakes to look for in your own writing and shows you how to correct each error.

Common Errors	Examples	Corrected Sentences
Using an apostrophe in a plural noun	Some scientist's study fossils.	Some scientists study fossils.
Leaving out an apostrophe in a possessive noun	Each fossils history is interesting. The girls reports are long.	Each fossil's history is interesting. The girls' reports are long.
Putting an apostrophe in the wrong place in a possessive noun	The childrens' class learned about the past.	The children's class learned about the past.

Nouns

Why is it important to write plural nouns and possessive nouns correctly? Write your answer in your journal.

REVIEW THE RULES

PLURALS AND POSSESSIVES

A plural noun names more than one person, place, or thing. A possessive noun shows who or what owns or has something.

- To form the possessive of a singular noun, add an apostrophe and *s* (*'s*).
- To form the possessive of a plural noun that ends in *s*, add an apostrophe (').
- To form the possessive of a plural noun that does not end in *s*, add an apostrophe and *s* (*'s*).
- Remember Most plural nouns are formed by adding *s* or *es*.

Practice

A. Read each sentence. Write whether the underlined word is a *plural noun*, a *singular possessive*, or a *plural possessive*.

1. Fossils tell a story.
2. Those are dinosaurs' eggs.
3. Can you guess the plant's age?
4. The scientists study fossils.
5. You can see the oxen's footprints.

B. Write each sentence. Correct each underlined plural or possessive noun.

6. We learn about earths history from fossils.
7. A footprint is a clue to an animals size.
8. Students found many bone's in a tar pit.
9. The scientists measured two bones lengths.
10. The mens' report described the fossils.

C. Write each sentence correctly. Correct errors in plural nouns and possessive nouns.

11. We learned about two scientists discoveries in a museum.
12. The womens' research was important.
13. The guide told us about ancient plant's.
14. One plants edges were sharp.
15. We studied many flowers shapes.

Handbook
pages 530–531

Grammar Troubleshooter, pages 510–511.

Writing Activity Descriptive Labels

Choose two objects in your room. Write a label for each one that explains what the object tells about you. Use vivid words.
APPLY GRAMMAR: Be sure to use apostrophes correctly to form singular and plural possessive nouns. Check that you have spelled plural nouns correctly.

Mechanics and Spelling

Directions

Read the passage and decide which type of mistake, if any, appears in each underlined section. Choose the letter for your answer. If there is no error, choose "No mistake."

Add an apostrophe and s to a singular noun to make it possessive.

The main words in a proper noun must begin with a capital letter.

When a word ends in silent e, drop the e when adding an ending that begins with a vowel.

Sample

We have a new boy in my class. The boys name (1) is Harold Ling. His mother, Dr. Ling, is a dentist. Her office is on hillcrest avenue near (2) the school. The Lings' house is next door to the office. I think Harold and I will be good friends. He plays soccer, and he loves spaghetti. He inviteed me to come (3) over this Friday after school. I can't wait.

1 **A** Spelling
B Capitalization
C Punctuation
D No mistake

2 **F** Spelling
G Capitalization
H Punctuation
J No mistake

3 **A** Spelling
B Capitalization
C Punctuation
D No mistake

Test Tip
When you have finished, reread all the answer choices to be sure you marked the choice you intended.

Grammar and Usage

Directions

Read the passage and choose the word or group of words that belongs in each space. Choose the letter for your answer.

Sample

Volunteering is a __(1)__ way to spend a Saturday. Recently, my aunt and I helped clean up a community center. First we __(2)__ everything outside. There, some other volunteers sorted through the items and decided what should be thrown out. Meanwhile, my aunt and I went inside to scrub the rooms from top to bottom. Then __(3)__ painted the walls a bright white. After all the volunteers had __(4)__ their work, the community center looked beautiful.

Adjectives that compare are only used to compare two or more things.

The verb must match the tense of the passage.

Use a subject pronoun as the subject of a sentence.

Use the past-tense form of a verb with had.

1 **A** more useful
B usefuler
C useful
D more usefuler

2 **F** move
G will move
H are moving
J moved

3 **A** us
B our
C them
D we

4 **F** finished
G finish
H finishes
J finishing

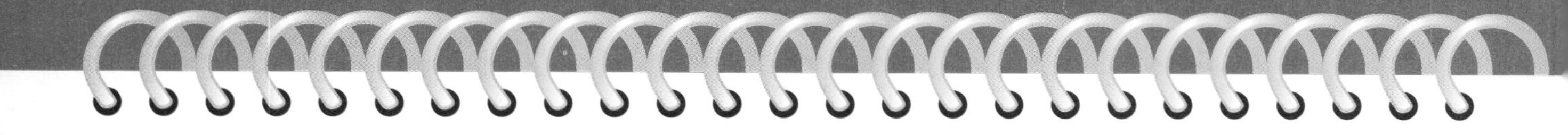

TIME FOR KIDS Writer's Notebook

RESEARCH

RESEARCH

When I do research with books, the first thing I do is check the **table of contents, index,** or **glossary**. These book parts help me find the information I need quickly.

COMPOSITION SKILLS

WRITING WELL

When I write **descriptions,** I think of comparisons that my readers will understand, like "as heavy as a backpack" or "a dinosaur egg the size of a grapefruit." I make sure my words give the clearest picture possible.

VOCABULARY SKILLS

USING WORDS

Words like eggshell and grapefruit are compound words. A **compound word** is made from two separate words. I use them to explain a specific idea. What compound words do you know?

Read Now!

As you read the dinosaur photo essay, jot down any descriptions that make it easier for you to better understand what you are reading.

TIME FOR KIDS

PHOTO ESSAY

Dino-mite Discovery!

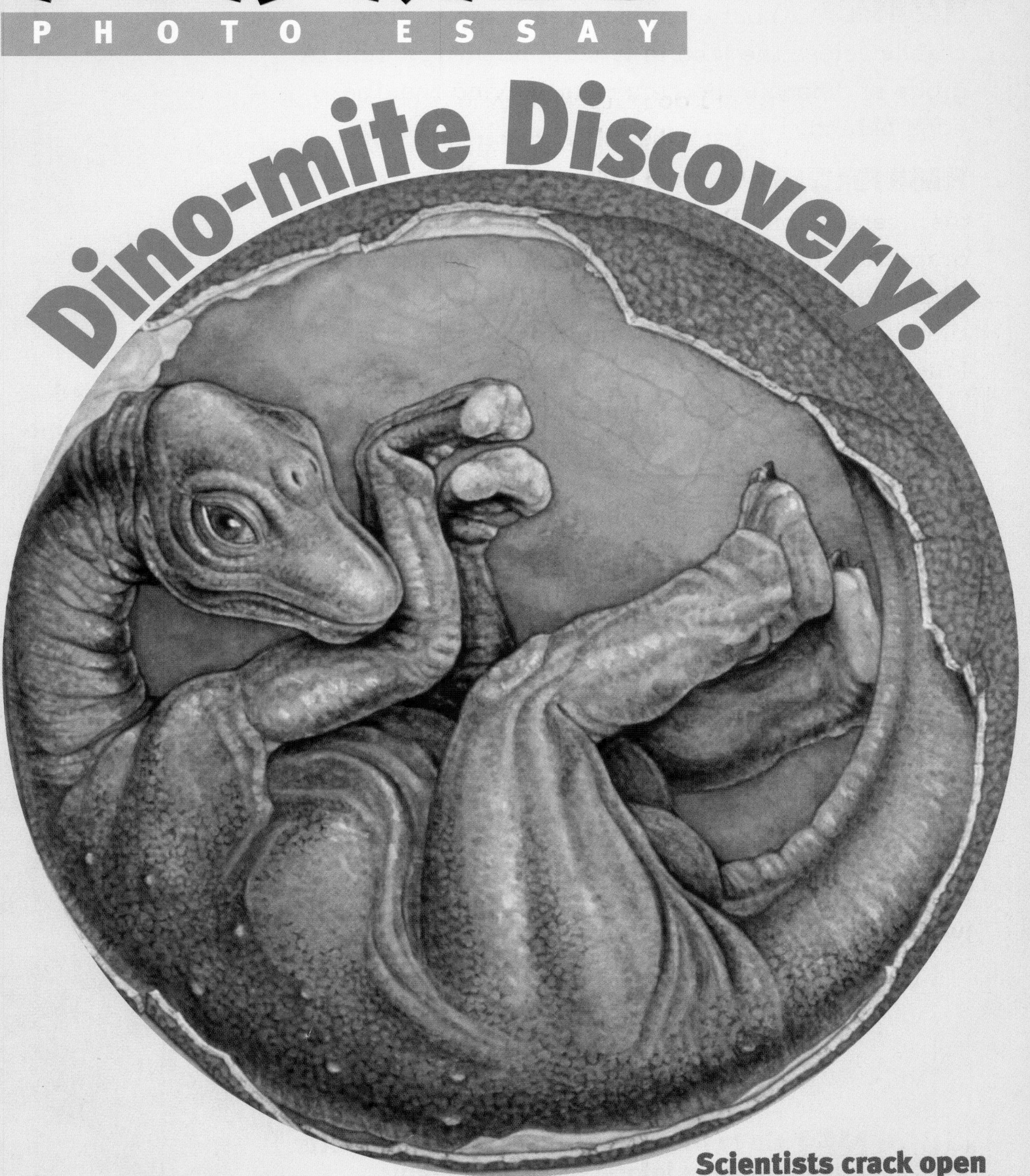

Scientists crack open giant nests of dinosaur eggs.

Eggs-citing News!

A discovery in Argentina is helping scientists learn more about dinosaur mothers and their young.

FLASHBACK: About 80 million years ago, a flood rushes across the land in what is now Argentina. A group of dinosaur mothers runs, leaving their baby eggs behind.

FLASH FORWARD: In 1997, a group of scientists discovered a pile of rocks. Each was the size of a grapefruit. But the "rocks" were not rocks at all. They were fossilized dino eggs! "There were thousands of eggs all over the place," says scientist Luis Chiappe.

When the flood hit, "everything seems to have been buried quickly," says Chiappe. "The dinosaurs probably suffocated."

The eggs were in excellent shape. In fact, many of them held the remains of small, unborn dinosaurs. The eggs belonged to a kind of dinosaur called a titanosaur (tuh-TAN-uh-sor). It was a plant-eating creature with a long tail, long neck, and small head. Titanosaurs grew to be 50 feet long.

Scientists hope their discovery will answer some questions about dino mothers and how they cared for their young. With so many eggs yet to be studied, the answers may be just inside those ancient eggshells.

This magnified patch of skin once covered part of a baby dinosaur still in its egg.

A researcher carefully scrapes away clay from a cluster of eggs.

*inter***NET** **CONNECTION** **Go to www.mhschool.com/language-arts for more information on the topic.**

Beneath a hot sun, Luis Chiappe searches for more eggs. Some of the babies were about to break through their eggshells when the flood came.

EGG COMPARISON CHART

(All sizes are approximate.)

Dinosaur	Elephant Bird	Ostrich	Chicken	Hummingbird
18"	14"	6"	2"	$\frac{1}{2}$"

Cover: Mick Ellison/National Geographic Society; all other photos: L. Meeker/American Museum of National History

Write Now!

Not all eggs are the same size! Write to compare the size of the eggs on the chart. Which is the biggest? Which is the smallest?

Parts of a Book

Suppose you want to find information for a report about animals. How can you tell if a book contains the facts that you need without reading it cover to cover?

There are many different **parts of a book**. Knowing the purpose of each part can help you find information quickly and easily. At the front of a book, the **title page** tells you the title, the author, and the publisher of the book. The **copyright page** tells you the date the book was published. The **table of contents** lists the titles of the chapters and the page numbers on which they begin. At the back of a book, a **glossary** gives the meaning of special words used in the book. It is like a small dictionary. An index lists all the topics in the book in alphabetical order. The information below shows some of the important parts of a book.

Table of Contents

Chapter number and chapter title

Page on which the index begins

Index

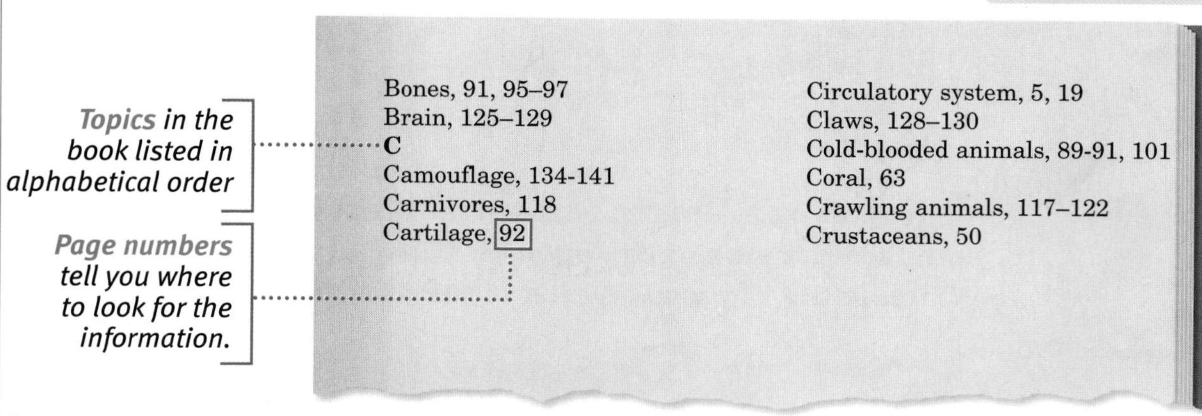

Build Skills

Glossary

adaptation-bacteria

adaptation (ad' əp tā' shən) A special trait that helps an organism survive. (p.142)
amber (am' bər) Hardened tree sap, yellow to brown in color, often a source of insect fossils. (p.57)
amphibian (am fib' ē ən) A cold-blooded vertebrate that spends part of its life in water and part of its life on land. (p.99)
arthropod (är' thrə pod') An invertebrate with jointed legs and a body that is divided into sections. (p.48)
atmosphere (at' məs fîr') Gases that surround Earth. (p.165)

Guide words tell you what terms you will find on the page.

Definitions of special terms listed alphabetically

Pronunciation of the word

Page number where term can be found

Practice

A. Use the sample contents, index, and glossary to answer the questions.

1. Which chapter would tell you how many California condors are left in the world?
2. Where does an amphibian live?
3. On which page would you find information about coral?
4. How many pages talk about cold-blooded animals?
5. Which chapter would tell you what all animals have in common?

B. Write which part of a book you would use to find each piece of information.

6. The date the book was published
7. The definition of a special term
8. The way the chapters in the book are organized
9. The correct spelling of the author's name
10. The pages on which you can find specific facts

interNET CONNECTION

Go to: www.mhschool.com/language-arts for more information on the topic.

Writing Activity A Fact Sheet

Find a nonfiction book about a favorite topic. Write the title, the author, and the date of the book. Use the contents, index, and glossary to find facts about your subject. Then use the information to write a fact sheet about the topic.

Vocabulary: Compound Words

DEFINITION

A compound word is a word made from two or more smaller words that are joined together.

light + house = lighthouse
cow + boy = cowboy
any + where = anywhere

afternoon	after + noon	after 12:00 P.M.
backpack	back + pack	pack worn on the back
blueberry	blue + berry	berry that is blue
homemade	home + made	made at home
mailbox	mail + box	box where mail goes
newspaper	news + paper	paper that contains news
skateboard	skate + board	board to skate on
swimsuit	swim + suit	clothing for swimming
teammate	team + mate	person on your team
weekend	week + end	end of the week

Compound Words

How can you figure out the meaning of a compound word? In your journal, include examples in your answer.

Look at the highlighted words in the paragraph below. What two smaller words make up each compound word?

Last weekend, my family participated in a baking contest at the county fair. My mom and I baked a homemade blueberry pie. In the afternoon, the judges announced the winners. We came in second, but the newspaper printed all of our names!

Practice

A. Write the compound word in each sentence.

1. Lynne and Mateo rode their skateboards to the beach.
2. They rode all the way to the seashore.
3. Mateo wore his new swimsuit.
4. They ate homemade sandwiches.
5. Then they took a walk on the boardwalk.

B. Write the sentences. Complete each sentence with a compound word formed from a word in the top row and a word in the bottom row.

after	back	sun	news	sea
set	paper	noon	shell	pack

6. Lynne read the ______.
7. Mateo found a ______ in the sand.
8. Mateo put the shell in his ______.
9. Lynne swam in the ocean all ______.
10. Mateo and Lynne went home at ______.

C. Grammar Link **Write each sentence and underline the two nouns it contains. Then write a compound word formed from the two underlined nouns.**

11. It was time for lunch.
12. She attached the paper to the wall.
13. He read the news from the paper.
14. The club meets in the old house.
15. Her class meets in that room.

Writing Activity A Paragraph

Write a paragraph about Lynne and Mateo. Tell why you think they are friends. What do they have in common? Use two compound words in your paragraph.

APPLY GRAMMAR: Include three plural nouns that are formed in three different ways. Make sure proper nouns begin with a capital letter.

Composition: Writing Descriptions

A writer uses **description** to create a picture, in words, or what a person, place, or thing is like.

GUIDELINES

- A description creates a clear and vivid picture of a person, place, or thing.
- A good description makes the reader feel as if he or she is actually there.
- Include a sentence that gives a general idea, or overall impression, of the person, place, or thing you are describing.
- Use vivid specific details to tell more about the overall idea.
- Use words that appeal to the senses: sound, sight, smell, touch, and taste.
- Arrange the description in a logical order, such as from top to bottom or side to side.

Writing Descriptions

What kinds of writing use description? What kinds of words would you use in a description? Write your ideas in your journal.

Read this **description**. Notice how the writer creates an overall impression that is supported by details.

The first sentence gives a general idea, or overall impression, of the skyscraper.

The skyscraper is described in logical order, from top to bottom.

Words appeal to the senses of touch and sight.

At dusk the skyscraper looked like a giant glittering robot. Two tall towers on the top of the building reached toward the sky. Bright red lights flashed from the towers. Below the towers a huge balcony reached like arms around the building. White light from hundreds of windows beneath the balcony twinkled brightly. They were like stars set in the cold, smooth surface of the building's dark walls.

Practice

A. Copy the sentences below. Underline the descriptive sentences.

1. Some people think that frogs and toads are alike.
2. A frog is a slimy, tailless animal with bulging eyes.
3. Frogs live in or near water, and toads live mostly on land.
4. A toad has a broader, flatter body and darker, drier skin than a frog.
5. Frogs live on all continents except Antarctica.

B. Write each sentence. Add descriptive words or phrases to make the sentences clearer and more vivid.

6. An octopus has a ______ body and ______ arms.
7. It clings ______ to rocks by using the suckers ______.
8. The ______ eyes of an octopus are on ______ its head.
9. The ______ octopus can measure twenty feet ______.
10. The octopus escapes ______ enemies by ______ changing colors.

C. Grammar Link **Rewrite each sentence. Underline the nouns. Add words to describe them.**

11. Bees carry pollen to flowers.
12. A queen bee makes a nest of grass.
13. A coat keeps bees warm.
14. A bumblebee nest is the size of a grapefruit.
15. The nest can hold over 200 bees!

Writing Activity A Field Guide

Imagine that you are writing a field guide to describe animals that you see on a trip to the meadow, the lake, or the woods. In your field guide, compare and contrast two animals that you see. Describe them so that your readers can see them clearly.

APPLY GRAMMAR: Include two or more proper nouns in your field guide. Be sure that you capitalize them.

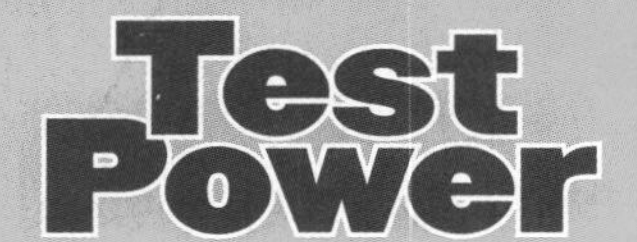

Better Sentences

Directions

Read the passage. Some sections are underlined. The underlined sections may be one of the following:

- **Incomplete sentences**
- **Run-on sentences**
- **Correctly written sentences that should be combined**
- **Correctly written sentences that do not need to be rewritten**

Choose the best way to write each underlined section. If the underlined section needs no change, choose "No mistake."

Combine sentences by joining words in the subject or predicate of the two sentences.

A correct sentence may contain several prepositional phrases.

Sample

Tina and Jill decided to start their own recycling program. Tina gathered paper to be recycled. Jill gathered paper to be recycled. **(1)** The girls called a recycling center and arranged to have the paper picked up. Soon they created a successful program with the help of their friends. **(2)**

1 **A** Tina gathered paper to be recycled, and Jill gathered paper to be recycled.

B Tina and Jill, they gathered paper to be recycled.

C Tina and Jill gathered paper to be recycled.

D No mistake

2 **F** Soon they created a successful program. With the help of their friends.

G Soon they created a successful program, and they did it with their friends.

H Soon they created a successful program. Their friends helping.

J No mistake

Test Tip

Look through a test first to see what skills are covered.

Vocabulary and Comprehension

Directions

Read the passage. Then read each question that follows the passage. Decide which is the best answer to each question. Choose the letter for that answer.

Sample

Justin watched as Lisa and Sid rode their skateboards. "Do you want to skate with us?" Lisa asked.

"No thanks," Justin replied. Justin wanted to join them more than anything. He was just embarrassed to say that he didn't know how to skate.

Suddenly Sid lost his balance and fell.

"Are you okay?" Justin asked.

"Yes," Sid replied. "I'm still learning how to skate."

Justin jumped up. He wasn't embarrassed anymore. He asked, "Will you teach me?"

"Sure," Sid answered. "Let's go!"

To define a compound word, look at the meaning of the words that form the compound.

1 How do you think Justin feels at the end of the story?

A embarrassed

B sad

C excited

D angry

2 In this passage, the word *skateboards* means—

F roller skates

G boards used for skating

H areas where people skate

J a park for skating

Seeing Like a Writer

How are the pictures similar? In what ways are they different? What ideas for writing do the pictures give you?

Haymaking by Pieter Brueghel, the Elder

Writing from Pictures

1. Make a list of the people, places, and things that you see in the three pictures. Write *person, place*, or *thing* next to each.
2. Write a caption to describe one of the pictures. Include clear details that are easy to understand.
3. Choose two pictures. Imagine they are both in a display. Write a title for the display that will tell about both pictures. Then write a short paragraph that compares the two pictures.

   Apply Grammar: Include proper nouns in your writing. Underline each proper noun you use.

Writing That Compares

When you tell how two things are alike and how they are different, you are comparing and contrasting. Writing that compares includes details to show readers how items are similar and different.

THINK AND WRITE

Purpose

Why would you want to compare and contrast two items? Write your ideas in your journal.

Learning from Writers

Read the following examples of writing that compares. What two things is the writer comparing and contrasting? As you read, think about the similarities and differences between the two things.

A Dinosaur Discovery

As a paleontologist, James Kirkland has examined thousands of different dinosaur bones. But even he wasn't prepared for what he saw when he was called to investigate some new fossils found near Salt Lake City, Utah. A fossil bed there held the bones of two never-before-seen species of ankylosaur.

Both of the newly discovered creatures belong to a group of plant-eating dinosaurs called ankylosaur, which means "fused lizards." The name comes from the heavy armor-like plates attached or fused to their heads. Some grew more than 30 feet long.

"These two dinosaurs were very similar animals in many respects," says Kirkland. One is an ankylosaurid. Ankylosaurids had big armored plates around their head and a long tail with a heavy club at the end. They would swing the club-tail to fight bigger animals. . . .

The other new species, the nodosaurid, was also well armed. It had spikes on its shoulders. "It used to ram larger creatures," says Kirkland. "These dinosaurs were built like tanks."

—From "A New Dino Duo" in *Time for Kids*

Francis Beach and Marquette Beach

Two beaches near my town show the difference pollution can make. Francis Beach is near a canal. Some factories send waste directly into the canal. Marquette Beach, which is the same size as Francis Beach, is in the town of Lee. In Lee, waste from factories is strictly controlled.

There are no birds at Francis Beach. However, at Marquette Beach, seagulls and sandpipers are everywhere. There are also no bluefish at Francis Beach. On the other hand, Marquette Beach has bluefish and many other fish.

Pollution has made a difference in the wildlife population at Francis Beach. Nothing seems to live there, while Marquette Beach, with its strict laws about pollution, is full of life.

–Sarah Park

Practice and Apply

Thinking Like a Reader

1. How are the dinosaurs in "A Dinosaur Discovery" similar?
2. How are Francis Beach and Marquette Beach different?

Thinking Like a Writer

3. What facts does the author include to show how the dinosaurs are similar?
4. How does Sarah Park organize the information about beaches?

5. **Reading Across Texts** What is the author of each essay trying to show through the comparisons? How are the authors' goals different?

Features of Writing That Compares

DEFINITIONS AND FEATURES

Writing that compares is a form of writing that explains how two things are alike and different. A good example of writing that compares:

- Explains how two things are **similar.**
- Explains how two things are **different.**
- Organizes details and facts in a **logical order.**
- Uses **compare and contrast words** to point out similarities and differences.

Similarities

Reread "A Dinosaur Discovery" on page 130. An important part of writing that compares is explaining how two things are similar. How are the dinosaurs similar?

> Both of the newly discovered creatures belong to a group of plant-eating dinosaurs called ankylosaur, which means "fused lizards."

Similarities tell how two things are the same. Both of the new dinosaurs belonged to the ankylosaur group.

Differences

Another important part of writing that compares is explaining how two things are different. How are the newly discovered dinosaurs different?

> One is an ankylosaurid. Ankylosaurids had big armored plates around their head and a long tail with a heavy club at the end. . . .
>
> The other new species. . . had spikes on its shoulders.

The two new species of dinosaur looked different in certain ways.

▶ Logical Order

Presenting ideas in a logical order can help readers better understand your writing. The author of "A Dinosaur Discovery" begins by introducing the things that will be compared.

> A fossil bed there held the bones of two never-before-seen species of ankylosaur.

The author next talks about the two dinosaurs together, and then gives details about each one. Do you think the order the writer chose is a good one? Why or why not?

▶ Compare and Contrast Words

To help readers clearly understand writing that compares, writers include words that point out that things are alike or different. Some compare and contrast words are *similar*, *both*, *also*, and *other*.

> The other new species, the nodosaurid, was also well armed.

What other compare and contrast word does the author use in the article?

Practice and Apply

Create a Features Chart

1. List the features of a good example of writing that compares.
2. Reread "Francis Beach and Marquette Beach" by Sarah Park on page 131.
3. Write one example of every feature in Sarah's writing.
4. Write what you have learned from reading Sarah's piece.

Features	Examples

Prewrite

In writing that compares, the writer explains how two things are similar and how they are different. Comparing and contrasting is a good way to share your ideas about two different things.

Purpose and Audience

The purpose of writing that compares is to show how two people, places, things, or ideas are alike and different.

Before writing, you need to think about your audience. Who will be reading your writing that compares? How will you organize the facts in your writing so they will be easy to understand?

Choose a Topic

Start by **brainstorming** a list of things that are similar in some ways but different in others. Then choose one pair of items that interests you most.

Explore ideas by making a list of details about each item that you can compare and contrast.

Audience

Write how your audience will affect the way you plan and write your comparison.

How Lakes and Swimming Pools Are Alike and Different

Both are filled with water.
Lakes are always outdoors.
My granddad has a pool.
Both are used for swimming.
I love swimming in lakes.
Both come in many shapes and sizes.
Pools are made by humans, but lakes are not.
Lakes are very deep.
The deepest pools are only nine or ten feet.
Pools have only one use.

Organize • Classifying

When you write a comparison, you need to classify your details into two groups. One group of details should tell how the items are alike, and one group of details should tell how they are different. To plan your writing, you can use a compare-and-contrast chart.

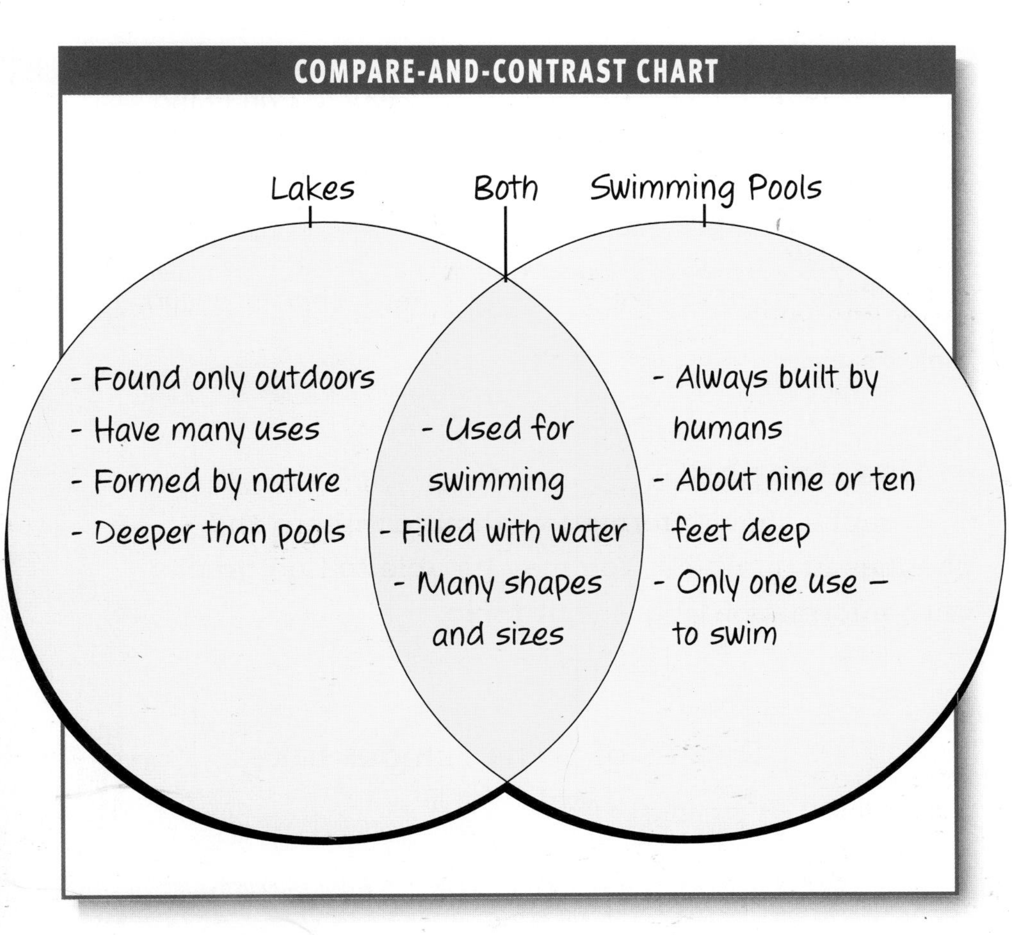

Practice and Apply

Plan Your Own Writing That Compares

1. Think about your purpose and audience.
2. Brainstorm ideas about things that are the same and different.
3. Choose two things to compare, and explore your ideas.
4. Organize your ideas.

Checklist

Prewriting

- Did you think about your purpose and audience?
- Have you chosen two things that are similar in some ways and different in others?
- Have you listed details about both things?
- Can you use those details to compare and contrast?
- Have you used your chart to organize your ideas?
- Do you need to do research to check any of your details?

Writing PROCESS

Prewrite • Research and Inquiry

▶ Writer's Resources

You may have to do research to get more information for your writing. First, make a list of questions. Then, decide what resources you need to answer the questions.

What Else Do I Need to Know?	Where Can I Find the Information?
Are any lakes created by people?	Find a book about lakes.
How deep are most lakes?	Look for a chart or graph.

▶ Use Graphs

Graphs show information about numbers and changes in numbers. You may be able to find graphs with information about your topic.

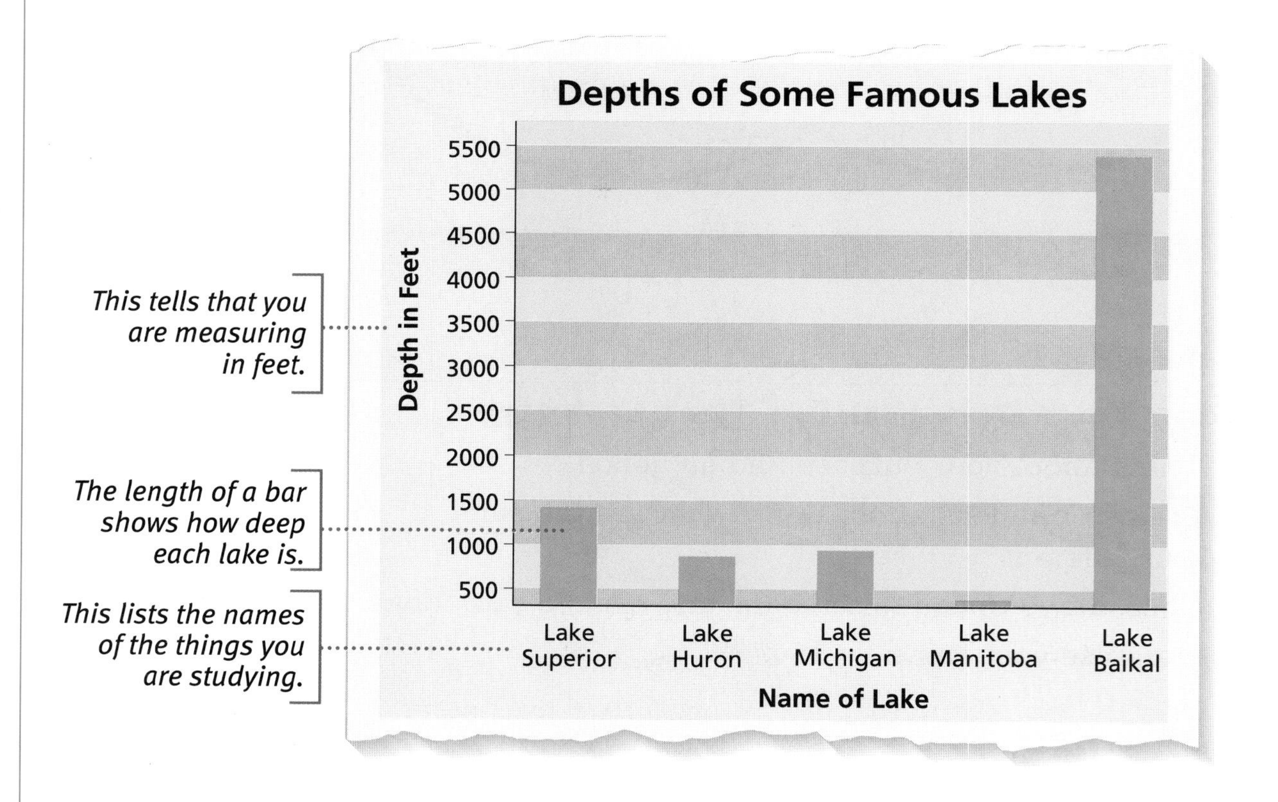

▶ Use Parts of a Book

You can find information about almost any topic in a book. To locate the information you need, you can use the table of contents.

The table of contents is in the front of a book. It lists chapters or units in the book and gives the page numbers on which they begin. Another way to find information is to skim through a book looking at the headings. A heading is a word or group of words that stands out at the top of a page or at the beginning of a paragraph.

pages 565, 566

▶ Use Your Research

New information gathered from your research can go into your compare-and-contrast chart. This writer learned some important information while doing research. How did it affect his chart?

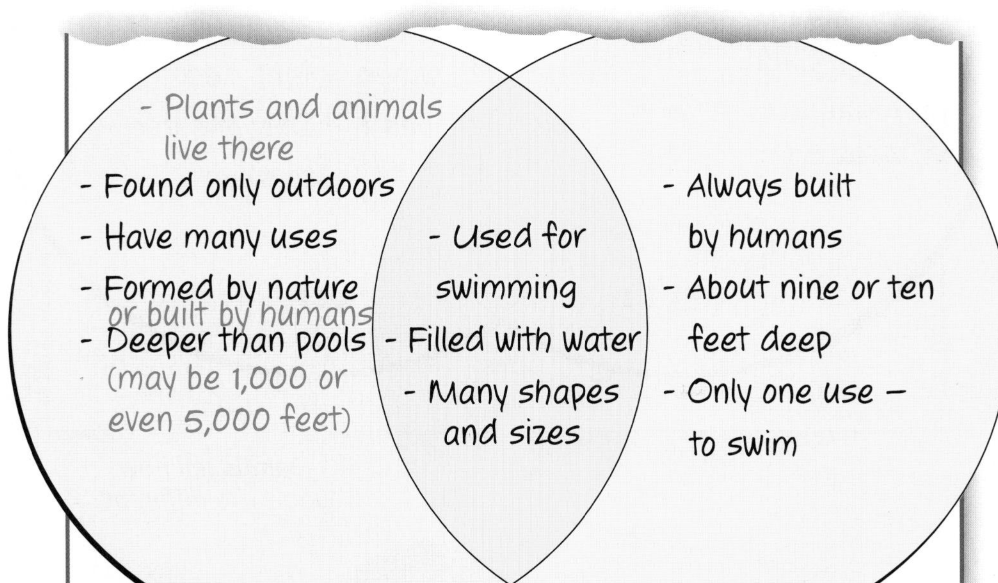

Practice and Apply

Review Your Plan

1. Look over your compare-and-contrast chart.
2. List any questions you have about your topic.
3. Identify the resources you will need to help answer your questions.
4. Add new information you gather to your chart.

Checklist ✓

Research and Inquiry

- Did you list additional questions?
- Did you identify resources you might use?
- Did you take notes?

Draft

Before you begin writing your comparison, review your chart. Think about making a paragraph for similarities and a paragraph for differences. You will want to include specific details in each paragraph.

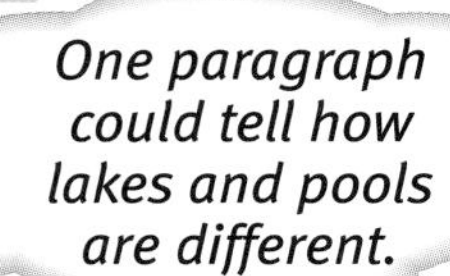

COMPARE-AND-CONTRAST CHART

Lakes

- Plants and animals live there
- Found only outdoors
- Have many uses
- Formed by nature or built by humans
- Deeper than pools (may be 1,000 or even 5,000 feet)

Both

- Used for swimming
- Filled with water
- Many shapes and sizes

Swimming Pools

- Always built by humans
- About nine or ten feet deep
- Only one use – to swim

✓Checklist

Drafting

- Does your writing fit your purpose and audience?
- Have you explained how two things are similar and how they are different?
- Are your details organized in logical order?
- Have you included compare and contrast words to help your readers follow your organization?

Look at how this writer used the ideas in his chart to write a first draft. He organized the information into paragraphs. He included specific details to describe lakes and swimming pools.

PREWRITE
DRAFT
REVISE
PROOFREAD
PUBLISH

DRAFT

Lakes and swimming pools are different in many wayes. My granddad has a pool. Pools may be nine or ten feet deep, but lakes are much deeper. For example, lake superior is over 1,000 feet deep, and lake Baikal in russia is over 5,000. Lakes are always found outdoors. Lakes can be formed by nature or made by men and womans. All pools are human-made. Lakes have more uses than pools. Finally, plants and animals live in lakes.

Lakes and pools are also alike. They come in many shapes and sizes, and they are filled with water. They can be used for swimming and are often crowded in july and august. Even though Lakes and Pools are different, they are both places to have fun!

First paragraph tells how lakes and pools are different.

Details give a description of pools and lakes.

Second paragraph tells how they are similar.

Practice and Apply

Draft Your Own Writing That Compares

1. Review your prewriting chart.
2. Include details that compare and contrast.
3. Organize similarities and differences logically.
4. Use exact, vivid words to describe the things you are comparing and contrasting.

TECHNOLOGY

Save your document every few minutes. Then, if your computer shuts down or if you lose power, you won't lose all your work.

Writing PROCESS

Revise

Elaborate

Elaborating will help you to improve your writing. To elaborate means to add examples and details that further support your ideas. As you revise your comparison, you should add some details to explain some of your ideas more clearly.

The detail that the writer added made the difference between pools and lakes clearer.

> , while pools can be indoors or outdoors
> Lakes are always found outdoors.

The writer added details to support a point.

> For example, you can go fishing or boating on a lake.
> Lakes have more uses than pools.

COMPARE AND CONTRAST WORDS

- different
- same
- similarly
- as well as
- alike
- but
- although
- both
- neither
- also
- however
- on the other hand

Word Choice

When you are writing, it is important to choose words that make your ideas clear.

In a comparison, you can use compare and contrast words to show the similarities and differences between things and to make transitions from one idea to the next.

> On the other hand, Both
> Lakes and pools are also alike. ~~They~~ come in many
> both
> shapes and sizes, and ~~they~~ are filled with water.

PREWRITE
DRAFT
REVISE
PROOFREAD
PUBLISH

Better Paragraphs

As you continue to revise your draft, check your paragraphs to make sure each one has a topic sentence that states the main idea. Do the facts in each paragraph support the main idea? Is there any information that you can add? Is there any information you do not need to include? You can make your writing clearer by taking out information that does not contribute to your main idea.

> Lakes and swimming pools are different in many wayes. ~~My granddad has a pool.~~

Practice and Apply

Revise Your Own Writing That Compares

1. Add details about your topic to make your writing more interesting.
2. Add words or phrases that help you compare and contrast things.
3. Take out facts that don't support your main idea.
4. **Grammar** Have you formed all plural nouns correctly?

TECHNOLOGY

Sometimes paragraphs sound better and make more sense when you change the order of sentences. Use the cut-and-paste feature to move sentences around.

Revise • Peer Conferencing

Take some time out from your writing. Exchange drafts with a partner. Someone reading your paper for the first time may be able to help you communicate your ideas more clearly.

Interesting details!

You could add a contrast word to this sentence.

You should tell how pools are different.

Lakes and swimming pools are different in many wayes. My granddad has a pool. Pools may be nine or ten feet deep, but lakes are much deeper. For example, lake superior is over 1,000 feet deep, and lake Baikal in russia is over 5,000. Lakes are always found outdoors. Lakes can be formed by nature or made by men and womans. All pools are human-made. Lakes have more uses than pools. Finally, plants and animals live in lakes.

Lakes and pools are also alike. They come in many shapes and sizes, and they are filled with water. They can be used for swimming and are often crowded in july and august. Even though Lakes and Pools are different, they are both places to have fun!

Conferencing for the Reader

- Are features of writing that compares included in your partner's piece?
  - how things are similar
  - how things are different
  - logical order
  - compare and contrast words
- Don't forget to tell your partner what you like about the piece, as well as suggestions to improve it.

Think about your partner's suggestions as you revise your draft. Use the ideas that you feel would help your paper. This writer revised his paper using some of his partner's comments.

REVISE

Lakes and Swimming Pools

Lakes and swimming pools are different in many wayes. ~~My granddad has a pool.~~ Pools may be nine or ten feet deep, but lakes are much deeper. For example, lake superior is over 1,000 feet deep, and lake Baikal in russia is over 5,000. Lakes are always found outdoors, while pools can be indoors or outdoors. Lakes can be formed by nature or made by men and womans. All pools, however, are human-made. Lakes have more uses than pools. For example, you can go fishing or boating on a lake. Finally, plants and animals live in lakes but not in pools.

On the other hand, Lakes and pools are also alike. ~~They~~ Both come in many shapes and sizes, and ~~they~~ both are filled with water. They can be used for swimming and are often crowded in july and august. Even though Lakes and Pools are different, they are both places to have fun!

PREWRITE

DRAFT

REVISE

PROOFREAD

PUBLISH

Practice and Apply

Revise Your Own Writing That Compares

1. Share your draft with your partner.
2. Think about your partner's comments as you revise.
3. Add descriptive details to tell more about the things you are comparing and contrasting.
4. Add a short title to tell readers what the writing is about.

Checklist

Revising

- Have you kept your purpose and audience in mind?
- Do you need to elaborate on any other facts in your writing?
- Did you use a variety of words to show you are comparing and contrasting?
- Did you take out facts that don't support your main idea?
- Did you include a title that tells about the subject?

Writing PROCESS

Proofread

After you have revised your comparison, you will need to proofread it to find and correct any errors in mechanics, grammar and usage, and spelling.

STRATEGIES FOR PROOFREADING

- **Reread your revised paper several times, each time looking for a different type of error.** This will help you find all your errors.
- **Read for correct capitalization.** All proper nouns must begin with a capital letter.
- **Read for spelling mistakes.** Starting with the last word and reading backward will help you spot errors.

REVIEW THE RULES

GRAMMAR

- The plural of most nouns is formed by adding *-s* or *-es*. Some nouns have special plural forms.

MECHANICS

- A proper noun names a special person, place, or thing. It always starts with a capital letter.
- Names of days, months, and holidays begin with a capital letter.

Spelling

If a noun ends with a consonant and *y*, change *y* to *i* and add *-es*. If it ends with a vowel and *y*, just add *-s*.

Look at the proofreading corrections made on the draft below. Why does the writer use the symbol ≡ several times?

PROOFREAD

Lakes and Swimming Pools

Lakes and swimming pools are different in many ways. Pools may be nine or ten feet deep, but lakes are much deeper. For example, Lake Superior is over 1,000 feet deep, and Lake Baikal in Russia is over 5,000. Lakes are always found outdoors, while pools can be indoors or outdoors. Lakes can be formed by nature or made by men and women. All pools, however, are human-made. Lakes have more uses than pools. For example, you can go fishing or boating on a lake. Finally, plants and animals live in lakes but not in pools.

On the other hand, lakes and pools are also alike. Both come in many shapes and sizes, and both are filled with water. They can be used for swimming and are often crowded in July and August. Even though lakes and pools are different, they are both places to have fun!

Practice and Apply

Proofread Your Own Writing That Compares

1. Check your spelling and correct any mistakes.
2. Check to be sure that all plural nouns have been formed correctly.
3. Capitalize proper nouns.
4. Indent each paragraph.

PREWRITE
DRAFT
REVISE
PROOFREAD
PUBLISH

Checklist

Proofreading

- Did you check the spelling of plural nouns?
- Did you capitalize proper nouns?
- Did you capitalize names of days, months, and holidays?

PROOFREADING MARKS

- ¶ new paragraph
- ^ add
- take out
- ≡ Make a capital letter.
- / Make a small letter.
- (SP) Check the spelling.
- ⊙ Add a period.

Publish

Before you publish, review your writing one last time. Use a checklist to make sure you go over all the important details.

Self-Check Writing That Compares

- ❑ Who was my audience? Will my writing be clear to the audience?
- ❑ What was my purpose? Did I tell how two things were alike and how they were different?
- ❑ Did I present my ideas in a logical order?
- ❑ Did I present accurate and complete details?
- ❑ Did I use words that compare and contrast?
- ❑ Did I write all plural and possessive nouns correctly?
- ❑ Did I proofread and correct errors in capitalization, spelling, and punctuation?

The writer used the checklist to review his writing that compares. Read "Lakes and Swimming Pools" with your classmates. Discuss the writer's published piece. Do you think it was ready to publish? Tell why or why not.

Lakes and Swimming Pools

By Kevin Jamison

Lakes and swimming pools are different in many ways. Pools may be nine or ten feet deep, but lakes are much deeper. For example, Lake Superior is over 1,000 feet deep, and Lake Baikal in Russia is over 5,000. Lakes are always found outdoors, while pools can be indoors or outdoors. Lakes can be formed by nature or made by men and women. All pools, however, are human-made. Lakes have more uses than pools. For example, you can go fishing or boating on a lake. Finally, plants and animals live in lakes but not in pools.

On the other hand, lakes and pools are also alike. Both come in many shapes and sizes, and both are filled with water. They can be used for swimming and are often crowded in July and August. Even though lakes and pools are different, they are both places to have fun!

TECHNOLOGY

Do you have an e-mail address? Learn how to e-mail your document to a friend by adding an attachment to an e-mail letter that you have written.

Practice and Apply

Publish Your Own Writing That Compares

1. Check your revised draft one last time.
2. Make a neat, final copy.
3. Add photos, charts, or graphs to illustrate facts about your topic.

LISTENING

SPEAKING

VIEWING

REPRESENTING

Present Your Writing That Compares

To deliver a good presentation, you need to do some planning. Here are some things you can do to make your presentation successful.

STEP 1

How to Explain Your Report

Strategies for Speaking As you plan your presentation, remember that your purpose is to explain how two things are alike and different.

- Create note cards that include the main topics of each paragraph and brief reminders or details.
- Decide how fast you should speak. Remember, it is hard for people to follow you if you speak too quickly.
- Practice making eye contact with your audience so that they will feel that you are talking to them.

Listening Strategies

- **Set a purpose. Are you listening for new information or for enjoyment?**
- **Listen for comparisons and contrasts to help you understand important information.**
- **Write questions in your journal that you may want to ask or think about later.**
- **Listen actively. Keep your eyes focused on the speaker.**

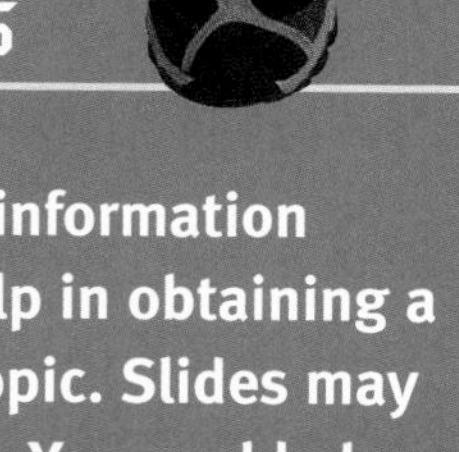

Multimedia Ideas

You may wish to *use slides* that illustrate information from your writing. Ask your teacher for help in obtaining a slide projector as well as slides on your topic. Slides may be available in your school or local library. You could also use slides of your own.

STEP 2

How to Show Your Comparison

Suggestions for Visuals Give your audience more information about your topic by adding visuals. You can display them as your audience listens.

- A diagram can show a lot of facts in a short amount of time.
- Photographs and drawings can clearly illustrate how things are similar and different.
- Graphs and charts can show facts about your topic.

STEP 3

How to Share Your Comparison

Strategies for Rehearsing The more you practice, the more comfortable you'll feel on the day of your presentation.

- Practice your speech in front of a mirror. Notice your hand and facial gestures.
- Practice in front of a friend, classmate, or family member. Ask for suggestions.
- Rehearse several times straight through.

TIP!

Viewing Strategies

- Study the visuals carefully.
- Look for details in the visuals that the speaker has not stated.
- Ask questions about the visuals.

PRACTICE AND APPLY

Present Your Own Writing That Compares

1. Prepare note cards that include ideas and important details.
2. Find diagrams, graphs, or photographs to illustrate your points.
3. Practice in front of an audience. Ask for suggestions.
4. Present your comparison using your notes and visuals.

Writing Tests

On a writing test, you are required to write a composition in response to a prompt. Remember to read the prompt carefully. Look for key words and phrases that describe the topic of your composition and explain how you should present your ideas.

Are you writing to entertain, inform, or influence your audience?

Look for words or phrases that tell you what kind of information to include in your writing.

Check for clues that tell you who your audience is.

Prompt

Think about what you like and don't like about being a child.

Write a composition explaining what you think is better about being a child or an adult. Include specific details.

How to Read a Prompt

Purpose Read the prompt again. Look for words that tell about the purpose of your writing. The words "composition" and "explaining" tell you that your purpose will be to inform.

Audience Sometimes a prompt will name your audience. When it does not, think of your audience as your teacher.

Writing That Compares When you are asked to explain the similarities and differences between two things, you are writing a composition that compares. When the prompt tells you to explain "what you think is better about being a child or an adult," you are being asked to compare adults and children by describing the differences between them. Use specific details to make your comparison clear.

Test Tip
Before you begin writing, make a list of the ideas you want to include in your composition.

How to Write to a Prompt

Here are some ideas to keep in mind when you are given a prompt on a writing test.

Before Writing **Content/Ideas**	• Think about your writing purpose. • Remember your intended audience. • If you are writing to compare, make a list of similarities and differences. • Choose your most important ideas to include in your writing.
During Writing **Organization/ Paragraph Structure**	• Start with a topic sentence that explains the subject of your writing. • Organize your ideas so that they will make sense to your audience. • Elaborate on your ideas. • Write a strong conclusion.
After Writing **Grammar/Usage**	• Proofread your work. • Make sure that proper nouns are capitalized and common nouns are not. • Use apostrophes correctly in possessive nouns. • Check for spelling errors.

Apply What You Learned

When reading a prompt on a writing test, make sure you know the purpose of your writing, the audience, and the topic. Organize your ideas before you write.

Prompt

Do you like warm, sunny days or snowy days better?

Write a composition explaining which kind of day you enjoy more. Include specific details.

Unit 2 Review

Grammar and Writing Review

pages 88–89

Nouns

A. Write the sentences. Underline each noun.

1. The girl is fishing on the lake.
2. The boy is fishing with his friend.
3. Fish swim up the river near the lake.
4. The children place worms on the ends of their hooks.
5. After several hours, the friends return to the city.

pages 90–95

Singular and Plural Nouns

B. Write the sentences. Underline the nouns. Then write the plural form of each noun you underlined.

6. My friend wrote a letter.
7. The note went to the hospital.
8. The child asked about a party.
9. The boy wants to bring lunch.
10. The student hopes to help a sick woman.
11. A lady works at the clinic.
12. The worker talked to her boss.
13. The man invites the class.
14. Each guest brings a snack.
15. The member tells a funny story, too.

pages 96–97

Common Nouns and Proper Nouns

C. Write the sentences. Underline the common nouns. Circle the proper nouns.

16. The girl loves to swim at Jensen Beach.
17. Her friend prefers to swim at Looloo Lake.
18. Julie Adams swims almost every day.

19. Max will go with Julie this Labor Day.

20. The beach is closed on Tuesday and Thursday.

21. The lake is open every day except Monday.

22. Professor Adams takes the kids to the ocean.

23. On Friday, Max and Julie will swim at the lake.

24. Max will bring his dog Butch.

25. From November through March, the park and pool are closed.

pages 98–99

Mechanics and Usage: Capitalization

D. Rewrite the sentences using the correct capitalization.

26. Jan and aunt doris pick apples in the orchard.

27. The green apples from maine taste the best.

28. Jan, mom, and uncle fred take the apples to the market.

29. By thanksgiving, the stores will be filled with apples.

30. Jan returns every october to help pick the apples.

31. She rides the bus up from new york on a friday afternoon.

32. Her cousin steve picks her up in the center of town.

33. The drive to the baileys' farm takes half an hour.

34. When jan arrives, her aunt and uncle are pleased to see her.

35. On sunday, they give her a book titled *an apple a day*.

Unit 2 Review

pages 102–105

Possessive Nouns

E. Write each phrase another way. Use the possessive form of the underlined singular or plural noun.

36. the notebook of Jan

37. the playground of the children

38. the homework of my friends

39. the baseball cap of another friend

40. the car of her parents

pages 106–107

Combining Sentences: Nouns

F. Combine each pair of sentences into one sentence by joining nouns with *and* or *or*.

41. Jane lived in the white house. Peter lived in the white house.

42. Jane mowed the lawn. Her mother mowed the lawn.

43. Peter vacuumed the living room. Dad vacuumed the living room.

44. The kitchen had been cleaned. The bedroom had been cleaned.

45. The dog ruined our dinner. The dog ruined our dessert.

pages 108–109

Mechanics and Usage: Abbreviations

G. Write each group of words. Use abbreviations when possible.

46. Mister Murphy

47. Doctor Sanchez

48. Sunday morning

49. February 25, 2001

50. Senator Lucy Fields

Unit 2 Review

pages 122–123

Vocabulary: Compound Words

H. Find the compound word in each sentence. Then write the two smaller words that make up the compound word.

51. Meg woke up early that morning in Ellen's guest bedroom.

52. She and Ellen were going to pick blueberries.

53. Ellen prepared homemade sandwiches.

54. The friends put their lunches into two backpacks.

55. The newspaper said it was going to rain.

pages 124–125

Composition: Writing Descriptions

I. Rewrite each sentence. Add descriptive words to make the writing more interesting.

56. Janet wanted to sell a drink.

57. She decided to sell lemonade.

58. Ronald bought a glass of juice.

59. He said the treat was refreshing.

60. Janet purchased more lemons.

pages 134-149

Proofreading Writing That Compares

J. Write the following paragraph. Correct the ten mistakes in punctuation, capitalization, grammar, and spelling.

We went on a family camping trip last july. In many ways, the trip was different from the time my brother and I slept in the backyard on a saturday night. The tent we used for the camping trip, which we borrowed from Mr. roth, was larger than our backyard tent. Also, our entire family went on the camping trip, and only joe and I slept in the backyard. On the camping trip, the night noises lulled me to sleep. I heard an owls hoot and crickets chirping. I watched some deers, and I saw familys of mouses. At home, there were no animales, and several neighbors stereos kept me awake. In contrast, our family camping trip was interesting and peaceful.

Project File

ACTIVITY 1 A Book Review

A book review tells whether or not you liked a book you have read and why you think others should read it. Study the parts of a book review in this sample. How did the writer use them?

You will need to know the form of a book review when your write your persuasive book review in the next unit.

A Boy's Unusual Adventures

By Vincent Citta

Edgar Aaron Pond's Orson Wellesly is a story of a boy's unusual adventures. Orson went to live with his aunt and uncle in their old house in the middle of nowhere. At night, Orson would hear faint scrapings, tiny whispers, and stray words as he sat alone in the dark.

One day, Orson heard his name. He traced the voice to a hidden room in the attic. Yet, there was no one there, just a dusty old trunk. Was the voice coming from the trunk? Who or what was inside? I followed Orson's adventures breathlessly.

I thought this book was wonderful. It was scary, sad, and funny, all at the same time. I think you'll like it, too.

Introduction Grabs your reader's attention.

Body Gives the setting, the main character, and an important event in the story.

Conclusion Tells why you did or did not like the book and why you would recommend it to others.

Write a Book Review Think about two books you have read. Was one funny and the other one sad? Were they both adventure stories? Compare the books. Then choose one book, and write a book review about it for your classmates to read. Look at the model on page 156 to make sure you include all the important parts of a book review. Would you recommend this book to others to read? Why or why not?

A Poster

According to "Dino-mite Discovery," scientists believe titanosaurs grew to be 50 feet from head to tail. How big are the eggs of a titanosaur compared to the eggs of a chicken? Use several sources to do research about titanosaur eggs and chicken eggs.

Dinosaurs Versus Chickens Make a poster that compares both kinds of eggs. Be sure to include words and pictures, such as diagrams, to show how the eggs are alike and different.

Extra Practice

Nouns

A. Write whether each underlined noun names a person, place, or thing.

1. The students are going to the mall.

2. The children are learning about money.

3. The boy has a pocket full of coins.

4. Let's go into this shop.

5. Leanne buys a shirt.

6. The clerk takes her coins and bills.

7. Two friends look at games for their computer.

8. The boxes are high on a shelf.

9. Parents wait in the restaurant.

10. Shoes, clothing, and games are expensive.

B. Write each noun. Write *person*, *place*, or *thing* after each one to tell what kind of noun it is.

11. The people here do not want a mall.

12. Their town has a big park.

13. In the playground are a slide and swings.

14. Children climb up the steps.

15. One child flies a kite.

16. Friends have picnics in the meadow.

17. One woman sells lemonade and hot dogs.

18. Her stand is next to the pond.

19. Visitors buy sandwiches, too.

20. Is a park better than a mall?

C. Write the sentences. Fill in each blank with a different noun.

21. There are seven ______ in the town.

22. Our ______ has many trees.

23. Let's buy a ______ in this shop.

24. When does the ______ begin?

25. The ______ are proud of their town.

Singular and Plural Nouns

A. Write the nouns in each sentence. Write whether each one is singular or plural.

1. Three boys made cookies.
2. An adult helped with the recipe.
3. How many batches did the girl make?
4. Let's give a box to your grandmother.
5. The boy carried two boxes.
6. One girl frosted a dozen cupcakes.
7. Who will make the pies?
8. The child has many peaches.
9. Use one bowl and two forks.
10. These desserts will win a prize.

B. Write the plural form of each underlined noun.

11. I have stirred this for one minute.
12. Look at your watch to be sure.
13. Please don't make a mess!
14. What is your guess about the menu?
15. The cook always makes a surprise.
16. Will you have a salad with your meal?
17. I will take this bunch of grapes.
18. Let's have fajitas for our lunch.
19. Have you ever had a fried pickle?
20. Please just give me a plain sandwich.

C. Decide which noun in parentheses ( ) correctly completes each sentence. Then write the sentence.

21. Many (school, schools) have their own cafeteria.
22. A cafeteria might serve 500 (lunch, lunches) every day.
23. My mother is the (cook, cooks) at my school.
24. She makes many tasty (dish, dishes)!
25. We eat our lunch on a (bench, benches) under a tree.

Extra Practice

Nouns Ending with *y*

A. Write the plural noun in each sentence.

1. Texas is larger than some countries.
2. Its biggest cities are Dallas and Houston.
3. Families like the seashore on the Gulf of Mexico.
4. Now and then you can see a shrimp boat in its bays.
5. There are many activities in every season.
6. Long summer days are good for swimming.
7. Texas is famous for its cowboys.
8. I love to spend the holidays there.
9. Many companies have their home office in Texas.
10. What do you think about the highways in Houston?

B. Write the correct plural form of each noun.

11. community
12. library
13. play
14. family
15. buggy
16. lady
17. toy
18. cherry
19. daisy
20. day

C. Use the plural form of the noun in parentheses ( ) to complete each sentence.

21. There are many ______ about the Alamo. (story)
22. Spanish ______ built the Alamo. (missionary)
23. I have seen ______ about the battle. (play)
24. The Mexicans and the Texas settlers were ______. (enemy)
25. One of the most famous battle ______ is "Remember the Alamo!" (cry)

More Plural Nouns

A. Write the plural noun in each sentence.

1. Our science museum has an animal display for children.
2. They have a petting zoo that includes live sheep.
3. Be careful not to scare the geese.
4. I enjoyed watching a team of oxen pull a heavy sled.
5. Inside, the forest exhibit shows moose in winter.
6. Have you ever seen such big teeth?
7. I can't believe how graceful these deer are!
8. A video explained how early men used to hunt.
9. Sometimes they wore nothing on their feet.
10. I liked the white mice best of all.

B. Write each sentence. Use the plural form of each word in parentheses ( ).

11. Two (woman) told us about small animals.
12. One of them put her hand in a large cage of (mouse).
13. She showed us their (tooth).
14. Some (child) keep rodents as pets.
15. I'd rather have (goose) on my farm.
16. I like mice's (foot) though.
17. Several (sheep) were in a herd.
18. Two (man) will feed them soon.
19. (Child) under twelve can fish in the pond.
20. Do all animals have (tooth)?

C. Complete each sentence with the plural form of a word from the list.

woman tooth foot man child

21. The kindergarten ______ will go to a farm next week.
22. Some ______ will show them how to shear sheep.
23. The ______ will take them to the pasture to see the cows.
24. Cows do not have sharp ______.
25. Their ______ are really hooves.

Extra Practice

Common and Proper Nouns

A. For each underlined noun, write *common* or *proper*.

1. Once upon a time, there was a girl named Alice.
2. One day, the girl fell down a rabbit hole.
3. She landed in a land called Wonderland.
4. Lewis Carroll wrote about her adventure.
5. My class began the book on Monday.
6. We read about Tweedledum and Tweedledee.
7. What did the teacher think of the Queen of Hearts?
8. What story tells about Aunt Sponge and Aunt Spiker?
9. I like that book by Roald Dahl.
10. James had an adventure inside a giant peach.

B. Write each sentence. Draw one line under the common nouns. Draw two lines under the proper nouns.

11. James Henry Trotter lived with his two aunts.
12. His family lived on Proudfoot Avenue in Stillwater.
13. Their house was on a high hill in England.
14. One day, a large box arrived from Admiral Drake in Antarctica.
15. Inside was a penguin named Captain Cook.
16. That penguin caused a lot of trouble in Stillwater.
17. Imagine that James and Alice met.
18. Didn't the two children live near London?
19. Would the boy and the girl visit Mr. Popper?
20. People in the United States love these two characters.

C. Write each sentence. Capitalize each proper noun.

21. My favorite author is e. b. white.
22. White was born in mount vernon, new york.
23. He went to cornell university and graduated in 1921.
24. Have you ever heard of a mouse named stuart little?
25. This mouse liked to stroll on fifth avenue in new york city.

Capitalization

A. Write the noun or nouns that should begin with a capital letter.

1. Our teacher, miss ramos, has given us a good assignment.
2. We are mapping our town, east pine.
3. On wednesdays we work on the map.
4. We put our school, martin luther king school, in the middle.
5. Our school is on shannon drive.
6. Two of my friends, stacey and ryan, are on the committee.
7. We will show the map in january at the county fair.
8. I asked mother to help illustrate the map.
9. She illustrated a children's book called *the rabbit and the fox*.
10. She will draw our famous landmark, nightingale park.

B. Write each sentence. Correct the nouns that should begin with a capital letter.

11. We began the map in november, after thanksgiving.
12. We are studying the geography of the united states.
13. Last summer we traveled by bus to missouri and illinois.
14. Our science teacher, miss jackson, went with us.
15. We crossed the mississippi river and saw lake michigan.
16. I helped jonathan adams and ashley parks read the maps.
17. We got lost in st. louis, missouri.
18. Do you want to see the gateway arch and busch stadium?
19. Our little town of east pine is just right for mapping.
20. Our two main streets are broadway and elm street.

C. Write each sentence. Use a proper noun that fits the description shown in parentheses ( ).

21. Will the map be ready by ______? (month of the year)
22. We may have to work on ______ to finish it. (day of the week)
23. The teacher and ______ will check the map. (name of person)
24. The map will hang in the hallway at ______. (name of a school)
25. The school is on ______. (name of a street)

Grammar

Extra Practice

Singular Possessive Nouns

A. Write the possessive form of each singular noun.

1. grandmother
2. Sarah
3. boy
4. boss
5. baby
6. bicycle
7. cat
8. uncle
9. father
10. Tom

B. Rewrite each phrase. Use the possessive form of the underlined noun.

11. the recipe of the family
12. the fruit pies of my sister
13. the hot dogs of David
14. the pickled cucumbers of Mom
15. the favorite dish of your boss
16. the cookbooks that belong to my friend
17. the recipe that Aunt Gail uses
18. the cabin that my grandmother owns
19. the yard of my neighbor
20. the recipes in the book

C. Write each sentence. Use the singular possessive form of the noun in parentheses ( ) to complete each sentence.

21. ______ soup is a big hit in his family. (Kevin)
22. It really is our ______ recipe. (grandfather)
23. The ______ name is "Garbage Soup." (recipe)
24. We always add many vegetables from ______ kitchen. (Mom)
25. The ______ big secret is the variety of spices used. (dish)

Plural Possessive Nouns

A. Rewrite each group of words. Use the possessive form of the underlined plural noun.

1. the pets of the girls
2. the mice of the children
3. the antlers of the elks
4. the eyes of the adults
5. the clothes of the men
6. the tails of the mice
7. the tree house of the boys
8. the club of the members
9. the strength of the oxen
10. the dresses of the women

B. Write each sentence. Use the possessive form of the plural noun in parentheses ( ) to complete each sentence.

11. In the Black Forest, we saw ______ small farms. (people)
12. We heard the ______ honks first. (geese)
13. Two ______ horses were in a lush pasture. (farmers)
14. The ______ harness is no longer used. (oxen)
15. Along the trail we saw two ______ tracks. (deer)
16. Where are the ______ gardens? (children)
17. They enjoy the ______ questions. (visitors)
18. Look at these ______ tiny ears. (kitties)
19. Please get the ______ feed from the barn. (horses)
20. That is the gate to the ______ pen. (sheep)

C. Write each sentence. Replace the underlined words, using a plural possessive noun.

21. Andrew sees the homes of two mice.
22. The mice see claws of four cats.
23. The wheels of the tractors are stuck in the mud.
24. Are those the quilts of the women?
25. Soon they will shear the wool of the sheep.

Grammar

Extra Practice

Combining Sentences: Nouns

A. Read the pairs of sentences. Write *and* or *or* to show how you would combine the underlined nouns.

1. Monica worked in a magazine office. Sean worked in a magazine office.
2. They liked the editor. They liked the writers.
3. Did Sean start first? Did Monica start first?
4. Was the editor Dr. Reyes? Was the editor Mrs. Hart?
5. Dr. Reyes writes about food. Dr. Reyes writes about science.
6. Is he a scientist? Is he a cook?
7. Mrs. Hart got a pot. Mrs. Hart got water.
8. Dr. Reyes added water. Dr. Reyes added salt.
9. Monica boiled an egg. Sean boiled an egg.
10. Did they poke the big end? Did they poke the small end?

B. Write the nouns that could be combined. Then write *and* or *or* to show how you would combine them.

11. Dr. Reyes baked a cake. The children baked a cake.
12. They put eggs in the bowl. They put milk in the bowl.
13. Then they added flour. Then they added salt.
14. You can use butter. You can use oil.
15. Do you prefer walnuts? Do you prefer pecans?
16. Dr. Reyes will slice the cake. Mrs. Hart will slice the cake.
17. The butter will melt. The chocolate will melt.
18. Dr. Reyes wrote an article. Dr. Reyes wrote a book.
19. Do they work Monday? Do they work Tuesday?
20. Science can be a hobby. Science can be a career.

C. Write each pair of sentences as one by joining two nouns.

21. I like bacon. I like eggs.
22. Do you like eggs for breakfast? Do you like eggs for dinner?
23. Mom made breakfast. Dad made breakfast.
24. Do you want salt? Do you want pepper?
25. Here are the forks. Here are the napkins.

Abbreviations

A. Write the abbreviation for each underlined word.

1. Wednesday afternoon
2. Mister Miguel Suarez
3. Governor Atkins
4. February 12
5. Senator Sam Allen West
6. Doctor Alicia North
7. Tuesday, August 1
8. September 14
9. Sunday in January
10. Senator Tom O'Rourke

B. Write each group of words. Replace the words in parentheses with abbreviations.

11. early (Friday) morning
12. (Governor) Michael Johnson
13. (a married woman) Gloria Ramirez
14. (Mister) Paul Abrams
15. (Doctor) Ann McCoy
16. last (Monday)
17. (Thursday), (December) 7
18. (Senator) Anthony Aurelio
19. (any woman) Lila Stein
20. a date in (April)

C. Rewrite each sentence. Abbreviate as many words as possible.

21. Mister Hanson took us to the state capitol.
22. We met with Governor Edward Soames.
23. This chart lists February and March as the best months to visit.
24. Senator Leanne Ross set up the trip for us.
25. She wrote herself a note that said, "Monday, February 22."

Theme Speak Out

UNIT 3

Verbs and Persuasive Writing

In this unit you will learn about verbs. You will also learn how to write persuasively. Persuasive writing gives an opinion and tries to influence the reader.

Science Link *Read about the fascinating world of whales. The future of these magnificent animals may be in the hands of people.*

In 1946, the International Whaling Commission (IWC) was set up to establish rules to limit whaling. Despite the rules, the numbers of whales steadily shrank. Some kinds of whales may be about to become extinct. Because of a worldwide movement to save the whales, the IWC banned all commercial whaling, beginning in 1985. But the governments of a few countries still allow their citizens to hunt whales.

Whales are one of the few wild animals that are commonly friendly to humans they encounter. Many people feel that we have an obligation to preserve these intelligent and special animals.

Will whales be allowed to remain to share the world with us? The choice is ours.

from ***Whales*** by Seymour Simon

Thinking Like a Writer

Persuasive Writing In persuasive writing, the author tries to convince the reader to share his or her opinion. Reread the passage.

- What is the author's opinion about whales?

Verbs The author uses several verbs that show action in the passage. Read the passage again.

QUICK WRITE What are some action verbs the author uses?

Grammar

Action Verbs

RULES

An action verb is a word that expresses action.

Pen pals write letters to each other.

Felicia told her pen pal about her friends.

An action verb tells what the subject does or did.

subject → Pamela, verb → sent

Pamela sent a letter to Felicia.

subject → Felicia, verb → read

Felicia read the letter to her father.

Verbs

In your journal, write to tell how you know which word in a sentence is an action verb.

Guided Practice

Name the action verb in each sentence.

EXAMPLE: Felicia's pen pal collects stamps.
collects

1. Felicia writes to her pen pal, Pam Rogers.
2. Pam lives in Arizona.
3. Felicia visited Pam last summer.
4. The pen pals played soccer with Pam's friends.
5. Pam and Felicia's team scored the most goals.
6. The girls wrote a script for a play.
7. Pam sewed costumes for the play.
8. They took the parts of the main characters.
9. Felicia directed the actions of the characters.
10. The girls enjoyed their week together.

REVIEW THE RULES

- An action verb is a word that expresses action. It tells what the subject does or did.

Grammar

More Practice

A. Write each sentence. Draw one line under the action verb.

11. Felicia flew home from Arizona.

12. She wrote a thank-you note to Pam's mother.

13. Felicia enjoyed her time in Arizona.

14. Felicia invited Pam to her house next summer.

15. She plans a tour of the historic places in her city.

B. Write each sentence. Fill in each blank with an action verb that makes sense.

16. Pam ______ Felicia's letter.

17. Pam ______ upstairs to her mom's room.

18. Pam ______ if she could visit her pen pal.

19. Pam's mom ______ quickly.

20. Pam ______ Felicia to tell her the good news.

Handbook page 532

C. Spiral Review Write each sentence adding apostrophes in possessive nouns. Draw a line between the complete subject and complete predicate. Circle the action verbs.

21. Pam planned a trip to her friends house.

22. Pams mother drove her there.

23. Her mothers car moved slowly down the avenue.

24. They reached Kristens house in ten minutes.

25. Big smiles appeared on both girls faces.

Extra Practice, page 244.

Writing Activity A Letter

Write a letter to an imaginary or real pen pal. Invite the pen pal to visit you. Offer convincing reasons for visiting.

APPLY GRAMMAR: Include action verbs in your letter. Draw a line under each action verb.

Grammar

Verb Tenses

RULES

A verb in the present tense shows an action that happens now.

We learn about fossils and dinosaurs.

A verb in the past tense shows an action that has already happened.

We learned about dinosaurs yesterday.

A verb in the future tense shows an action that will happen.

We will learn about dinosaur fossils tomorrow.

Verbs

In your journal, write how you can tell the difference between a verb in the present tense and a verb in the past tense.

The **tense** of a verb tells when an action takes place. Most verbs in the past tense end in *-ed*, although some do not. The special verb *will* is used to form the future tense.

Present	Past	Future
talk, talks	talked	will talk
find, finds	found	will find
learn, learns	learned	will learn

Guided Practice

Tell whether the underlined verb is in the present, past, or future tense.

EXAMPLE: Fossils give us clues about the past.
Present tense

1. Fossils tell us about plants and animals of long ago.
2. Our teacher studied dinosaur fossils.
3. Dinosaurs lived on Earth long ago.
4. Fossils provide information about dinosaur sizes.
5. I will ask questions about the dinosaurs' diet.

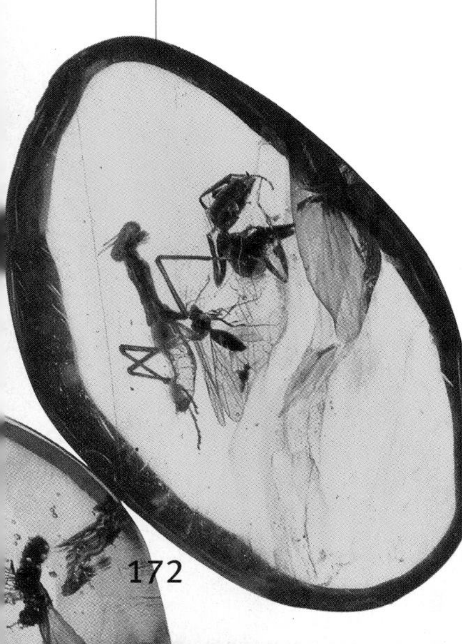

REVIEW THE RULES

- The tense of a verb shows whether the action takes place in the present, past, or future.

Grammar

More Practice

A. Write each sentence. Then write *present*, *past*, or *future* to tell the tense of the underlined verb.

6. Workers found fossils in layers of rock.
7. Scientists studied these fossils carefully.
8. They learned what dinosaurs ate.
9. People continue to study dinosaurs today.
10. They will search for more clues about the past.

B. Write each sentence. Underline the verb. Then write *present*, *past*, or *future* to tell the tense of the verb.

11. Our class left for a field trip at 8:00 A.M.
12. We traveled by bus to the park.
13. We search a riverbank for fossils.
14. We eat a picnic lunch under a big tree.
15. We will leave the park at 2 o'clock.

C. Spiral Review Write the paragraph. Use capital letters where they are needed. Fill in each blank with a verb in the tense shown in parentheses ( ).

16–20. Kevin ______(past) a fossil of an insect last tuesday. He took it to his science teacher, ms. Jakes. She ______(present) fossils. Kevin ______(future) a book about fossils in the library.

Handbook page 532

Extra Practice, page 245.

Writing Activity An Advertisement

Write an ad for a job that requires a worker to search for fossils at a fossil site. Use opinion words to convince readers that the job is interesting and fun.

APPLY GRAMMAR: Include a variety of verb tenses in your ad. Draw one line under each verb in the present tense and two lines under each verb in the past tense. Circle each verb in the future tense.

Science Link

Grammar

Subject-Verb Agreement

RULES

A present-tense verb must agree with the subject of a sentence. Add *-s* to most verbs if the subject is singular.

My dad writes business letters on a computer.

Add *-es* to verbs that end in *s*, *ch*, *sh*, *x*, or *z*.

He reaches his customers with the Internet.

Do not add *-s* or *-es* if the subject is plural or if it is *I* or *you*.

We write letters to our friends.

Verbs

In your journal, write how you know when to add *-s* or *-es* to a verb.

The subject and verb in a sentence must work together.

Singular noun he, she, it	*Add* -s *or* -es *to verb.*
Plural noun I, we, you, they	*Do not add* -s *or* -es.

Guided Practice

Name the verb form in parentheses that agrees with each underlined subject.

EXAMPLE: Cara's letter (tell, tells) about her fun day. *tells*

1. Cara and Sol (ride, rides) bikes around the park.
2. They (stop, stops) at the water fountain.
3. Sol (catch, catches) a runaway balloon.
4. He (give, gives) the balloon to a little boy.
5. A bumblebee (buzz, buzzes) around Cara's head.

REVIEW THE RULES

- The subject and verb in a sentence must agree.
- Add *-s* to most present-tense verbs if the subject is singular. Add *-es* to verbs that end in *s*, *ch*, *sh*, *x*, or *z*.
- Do not add *-s* or *-es* if the subject is plural or if it is *I* or *you*.

Grammar

More Practice

A. Write each sentence. Use the present-tense verb form that agrees with the underlined subject.

6. Jake and Jane (call, calls) Cara on the phone.

7. The twins (want, wants) to come for a visit.

8. Jake (wax, waxes) cars in his neighborhood.

9. Jane (watch, watches) smaller children.

10. They (earn, earns) money for a trip to Cara's house.

Handbook
page 533

B. Write each sentence. Write the correct form of the verb in parentheses ( ).

11. Many people (send) messages with a computer.

12. They (write) e-mail messages to friends.

13. An e-mail message (travel) all over the world.

14. Jack (wish) for a message from his pen pal.

15. The Internet (rush) Cara's message to Jack's computer.

C. Spiral Review Write the paragraph. Choose the correct verb or noun form in parentheses ( ).

16–20. Cara (start, starts) her journal. "Two (woman, women) wait for the bus with me. The bus (pass, passes) through the desert. We (see, sees) many (rabbit, rabbits) from the bus window."

Extra Practice, page 246.

Writing Activity An E-mail Message

Write an e-mail message to an imaginary friend in another state. Describe your school in the message. Tell why your school is great. Provide facts in a logical order.

APPLY GRAMMAR: Make sure that the subjects and verbs in your sentences agree.

Grammar

Spelling Present-Tense and Past-Tense Verbs

RULES

The spellings of some verbs change when *-es* or *-ed* is added.

For verbs ending in a consonant and *y*, change the *y* to *i* before adding *-es* or *-ed*.

Monty tries to call. Monty tried to call.

For one-syllable verbs ending in one vowel and one consonant, double the final consonant before adding *-ed*.

The phone stopped ringing.

For verbs ending in *e*, drop the *e* before adding *-ed*.

Toni smiled at her friend.

THINK AND WRITE

Verbs

In your journal, write how you know whether a verb changes its spelling when *-es* or *-ed* is added.

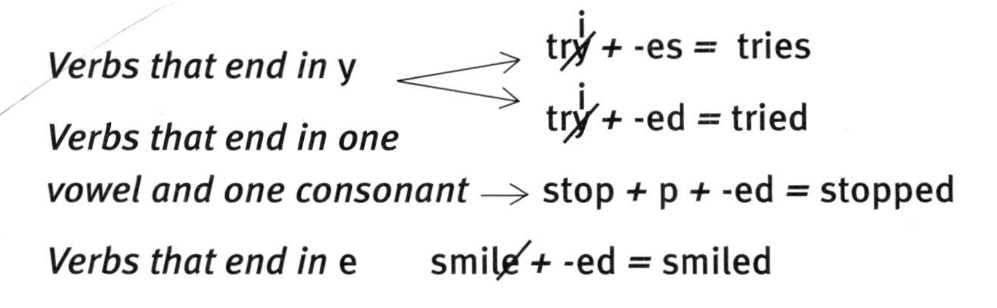

Guided Practice

Read each sentence. Spell the present-tense and past-tense form of the verb in parentheses.

EXAMPLE: Erica (use) paper and pencil to communicate.
Present: uses; past: used

1. Erica (shop) for writing paper and pens.
2. She (plan) to write to her friends.
3. The clerk (hurry) to ring up her purchases.
4. Erica (copy) names from the school directory.
5. She (hope) to get answers from everyone.

REVIEW THE RULES

- **Change the *y* to *i* before adding *-es* or *-ed* to verbs that end with a consonant and *y*.**
- **Double the final consonant and add *-ed* to one-syllable verbs that end in one vowel and one consonant. Drop the *e* and add *-ed* to verbs that end in *e*.**

Grammar

More Practice

A. Read each sentence. Write the correct present-tense or past-tense form of the verb in parentheses.

6. Students (reply) to Erica's messages.
7. Erica (grin) when she read Seth's note.
8. Seth (include) a funny drawing in his note.
9. Erica (clap) when she saw Becky's letter.
10. She (wish) Sarah would write to her, too.

Handbook
page 533

B. Write each sentence. Use the correct form of the verb in parentheses in the tense shown after the sentence.

11. Paul (try) to e-mail Erica. *present*
12. He (decide) to phone his message. *past*
13. Juanita (carry) a note to Erica. *present*
14. She (slip) in a compliment for Erica. *past*
15. People (notice) that Erica is a good artist. *past*

C. Spiral Review **Rewrite the paragraph. Correct run-on sentences. Spell verb forms and plural nouns correctly.**

16–20. Erica loved partys. She hurryed to see her friends. Seth arrived early he brought a CD player. Erica spoted him at the door they walked in together.

Extra Practice, page 247.

Writing Activity An Invitation

Write an invitation for a party that you would like to have. Select words that will really make your party sound fun.

APPLY GRAMMAR: Include verbs in the present and past tenses in your message. Check the spelling rules for these words.

Grammar

Commas in a Series

RULES

A comma tells the reader to pause between the words that it separates.

Use commas to separate three or more words in a series.

Do not use a comma after the last word in a series.

Amy sketches, draws, and paints pictures of animals.

If three or more words are listed in a sentence, the list is called a series. Commas are used to separate the items in a series.

commas   *no comma*

Lee, Amy, and Ben are best friends.

Commas

Why is it important to use commas in a series? Write your ideas in your journal.

Guided Practice

Name the sentences that need commas. Tell where the commas should be placed.

EXAMPLE: Bob Moe and Kit are planning a school newspaper. *Commas are needed after Bob and Moe.*

1. Bob and Kit report news about their school.
2. They talk to teachers students and school workers.
3. Moe writes stories jokes and facts for the paper.
4. Bob asks students and teachers their opinions.
5. Kit writes edits and types stories.
6. The paper is given to friends parents and teachers.
7. Everyone praises the boys and their newspaper.
8. Mrs. Magritte says they are smart careful and clever.
9. Mr. Jones wants to give Kit Bob and Moe a job.
10. He owns edits and publishes the Herald.

REVIEW THE RULES

- A comma is needed after each item in a series, except after the last item.

More Practice

A. Write each sentence. Add commas where they are needed.

11. Bob wants to write a story about Fluff Muff and Puff.

12. These kittens crept scurried and hid in the gym.

13. They looked cute and curious.

14. Tyler Steve and Jeff noticed the kittens under the lockers.

15. Bob will tell about the yellow white and gray kittens.

B. Write each sentence. Add commas where they are needed. Take them out where they are not needed.

16. Addy will draw pictures, cartoons and charts, for the paper.

17. Her art has been called clever pretty and colorful.

18. Parents donated a camera supplies and paper.

19. Students copy fold and staple their newspaper.

20. Bob, Moe, and Kit, are proud of their work.

C. Spiral Review Write the sentences. Add commas and periods where they are needed.

21. Sara, Jess and Jeni received a fax from the mayor.

22. Mrs Kerley praised the girls' good work.

23. The girls raised money and they donated it to the library.

24. The girls sold crafts candy and cards to raise money.

25. The librarian bought books and cassettes

Extra Practice, page 248.

Writing Activity A Story

Write a story about your class for a school newspaper. Use clear and interesting words to tell about something your class has done. **APPLY MECHANICS AND USAGE:** Include a list of three or more words in a series in your story. Circle each comma in the series.

Grammar

Handbook
pages 554–555

Mixed Review

REVIEW THE RULES

- An action verb is a word that expresses action.
- The present tense shows action that happens now.
- The past tense shows action that has already happened.
- The future tense shows action that will happen.
- Add *-s* to most present-tense verbs if the subject is singular. Add *-es* to verbs that end in *s*, *ch*, *sh*, *x*, or *z*. Do not add *-s* or *-es* if the subject is plural or *I* or *you*.
- For verbs ending in a consonant and *y*, change the *y* to *i* before adding *-es* or *-ed*.
- For verbs ending in one vowel and one consonant, double the consonant before adding *-ed*.
- For verbs ending in *e*, drop the *e* before adding *-ed*.
- Use commas to separate three or more words in a series.

Verbs

Write three sentences about a class project you would like to do. Use verbs in three different tenses: present, past, and future.

Practice

A. Write each sentence. Underline each action verb. Write *present*, *past*, or *future* over the verb to show the tense. Add commas where they are needed.

1. My pen pal Juan lives in Mexico City.
2. We send notes to each other over the Internet.
3. Juan's uncle introduced us last year.
4. Mr. Romez his wife and their son moved here from Mexico City.
5. They own the house next door.
6. Juan will visit his uncle in September.
7. He his sister and his mom will fly on a big jet.
8. I will greet Juan at the airport.
9. I plan to be the first person in line.
10. I will give Juan a big hug.

B. Write each sentence. Use the correct form of the verb in parentheses ( ) in the tense shown after the sentence.

11. People (greet) each other in different ways. *present*

12. Some people (touch) hands. *present*

13. A sailor (cry), "Ahoy, mate!" *present*

14. Soldiers (salute) each other. *past*

15. A child (clap) at her mom. *past*

16. My friend (pass) me a note. *present*

17. My dad (surprise) me with a hug. *past*

18. A pilot (fly) over his house. *present*

19. The police officer (tip) her hat. *past*

20. I (smile) and said, "Good day." *past*

C. **Challenge** **Rewrite the following paragraph. Correct mistakes in verb forms, punctuation, and spellings.**

21–30. Thea and Alicia studyed secret codes. They planed a code using lights colors, and sounds. The girls tests it today. Thea flashs red yellow and green lights. Alicia tap out signals on a glass a can and a box.

Grammar REVIEW

Handbook
pages
532–533, 554–555

Writing Activity A Dialogue

Write a conversation between two friends. Draw a line down the center of a sheet of paper. Write a greeting and dialogue for one friend on the left and greeting and dialogue for the other on the right. Check your sentences for correct punctuation.

APPLY MECHANICS AND USAGE: In your dialogue, include at least one sentence that has three or more words in a series.

Grammar

Main Verbs and Helping Verbs

RULES

The main verb in a sentence tells what the subject does or is.

A helping verb helps the main verb show an action or make a statement.

Mike's class is going on a field trip.

THINK AND WRITE

Verbs

Write how you can tell the difference between a main verb and a helping verb.

Verbs Often Used As Helping Verbs

have	am	was
has	is	were
had	are	will

In the sentences below, the main verbs are in blue and the helping verbs are underlined.

The workers have cut the leather.

Mr. Murphy is operating a machine.

They will produce the shoes.

Guided Practice

Name the main verb and the helping verb in each sentence.

EXAMPLE: American factory workers have made many products.
Main verb: made; helping verb: have

1. Mike's class is visiting a factory today.
2. The children have watched people at work.
3. Mike has seen several people from his neighborhood.
4. His teacher will show the class around.
5. Some workers are making the tops for sneakers.

Grammar

REVIEW THE RULES

- The main verb tells what the subject does or is.
- The helping verb is a verb that helps the main verb.

More Practice

A. Write each sentence. Draw one line under each main verb. Draw two lines under each helping verb.

6. My class is touring a shoe factory.
7. Workers have poured melted rubber into molds.
8. Machines are cutting shoe tops.
9. We were watching workers glue the shoes.
10. We will see the sewing department next.

B. Write each sentence. Add a helping verb.

11. My class ______ visited another factory.
12. Some workers ______ making ketchup.
13. Others ______ bottling ketchup.
14. The supervisor ______ help the workers.
15. I ______ enjoying our factory visits.

Handbook
page 534

C. Spiral Review Write each sentence, adding end punctuation if needed. Draw one line under each helping verb. Circle each noun.

16. The children are going on another tour.
17. The workers are making cornflakes.
18. The students taste the cereal
19. Maybe they will get a sample box.
20. The children love this tour

Extra Practice, page 249.

Writing Activity A Poster

Write and design a poster convincing people to tour your factory. Make sure your message is meaningful and clear.

APPLY GRAMMAR: Include main and helping verbs. Draw one line under each main verb and two lines under each helping verb.

Grammar

Using Helping Verbs

RULES

The helping verbs *has*, *have*, and *had* can be used with the past-tense form of a verb to show an action that has already happened.

Jack has visited the zoo.

I have visited many times.

Jack had visited the zoo twice before.

The verb *have* must agree with the subject of the sentence. When you use *have, has*, or *had* as helping verbs, use the past-tense form of the main verb.

Subject	Present	Past
he, she, it	has	had
I, you, we, they	have	had

Verbs

In your journal, write how you know whether to use *has* or *have*.

Guided Practice

Name the correct form of the helping verb.

EXAMPLE: We (have, has) traveled to the zoo.
have

1. The idea (have, had) come from Kim.
2. The animals (have, has) grown larger.
3. The baby deer (have, has) lost its spots.
4. I (have, has) decided to visit the giraffe.
5. It (have, has) grown a longer neck.

REVIEW THE RULES

- Use the helping verbs *has*, *have*, and *had* with the past-tense form of a verb to show an action that has already happened.

Grammar

More Practice

A. Write each sentence. Use the correct helping verb.

6. Animals (have, has) developed special parts for protection.
7. A bird (have, has) developed feathers.
8. Markings (have, has) protected moths.
9. Fur coats (have, has) kept bears warm in winter.
10. You (has, have) grown hair to keep warm, too.

B. Write each sentence. Use *has*, *have*, or *had* and the correct form of the main verb in parentheses ( ).

11. Butterflies ______ me for a long time. (interest)
12. A butterfly ______ a mouth like a tube. (develop)
13. I ______ a bush to attract butterflies. (plant)
14. A monarch butterfly ______ on the bush. (land)
15. The children ______ the butterflies for hours. (watch)

Handbook page 534

C. Spiral Review Write the sentences. Draw one line under each proper noun. Correct the incorrect verbs and add end punctuation where needed.

16. We has visited Cameron Park.
17. Lector has seen many rabbits near the pond
18. A duck have laid eggs in the underbrush
19. Lil have hidden behind a tree near the pond.
20. They has seen many animals at Mallard Pond.

Extra Practice, page 250.

Writing Activity A Debate

Take turns with a partner. Choose different animals. Write arguments about why your animal should be named "most special." Pass the paper back and forth until you have no more arguments. Be sure to use the "I" point of view.

APPLY GRAMMAR: Include helping verbs *have*, *has*, and *had* in some of your arguments. Underline each helping verb.

Grammar

Linking Verbs

RULES

An action verb tells what the subject does or did.

A linking verb links the subject of a sentence to a noun or an adjective in the predicate.

A linking verb does not express action.

Spiders are interesting creatures.

Forms of the verb *be* are often used as linking verbs.

FORMS OF *BE*	
Present	**Past**
am	was
is	were
are	

Verbs

In your journal, write how an action verb and a linking verb are different.

Guided Practice

Tell whether each underlined verb is an action verb or a linking verb.

EXAMPLE: A spider is an animal called an arachnid.
linking

1. The zoo is a home to many spiders.
2. Only a few spiders are dangerous to people.
3. Black widow spiders bite people only in defense.
4. Garden spiders eat harmful insects outdoors.
5. I am a friend of spiders.

REVIEW THE RULES

- A **linking verb** links the subject of a sentence to a noun or adjective in the predicate.

Grammar

Handbook
page 535

More Practice

A. Write each sentence. Write whether each underlined verb is a *linking verb* or an *action verb*.

6. Spiders eat harmful insects.

7. I was afraid of spiders once.

8. They were actually harmless.

9. Spiders catch insects in their silk webs.

10. Spider silk is stronger than steel.

B. Write each sentence. Underline the verb. Write *linking* or *action* to tell what kind it is.

11. A spider is an animal with eight legs.

12. Many spiders build webs.

13. Some spiders are helpful to people.

14. My first pet was a spider.

15. Today, my spider constructed a masterpiece.

C. Spiral Review Write the sentences. Circle each linking verb. Draw one line under each singular possessive noun and two lines under each plural possessive noun.

16. Spiders' webs are sticky.

17. *Charlotte's Web* is a book about a spider.

18. One spider's web is as big as a basketball.

19. Hundreds of spiders were "visitors" under the boys' house.

20. I am the world's biggest spider fan.

Extra Practice, page 251.

Writing Activity A Bumper Sticker

Write and design a bumper sticker to convince people that spiders are helpful. Make sure you write a persuasive and lively message.
APPLY GRAMMAR: Circle each linking verb you include.

Mechanics and Usage

Contractions with *Not*

RULES

A contraction is a shortened form of two words.
A contraction can be made by combining a verb with the word *not*.

An apostrophe (') shows a letter has been left out.

The Statue of Liberty wasn't made in America.

In most contractions with *not*, the apostrophe replaces the letter *o* in *not*. The verb *will* changes its spelling when it is combined with *not* in the contraction *won't*.

Verbs
Write how you can remember where to place the apostrophe when forming a contraction with *not*.

Contractions with *Not*

isn't	is + not	hasn't	has + not
aren't	are + not	haven't	have + not
wasn't	was + not	hadn't	had + not
weren't	were + not	can't	can + not
won't	will + not	couldn't	could + not
don't	do + not	shouldn't	should + not
doesn't	does + not	wouldn't	would + not
didn't	did + not		

Guided Practice

Name the contraction that can be formed by combining each of these pairs of words.

EXAMPLE: are not
aren't

1. is not
2. would not
3. should not
4. have not
5. will not
6. had not
7. do not
8. could not
9. did not
10. were not

Grammar

REVIEW THE RULES

- A contraction is a shortened form of two words.
- An apostrophe (') takes the place of one or more letters that are left out.

More Practice

A. Write the contractions for the following words.

11. are not
12. was not
13. cannot
14. has not
15. does not

B. Write each sentence. Write a contraction by combining the underlined words.

16. The Statue of Liberty is not in our nation's capital.
17. Perhaps you are not sure about this statue's location.
18. The statue can not be found on the mainland, either.
19. I had not seen it until I visited New York City.
20. I was not disappointed with this fascinating landmark.

Handbook page 553

C. Spiral Review Write the sentences. Add apostrophes where they are needed. Write *declarative*, *interrogative*, *imperative*, or *exclamatory*.

21. Look at the statue in the citys harbor.
22. This statue isnt a small monument.
23. Jason wont climb the 354 steps to the top.
24. What is Jasons favorite national monument?
25. Please visit the worlds most famous statue.

Extra Practice, page 255.

Writing Activity An Advertisement

Write an advertisement for a national monument. Be sure your ad will convince others to see the monument.

APPLY GRAMMAR: Include at least one contraction with *not* in your advertisement. Circle each contraction.

Grammar REVIEW

Mixed Review

REVIEW THE RULES

- The main verb in a sentence shows what a subject does or is.
- A helping verb helps the main verb show an action or make a statement.
- The helping verbs *have*, *has*, and *had* can be used with the past-tense form of a main verb to show an action that has already happened.
- A linking verb connects the subject of a sentence to a noun or adjective in the predicate.
- An irregular verb does not add *-ed* to form the past tense.
- A contraction is a shortened form of two words.

QUICK WRITE

Verbs

Write three sentences using helping verbs and three sentences using linking verbs.

Practice

A. Write each sentence. Draw one line under each main verb. Draw two lines under each helping verb. Circle each linking verb.

1. Jeff and I are best friends.
2. Jeff's dad is an animal doctor.
3. Dr. Locke was working at his office.
4. Jeff and I had taken our bikes from the garage.
5. We were riding over to see the animal hospital.
6. Dr. Locke was giving a collie a checkup.
7. He had taken the dog's temperature.
8. He was looking in the dog's throat and ears.
9. Dr. Locke is an animal lover.
10. Jeff and I are planning careers as veterinarians.

B. Write each sentence. Choose the correct word in parentheses.

11. Maria's grandmother (is, are) a zookeeper.

12. She has (took, taken) care of bears and monkeys.

13. Once she (was, were) a keeper of the big cats.

14. Maria and I (was, were) junior zookeepers last week.

15. We (hadn't, hadnt') seen meerkats before.

16. They (run, ran) around and darted in holes.

17. Maria (did'nt, didn't) like monkeys at first.

18. Now, monkeys (is, are) her favorite animals.

19. Mrs. Garcia (driven, drove) us around in a cart.

20. I had never (rode, ridden) in a zoo cart.

C. Challenge Rewrite the following paragraph. Correct the incorrect verbs and misspelled contractions.

21–25. A sea turtle is'nt a clumsy animal. These graceful reptiles has lived in the oceans for many years. Loggerhead turtles is huge animals. Some have grew to weigh 400 pounds. Dont female sea turtles swim to the beach to lay their eggs?

Handbook pages 534–535, 553

Writing Activity A Poem

Write a short poem about your favorite animal. Call your poem "The Best One." Your poem can be funny or serious. Remember to use colorful language and descriptive words.

APPLY GRAMMAR: In your poem, include at least one linking verb and one helping verb. Underline the linking verb and circle the helping verb.

Common Errors in Subject-Verb Agreement

Sometimes writers make mistakes in subject-verb agreement. Read the chart. Look closely at each error and the corrected sentence. Think about these rules when you write.

Common Errors	Examples	Corrected Sentences
Using a singular verb with a compound subject joined by and	Nikki and I collects rocks.	Nikki and I collect rocks.
Using the wrong verb with a compound subject joined by or	Either the students or the teacher sort the rocks. The size or the colors matches.	Either the students or the teacher sorts the rocks. The size or the colors match.

Verbs

In your journal, write to tell why it is important to follow the rules for subject-verb agreement.

REVIEW THE RULES

SUBJECT-VERB AGREEMENT

- When the parts of a compound subject are joined by *and*, use a plural verb.
- When the parts of a compound subject are joined by *or*, the verb agrees with the subject that is closer to it.
- Remember When a verb ends with a consonant and *y*, change the *y* to *i* and add *-es* to form a singular verb.
- Remember When a verb ends with a vowel and *y*, add *s* to form a singular verb. Do not change the spelling of the verb.

Practice

A. Write the verb in parentheses ( ) that agrees with the compound subject of each sentence.

1. Rocks and minerals (is, are) found in nature.
2. Limestone and marble (contains, contain) only one mineral.
3. Pressure or weather (causes, cause) rocks to change.
4. Rivers and oceans (moves, move) rocks to new places.
5. A magnifying glass or magnets (is, are) useful tools for collecting rocks.

B. Write each sentence. Change the underlined verbs so that they agree with their compound subjects.

6. Sean and Sylvia hurries to the mine.
7. They and their friends enjoys collecting rocks.
8. Either rock collectors or a geologist give a tour of the mine.
9. A bus or a jeep take people to the bottom of the mine.
10. Either the colors or the shape vary from one rock to another.

Handbook
page 533

C. Write each sentence. Use the correct form of the verb in parentheses ( ).

11. Metals and gems ______ from rocks. (come)
12. The builder and the artist ______ rocks in their work. (use)
13. Either Holly or Luis ______ stones to the garden. (carry)
14. Pebbles or colored sand ______ the path. (mark)
15. Either a stone or pretty shells ______ down the papers on my mother's desk. (hold)

Grammar Troubleshooter, pages 512–513.

Writing Activity An Advertisement

Write an advertisement encouraging the reader to use an everyday object in a special way. Use colorful words in your ad. **APPLY GRAMMAR:** Check that the verbs in your advertisement agree with their subjects. Make sure that you spell verbs ending in *y* correctly.

Mechanics and Spelling

Directions

Read the passage and decide which type of mistake, if any, appears in each underlined section. Choose the letter for your answer. If there is no error, choose "No mistake."

Check that a contraction has an apostrophe in the correct place.

Use commas to separate words in a series.

A proper noun must always start with a capital letter.

Sample

Whenever Mary rides her bicycle, she keeps several safety rules in mind. She always wears a helmet so that she won't get hurt if **(1)** she falls down. She also has placed reflectors a horn and a light **(2)** on her bike. When she is in a group of riders, she makes sure that they all ride in single file. If you remember the rules that mary **(3)** follows, you'll be safe on your bicycle, too.

1 **A** Spelling
B Capitalization
C Punctuation
D No mistake

2 **F** Spelling
G Capitalization
H Punctuation
J No mistake

3 **A** Spelling
B Capitalization
C Punctuation
D No mistake

Test Tip
Read the entire passage before you answer any of the questions.

Grammar and Usage

Directions

Read the passage and choose the word or group of words that belongs in each space. Choose the letter for your answer.

Sample

Electricity is a type of energy. People __(1)__ electricity in many ways. For example, electricity is used to run appliances at home and at work. It is important to conserve electricity whenever possible. Turn off the lights when you leave a room. Shut off the television when no one is watching __(2)__. Decide what you need from the refrigerator before you open the door. Close the door __(3)__. It is important for people to do __(4)__ part in conserving electricity.

Remember that the verb must agree with the subject of the sentence.

Make sure the pronoun matches the word it is replacing.

Use an adverb to describe how the door should be closed.

Do not use an apostrophe in a possessive pronoun.

1 **A** uses
B use
C is using
D has used

2 **F** them
G you
H it
J him

3 **A** quick
B quicker
C quickest
D quickly

4 **F** their
G their's
H theirs'
J theirs

TIME FOR KIDS Writer's Notebook

RESEARCH

RESEARCH

If I want to write a report on the environment, I go to the library media center. The **card catalog** helps me find any book I need. Most books are listed by author, by title, and by subject. The lists are in ABC order.

COMPOSITION SKILLS

WRITING WELL

Writing a good **lead**—or beginning—will make my readers want to read more. A good **ending** leaves my readers with an idea they will remember. Sometimes it takes two or three times to write good leads and endings. But working hard makes me a better writer.

VOCABULARY SKILLS

USING WORDS

Words like <u>recycle</u> and <u>imperfect</u> have **prefixes**—an extra syllable at the beginning of the word. Prefixes can change a word's meaning. They also help me to say exactly what I mean. What words can you think of that have prefixes?

Read Now!

Write down any leads or endings that you especially like in the following photo essay. Do the leads make you want to read more?

Kid Heroes!

Kids Are Doing It!

Here's a look at some super U.S. kids. One is helping out the environment. Another is a chess champ. And another is singing across America, setting records as she goes. It just goes to prove: You can do anything if you set your mind to it!

The Worm Turns

Taking out the trash is never a problem for Kevin Incikaya of Sierra Madre, California. Kevin loves litter! "I just like watching trash trucks," says the toy-truck collector.

Now Kevin is putting his passion for trash to use—with the help of wiggly worms. He runs a worm farm. Kevin feeds his worms food scraps and then records their eating habits. He plans to send the results of his study for use in a government report. It's a test to see if two California cities should use worms to help reduce the amount of food scraps that end up in landfills. Kevin digs his work. "The worms are fun to play with," he says. And they recycle too!

Mike Mulen/San Gabriel Valley Newspaper/AP

*inter*NET CONNECTION **Go to www.mhschool.com/language-arts for more information on the topic.**

Say, Can She Sing!

Jamie Lynn Bence lives in Wisconsin. But she has made herself heard all over the U.S. Jamie Lynn has visited every major-league baseball park in the U.S. The reason: "I just love to sing," says Jamie Lynn. What's the tune she's singing? *The Star-Spangled Banner.* In 1998, Jamie Lynn became the first person to sing that song at all 30 parks. It took her 15 months to set the record.

Richard Harbus/NYT Pictures

King of the Board

Hikaru Nakamura has all the right moves! At age 10, the preteen became the youngest American chess master ever. The title means he's earned more than 2,200 points in tournaments. Hikaru began playing chess at age 7. Hikaru's next goal is to be an international master. Does he ever get bored at the board? "Only when I'm losing." And for him, losing is pretty much impossible!

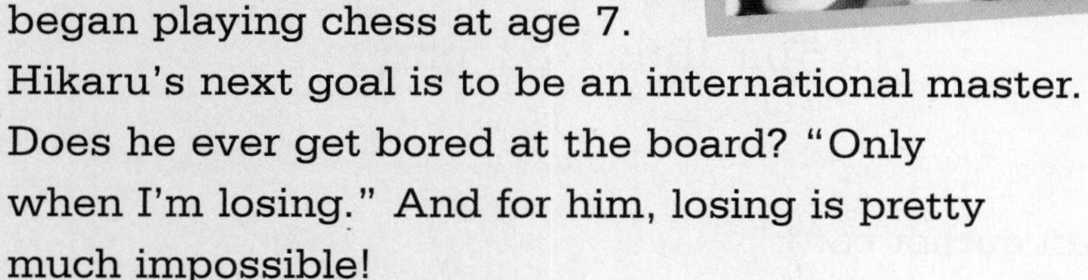

Write Now!

All of these kids spend time working on things that they care about. Choose something you care about. Write to tell why other people should care about it, too.

Card Catalog

In the library's **card catalog,** you will find cards that will help you locate any book in the library. The card catalog is found in a set of drawers or on a computer.

There are three kinds of cards: **subject cards**, **title cards**, and **author cards**. All three kinds of cards are arranged in alphabetical order.

Use the author cards when you know only the author of a book. Use the title cards when you know only a book's title. Subject cards will show you all the available books on a subject. A computer card catalog also allows you to search by author, title, or subject.

Cards and computer catalog entries give you similar information about a book, including a **call number** that will help you find the book on the library shelves. Here is a sample subject card. Notice the call number in the upper left corner.

Subject Card

J792.8 DANCE
K Krementz, Jill
A Very Young Dancer.
N.Y.: Alfred A. Knopf, ©1977.
126p.: illus.: 31 cm.

Here is an author card:

Author Card

J792.8 Krementz, Jill
K A Very Young Dancer.
N.Y.: Alfred A. Knopf, ©1977.
126p.: illus.: 31 cm.

Title cards are filed in alphabetical order by the title of the book. Here is a title card:

Title Card

J792.8 A Very Young Dancer.
K Krementz, Jill
N.Y.: Alfred A. Knopf,
©1977.
126p.: illus.: 31 cm.

Practice

A. Write your answers to these questions about the cards on pages 206–207.

1. Who is the author of the book?
2. What is the subject of the book?
3. What is the title of the book?
4. When was it published?
5. If you were to look for this book in the library, would you find it closer to books with the call number 790 or 820?

B. Write your answers to these questions.

6. What kind of card would you use to find a book about soccer?
7. Which card will help you find books by E. B. White?
8. Which card will help you find the book *Stuart Little*?
9. What part of a card would you use to find the book on the library shelf?
10. What does it mean if there are no cards about a book in the card catalog?

Go to: www.mhschool.com/language-arts for more information on the topic.

Writing Activity A Speech

Next week you will be speaking to your classmates about a subject that interests you. You must convince them to agree with your point of view. Choose the subject. Then use your library's card catalog to find books about it. List the titles and the call numbers of books that might be useful. Then use the books to write your speech.

Vocabulary: Prefixes

DEFINITION

A prefix is a word part added to the beginning of a base word. It changes the meaning of the base word.

re- + read = reread *un- + happy = unhappy*

pre- + view = preview

Prefix	Meaning	Example
re-	again	rewrite
dis-	not, opposite of	disapprove
un-	not	untie
non-	without, opposite of	nonsense
mis-	badly or wrong	misspell
pre-	before	preview
im-	not, without	impossible
in-	not, without	insecure
multi-	many	multicultural
post-	after	postwar

Prefixes

How can knowing the meaning of a prefix help you figure out the meaning of a word? In your journal, explain how you would determine the meaning of a word with a prefix.

Look at the highlighted words in the paragraph below. Which prefix does each word contain?

My dad and I built a tree house in the backyard this summer. After the big storm last week, we had to rebuild it. Each of us thought about the changes we wanted to make, and we made a list of materials we would need. When Dad read my list, he looked at me in disbelief. "Gracie," he laughed, "either I misread this, or we're going to need a much bigger tree!"

Practice

A. Write each sentence. Underline the word with a prefix. Circle the prefix.

1. My friend has an unbelievable imagination!
2. She worked nonstop planning the puppet show.
3. First, we had to repaint an old puppet theater.
4. We were unable to use our old puppets.
5. We made beautiful new multicultural puppets.

B. Choose a word from the Word Bank to complete each sentence. Write the sentence.

rearrange	unable	distrust	misspelled	impossible

6. No one could finish that on time; it's ______.
7. I will have to ______ those books in the proper order.
8. Proofread your paper for ______ words.
9. She is ill and is ______ to go on the field trip.
10. He had learned to ______ strange dogs.

C. Grammar Link Underline the verb in each sentence. Then add a prefix to the verb to form a new word. Rewrite the sentence with the new verb.

11. We had to make the puppets for the show.
12. We checked the props and the stage.
13. Lori spelled some words on the flyer.
14. People may want to view the story first.
15. I read my first line!

Writing Activity A Review

Imagine that you are writing a newspaper review of a puppet show you have just seen. Write about the performance. Tell something about the show and give three reasons for recommending or not recommending it to others.

APPLY GRAMMAR: Use the correct forms of past-tense verbs.

Build Skills

Composition: Leads and Endings

Good writing starts with an interesting lead, or beginning, and finishes with a strong ending. A good lead and ending help you interest your reader in your topic.

GUIDELINES

- A lead is the first part of a piece of writing.
- Write a strong lead to capture your reader's attention.
- You may state your main idea in the lead.
- An ending is the last part of a piece of writing.
- Write a good ending to give your reader a feeling of closure, or completeness.
- Use the ending to draw a conclusion, summarize your main points, or restate the main idea.

Leads

Why is it important to write a good lead if you want your reader to keep reading? Explain your answer in your journal.

Read this advertisement. Find the lead and ending. How does the lead grab your attention and help you focus on the writer's purpose? How does the ending summarize the main idea?

The lead grabs the reader's attention right away. It introduces the main idea of the advertisement.

Would you like to have the cleanest car on the block and help our school at the same time? This Saturday, come to Parkview Elementary School between 10:00 a.m. and 2:00 p.m. for our annual car wash.

The total cost is only $2.00. The money will be used to help buy new band instruments for our school. Did you know that a single tuba costs about $800? I know you will agree that this is a good cause. You can help our school band make beautiful music by coming to our car wash!

The ending restates the main idea.

Practice

A. Write *lead* or *ending* to identify each sentence.

1. What is it like to win a gold medal in bobsledding?
2. As I turned off the light, I knew I would remember this day forever.
3. These facts show that honeypot ants and aphids help each other survive.
4. This month, our class will be holding a mouth-watering event you won't want to miss.
5. So, as stated, your involvement in student council can greatly benefit the school.

B. Write a lead sentence for each main idea.

6. An Unforgettable Day
7. Why Recycle?
8. My Favorite Team Sport
9. The Importance of a Balanced Diet
10. How You Met Your Best Friend

C. Grammar Link **Complete each lead or ending sentence with the correct form of the verb in parentheses. Write each new sentence.**

11. How can I ever (forget, forgot) the first time I rode a horse?
12. As the facts support, our nation's waterways (need, needed) to be free of pollution.
13. My favorite fruit (is, was) peaches for a lot of reasons.
14. For these reasons, we should (plant, planted) trees on Arbor Day.
15. Why should you (participate, participated) in the school play?

Writing Activity A Letter to the Editor

Write a letter to the editor of a newspaper that tells why it is important for children in your community to use crosswalks with crossing guards as they walk to and from school. Be sure your letter has an attention-getting lead as well as a summarizing ending.

APPLY GRAMMAR: Make sure you use the correct verb tense in each of your sentences. Circle the verbs you use. Write *past*, *present*, or *future* above each verb to show the tense.

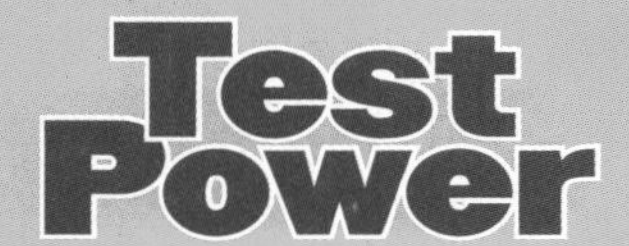

Better Sentences

Directions

Read the passage. Some sections are underlined. The underlined sections may be one of the following:
- **Incomplete sentences**
- **Run-on sentences**
- **Correctly written sentences that should be combined**
- **Correctly written sentences that do not need to be rewritten**

Choose the best way to write each underlined section. If the underlined section needs no change, choose "No mistake."

Look for sentences that should be joined with and, but, *or* or *and a comma.*

Sometimes you can correct a sentence fragment by attaching it to a complete sentence.

Sample

Most mammals use their legs to move. Bats use their wings. **(1)** Bats are the only mammals that can fly. They have wings made of thin skin. The lightweight material helps them fly with ease. When bats fly. They hunt for insects to eat. **(2)**

1 A Most mammals use their legs to move, bats use their wings.

B Most mammals use their legs to move, but bats use their wings.

C Most mammals use their legs to move, or bats use their wings.

D No mistake

2 F When bats fly, they hunt for insects to eat.

G When bats fly, they hunt. For insects to eat.

H When bats fly and hunt for insects and eat.

J No mistake

Test Tip

After you finish a test, always check each answer carefully.

Vocabulary and Comprehension

Directions

Read the passage. Then read each question that follows the passage. Decide which is the best answer to each question. Choose the letter for that answer.

Sample

The arctic tern is a champion flier. In the summer, this small bird lives near the North Pole. As winter approaches, it flies 11,000 miles to the South Pole. Since these birds are not good swimmers, they swoop down to catch fish only occasionally. Usually they catch insects in the air and keep flying. Each year these birds travel a distance that seems impossible. They fly more than 22,000 miles, which is farther than any other bird migrates.

To determine the meaning of a word with a prefix, identify the base word first.

1 In this passage, the word *impossible* means—

A very possible

B not possible

C usual

D more possible

2 What main point is the author trying to make?

F The arctic tern eats fish and insects.

G The arctic tern is a very small bird.

H The arctic tern does not swim well.

J The arctic tern migrates a greater distance than any other bird.

Seeing Like a Writer

Which picture do you like best? What would you write to convince a friend to feel the same way?

Clean Water Poster, Kingsfield Elementary School

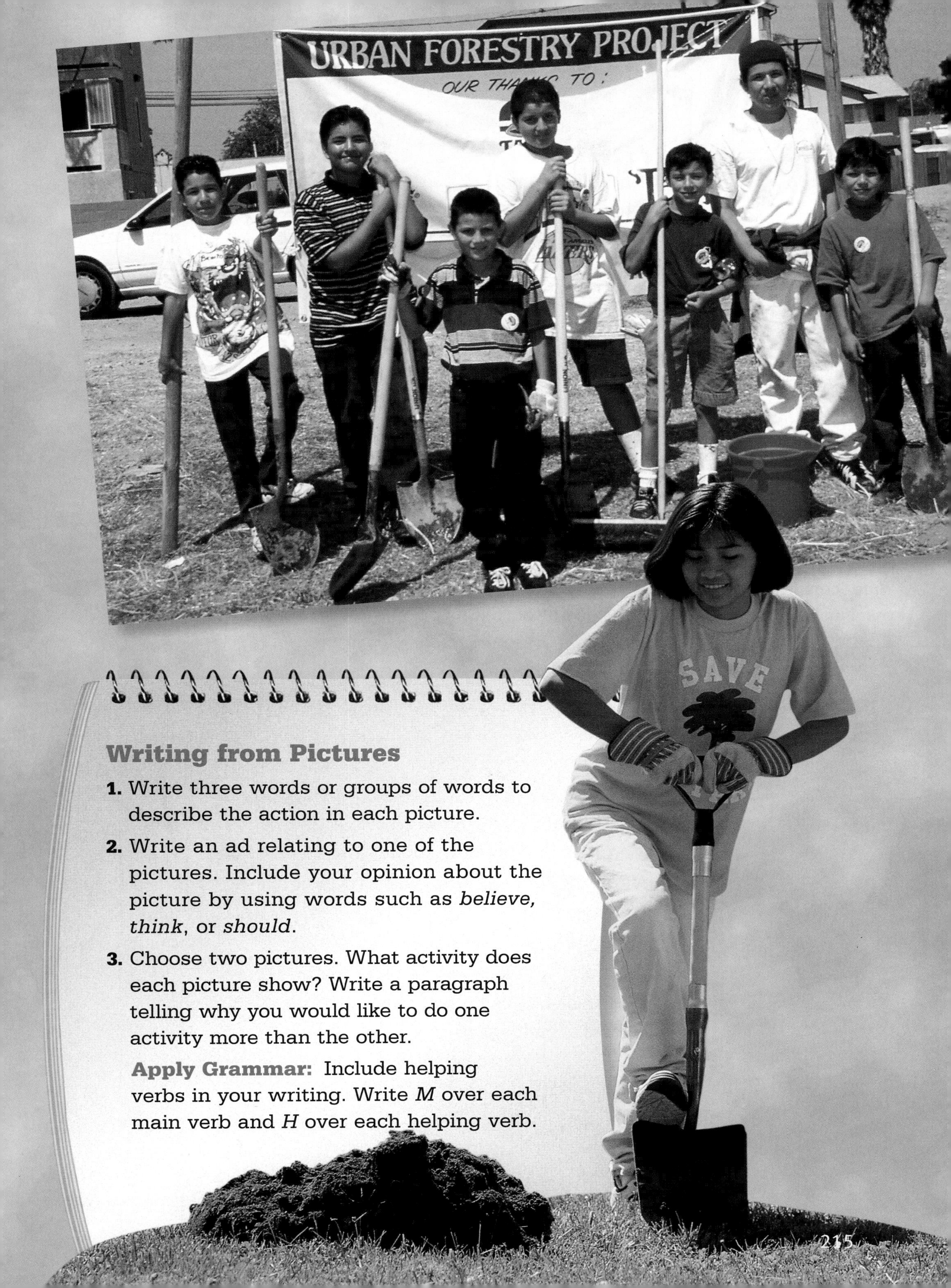

Writing from Pictures

1. Write three words or groups of words to describe the action in each picture.
2. Write an ad relating to one of the pictures. Include your opinion about the picture by using words such as *believe*, *think*, or *should*.
3. Choose two pictures. What activity does each picture show? Write a paragraph telling why you would like to do one activity more than the other.

   Apply Grammar: Include helping verbs in your writing. Write *M* over each main verb and *H* over each helping verb.

Persuasive Writing

Have you ever read a piece of writing in which the author tries to convince you to feel or think a certain way? This type of writing is called persuasive writing. In persuasive writing, an author states an opinion in order to influence readers.

Purpose

Why would you write a persuasive piece? When would you read a persuasive piece? Write your ideas in your journal.

Learning from Writers

Read the following example of persuasive writing. What is the writer trying to influence readers to think or feel? As you read, look for convincing ideas the author presents.

A Power-ful Sun!

A lot of our energy comes from fuels like oil, coal, and gas. One day we'll run out of them, but what can we do? We should use energy from the Sun!

When the Sun heats air, it rises and cooler air rushes in to take its place. The Sun's energy is now wind energy! It can turn windmills that, in turn, can produce electrical energy!

The Sun also warms water. It rises and evaporates. Then it falls as rain or snow. Now the Sun's energy fills rivers. We can use this water to run generators that produce electricity!

Solar panels on houses collect the Sun's energy. It can warm a house and heat its water supply.

Special cells collect the Sun's energy and change it into solar energy.

The more we use the Sun, the less we'll need other fuels, and the cleaner our air will be!

—From a science textbook

Make Earth Day a Town Holiday

Nothing is more important than cleaning our environment. Our town sends 5,000 tons of trash to the landfill every year. The landfill is nearly full. Last year's bacteria scare showed that even our water is not safe. If we made Earth Day a town holiday, everyone in town could spend that one day a year cleaning up the mess.

If townspeople spent one whole day working together, we could do amazing things. The citizens of Midville–a town smaller than ours–cleaned the whole shoreline. Just imagine how much good we could do!

We should write to the mayor and ask her to declare Earth Day a town holiday. Then we should work together to make our town the cleanest in the state!

–Mark Harmond

Practice and Apply

Thinking Like a Reader

1. What does the author of "A Power-ful Sun!" think about using energy from the Sun?
2. Why does Mark Harmond want Earth Day to be a town holiday?

Thinking Like a Writer

3. How do the reasons given in "A Power-ful Sun!" influence the reader about using solar energy?
4. What reasons does Mark Harmond give to support his opinion?

5. **Reading Across Texts** Read both literature models again. List specific words and phrases the authors use to convince readers to agree with them.

Features of Persuasive Writing

DEFINITIONS AND FEATURES

Persuasive writing **gives the opinions of the writer and encourages the audience to share the writer's opinions. A good persuasive writing piece:**

- Clearly states the **author's opinion** on a topic.
- Supports the opinion with **convincing reasons** and arguments.
- Organizes reasons in a **logical order**, often saving the strongest reason for last.
- Includes **opinion words.**

Author's Opinion

Reread "A Power-ful Sun!" on page 216. The author's opinion is stated in the first paragraph.

> A lot of our energy comes from fuels like oil, coal, and gas. One day we'll run out of them, but what can we do? We should use energy from the Sun!

The author's opinion is that we should use the Sun for energy instead of other fuels.

Convincing Reasons

It is important to support an opinion with convincing reasons.

> Now the Sun's energy fills rivers. We can use this water to run generators that produce electricity!

The author explains how heat from the Sun helps make rivers and how the energy from rivers can run machines that create electricity. The explanation helps convince us that the Sun's power could replace other fuels, such as oil, coal, or gas.

▶ Logical Order

Presenting ideas in a logical order can make your writing more persuasive. Often writers save their strongest points for last so that they end their pieces on a powerful note. Read the author's final sentence. Why is it a good way to end the piece?

> The more we use the Sun, the less we'll need other fuels, and the cleaner our air will be!

The writer ends with a persuasive point. If we use energy from the Sun, we will not only save other fuels but also help the environment.

▶ Opinion Words

Reread the third sentence in the article.

> We should use energy from the Sun!

The word *should* is a word that shows the author's opinion. The author wants to convince readers to use energy from the Sun.

Practice and Apply

Create a Persuasive Writing Chart

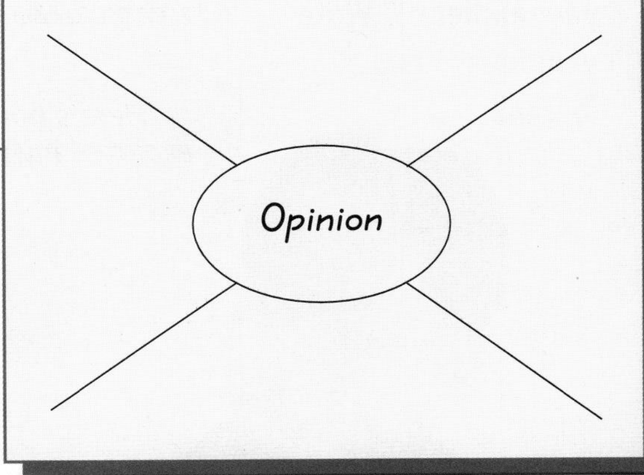

1. Reread "Make Earth Day a Town Holiday," on page 217.
2. In a circle, write Mark Harmond's opinion. Include an opinion word.
3. Draw "arms" from the circle. On each arm, write a reason Mark presents to convince readers to support his opinion. Number the reasons to show the order in which the author gives them.
4. Write whether Mark's reasons convinced you to support his plan.

Writing PROCESS

Prewrite

In persuasive writing, the writer tries to convince readers to agree with his or her ideas. Writing a persuasive piece is one good way to share an opinion about something that is important to you.

Purpose and Audience

The purpose of persuasive writing is to influence the audience's opinion about a topic. A book review is one type of persuasive writing.

Before you begin, think about your audience. What ideas can you use to convince readers to agree with you? What special words can help you write persuasively?

Audience

To plan your book review, what do you need to know about your audience? Write your ideas in your journal.

Choose a Topic

Brainstorm a list of books you have enjoyed reading. Think about which one would be the best choice for your book review.

After you choose a book, **explore ideas** by listing reasons that your book is a good choice. Later, you will organize your ideas.

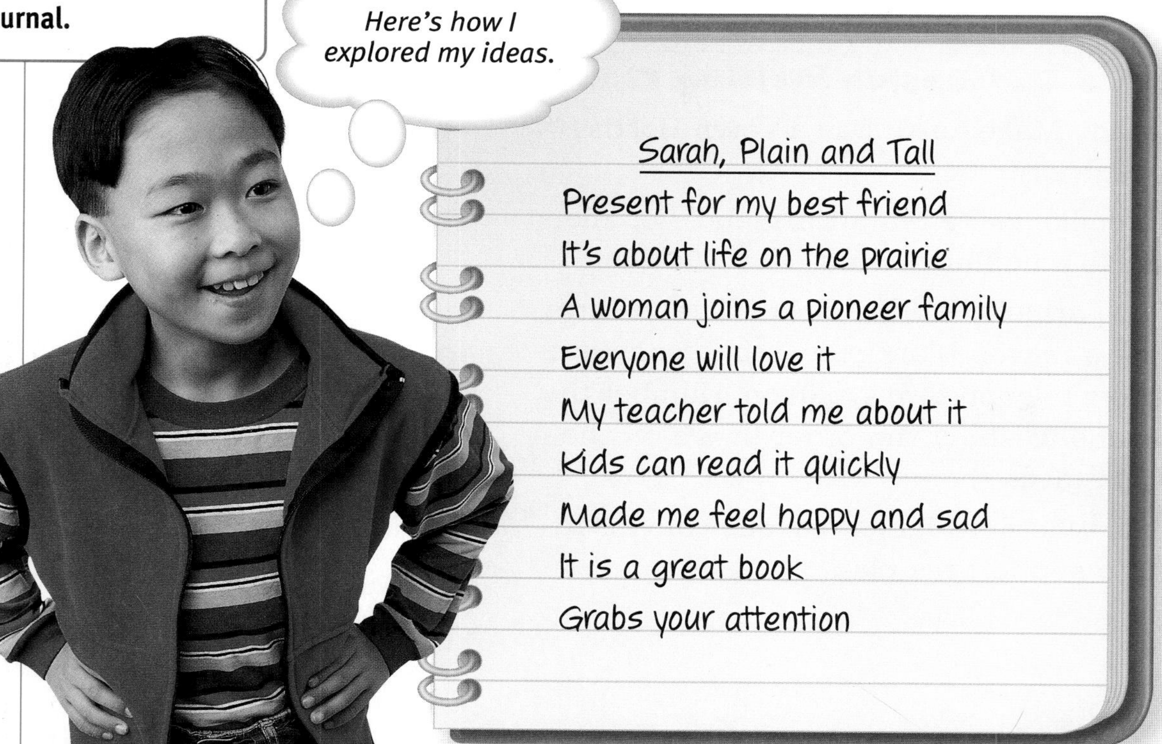

Organize • Facts and Opinion

A writer uses both facts and opinions to support his or her position. To plan your persuasive writing, you can list facts and opinions on a chart. Which information from the list did this writer decide not to include on his chart?

FACT-AND-OPINION CHART

Facts	Opinions
Present for my best friend	Everyone will love it
It's about life on the prairie	Made me feel happy and sad
A woman joins a pioneer family	It is a great book
	Grabs your attention

PREWRITE
DRAFT
REVISE
PROOFREAD
PUBLISH

Practice and Apply

Plan Your Own Persuasive Writing

1. Think about your purpose and audience.
2. Choose a book your audience would enjoy reading.
3. List convincing facts and opinions on a chart.
4. Leave out ideas that do not support your purpose.

Checklist

Prewriting

- Did you think about your purpose and audience?
- Did you identify your favorite book?
- Did you think about how you would convince others to read it?
- Are your ideas organized in a chart?
- Should you do any research?

Prewrite • Research and Inquiry

▶ Writer's Resources

You can do some research to get more information for your book review. First, make a list of questions to direct your research. Then, decide what resources you need to answer your questions.

What Else Do I Need to Know?	Where Can I Find the Information?
Does our library have copies of the book?	Library card catalog
What do others think of it?	Reviews in periodicals

▶ Use the Library Card Catalog

One way to find a book in the library is to look in the card catalog. Some card catalogs contain cards, but others are on the computer. Each book is listed by title and author. Every nonfiction book and some fiction books are also listed by subject. To use an electronic card catalog, follow the instructions on the computer.

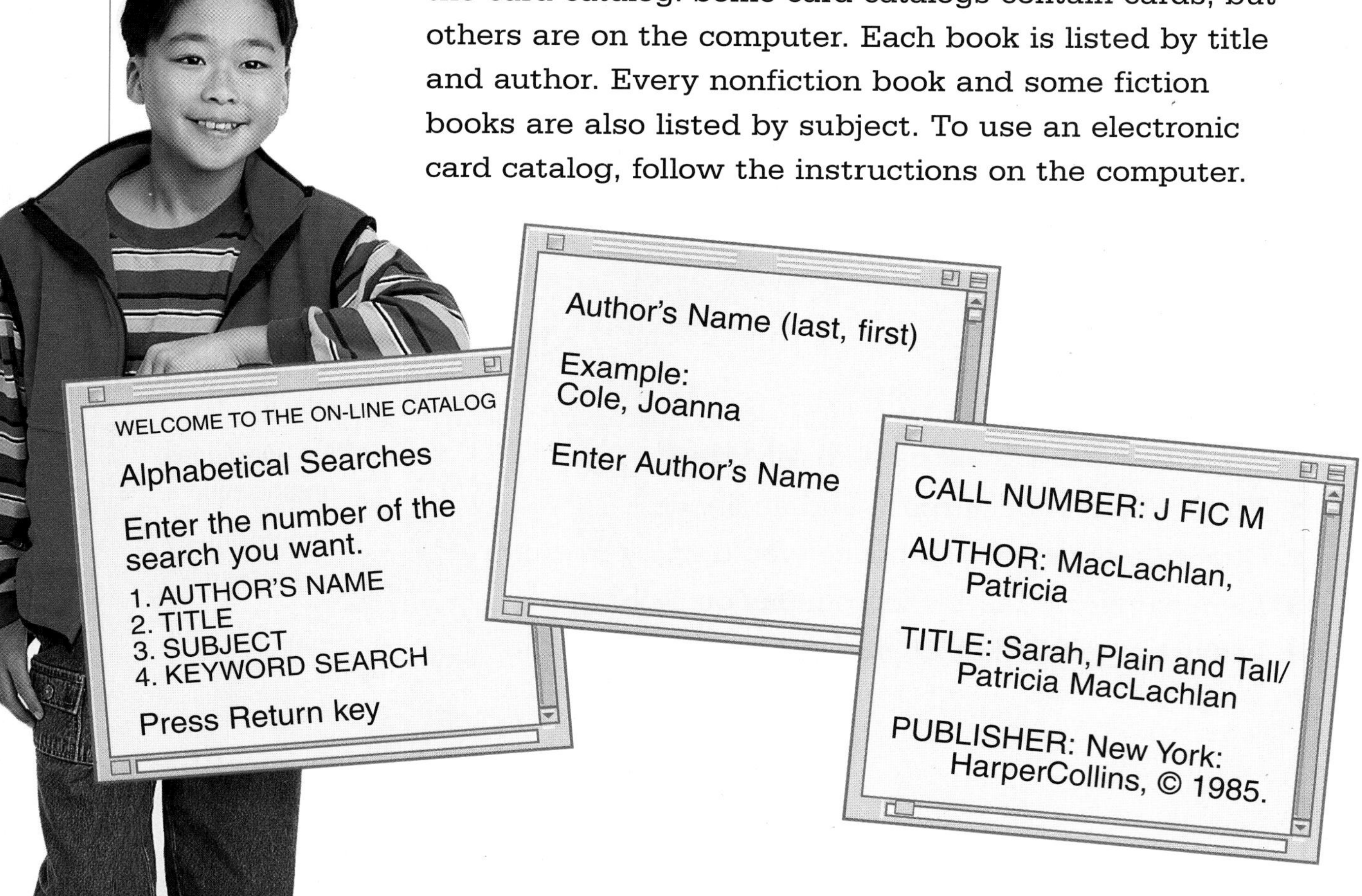

▶ Read Periodicals

Check your library for periodicals that review children's books. A book review expresses a writer's opinion about a book. Sometimes, reviews include interesting information about the book or the author. These details may help you write a more persuasive book review.

▶ Use Your Research

The information you gathered from your research can be added to your fact-and-opinion chart. This writer learned something interesting that he wants to include in his writing. What did he add to his chart?

A woman joins a pioneer family	It is a great book.
Local library has 6 copies	Grabs your attention
Reviewers liked it	
Won a Newbery Award	

PREWRITE

DRAFT

REVISE

PROOFREAD

PUBLISH

Handbook
pages 567–568

Checklist ✓

Research and Inquiry

- Did you list your questions?
- Did you find possible resources?
- Did you take notes?

Practice and Apply

Review Your Plan

1. Look at your fact-and-opinion chart.
2. Think of questions you have about your book.
3. Identify the resources that will help you answer your questions.
4. Take notes and add new information to the chart.

Writing PROCESS

Draft

Before you begin your persuasive writing, take a look at the chart you made. Think about placing each main idea in a separate paragraph. Include facts and opinions that support each main idea.

FACT-AND-OPINION CHART

Facts	Opinions
Present for my best friend	Everyone will love it.
It's about life on the prairie.	Made me feel happy and sad
A woman joins a pioneer family.	It is a great book.
Local library has 6 copies	Grabs your attention
Reviewers liked it.	
Won a Newbery Award	

An important fact to use in third paragraph

Main idea for second paragraph: Others like the book

A good idea for the lead, or beginning

Checklist

Drafting

- **Does your writing fit your purpose and audience?**
- **Do you capture the reader's attention with your beginning?**
- **Have you stated your opinion clearly?**
- **Did you give strong reasons for your opinion?**
- **Did you organize your reasons in a logical order?**
- **Did you close with a strong ending?**

This writer used his fact-and-opinion chart to write a first draft. He included details to support his main ideas.

DRAFT

A Book Review

When was the last time you read a book that grabed your attention right from the start? Sarah, Plain and Tall by Patricia MacLachlan will keep you reading. It will make you happy and sad at the same time. It's about a woman who joins a pioneer family that has lost its mom.

Some people think this is a great book. An important committee awarded it the Newbery Medal. I gived it to my best friend for her birthday.

You can read this book if you enjoy learning about life on the prairie family life and animals. Our local library has six copies of the book, so you can get it easily. You wont be disappointed.

main idea for first paragraph

A supporting detail shows how the writer feels about the book.

main idea of second paragraph

A supporting detail shows how others feel about the book.

Practice and Apply

Draft Your Own Persuasive Writing

1. Review your prewriting chart.
2. Express your opinions clearly.
3. Use convincing reasons to support your opinions.
4. Place your ideas in a sensible order.

TECHNOLOGY

When you write your first draft on the computer, focus on getting your ideas down, not on fixing spelling or typing errors.

Writing PROCESS

Revise

Elaborate

One way to improve your writing is to elaborate. When you elaborate, you add important ideas and details that might be missing from your writing. When you revise your persuasive writing, you may need to add details to help you prove your point.

The writer added details to show how much you will enjoy reading the book.

> Sarah, Plain and Tall by Patricia MacLachlan will keep you reading eagerly until the last page. It will make you happy and sad at the same time.

The writer added his best friend's opinion about the book to show how much other people like the story.

> I gived it to my best friend for her birthday. She loved it!

Word Choice

When you write, the words you use affect how your audience feels about your topic. In persuasive writing, you need to use words that will convince your reader to share your opinion.

> You ~~can~~ should read this book if you enjoy learning about life on the prairie family life and animals.

OPINION WORDS

- I believe
- In my opinion
- Everyone agrees
- Everyone knows
- must
- should
- ought
- never
- always
- most

Better Paragraphs

As you revise, check that the ideas and sentences fit together in each paragraph. Have you arranged information in a logical order?

Look at the sentence below. The writer needs to tell you what the book is about before he can tell you how the book will make you feel. Once you know the subject of the book, you can understand why the story will make you happy and sad.

> Sarah, Plain and Tall by Patricia MacLachlan will keep you reading eagerly until the last page. It will make you happy and sad at the same time. It's about a woman who joins a pioneer family that has lost its mom.

Practice and Apply

Revise Your Own Persuasive Writing

1. Elaborate on your ideas by adding important details.
2. Choose words that will help you convince your reader to share your opinion.
3. Check your paragraphs to see if you presented information in a logical order.
4. **Grammar** Have you used the correct form of verbs?

TECHNOLOGY

It is easy to revise your work on the computer. Highlight information you no longer want and press the *delete* key. To add new information, click your mouse where you want to insert words, and then type.

Writing PROCESS

Revise • Peer Conferencing

Pair up with a partner and share your thoughts about each other's first draft.

A Book Review

When was the last time you read a book that grabed your attention right from the start? Sarah, Plain and Tall by Patricia MacLachlan will keep you reading. It will make you happy and sad at the same time. It's about a woman who joins a pioneer family that has lost its mom.

Some people think this is a great book. An important committee awarded it the Newbery Medal. I gived it to my best friend for her birthday.

You can read this book if you enjoy learning about life on the prairie family life and animals. Our local library has six copies of the book, so you can get it easily. You wont be disappointed.

You capture your audience's attention with this beginning.

Use strong opinion words to make this more persuasive.

Include another convincing reason to support your argument.

Conferencing for the Reader

- Are features of persuasive writing included in your partner's piece?
  - states the author's opinion
  - convincing reasons
  - logical order
  - strongest reason for last
  - opinion words
- Make sure to tell your partner what's good about the piece, as well as what needs improvement.

Think about your partner's suggestions. This writer made some changes based on his partner's ideas.

REVISE

A Must Read!
~~A Book Review~~

When was the last time you read a book that grabed your attention right from the start? Sarah, Plain and Tall by Patricia MacLachlan will keep you reading eagerly until the last page. It's about a woman who joins a pioneer family that has lost its mom. It will make you happy and sad at the same time.

~~Some people think~~ Everyone agrees that this is a great book. An important committee awarded it the Newbery Medal. I gived it to my best friend for her birthday. She loved it!

You ~~can~~ should read this book if you enjoy learning about life on the prairie family life and animals. It's a realistic and exciting story. Our local library has six copies of the book, so you can get it easily. You wont be disappointed.

Checklist

Revising

- Does your writing suit your purpose?
- Should you elaborate more to convince your audience?
- Did you use opinion words to make your piece more persuasive?
- Do your sentences flow smoothly when you read the piece aloud?
- Did you add a good title?

Practice and Apply

Plan Your Own Persuasive Writing

1. Ask a partner to read your draft and summarize it. This will tell you if your main points are clear.
2. Use your partner's suggestions to revise your draft.
3. Check that the sentences in your revised draft flow smoothly.
4. Include an interesting title.

Writing PROCESS

Proofread

After you have revised your writing, you will need to proofread it to find and correct any errors in mechanics, grammar, and spelling.

STRATEGIES FOR PROOFREADING

- **Check each sentence for proper punctuation.** Make sure you have used commas and apostrophes correctly.
- **Read your work aloud to find errors in verb forms.** Sometimes you can hear mistakes that you may miss when you read to yourself.
- **Read for spelling errors.** Reading backwards from right to left may help you find mistakes.

Spelling

When a one-syllable word ends in a vowel followed by a consonant, double the consonant before adding an ending that begins with a vowel.

REVIEW THE RULES

GRAMMAR

- An **irregular verb** is a verb that does not add *-ed* to form the past tense. The spelling of an irregular verb changes to form the past tense and the past with *have*.

MECHANICS

- A **contraction** is a shortened form of a verb and a word such as *not*. An apostrophe is used to replace one or more letters.
- **Commas** are used to separate three or more words in a series. Do not use a comma after the last word in the series.

Look at the proofreading corrections made on the draft below. What does the symbol ^ mean? Why does the writer want to add an apostrophe?

PROOFREAD

A Must Read!
~~A Book Review~~

When was the last time you read a book that grabbed ~~grabed~~ your attention right from the start? Sarah, Plain and Tall by Patricia MacLachlan will keep you reading eagerly until the last page. ~~It will make you happy and sad at the same time.~~ It's about a woman who joins a pioneer family that has lost its mom.

Everyone agrees that ~~Some people think~~ this is a great book. An important committee awarded it the Newbery Medal. I gave ~~gived~~ it to my best friend for her birthday. She loved it!

You should ~~can~~ read this book if you enjoy learning about life on the prairie, family life, and animals. It's a realistic and exciting story. Our local library has six copies of the book, so you can get it easily. You won't be disappointed.

Practice and Apply

Proofread Your Own Persuasive Writing

1. Correct spelling errors.
2. Use the proper forms of verbs.
3. Use commas correctly.
4. Include apostrophes in contractions.

Checklist

Proofreading

- Are all contractions spelled correctly?
- Did you follow the rules for adding endings to verbs?
- Did you spell irregular verbs correctly?
- Did you use commas to separate three or more words in a series?

PROOFREADING MARKS

- # new paragraph
- ^ add
- take out
- ≡ Make a capital letter.
- / Make a small letter.
- (SP) Check the spelling.
- ⊙ Add a period.

Publish

Carefully look over your writing once more before you publish. A checklist can help you focus your attention on this task.

Self-Check Book Review

- ❑ Did I keep my audience in mind?
- ❑ Did I achieve my purpose? Will my readers agree with my opinion?
- ❑ Did I include several convincing reasons?
- ❑ Did I present my ideas in a logical order?
- ❑ Did I write a strong opening sentence and a good closing sentence?
- ❑ Did I use strong opinion words to help convince my readers?
- ❑ Do my sentences flow smoothly?
- ❑ Have I used the correct forms of verbs?
- ❑ Have I used correct punctuation in my sentences, including commas and apostrophes?

The writer used the checklist to review his writing. Read "A Must Read!" and decide if the writer has convinced you to read the book. Is this review ready to be published? Write your response in your journal.

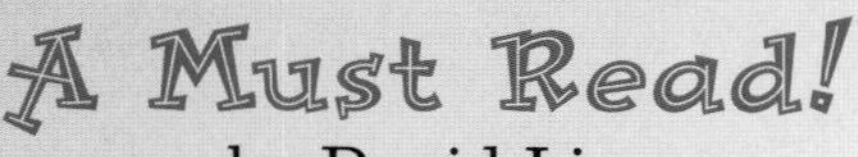

A Must Read!

by David Liu

When was the last time you read a book that grabbed your attention right from the start? Sarah, Plain and Tall by Patricia MacLachlan will keep you reading eagerly until the last page. It's about a woman who joins a pioneer family that has lost its mom. It will make you happy and sad at the same time.

Everyone agrees that this is a great book. An important committee awarded it the Newbery Medal. I gave it to my best friend for her birthday. She loved it!

You should read this book if you enjoy learning about life on the prairie, family life, and animals. It's a realistic and exciting story. Our local library has six copies of the book, so you can get it easily. You won't be disappointed.

PRACTICE AND APPLY

Publish Your Own Persuasive Writing

1. Check your revised work one last time.
2. Type or neatly write your final copy.
3. Add computer graphics or drawings.
4. Mount your work on an unusual background, such as wrapping paper.

Handwriting

Read your final draft carefully to make sure that you haven't left out any words or letters.

LISTENING
SPEAKING
VIEWING
REPRESENTING

Present Your Persuasive Writing

Think of a plan for your oral presentation. Planning ahead and practicing can help you make a successful presentation.

STEP 1

How to Give Your Book Review

Strategies for Speaking As you prepare your speech, remember that you want to persuade your audience to read the book.

- Pay attention to the tone of your voice. Try to speak with expression and confidence.
- Imagine making eye contact with listeners.
- Plan gestures that would help you make your points.

Listening Strategies

- Set a purpose. What do you want to learn?
- Make notes as you identify the speaker's main points.
- Ask questions when the speaker is finished.
- Decide whether or not you agree with the speaker's opinion.

Multimedia Ideas

You might want to play taped reviews by other students who have read and liked *Sarah, Plain and Tall* for the conclusion to your speech. Beforehand, record student comments to support your position. Have speakers keep their comments brief and to the point.

STEP 2

How to Show Your Book Review

Suggestions for Visuals Your presentation will be more interesting to your audience if you add visuals to bring your points to life.

- Display a copy of the book as you introduce it.
- Illustrate some of your favorite parts of the book to draw your audience into the story.
- Make a poster that includes reviewers' comments about the book.

STEP 3

How to Share Your Book Review

Strategies for Rehearsing The more you practice, the more comfortable you'll feel on the day of your presentation.

- Have your family or friends listen to your speech. Use their suggestions the next time you practice.
- Refer to prepared note cards if you forget what you want to say.
- Tape-record yourself giving your speech to hear how you sound.

Viewing Strategies

- Look at the visuals as the speaker presents them.
- Link the visuals with the speaker's ideas as he or she talks.
- View the visuals again when the speech is over if you need more information.

PRACTICE AND APPLY

Present Your Own Book Review

1. Speak with expression and confidence.
2. Make illustrations of the story to create extra interest for your audience.
3. Practice giving your speech in front of others.
4. Watch your listeners for clues about how convincing you are. Adjust your presentation to match their reactions.

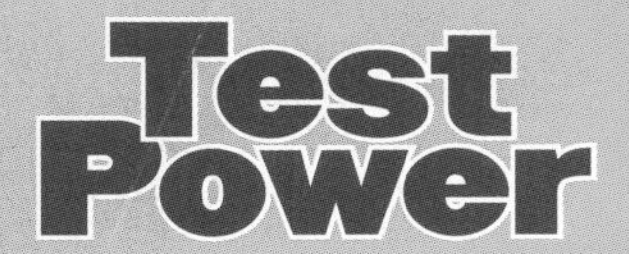

Writing Tests

On a writing test, you are asked to write a composition in response to a prompt. Be sure to read the prompt carefully. Look for key words and phrases that describe the topic of your composition and explain how you should present your ideas.

Look for words or phrases that name your audience.

Look for clues that tell you the purpose of your writing.

This sentence describes the kind of information you should include in your letter.

Prompt

You have always wanted a pet, but your family is not sure that you should have one.

Write a letter <u>to your family</u>. <u>Give your opinion</u> about why you should have a pet. <u>Support your opinion with convincing reasons</u>.

How to Read a Prompt

Purpose Read the prompt again. Look for key words that explain your purpose for writing. The phrase "Give your opinion" tells you that the purpose of your letter is to influence.

Audience Sometimes a prompt tells you who your audience is. This time, your audience is your family. If a prompt does not name your audience, write for your teacher.

Persuasive Writing When you are writing to persuade, you give your opinion about a topic and try to influence your audience. Include convincing reasons in your persuasive writing. Save your strongest argument for last.

Test Tip

Reread the prompt to be sure you are staying focused on the task.

How to Write to a Prompt

Listed below are some points to remember when you are given a prompt on a writing test.

Before Writing Content/Ideas	• Think about the purpose of your writing. • Remember your audience. • List your ideas. • Choose your strongest ideas to include in your writing.
During Writing Organization/ Paragraph Structure	• If you are writing to persuade, begin with a topic sentence that tells your opinion. • Save your strongest argument for last in your persuasive writing. • Give details to support your ideas. • End with a convincing conclusion.
After Writing Grammar/Usage	• Proofread your work. • Be sure your subjects and verbs agree. • Be sure that you have used commas in a series. • Check the spelling of all verbs, especially irregular ones.

Apply What You Learned

As you read a prompt in a writing test, look for the purpose and the audience. Think about the topic and the best way to organize your ideas.

Prompt

If you could start a new club in your school, what would it be?

Write a letter to your principal. Tell why you think this club should be created. Support your opinion with convincing reasons.

Unit 3 Review

Grammar and Writing Review

pages 170–171

Action Verbs

A. Write each sentence. Underline the action verb.

1. Ana scored the winning goal.
2. The fans cheer throughout the game.
3. Cheri raced across the field.
4. A goalie blocked many shots.
5. The sun shone brightly during the game.

pages 172–173

Verb Tenses

B. Write each sentence. Underline the verb. Write *present*, *past*, or *future* to tell the verb's tense.

6. We ate pizza after the game.
7. Byron picked a cheese pizza.
8. The manager takes our drink orders.
9. Jacob joins us at the restaurant.
10. He will play next week.

pages 174–175

Subject-Verb Agreement

C. Write each sentence. Choose the correct verb.

11. The library (sponsor, sponsors) a summer reading program.
12. Adrien (participate, participates) every year.
13. Adrien and her sister (enjoy, enjoys) reading.
14. Fourth graders (read, reads) ten books during the summer.
15. The children (receive, receives) sports tickets.

pages 176–177

Spelling Present-Tense and Past-Tense Verbs

D. Write each sentence. Use the correct form of the verb in parentheses ( ) in the tense given.

16. Erin (plan) to visit her uncle's farm every summer. (present)
17. She (carry) food to the animals. (present)
18. Last summer, she (hoe) the vegetable garden. (past)
19. Erin and her uncle (stop) the pigs from escaping. (past)
20. Her uncle (trip) over a pig. (past)

Unit 3 Review

pages 178–179

Mechanics and Usage: Commas in a Series

E. Write each sentence. Use commas where they are needed.

21. Mark watched fed and photographed animals at the zoo.

22. The monkeys gorillas and apes are primates.

23. The zookeeper was feeding seals sea lions and walruses.

24. Students had sandwiches fruit and milk for lunch.

25. Mario Jeff and José ate lunch together.

pages 182–183

Main Verbs and Helping Verbs

F. Write each sentence. Draw one line under each main verb and two lines under each helping verb.

26. The sun is shining down.

27. Children are playing on the playground.

28. Teachers are watching the children.

29. Everyone has enjoyed the beautiful day.

30. They will play outside again tomorrow.

pages 184–185

Using Helping Verbs

G. Write each sentence. Use *has, have*, or *had* and the correct form of the verb in parentheses ( ).

31. Each student in the class ______ with the butterfly project. (help)

32. I ______ plants that attract butterflies. (study)

33. Megan ______ the teachers at the nature center. (interview)

34. Earlier this year, our class ______ a greenhouse. (visit)

35. Our class ______ a garden to attract butterflies. (plant)

pages 186–187

Linking Verbs

H. Write each sentence. Underline the verb. Write *action* or *linking*.

36. Canada is a beautiful country.

37. The winters in Canada are very cold.

38. Many farmers in Canada grow wheat.

39. Some people in Canada speak English and French.

40. Toronto is a large city in Canada.

Unit 3 Review

pages 188–189

Using Linking Verbs

I. Write each sentence. Use the correct form of the verb in parentheses to complete each sentence.

41. My pen pal (is, are) from Mexico.

42. Her letters (is, are) always exciting.

43. She (is, were) very funny.

44. Her family (is, am) bilingual.

45. I (are, am) glad that she is my pen pal.

pages 190–191

Irregular Verbs

J. Write each sentence. Use the correct form of the verb in parentheses ( ) to complete the sentence.

46. Mom (given, gave) me a package from Grandpa.

47. I (ran, runs) inside to get scissors so I could open it.

48. As I opened the package, I (seen, saw) an envelope fall out.

49. It had airline tickets, so I (gone, went) to visit Grandpa.

50. My grandfather was very glad that I had (came, come).

pages 192–193

More Irregular Verbs

K. Write each sentence. Use the correct past-tense form of the verb in parentheses ( ) to complete the sentence.

51. My parents and I had ______ a train into the city. (ride)

52. We ______ a taxi to the airport. (take)

53. We boarded a jet, and ______ to my uncle's house. (fly)

54. I ______ every day in my uncle's pool. (swim)

55. I have ______ postcards to all my friends back home. (write)

pages 194–195

Mechanics and Usage: Contractions with *Not*

L. Write each sentence. Use a contraction to combine the underlined words.

56. John had not ever been to Washington, D.C.

57. He did not know it was not located in the state of Washington.

58. You will not find Washington, D.C., on the West Coast at all.

59. Our nation's capital is not even in a state.

60. Who still does not know where this unusual city is?

Unit 3 Review

pages 208–209

Vocabulary: Prefixes

M. Write each sentence. Add a prefix in each blank that makes sense with the word and sentence.

dis-	mis-	re-	un-	non-

61. Mr. Potter read the directions for ______ heating his dinner.

62. Still, he was ______certain of what to do.

63. His wife looked at the directions and said, " ______sense!"

64. "You just ______understood this part," she explained.

65. "If you ______regard the picture, it will be easy," she said.

pages 210–211

Composition: Leads and Endings

N. Write a lead sentence for each main idea.

66. The Very Best Pet

67. Visiting Sea World

68. My Favorite Restaurant

69. The Perfect Season

70. A Great Dessert

pages 220–235

Proofreading Persuasive Writing

O. Write the following paragraphs. Correct ten mistakes in capitalization, punctuation, grammar, and spelling.

My science teacher have been teaching us about the environment. You can help take care of our environment by remembering to reduce reuse and recycle.

First, you should try to reduce the amount of garbage. For example, when you packs your lunch for school, choose a container that can be washed and used again. Second, reuse items. Ill bet you throwed away your last peanut butter jar when it was empty. Why not use it as a bug container. Third, recycle all your plastic, glass and paper products. This material doesnt need to take up space in our landfills. If we all try to do these things, we'll have a much niser world in which to live.

Project File

ACTIVITY 1 A Friendly Letter

You have probably written letters to friends, to people in your family, or to pen pals. You may already know that a friendly letter has five parts. Think about what each part of the letter does.

You will need to know the form for a letter when you write a letter in the next unit.

11 Main Street
Austin, Texas 78703
July 11, 2002

Dear Lee,

I have really enjoyed my summer. I was worried last spring that the new pool wouldn't be ready in time, but it was. It's great!

I took swimming lessons in June, and now I can swim the whole length of the pool. You have to be able to swim the whole length to go into the deep end and to slide on the tube slide. The lifeguards tested me, and I passed on the first try!

I'm also playing softball this summer. We have won only a few games, but Dad says that winning isn't everything. I agree with him. I have so much fun playing that I sometimes forget the score.

Next time you come to visit, maybe you can come to a game. That would be so much fun! Please write to me soon.

Your friend,
Barb

Heading Gives the address of the person writing the letter.

Greeting Usually starts with Dear and includes the name of the person who will receive the letter.

Body Is the main part of the letter.

Closing Tells that the letter is about to end.

Signature Is the name of the person writing the letter.

For more information, see Handbook page 587.

Write a Friendly Letter Imagine that one of your friends has moved away. How would you feel? What would you write in your first letter? Write a friendly letter to your friend who has moved away. Say how much you miss him or her, and persuade your friend to come for a visit. Look at the model on page 242 to make sure that you include all the parts of a friendly letter.

ACTIVITY 2

A Newspaper Article

Each of the children described in "Kid Heroes" works hard toward a goal. Choose one of the children from the article, and do research to find out more about the activity described.

You Can Do It, Too! Write a newspaper article that tries to persuade other children to do what the child does. Be sure to give reasons why the activity is worthwhile as well as fun.

Grammar

Extra Practice

Action Verbs

A. Write the sentences. Underline the action verb in each sentence.

1. Mrs. DeMarco teaches a crafts class after school.
2. Justin and Emily print a still life.
3. The still life contains fruit and flowers.
4. Two girls poured several candles.
5. The hot wax dripped into the sink.
6. The girls cleaned the mess.
7. These candles make nice gifts.
8. Everyone made a clay pot this month.
9. I finished this clay pot last week.
10. I glazed the pot in blue and white.

B. Write each sentence. Replace each underlined action verb with a different action verb.

11. I enjoy working with clay.
12. Darice carved a statue of her parrot.
13. She gave the statue to her mother.
14. We made jewelry from beads and wire.
15. Mrs. DeMarco collected our artwork.
16. She displayed the art near the school office.
17. Everyone loved my green bead necklace.
18. We started a mural design.
19. Mrs. DeMarco thinks the mural is great.
20. She asked the principal about it.

C. Write each sentence. Fill in each blank with an action verb that makes sense.

21. The principal ______ a great place for the mural.
22. The kindergarten wing ______ more color.
23. Mrs. DeMarco ______ all the paints.
24. Justin ______ a striped circus tent.
25. Caitlin ______ animals very well.

Verb Tenses

A. Write each sentence. Then write *present*, *past*, or *future* to tell the tense of the underlined verb.

1. My new kitten likes his toys.
2. The older cat looks confused.
3. The cat will watch the kitten at play.
4. I showed the kitten to my class.
5. The kitten escaped from my arms.
6. He jumped back into his box.
7. The kitten purrs when he is happy.
8. He hisses at me when he is angry.
9. I will feed my cats in the morning.
10. I will take him home now.

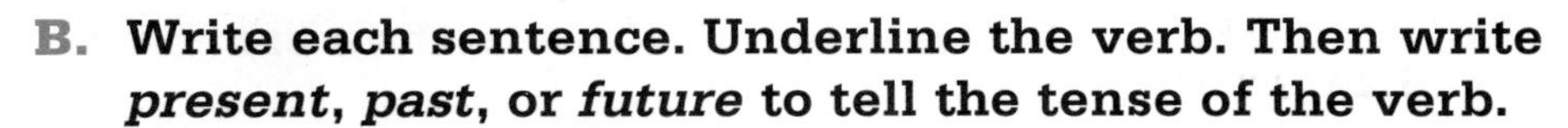

B. Write each sentence. Underline the verb. Then write *present*, *past*, or *future* to tell the tense of the verb.

11. I watch the actions of the cat and kitten.
12. The cat teaches the kitten many things.
13. The kitten pounced on a piece of yarn.
14. The kitten practices his climbing skills.
15. He ran under the chair.
16. Then the cat will move past the kitten.
17. The kitten will jump at its mother.
18. The kitten scampers away.
19. The kitten eats a little food at a time.
20. The cat shows the kitten how to play.

C. Write each sentence. Complete the sentence with the correct verb form.

21. Now the cat (sees, saw) something moving.
22. Yesterday the kitten (sleeps, slept) all day.
23. Tomorrow I (took, will take) my kitten to the vet.
24. Right now he (needed, needs) a nap.
25. Later today I (fed, will feed) him cat food.

Grammar

Extra Practice

Subject-Verb Agreement

A. Write *agrees* or *does not agree* to show if the verb in parentheses agrees with the underlined subject.

1. The Invention Lab (opens) today.
2. Students (create) any kind of gadget they want.
3. The lab (contain) interesting building materials.
4. I (want) to make a spacecraft.
5. These plastic tubes (looks) good for the fuel tanks.
6. Evan (draws) a picture of his robot.
7. He (collect) some cardboard pieces.
8. These rubber bands (connect) the parts.
9. Megan (makes) a silly monster.
10. She (finds) some interesting shiny paper.

B. Write each sentence. Use the correct form of the verb in parentheses ( ).

11. Ms. Barone (decide, decides) to make a satellite.
12. Two other teachers (work, works) together.
13. Silvia (brush, brushes) the dust away.
14. She (build, builds) a space shuttle.
15. My spacecraft (need, needs) solar panels.
16. These wood chips (look, looks) pretty good.
17. My dad (wash, washes) off the piece of wood.
18. He (like, likes) to build things, too.
19. We (know, knows) about making things.
20. Shannon (watch, watches) me work on my project.

C. Write each sentence. Use the correct present-tense form of the verb in parentheses ( ).

21. They ______ a thank-you note to the museum. (send)
22. Jake ______ the Invention Lab with his dad. (visit)
23. The inventions ______ great on display. (look)
24. Ms. Barone ______ pictures of all of the inventions. (take)
25. Jake ______ he could spend all day at the museum. (wish)

Spelling Present-Tense and Past-Tense Verbs

A. Write *present* or *past* to name the tense of each verb.

1. shopped
2. donates
3. rushed
4. replies
5. clap
6. finish
7. copied
8. invite
9. blushes
10. included

B. Read each sentence. Write the correct present-tense and past-tense forms of the verb in parentheses.

11. Mom (notice) something missing.
12. She (hurry) back into the store.
13. The cashier (grin) at her.
14. Mom (blush) with embarrassment.
15. Sally (carry) the bag to the car.
16. Mom (breathe) a sigh of relief.
17. She (stop) once more on the way home.
18. Mom (hope) her new glasses fit well.
19. The technician (like) the glasses she chose.
20. Mom (try) on the glasses.

C. Write each sentence. Use the correct form of the verb in parentheses ( ) in the tense shown after the sentence.

21. Sally (decide) these glasses look great on her. *past*
22. The technician (study) the fit of the glasses. *present*
23. Mom (hope) for new glasses for a long time. *past*
24. The technician (finish) the sale. *present*
25. Mom (hurry) out of the store. *present*

Grammar

Extra Practice

Commas in a Series

A. Write each sentence. Use commas where they are needed in each underlined phrase.

1. Nathan Zack and I went tubing last summer.
2. My sister brought Ellen Nadia and Linda with her.
3. My parents Zack's parents and Nadia's parents went, too.
4. The truck was loaded with coolers food blankets and towels.
5. We drove past the mall the park and the school.
6. The van the car and the truck followed Mrs. Morton.
7. All of us stopped to get tubes rafts and life jackets.
8. Ellen Nadia and Marie rented large tubes.
9. Mom Dad and Mr. Morton rented double tubes.
10. Zack's sister brother and friend each got a raft.

B. Write each sentence, and include the necessary commas. If no commas are needed, write *no commas* next to the sentence.

11. It was a hazy hot and humid day.
12. Zack and Marie checked the water temperature.
13. We left the food drinks towels and blankets in the truck.
14. Are there any alligators or turtles in the river?
15. The Ichetucknee River has lots of animals plants and rocks.
16. The children shrieked and screamed on their way to the river.
17. The parents smiled laughed and chuckled.
18. It's a good thing the weather was sunny hot and humid.
19. The river is not very deep or wide.
20. Marie Nadia and Ellen watched as Dad checked the tubes.

C. Write each sentence. Add commas where they are needed. Take them out where they are not needed.

21. Zack's sister, brother, and mother, stayed together.
22. The ropes helped the boys the girls and their parents.
23. We did a run in the morning the afternoon and the evening.
24. After that, we ate sandwiches, fruit, and chips, for lunch.
25. The hot sun felt great after sitting in the cold wet and rolling river.

Main Verbs and Helping Verbs

A. Write each sentence. Circle the helping verb that goes with the underlined main verb.

1. All of the fourth graders are studying history.
2. I am writing a report about camels in the military.
3. In the mid-1800s, horses and mules had served as pack animals.
4. The U.S. Army had heard about camels' great abilities.
5. Camels will endure long distances of travel in the desert.
6. They have developed ways to survive the hot and dry climate.
7. In 1855, the Army had sent two officers to the Middle East.
8. The two officers had purchased 33 camels for the Army.
9. They had loaded the camels on the *USS Supply*.
10. People were commenting on the camels' great strength.

B. Write each sentence. Underline the main verb and circle the helping verb.

11. The Army had moved a herd of camels to Fort Camp Verde.
12. A second herd was coming the following year.
13. The camels were working alongside horses and mules.
14. A camel's strong legs will allow it to carry heavy loads for long distances.
15. Camels have traveled up to 25 miles a day with little food or water.
16. Sometimes rocky soil has injured a camel's soft, padded feet.
17. A fire had destroyed Fort Camp Verde in 1910.
18. During the Civil War, the Army was selling the camels.
19. Some camels had escaped.
20. A few were roaming the west Texas desert.

C. Write each sentence. Add a helping verb to each main verb.

21. Some camels ______ survived until the end of the 1800s.
22. They ______ never tried the camel project again.
23. I ______ finishing my report today.
24. I ______ learned a lot about these camels.
25. They ______ kick if they have to work too hard.

Extra Practice

Using Helping Verbs

A. Write each sentence. Use the correct helping verb in parentheses ( ).

1. Sea turtles (has, have) appeared on the beach.
2. The fourth grade (has, have) learned about sea turtles.
3. The turtles (has, have) nested on Florida beaches for years.
4. Three different types (has, have) nested at Melbourne Beach.
5. The Science Center (has, have) a turtle field trip.
6. My dad (has, have) taken me on the trip before.
7. I (has, have) wanted to see a turtle.
8. Scientists (has, have) found many turtle nests.
9. I (has, have) read a book about loggerhead, green, and leatherback turtles.
10. Those three kinds (has, have) nested in Florida.

B. Write each sentence. Use the correct form of the verb in parentheses ( ).

11. Female sea turtles have ______ onto the beach at night. (crawl)
12. Last night the female had ______ her eggs in the sand. (bury)
13. The nest has ______ untouched by other animals. (remain)
14. People have ______ as many as 150 eggs in a nest! (notice)
15. The eggs had ______ late last week. (hatch)
16. Scientists have ______ many of the nests on the beach. (mark)
17. I have ______ for the turtle nests on the beach. (look)
18. I have ______ the turtle tracks in the sand. (examine)
19. My dad had ______ loggerhead turtles. (study)
20. He has ______ loggerheads closely. (watch)

C. Write each sentence. Use *has*, *have*, or *had* and the correct form of the verb in parentheses ( ).

21. We ______ patiently for an hour. (wait)
22. Turtles ______ me for a long time. (interest)
23. I ______ to see a turtle make a nest. (want)
24. A loggerhead ______ her nest at last. (finish)
25. Then she ______ slowly back to the sea. (walk)

Linking Verbs

A. Write each sentence. Draw a line under the linking verb.

1. We are excited about Health and Safety Day.
2. I am a helper during science.
3. Two police officers are experts about personal safety.
4. Coach Carter is helpful in our class.
5. This video on safety was interesting.
6. The first graders were happy after the puppet show.
7. Everyone is fascinated by the police horses.
8. The horses were so gentle and smart.
9. The firefighters are the leaders of our tour.
10. Bus safety is important.

B. Write each sentence. Write *linking verb* or *action verb* for each of the underlined verbs.

11. The sheriff's helicopter landed in the back field.
12. That was very exciting!
13. Bike riders learned about bicycle safety.
14. My class made a poster about dental care.
15. Nutrition is important for good health.
16. Mrs. Fields dressed in a tooth costume!
17. We were happy that so many parents came.
18. This is such a good idea.
19. Everyone appreciated the enjoyable activities.
20. The cafeteria staff made special lunches that day.

C. Write each sentence. Draw a line under the verb. Write *linking* or *action* to tell what kind of verb it is.

21. Peter won a prize for his display.
22. He is very clever.
23. Most of the displays were beautiful.
24. Ali and Hayley worked on their project together.
25. Many students are busy on the playground.

Grammar

Extra Practice

Using Linking Verbs

A. Write each sentence. Choose the correct form of *be* in parentheses ( ).

1. I (is, am) a student in the fourth grade.
2. My favorite subject (is, are) math.
3. Last year my favorite subject (was, were) reading.
4. We (is, are) ready for the math test.
5. Multiplication (is, are) easier this year.
6. My teacher (is, are) really great.
7. The spelling lists (is, are) longer in fourth grade.
8. Some of the words (was, were) difficult.
9. I (is, am) careful when I write the words.
10. Wesley (was, were) happy with his score.

B. Write each sentence. Use *am*, *is*, or *are* to complete the sentence.

11. My favorite books ______ *Mr. Popper's Penguins* and *Fudgemania*.
12. Reading ______ my favorite activity.
13. Reading ______ hard for me when it is noisy.
14. I ______ a good student in math.
15. My parents ______ very patient with me.
16. My dad ______ a music teacher.
17. Reading music ______ easy for me.
18. My mom and dad ______ musicians.
19. I ______ a good singer.
20. Singing ______ a good way to practice reading.

C. Write each sentence. Use a form of *be* to complete the sentence.

21. I ______ always careful with library books.
22. Last year nonfiction ______ my favorite kind of book.
23. Now fiction about dolphins ______ special to me.
24. Dolphins ______ smart animals in many ways.
25. These books ______ donations last month.

Irregular Verbs

A. Write each sentence. Draw a line under the irregular verb.

1. The Brown family did not unpack yet.
2. They came to the neighborhood yesterday.
3. I made three dozen cookies.
4. Mom brought a roasted chicken.
5. Mrs. Gonzalez came to help, too.
6. We saw all the boxes.
7. The neighbors gave them some food.
8. My mom and I went over to help them unpack.
9. We brought some food, too.
10. I ran outside to play with the children.

B. Write each sentence. Choose the correct verb in parentheses ( ).

11. I have (did, done) some unpacking, too.
12. The children have (ate, eaten) all the chicken.
13. Mom (given, gave) me a broom for sweeping.
14. Where have those children (went, gone)?
15. They have (ran, run) outside to play again.
16. We (gone, went) over to help for a while.
17. Mrs. Brown (seen, saw) an unmarked box.
18. Her little boy (run, ran) to the box.
19. He asked if I had (saw, seen) his teddy bear.
20. His mother had (gave, given) him the teddy bear.

C. Write each sentence. Use the correct past-tense form of the verb in parentheses ( ).

21. You have ______ a very good job today. (do)
22. The children have ______ me a present. (make)
23. Little Christopher ______ me a big hug. (give)
24. His sisters ______, too. (come)
25. They have ______ me a cookie. (bring)

Extra Practice

More Irregular Verbs

A. Write each sentence. Draw a line under the irregular verb.

1. My parents took us to the basketball game.
2. We rode there in the car.
3. My dad drove our new car.
4. We took our seats as the game started.
5. My dad had begun to cheer.
6. The referee threw the ball for the jump shot.
7. The players began passing the ball.
8. The ball flew from player to player.
9. The crowd had grown restless.
10. I wrote an article about the game for our school paper.

B. Write each sentence. Choose the correct form of the verb in parentheses ( ).

11. Yesterday I (swam, swum) in a competition.
12. My event had (began, begun) at noon.
13. Tyler's mom (drove, driven) four of us to the pool.
14. The coach had (wrote, written) our names on a chart.
15. I (took, taken) my place in the first lane.
16. The other team's swimmer had (took, taken) the other lane.
17. At the signal, I (threw, thrown) myself into the water.
18. I (flown, flew) through the water toward the finish.
19. The other swimmer had (drew, drawn) up close to me.
20. The crowd (began, begun) to cheer wildly.

C. Write each sentence. Use the correct past-tense form of the verb in parentheses ( ).

21. The reporter ______ about the game. (write)
22. He had ______ by congratulating the teams. (begin)
23. The article ______ up half of a page. (take)
24. My friends have ______ proud of my success. (grow)
25. They ______ a party for my team. (throw)

Contractions with *Not*

A. Write the two words that the following contractions replace.

1. hadn't
2. don't
3. weren't
4. wasn't
5. isn't
6. aren't
7. doesn't
8. won't
9. haven't
10. didn't

B. Write a contraction for each of the following pairs of words.

11. is not
12. will not
13. have not
14. has not
15. did not
16. were not
17. are not
18. does not
19. had not
20. do not

C. Write each sentence. Write a contraction by combining the underlined words.

21. This computer game <u>is not</u> much fun.
22. I <u>do not</u> like confusing directions.
23. It <u>was not</u> hard to use this game.
24. I <u>will not</u> play the other one again.
25. My friends <u>are not</u> using the computer right now.

Cumulative Review

Unit 1 Sentences

A. **Read each group of words. Write whether it is a *sentence* or *sentence fragment*.**

1. The bald eagle is found only in the United States and Canada.
2. Unknown in Europe.
3. Bald eagles are a protected species.
4. In 1978, scientists feared that this eagle might become extinct.
5. Today more than 5,800 breeding pairs of bald eagles.

B. **Write each sentence correctly. Add capital letters and end punctuation. Label each sentence as *declarative*, *interrogative*, *imperative*, or *exclamatory*.**

6. many bald eagles live at Chilkat Bald Eagle Preserve in Alaska
7. why do so many bald eagles live there
8. look at all the salmon and small mammals on the preserve
9. did you know that an eagle can spot a fish from a mile away
10. what an exciting creature the bald eagle is

C. **Combine each sentence pair by forming a compound subject, compound predicate, or compound sentence. Use commas and *or*, *and*, or *but* where needed.**

11. Worker ants live in a colony. Queen ants live in a colony.
12. There is only one queen ant in a colony. There are many worker ants.
13. Worker ants search for food. Worker ants protect the queen.
14. Would you watch an ant farm? Would you watch a bee hive?
15. Some people think ants are fascinating. Other people think they are pests.

D. **Write each sentence. Draw a line between the complete subject and the complete predicate. Draw one line under the simple subject and two lines under the simple predicate.**

16. Kelsey had a birthday party today.
17. She invited six friends to her party.
18. Her favorite aunt planned a bowling party for the children.
19. The friends met at the bowling alley after school.
20. The group ate pizza, hot dogs, and chocolate cake.

E. Write each sentence correctly. If the sentence is a run-on, write it as a compound sentence or as two separate sentences.

21. The children bowled first then they ate cake.

22. Dad took the drink orders Jeff passed out the drinks.

23. Mom grabbed her camera the girls posed for pictures.

24. It was time to leave no one was ready to say good-bye.

25. Kelsey thanked her friends for coming she gave each one a gift.

Unit 2 Nouns

A. Write each sentence. Draw one line under each singular noun. Then write the plural form of each noun you underlined.

26. Our class entered the cafeteria.

27. Each child sat at a table.

28. Gloria opened her lunchbox.

29. Brett ate a sandwich.

30. Tyler bit into an apple.

31. His front tooth fell out.

32. Steven had a banana and an orange.

33. My buddy Sam had a cookie shaped like a moose.

34. Ryan's dish fell on the floor and broke.

35. A man helped him clean up the broken plate.

B. Write each sentence. Use capital letters where they are needed. Replace the words in parentheses ( ) with the correct abbreviations.

36. There are fifty states in the united states.

37. (Mister) kirk has talked to us about texas, maine, and florida.

38. Now he is reading us a book called *the great states of america*.

39. On presidents' day, we read about virginia and kentucky.

40. A special visitor, (senator) watson, will tell us about oregon.

Cumulative Review

C. Write each phrase using the possessive form of the underlined noun.

41. the toys for the cats

42. the computer belonging to the student

43. the photos belonging to the men

44. the papers from Sue

45. the cars belonging to the families

D. Combine the sentences by joining the nouns in the subject or the predicate. Then write the new sentence.

46. Cory went to the play. Lauren went to the play.

47. The play was about a knight. The play was about a prince.

48. The prince had a dragon. The prince had a unicorn.

49. He rode to school on his dragon. He rode to school on his unicorn.

50. The friends enjoyed the characters. The friends enjoyed the costumes.

Unit 3 Verbs

A. Write each sentence. Underline the verb. Write *present*, *past*, or *future* to tell the tense of the verb. Then write *linking* if it is a linking verb.

51. I enjoy fishing with my grandfather.

52. This morning we took his boat to the pond.

53. We baited our hooks carefully.

54. My grandfather is a great fisherman.

55. We will catch a lot of fish.

B. Write each sentence. Draw one line under each main verb. Draw two lines under each helping verb.

56. Granddad will teach me to fish.

57. He is waiting for a big fish.

58. We are wearing our life jackets.

59. We have used all of our bait.

60. A fish is tugging on my line now.

Cumulative Review

Grammar

C. Write each sentence. Use the verb in parentheses ( ) that agrees with the subject.

61. Marc (try, tries) out for a part in the school play.

62. The director (select, selects) Marc to play the main character.

63. I (was chosen, were chosen) to be the musician's helper.

64. I (works, work) hard to learn my part.

65. On the night of the play, our teacher (coach, coaches) us from behind the stage.

66. He (worry, worries) that the actors may forget their lines.

67. Marc and Tami (has starred, have starred) in every play this year.

68. They (smile, smiles) as soon as they come onstage.

69. Our play (is, are) a great success.

70. The parents (clap, claps) loudly at the end.

D. Write each sentence. Use the correct form of the verb in parentheses ( ).

71. Bob (gone, went) to see the circus with his family.

72. The show (began, begun) at exactly 2:00.

73. The clowns (sang, sung) and danced first.

74. Bob's family has (saw, seen) the tigers jump through hoops.

75. They even watched as bears (ride, rode) little motorcycles.

E. Write the sentences correctly. Replace the words in parentheses ( ) with contractions. Add commas in a series where necessary.

76. What do an ostrich a peacock and a parrot have in common?

77. They have feathers to protect them from the rain cold and heat.

78. No, these animals (are not) all able to fly.

79. The ostrich (does not) fly at all.

80. The crow the bluejay and the sparrow are birds, too.

Theme
Find Out More

UNIT 4

Adjectives and Explanatory Writing

In this unit you will learn about adjectives. You will also learn how to write an explanatory piece. Explanatory writing informs the reader how to do something by explaining a step-by-step process.

Science Link *Roald Dahl's book* James and the Giant Peach *has been a children's favorite for over 35 years. Read about how filmmakers created an animated movie version of this beloved book.*

The main story was filmed in stop-motion animation, which makes doll-like puppets appear to move by themselves. Filmmakers fashioned dolls of James, the bugs, and 50 peaches. The peach models ranged from 3 inches to 20 feet across.

The animators posed the puppets in a miniature set, took one picture, then moved the puppets just slightly for the next shot. The pictures were then put together to create the movie. Shooting only 12 seconds of the movie took up to 6 days of work.

from "A Boy and His Bugs" from ***Time for Kids***

Thinking Like a Writer

Explanatory Writing Explanatory writing tells the reader how to do something. Reread the passage.

- How did the filmmakers make the puppets seem like they were moving?

Adjectives The author uses adjectives to describe items used in the film.

QUICK WRITE Which adjectives are used to describe items in the film? How do these words help you visualize what these items looked like?

Grammar

Adjectives

RULES

An adjective is a word that describes a noun. An adjective can tell *what kind* or *how many*.

I live in a yellow house.

There are two new families on my street.

Adjectives help make your writing more descriptive.

Without an Adjective	With an Adjective
I live in a house.	I live in a big house.
My house has windows.	My house has ten windows.

Adjectives

In your journal, write how you can tell if a word is an adjective.

Guided Practice

Name the adjective in each sentence. Tell which noun each adjective describes.

EXAMPLE: We moved into a new house.
adjective: new; noun: house

1. The house has eight rooms.
2. I live in a quaint neighborhood.
3. Plants grow in a spacious yard.
4. The kitchen has two doorways.
5. My bedroom has a roomy closet.
6. The house has a dusty attic.
7. My big sister and I explored the attic.
8. We found a plastic box in a corner.
9. There were several photographs in the box.
10. One photograph showed a house in a tree!

REVIEW THE RULES

- **Adjectives** are words that describe nouns.
- Adjectives can tell *what kind* or *how many*.

Grammar

Handbook page 536

More Practice

A. Write each sentence. Draw a line under the adjective. Circle the noun it describes.

11. There is a big tree in the yard.

12. Yesterday we climbed the beautiful tree.

13. We used a tall ladder.

14. My sister discovered wide boards in the tree.

15. She found a flat floor for a house.

B. Complete each sentence. Use an adjective in each blank.

16. The ______ house needed work.

17. ______ walls were missing.

18. We found ______ tools in the basement.

19. We started working on our ______ discovery.

20. Three days later, we had a ______ place to play!

C. Spiral Review **Write each sentence. Fill in the blank with the kind of word shown in parentheses ( ).**

21. We built a ______ tree house. (adjective)

22. We used ______ nails to build it. (possessive noun)

23. ______ the ladder to see our tree house. (action verb)

24. Slide on the ______ rope to get back down. (adjective)

25. We'll all have a ______ time in the tree house. (adjective)

Extra Practice, page 332.

Writing Activity A Paragraph

Write a paragraph explaining how you would build a tree house. Explain what it will look like. Organize your points.

APPLY GRAMMAR: Use at least six adjectives in your paragraph. Underline the adjectives you use.

Grammar

Articles: *a, an, the*

RULES

The words *a*, *an*, and *the* are special adjectives called articles.

Use *a* and *an* before singular nouns. Use *a* if the next word begins with a consonant sound. Use *an* if the next word begins with a vowel sound.

Please take a napkin. Would you like an apple?

Use *the* before plural nouns and before singular nouns that name a particular person, place, or thing.

Let's wipe off the chairs. Then we can sit at the table.

Articles

Write how you can decide when to use *a*, *an*, or *the*.

Notice how the article *a* is used to refer to any trip in general.

Let's take a trip.

The article *the* is used to refer to a particular trip.

The trip to Arizona was delightful.

Guided Practice

Name the article or articles in each sentence.

EXAMPLE: The Grand Canyon is in Arizona.
The

1. A canyon is a deep, narrow valley.
2. A river flows at the bottom of the canyon.
3. The canyon was created by the river.
4. The river carved a path through the rocks.
5. The Grand Canyon is an awesome sight.
6. A desert is near the Colorado River.
7. The Colorado River flows through the Grand Canyon.
8. The family took a raft trip on the river.
9. The state of Arizona has a dry climate.
10. There is a dangerous river in the Southwest.

REVIEW THE RULES

- *A*, *an*, and *the* are special adjectives called articles.
- Use *a* before singular nouns that begin with a consonant sound. Use *an* before singular nouns that begin with a vowel sound.
- Use *the* before singular nouns that name a particular person, place, or thing and before all plural nouns.

Grammar

More Practice

A. Write each sentence. Draw a line under each article.

11. Tourists visit the Grand Canyon.

12. They swim in the pools below the falls.

13. They see the squirrels and other wildlife.

14. One kind of squirrel is called an Abert squirrel.

15. The Abert squirrel has a gray tail.

Handbook
page 536

B. Write each sentence. Choose the correct article.

16. (The, A) Grand Canyon is a beautiful place.

17. The canyon's colors change as (a, the) sun rises.

18. (A, An) artist painted that picture of the Grand Canyon.

19. Visitors can hike on (a, the) trails.

20. Tourists can view the canyon from (a, an) airplane.

C. Spiral Review **Write each sentence. Circle articles. Underline common nouns. Capitalize proper nouns.**

21. Our trip to the grand canyon was exciting.

22. My family hiked across a bridge.

23. On monday, eva rode a raft down the colorado river.

24. Mules walked slowly down a steep path.

25. In august,chris spent an evening at a ranch.

Extra Practice, page 333.

Writing Activity Directions

Write directions for a nature walk. Tell the route and describe what you will see. Use precise words.

APPLY GRAMMAR: Underline each article you use.

Science Link

Grammar

Adjectives After Linking Verbs

RULES

Sometimes an adjective follows the noun it describes.

The day was hot.

When an adjective comes after the noun it describes, the noun and the adjective are connected by a linking verb.

Many of the customers were thirsty.

Adjectives

What is similar about an adjective that comes after a linking verb and one that comes before a noun? Write your response in your journal.

The linking verb is usually a form of the verb *be*.

The day is hot. The people are uncomfortable.

The lemonade was sweet. The glasses were cool.

Guided Practice

Name the adjective in each sentence. Then name the noun it describes.

EXAMPLE: The lemonade was cold.
adjective: cold; noun: lemonade

1. The lemons are yellow.
2. The ice is cold.
3. Sylvia's sign is colorful.
4. The cups are clean.
5. The lemonade is sour.
6. The drink was delicious.
7. The clouds were gray.
8. The rain is refreshing.
9. The project was successful.
10. The customers were friendly.

REVIEW THE RULES

- When an adjective comes after the noun it describes, the two are connected by a linking verb.

Grammar

More Practice

A. Write each sentence. Draw one line under the adjective. Draw two lines under the noun it describes.

11. The afternoon was sunny.
12. José was bored.
13. The children were curious about making lemonade.
14. Mom's cookbooks were great for recipes.
15. The recipe was easy.

B. Write each sentence. Use an adjective in each blank to complete the sentence.

16. The new customer is ______.
17. The lemonade is ______.
18. We are ______ about the lemonade stand.
19. The sidewalk is ______ with people.
20. Our lemonade stand is ______.

Handbook page 536

C. Spiral Review Write the paragraph. Draw one line under action verbs and two under linking verbs. Circle adjectives.

21–30. Ken painted a picture of the ocean. The ocean was blue and green. Pam wove a basket out of straw. Both projects were beautiful. Ken and Pam were happy. They displayed their work at the fair.

Extra Practice, page 334.

Writing Activity An Explanation

Write a paragraph explaining how you would make a specific product and sell it at a sidewalk stand. Use descriptive language.
APPLY GRAMMAR: Write at least two sentences containing a linking verb followed by an adjective.

Grammar

Proper Adjectives

RULES

A proper adjective is an adjective formed from a proper noun.

Tom is Chinese.

We flew the American flag.

The suffix *-an*, *-ish,* or *-ese* may be added to proper nouns to form proper adjectives. Notice that a proper adjective is always capitalized.

Proper Noun	Proper Adjective	Proper Noun	Proper Adjective
Africa	African	Japan	Japanese
America	American	Korea	Korean
Canada	Canadian	Mexico	Mexican
China	Chinese	Poland	Polish
Egypt	Egyptian	Russia	Russian
England	English	Spain	Spanish
Hawaii	Hawaiian	Sweden	Swedish
Italy	Italian	Turkey	Turkish

Adjectives

Write why a proper adjective is always capitalized.

Guided Practice

Name the proper adjective in each sentence. Name the noun it describes.

EXAMPLE: The Turkish delegates met at the United Nations.
proper adjective: Turkish; noun: delegates

1. There is a Russian translator at the United Nations.
2. The Polish ambassador is an interesting man.
3. Some Spanish diplomats are going to the meeting.
4. The Mexican flag flies outside the building.
5. A Japanese restaurant is on the corner.

REVIEW THE RULES

- Proper adjectives are formed from proper nouns.
- Proper adjectives are always capitalized.

More Practice

A. Write each sentence. Draw a line under each proper adjective. Circle the noun it describes.

6. The Egyptian lawyer is downstairs.
7. An Italian man is speaking now.
8. The Turkish embassy is nearby.
9. The Chinese spokesperson is about to leave.
10. A Swedish representative is taking notes.

Handbook
page 536

B. Write each sentence. Capitalize the proper adjectives.

11. The korean language is spoken here.
12. The african writer was given an award.
13. We discussed english history.
14. Many canadian families came to the city.
15. The hawaiian leader spoke at the banquet.

C. Spiral Review Rewrite each sentence correctly, using capital letters where needed. Add correct end punctuation.

16. are chinese newspapers sold in chinatown
17. The canadian border is north of us
18. does new york have many russian residents
19. the exhibit of mexican art was beautiful
20. many americans are of african descent

Extra Practice, page 335.

Writing Activity A Plan

Write a plan for teaching someone how to speak your native language. Be sure to organize the steps in your plan in a logical way. **APPLY GRAMMAR:** Use proper adjectives in your plan. Underline each proper adjective you use.

Grammar REVIEW

Mixed Review

REVIEW THE RULES

- An adjective is a word that describes a noun.
- Adjectives can tell *what kind* or *how many*.
- *A*, *an*, and *the* are special adjectives called articles.
- Use *a* before singular nouns that begin with a consonant sound. Use *an* before singular nouns that begin with a vowel sound.
- Use the article *the* before singular nouns that name a particular person, place, or thing and before all plural nouns.
- When an adjective comes after the noun it describes, the two are connected by a linking verb.
- A proper adjective is formed from a proper noun.
- Proper adjectives are always capitalized.

Adjectives
Write five sentences containing adjectives. Include at least one proper adjective and one adjective following a linking verb. Underline all adjectives and circle all articles.

Practice

A. Write each sentence. Underline each adjective. Capitalize proper adjectives. Circle the noun that each adjective describes.

1. Children play rugby in english schools.
2. The mexican teenagers played soccer in the park.
3. Let's go skiing in the italian mountains.
4. I swam in the sparkling water.
5. The lake was calm.
6. The russian gymnast won a medal.
7. The dancer was graceful.
8. An american teacher invented basketball.
9. The teacher hung large baskets in the gym.
10. The students tossed a heavy ball into the baskets.

B. Rewrite the sentences. Use an adjective or an article to complete each sentence.

11. It was ______ icy day.

12. The ______ students went into the gym.

13. The ______ gym echoed.

14. ______ baskets were on the floor.

15. One ball rolled into ______ corner.

16. The teacher nailed the ______ baskets to the balcony.

17. ______ players were curious.

18. Soon everyone was playing a ______ game.

19. The ______ teacher made up the rules.

20. Basketball is ______!

C. Challenge Rewrite the following paragraph. Correct any errors in the use of articles. Capitalize any proper adjectives.

21–25. James Naismith invented the game of basketball in 1891. He was born in Canada. As a canadian youngster, he was a excellent rugby player. Naismith invented basketball while he was the teacher in Massachusetts. Today basketball is a american tradition.

Handbook page 536

Writing Activity Captions

Write a series of captions that explain how to play your favorite game or sport. Be sure to include facts and details in your captions.
APPLY GRAMMAR: Include adjectives to help make your writing clear and precise. Use proper adjectives to explain where the game is played or where it was created.

Grammar

Adjectives That Compare

RULES

Adjectives can be used to compare two or more things.

- Add *-er* to most adjectives to compare two people, places, or things.

  A chimpanzee is smarter than a gorilla.

- Add *-est* to most adjectives to compare more than two people, places, or things.

  The chimpanzee is the smartest animal in the jungle.

Adjectives

How do you know which form of an adjective you should use to compare? Write your ideas in your journal.

Adjectives that compare are used to tell how things are alike and different.

Golden lion tamarins are one of the smallest monkeys. They are often mistaken for squirrels because of their size. Golden lion tamarins have rounder faces than squirrels. Their tails are longer than a squirrel's tail.

Guided Practice

Name the adjective that compares in each sentence.

EXAMPLE: That is the fastest monkey I have ever seen!
fastest

1. Monkeys swing from the tallest trees in the forest.
2. The orangutan has longer fur than the chimpanzee.
3. A spider monkey is lighter than a gorilla.
4. The baboon sat on the highest branch in the tree.
5. A gorilla is one of the strongest animals on Earth.

REVIEW THE RULES

- Add *-er* to most adjectives to compare two people, places, or things.
- Add *-est* to most adjectives to compare more than two.

More Practice

A. Write each sentence. Draw a line under the adjective that compares.

6. A monkey's tail is longer than its body.
7. Most monkeys will pick the sweetest bananas on a tree.
8. The chimpanzee made the loudest noise in the zoo.
9. The spider monkey is smaller than the gorilla.
10. The chimpanzee has shorter arms than the gorilla.

B. Write each sentence. Use the correct form of the adjective in parentheses ( ).

11. That monkey has the ______ eyes I have seen. (bright)
12. Which monkey has the ______ fur of all? (soft)
13. The little monkey was the ______ one in the cage. (mean)
14. A coconut is ______ than a peanut. (hard)
15. A pet cat is much ______ than a pet monkey. (neat)

C. Spiral Review Complete each sentence. Use the type of word in parentheses ( ).

16. Two monkeys ______ in a tall tree. (action verb)
17. One monkey was ______ than the other one. (adjective)
18. He swung from the ______ branch on the tree. (adjective)
19. The bold monkey reached for some ______. (plural noun)
20. He ______ the food and then chased his friend. (action verb)

Extra Practice, page 336.

Handbook page 536

Writing Activity A Postcard

Imagine visiting a zoo. Write a postcard describing some of the animals. Vary the way your sentences begin.

APPLY GRAMMAR: Use *-er* and *-est* forms of adjectives in your writing.

Science Link

Grammar

Spelling Adjectives That Compare

RULES

Use these spelling rules for adjectives that compare.

- When an adjective ends in a consonant and *y*, change the *y* to *i* and add *-er* or *-est*.

  happy + -er = happier

- When an adjective ends in *e*, drop the *e* and add *-er* or *-est*.

  nice + -est = nicest

- When an adjective has a single vowel before a final consonant, double the final consonant and add *-er* or *-est*.

  big + g + -est = biggest

Adjectives
How do you know if you need to change the spelling of an adjective when adding *-er* or *-est*? Write your answer in your journal.

Guided Practice

Name the adjective that compares. Tell the adjective that is the root word of the adjective that compares.

EXAMPLE: The tiniest ant in the colony ate my bread.
adjective that compares: tiniest; root word: tiny

1. My uncle is jollier than my father.
2. Today is hotter than yesterday.
3. A tortilla is thinner than a pancake.
4. That squirrel is the tamest one in the yard.
5. He was the hungriest of all my cousins.

REVIEW THE RULES

- Before adding *-er* or *-est*, change a final *y* to *i*, drop a final *e*, or double a final consonant after a single vowel.

More Practice

A. Write each sentence. Draw a line under the adjective that compares. Write the adjective that is the root word.

6. That was the loveliest picnic of all.
7. Falls Park is closer to my house than Bedford Park.
8. The playground was flatter than the field.
9. The stream was the widest one in the town.
10. The guests were the friendliest people I have ever met.

B. Write each sentence. Use the correct form of the adjective in parentheses ( ).

11. I ate the ______ tomato in the basket. (red)
12. My cousins were ______ than they were last year. (silly)
13. The lake was the ______ lake I have ever seen. (large)
14. The sack race was the ______ event of the day. (funny)
15. The food was ______ this year than it was last year. (tasty)

C. Spiral Review Write the paragraph. Complete each sentence using the type of word in parentheses ( ).

The Fourth of (**16.** ____) (proper noun) at the lake is the (**17.** ____) (adjective that compares) holiday of all. We (**18.** ____) (action verb) races until the summer sun (**19.** ____) (linking verb) too hot. Then we eat the (**20.** ____) (adjective that compares) watermelon you've ever tasted.

Extra Practice, page 337.

Writing Activity A Plan

Write a plan explaining what you need to do to prepare a picnic for your friends. Include precise details. **APPLY GRAMMAR:** Use adjectives that compare. Check the spelling of the words.

Grammar

Handbook
page 536

Grammar

Comparing with *More* and *Most*

RULES

For long adjectives, use *more* and *most* to compare people, places, or things.

Use *more* to compare two people, places, or things.

My trip to Washington, D.C., was more educational than last year's vacation.

Use *most* to compare more than two.

This was the most interesting trip of all.

Adjectives
Explain how you know when to use *more* or *most* to make a comparison.

Some two-syllable adjectives and most longer adjectives use *more* and *most* to form comparisons. When you use *more* or *most,* do not use the ending *-er* or *-est.*

polite	*more polite*	*most polite*
beautiful	*more beautiful*	*most beautiful*

Guided Practice

Name the word that should be used to complete each sentence.

EXAMPLE: Our guide was the ______ experienced of all.
most

1. The White House was ______ interesting than the Capitol.
2. The White House may be the ______ popular attraction in Washington, D.C.
3. The Washington Monument is the ______ famous sight in the city.
4. The National Zoological Park has the ______ spectacular collection of animals and birds in the world.
5. Constitution Avenue is ______ crowded than Maryland Avenue.

REVIEW THE RULES

- Use *more* to compare two people, places, or things.
- Use *most* to compare more than two.

Grammar

More Practice

A. Write each sentence. Add *more* or *most*.

6. I think zoos are ______ enjoyable than amusement parks.
7. Our city's zoo has the ______ creative exhibits of all.
8. The children's zoo is the ______ fascinating place to visit.
9. The gardens are ______ impressive than the playgrounds.
10. I saw some of the ______ unusual plants in the world.

B. Write each sentence. Use the correct form of the adjective in parentheses ( ).

11. The art museum is the ______ in the country. (splendid)
12. The mountains are ______ than the beaches. (scenic)
13. The fairs are ______ than the tours. (entertaining)
14. The cafe serves the ______ food of all. (delicious)
15. Visiting a television studio is one of the ______ things a tourist can do. (exciting)

Handbook page 537

C. Spiral Review Write the paragraph. Fix incorrect adjective forms. Capitalize proper nouns and correct run-on sentences.

16–20. We went on three tours when we were in new orleans. The boat tour was entertaininger than the walking tour. The tour guide on the bus told us great stories about the early days of jazz he showed us where louis armstrong used to play. This was the more interesting tour event ever!

Extra Practice, page 338.

Writing Activity A Newspaper Article

Write a newspaper article about a place you recently visited. Explain what you liked about this place. Be sure to use correct punctuation and capitalization.

APPLY GRAMMAR: Use *more* and *most* to compare.

Grammar

Comparing with *Good* and *Bad*

Adjectives

In your journal, write how you know when to use each form of *good* and *bad*.

RULES

The adjectives *good* and *bad* have special forms when used to compare.

Use *better* and *worse* when comparing two people, places, or things.

The ham is better than the chicken.

The lemonade is worse than the tea.

Use *best* and *worst* when comparing more than two.

The spaghetti is the best food in the restaurant.

The fruit punch is the worst drink I've ever tasted.

Adjective	Compare Two	Compare More Than Two
good	better	best
bad	worse	worst

Guided Practice

Name the form of *good* or *bad* used to compare in each sentence.

EXAMPLE: The state fair was the best ever.
best

1. Pierre was the best cook in the cooking contest.
2. The corn was better than the peas.
3. The asparagus was the worst vegetable of all.
4. The peach jam was worse than the apple jam.
5. The best dessert of all was the cherry pie.

REVIEW THE RULES

- Use *better* and *worse* to compare two things.
- Use *best* and *worst* to compare more than two.

More Practice

A. Write each sentence. Draw a line under the form of *good* or *bad* that is used to compare.

6. This is the best state fair in the country.
7. The weather was worse last year than this year.
8. The pony rides were the best activity at the fair.
9. The dog show was better than the singing contest.
10. Rain can be the worst problem of all.

B. Write each sentence. Use the correct form of the adjective in parentheses ( ).

11. Which game is the ______ of all? (good)
12. I think kickball is ______ than baseball. (good)
13. The beans were the ______ food of all. (bad)
14. The squash was ______ than the peas. (bad)
15. The tortillas tasted ______ than the crackers. (good)

C. Spiral Review Write the paragraph. Correct mistakes in forms of *good* and *bad*. Add commas where they are needed. Fix the run-on sentence.

16–20. The fair was over the children had played volleyball kickball and baseball. The food was even gooder than the games. The class had the goodest time they could remember.

Extra Practice, page 339.

Writing Activity A Poem

Write a poem about your favorite food. Compare it to other foods. Use words that make your food sound appealing.

APPLY GRAMMAR: Use forms of *good* and *bad* to compare.

Grammar

Handbook
page 537

Grammar

Combining Sentences: Adjectives

RULES

You can sometimes combine sentences by adding an adjective to one sentence.

Annie made a flower. She made a big flower.

Annie made a big flower.

Combining two short sentences can make your writing flow better. Sometimes you can combine two sentences when they are about the same person, place, or thing. Bring the adjective from one sentence into the other. Leave out the words that are repeated.

Ben had some paint.
The paint was blue.
→ *Ben had some blue paint.*

THINK AND WRITE

Adjectives
In your journal, explain when you might combine two sentences using adjectives.

Guided Practice

Tell what sentence can be formed from each pair of sentences.

EXAMPLE: Annie painted a cow. The cow was yellow.
Annie painted a yellow cow.

1. Annie hung up her painting. The painting was wet.
2. Ben added paint to Annie's cow. He added brown paint.
3. We made masks from paper and paste. Our masks were scary.
4. Cover the balloon with strips. The strips should be narrow.
5. Susan made a puppet. She made a colorful puppet.

REVIEW THE RULES

- You can combine sentences that tell about the same person, place, or thing.
- An adjective can be added to one of the sentences.

More Practice

A. Write each pair of sentences as one sentence.

6. Franco likes to carve animals. He makes funny animals.
7. Hal added water to the clay. The clay was dry.
8. Ben stirred the paint. The paint was thick.
9. Sally wove a rug. It was a colorful rug.
10. We made a scrapbook. The scrapbook was thick.

Handbook page 537

B. Write each pair of sentences, completing the second with an adjective. Then write the sentences as one.

11. Ben experimented with paints. The paints were ______.
12. Jen washed the brushes. The brushes were ______.
13. Pam painted a landscape. The landscape was ______.
14. The colors attracted attention. The colors were ______.
15. Yukiko knitted a cap. She knitted a ______ cap.

C. Spiral Review Write one sentence that combines each pair of sentences. Underline each action verb.

16. The children's paintings decorated the hall. The hall was long.
17. Ben's teacher hung them with tape. The tape was strong.
18. Pam's class created a mural. The mural was huge.
19. Artwork filled my school's halls. The artwork was colorful.
20. The artist's parents viewed the work. The work was excellent.

Extra Practice, page 340.

Writing Activity Directions

Write directions for creating a piece of art. Give step-by-step instructions in a logical order.

APPLY GRAMMAR: Look over your directions, and try to find sentences that can be combined.

Art Link

Letter Punctuation

RULES

The **greeting** and **closing** of a letter begin with a **capital letter**.

Use a **comma** after the greeting and the closing of a friendly letter.

Dear Jesse, *Love,*

Use a **comma** between the names of a **city** and a **state**.
Use a **comma** between the **day** and the **year** in a date.

Miami, Florida *May 5, 1999*

Letter Punctuation

Why is it important to use the correct punctuation in the letters you write? Write your ideas in your journal.

Here is a sample letter:

158 Northridge Drive
Austin, Texas 78723
May 10, 2001

Dear Aunt Mary,

I can't wait to come and visit you. I am looking forward to our hiking trips. I'll see you in June.

Your niece,
Janna

Guided Practice

Name the punctuation mark or capital letter that is missing in each letter part.

EXAMPLE: Your pal
comma

1. Dear Aunt Martha
2. sincerely,
3. March 2 2003
4. dear Rita,
5. Long Beach New York
6. yours truly,
7. Orono Maine
8. September 18 2000
9. with love,
10. Dear Mr. Hendrix

REVIEW THE RULES

- Begin the greeting and closing of a friendly letter with a capital letter, and end them with a comma.
- Use a comma between the names of a city and state, and between the day and year in a date.

Grammar

More Practice

A. Write these letter parts. Add the correct punctuation mark or capital letter.

11. Dear Jacob

12. July 18 2004

13. Sincerely

14. Boise Idaho

15. your friend,

B. Complete each letter part. Use capital letters and punctuation correctly.

16. ______ Mom,

17. 25 Pinecrest ______

18. October ______ 2001

19. Your ______

20. ______ Georgia

Handbook pages 547, 554

C. Spiral Review **Write the letter. Add capital letters and punctuation marks where they are needed.**

21–30.

552 Main Street
Troy Michigan 48098
april 4 2002

dear Mrs Taylor

I am really enjoying fourth grade. My teacher's name is mr. williams. He likes science as much as I do.

your student
Meg Stuart

Extra Practice, page 341.

Writing Activity A Letter

Write a letter to a friend, and explain the instructions to your favorite game. Be sure your sentences flow well together.

APPLY GRAMMAR: Make sure to use proper punctuation in the heading, greeting, and closing of your letter.

Grammar REVIEW

Mixed Review

REVIEW THE RULES

- Add *-er* to most adjectives to compare two people, places, or things. Use *more* with longer adjectives.
- Add *-est* to most adjectives to compare more than two. Use *most* with longer adjectives.
- Before adding *-er* or *-est*, change a *y* to *i*, drop a final *e*, or double a final consonant.
- Use *better* or *worse* to compare two people, places, or things. Use *best* or *worst* to compare more than two.
- You can sometimes combine sentences by adding an adjective to one sentence.
- Begin the greeting and closing of a letter with a capital letter, and end them with a comma.
- Use a comma between the names of a city and state, and between the day and year in a date.

QUICK WRITE

Adjectives
Write five sentences showing five different ways to use adjectives that compare.

Practice

A. Write each sentence. Choose the correct word.

1. Today's picnic is (nicer, nicest) than last year's.
2. The (more, most) serious problem we had was ants.
3. The ants were the (worse, worst) ever.
4. The ants liked bread (better, best) than meat.
5. Ants like the (tastier, tastiest) foods they can find.
6. The bite of a fire ant is (worse, worst) than a mosquito's.
7. The (better, best) advice of all is never to touch an ant.
8. Ants are the (more, most) common of all insects.
9. Large ants are (stronger, strongest) than small ants.
10. Red ants are (more, most) dangerous than black ants.

B. Write each pair of sentences as one sentence.

11. Dave went to the picnic. The picnic was crowded.

12. Kendra sat on a blanket. It was a striped blanket.

13. Li ate a sandwich. The sandwich tasted delicious.

14. Ants came to the picnic. They were red ants.

15. The ants marched in a line. They made a long line.

16. Sammy didn't want any pickles. The pickles were sour.

17. Sherry liked the lemonade. It was sweet lemonade.

18. Squirrels loved the muffin crumbs. They were gray squirrels.

19. The pitcher walked onto the field. The field was dusty.

20. Everyone watched the game. It was exciting.

C. Challenge Write the letter. Correct all punctuation, capitalization, and grammar errors. Combine two sentences into one.

21–30.

795 Redwood Lane
Menlo Park california 94025
September 16 2001

dear Bill

Yesterday was our family picnic. It was the better one we ever had! Unfortunately, there were lots of ants. The ants were red. These ants seemed to be quickest than black ants. I hope the ants go to a different picnic next year!

sincerely
Derek

Handbook
pages 536–537, 547, 554

Writing Activity An Invitation

Invite a friend to a picnic. Tell when and where the picnic will take place, and explain how to get there. Be sure to give detailed directions. You don't want your friend to get lost!

APPLY GRAMMAR: Make sure that your invitation has the proper punctuation.

Common Errors with Adjectives

Adjectives can make your writing interesting and fun to read. It is important to use adjectives correctly. This chart shows two errors writers sometimes make when they use adjectives to compare people, places, or things. Look at how each error can be corrected.

Common Errors	Examples	Corrected Sentences
Using -er *or* -est *instead of* more *or* most	The school fair is the excitingest event of the year.	The school fair is the most exciting event of the year.
Using -er *or* -est *with* more *or* most	The fair was more larger than last year's fair.	The fair was larger than last year's fair.

Adjectives

Why do you think we use *more* and *most* instead of *-er* and *-est* with some adjectives that compare? Write your answers in your journal.

REVIEW THE RULES

ADJECTIVES

- For most short adjectives, add *-er* to compare two nouns and *-est* to compare more than two nouns.
- For long adjectives, use *more* to compare two nouns and *most* to compare more than two nouns.
- Do not use *more* or *most* with an adjective ending with *-er* or *-est.*
- Remember When an adjective ends in a consonant and *y*, change the *y* to *i* before adding *-er* or *-est.*
- Remember When an adjective ends with a single vowel and a single consonant, double the consonant before adding *-er* or *-est.*
- Remember When an adjective ends in *e*, drop the *e* before adding *-er* or *-est.*

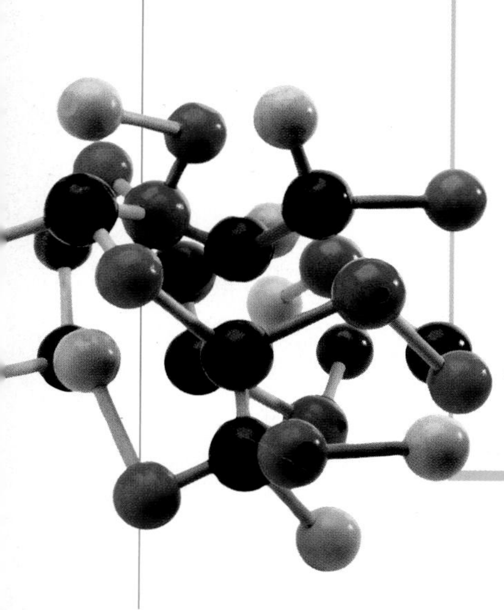

Practice

A. Rewrite each sentence using the correct form of the adjective in parentheses ( ).

1. This year's talent show was (entertaining) than last year's.
2. The science teacher won a prize for the (unusual) cake.
3. My score in the basketball toss was (high) than my father's.
4. In the band, the drums were (loud) than the trumpets.
5. Anthony's play was (dramatic) than Jessica's skit.

B. Write each sentence. To complete the sentence, use the correct form of an adjective in the word bank.

red graceful fine skillful funny

6. Kevin was the ______ juggler in the show.
7. The clown's act was ______ than the musician's act.
8. The clown's nose was the ______ nose I've ever seen!
9. The dancers were the ______ of all the performers.
10. Our class won first place for the ______ banner.

C. Write each sentence. Correct the errors in forms of adjectives.

11. The art club's display was the creativest of all.
12. The colors of our class mural were interestinger than the colors last year.
13. The fourth grade's hamster was the tinyest class pet at the fair.
14. The line for food was more longer than the line for the coin toss.
15. Maria's stilts made her the bigest person at the school fair.

Handbook pages 536–537

Grammar Troubleshooter, pages 516–517.

Writing Activity A Letter

How would you take part in your school fair? Write a letter to your teacher explaining what you would do and how you would do it. Organize your ideas logically.

APPLY GRAMMAR: Use the proper form of adjectives that compare. Make sure that you spell adjectives correctly when you add *-er* or *-est*.

Mechanics and Spelling

Directions

Read the passage and decide which type of mistake, if any, appears in each underlined section. Choose the letter for your answer. If there is no error, choose "No mistake."

Use a comma after the greeting when writing a letter.

When a word ends in a consonant and y, change the y to i before adding an ending that does not begin with i.

The pronoun I is always written with a capital letter.

Sample

Dear Sam (1)

Would you like some flowers? We have plenty. I think our roses are the lovelyest (2) of all. We also have mums, daisies, and pansies. Please come by sometime, and i'll make you a pretty (3) bouquet.

Your cousin,

Marty

1 **A** Spelling
B Capitalization
C Punctuation
D No mistake

2 **F** Spelling
G Capitalization
H Punctuation
J No mistake

3 **A** Spelling
B Capitalization
C Punctuation
D No mistake

Test Tip

Check your work to make sure that you haven't skipped any items.

Grammar and Usage

Directions

Read the passage and choose the word or group of words that belongs in each space. Choose the letter for your answer.

Sample

Both Mars and Earth __(1)__ planets in the same solar system. A day on Earth is about as long as a day on Mars. Yet the planets have several differences. People think Earth is __(2)__ than Mars because two-thirds of Earth is covered with water. People have a much __(3)__ chance of surviving on Earth than on Mars. Humans __(4)__ oxygen to breathe, and the air on Mars does not contain much oxygen. I wonder if we will ever figure out a way to live on Mars.

Choose a verb that agrees with the subject of the sentence.

Add -er *to an adjective or use* more *with an adjective to compare two things.*

The adjective good *has special forms when used to compare.*

Select a verb that matches the tense in the rest of the passage.

1 **A** are
B is
C was
D has been

2 **F** blue
G bluer
H bluest
J more bluer

3 **A** gooder
B more good
C better
D best

4 **F** needed
G were needing
H had needed
J need

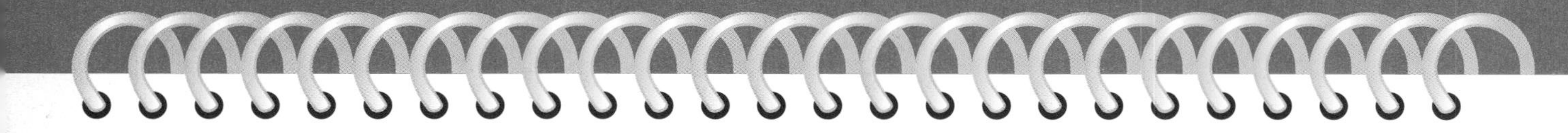

TIME FOR KIDS Writer's Notebook

RESEARCH

RESEARCH

When I write about a place, I like to use a **map** to illustrate what I'm writing. A map is like a picture full of information. It can tell my readers a lot with a few words.

COMPOSITION SKILLS

WRITING WELL

Telling a story well takes **organization**. Writing is easier if I have a plan. I use an outline to put my ideas in order, from start to finish. Then the story kind of writes itself, and my readers can understand it!

VOCABULARY SKILLS

USING WORDS

Huge and tiny are **antonyms**: a pair of words with opposite meanings. Identical and same are **synonyms**: words with the same meaning. Antonyms and synonyms make my writing more lively. What antonyms and synonyms can you think of?

Read Now!

As you read the photo essay and captions, refer to a map. Jot down any information you read that the writer might have found on a map.

TIME FOR KIDS

PHOTO ESSAY

A Blanket Statement

Kids picture the future in a quilt.

Sew Many Ideas!

What will life be like in the year 2050? That's what a museum asked students around the U.S. Pupils from more than 250 schools sent in their answers to that far-reaching question. The answers weren't written however. Kids sewed them!

Children stitched their dreams of the future into 19-inch squares. Judges picked one square from each state. Then the squares were sewn together into a 12-foot-high, 22-foot-wide quilt.

One of the squares showed a shopping trip to the moon. Another pictured a fishing expedition to an underwater hotel. War will be replaced by peace according to one of the kids. Some students predict that a female will replace a male as U.S. President. And another square shows alien ships landing in Wyoming!

What would you add to the quilt if you could?

WIDE-OPEN SPACES: Texan kids are ready to live on the moon, with a nice view of the folks back home!

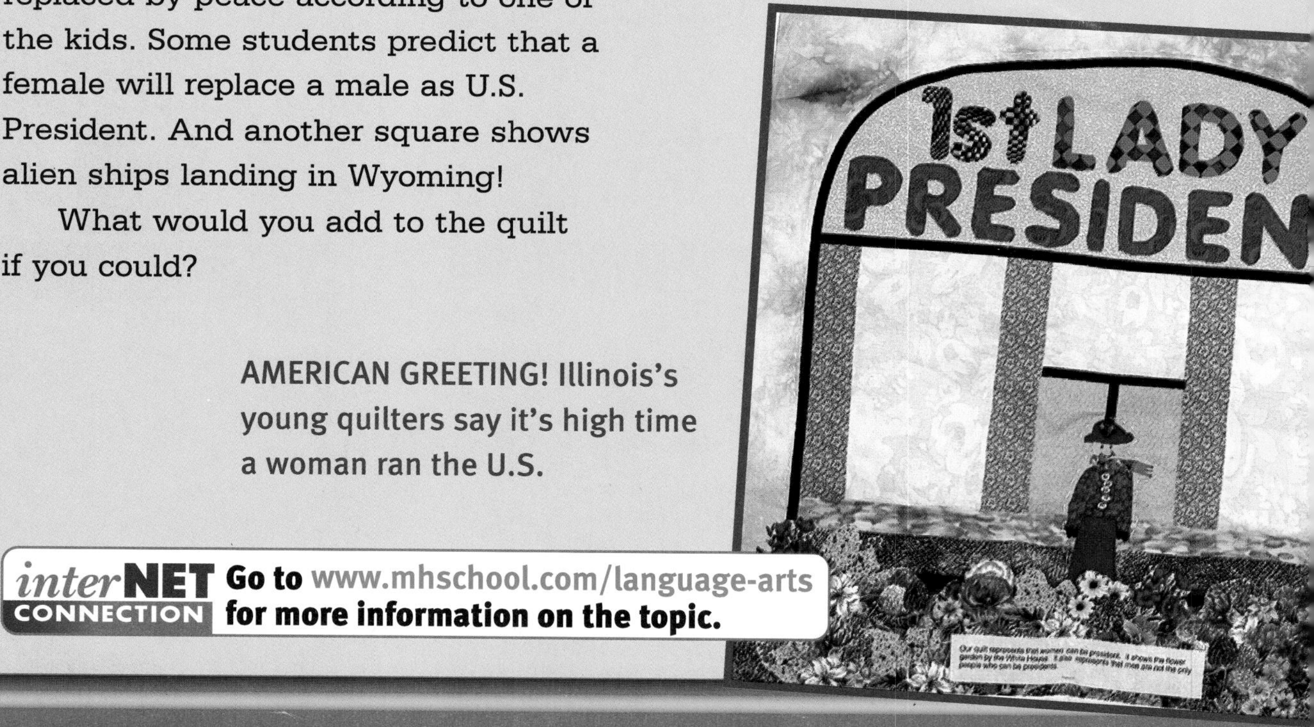

AMERICAN GREETING! Illinois's young quilters say it's high time a woman ran the U.S.

All photos: courtesy American Crafts Museum, New York

interNET CONNECTION Go to www.mhschool.com/language-arts for more information on the topic.

NATURE'S FUTURE: The Alaska square, with wildlife, mountains, and clean water.

HELLO, DOWN THERE: Will you check into a deep-sea hotel somewhere underwater in New Jersey?

WHAT A BUTTE! Wyoming provides a nice place for an alien spaceship to land.

Write Now!

If friendly aliens should land in the year 2050, how would they get to your home? Write directions for them, from a landmark in your town to where you live.

Maps

A **map** is a special way of looking at Earth or part of Earth. You can quickly find out many facts by looking at a map. Maps can show you how far one place is from another, how large your state and country are, what the capital of a state or a country is, and where a country's mountains are located. The map below shows important features of all maps.

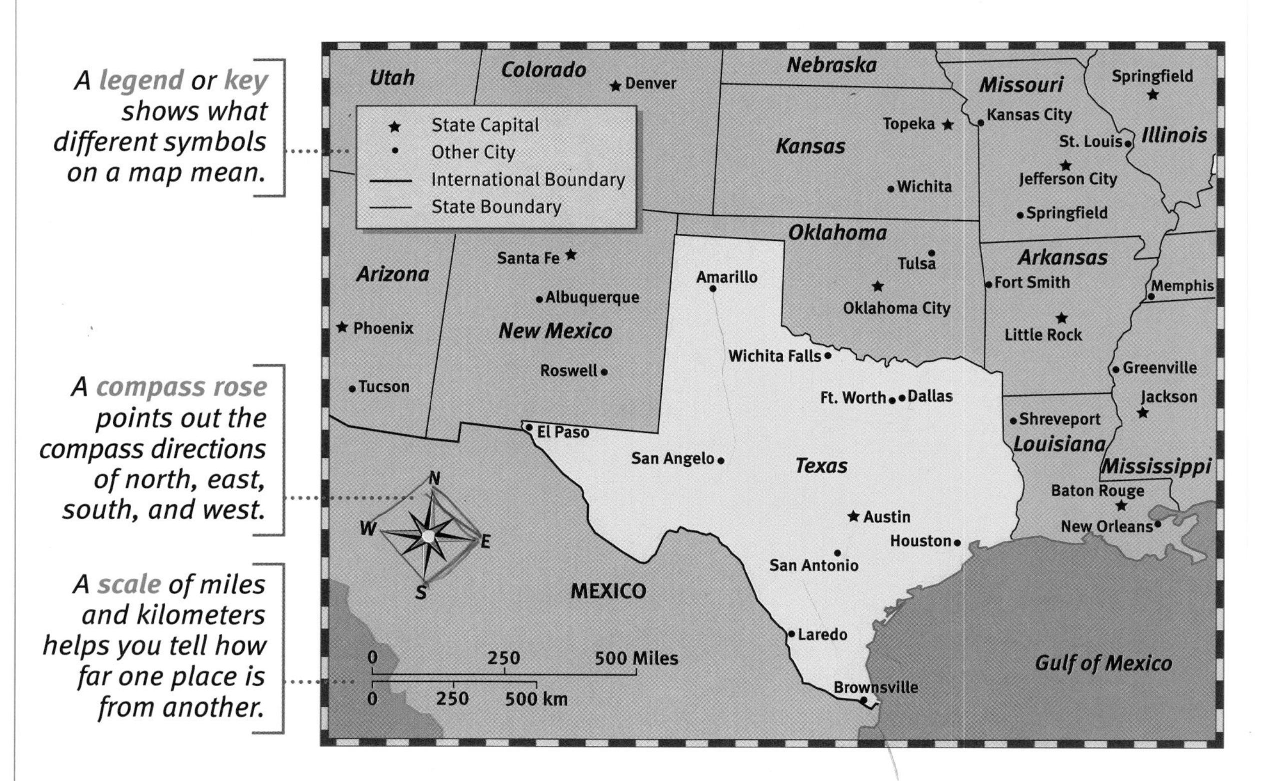

There is more than one type of map. A **political map** shows how the land is divided into political units such as states and countries. This type of map usually shows bodies of water like major rivers, lakes, and oceans that border the land. Another kind of map is a **physical map**. This type of map shows physical features of a place such as mountains, plains, deserts, and valleys.

A map that may be the most familiar to you is a **road map**. This type of map shows the many roads in an area.

Practice

A. Use the political map of Texas to answer these questions.

1. What is the capital of Texas?
2. Which state borders Texas on the west?
3. Which city in Texas is the farthest north on the map?
4. Which city in Texas is the farthest south on the map?
5. About how far is it from El Paso to San Angelo?
6. Which two cities are closest to each other?
7. Which city in Texas is closest to New Mexico?
8. If you lived in El Paso, which foreign country would you be near?
9. Which city in Texas is nearer to the Gulf of Mexico—Houston or Dallas?
10. Which two states have the longest border with Texas?

B. Write which type of map would tell you the following facts.

11. The best route to take to drive from your hometown to a city in another state
12. The name of a city located on the Mississippi River
13. The name of a mountain chain in the eastern United States
14. The location of the capital of the United States
15. The location of a desert in the Southwest

Go to: www.mhschool.com/language-arts **for more information on the topic.**

Writing Activity A Letter

A friend is planning a trip from Dallas to three other cities in Texas. Write your friend a letter describing the directions in which he or she should travel. Include the distance between the cities.

Vocabulary: Synonyms and Antonyms

DEFINITION

Synonyms are words that have the same, or almost the same, meaning. Antonyms are words that have opposite meanings.

Synonyms

big/large	happy/cheerful
tidy/neat	angry/mad
tiny/small	pretty/beautiful

Antonyms

old/new	true/untrue
fast/slow	tidy/messy
kind/unkind	happy/unhappy

THINK AND WRITE

Synonyms and Antonyms

How can you decide if words are synonyms or antonyms? Write your ideas in your journal.

Look at the highlighted words in the paragraph below. Which pairs of words are synonyms? Which are antonyms?

Everyone went to look at the new house. The kitchen was small, but sunny. The bedrooms were dark and tiny. The basement was dirty, and the garage was filthy. Nobody thought it was as nice as the old house.

Practice

A. Write whether the underlined words in each sentence are synonyms or antonyms.

1. Teresa is tall, but her sister is short.
2. I am pleased to be here and happy to help.
3. Decide whether the sentence is true or false.
4. He made a quick getaway in a fast car.
5. Can you tell the real bird from the fake bird?

B. Choose a word from the Word Bank that is a synonym or an antonym of the underlined word in each sentence. Write whether it is a synonym or an antonym.

large	nice	quiet	neat	beautiful	wide

6. Elm Street is very busy and narrow.
7. Our nearby neighbors are kind to us.
8. Lovely flowers grew in the green yard.
9. That park is noisy, but fun!
10. Those messy trash cans on the corner are full.

C. Grammar Link **Write each sentence. Underline the adjective. Then rewrite the sentence, replacing the adjective with a synonym or an antonym.**

11. Several houses were large.
12. The windows were clean.
13. The house was interesting because of its high roof.
14. The grass in the yard was tall.
15. The front door was heavy.

Writing Activity Analogies

An analogy is a comparison between pairs of things that show a relationship.

Some analogies use synonyms: *Tidy is to neat as tall is to high.*

Other analogies use antonyms: *Dark is to light as high is to low.*

Write three analogies using synonyms or antonyms.

APPLY GRAMMAR: Use adjectives in the analogies you write.

Build Skills

Composition: Organization

To create a well-organized paragraph, a writer must present all the sentences in a clear, logical order. This will make the information in the paragraph easier to read and understand.

GUIDELINES

- **Organization refers to the way ideas are put together in a paragraph.**
- **In a well-organized paragraph, sentences are arranged in a logical order.**
- **To organize a paragraph by time order, tell the order in which things happen or should be done. Use words such as *first, next, then, later, after that,* and *as soon as*.**
- **To organize a paragraph by spatial order, tell how things are arranged. Use words such as *inside*, *outside*, *over*, *beside*, *above*, *near*, *next to*, and *on top of*.**

Logical Order

How might logical order make directions easier to understand and follow? Write your answer in your journal.

Read these **directions**. Notice how the paragraph describes the steps in a logical order.

The first sentence states the main idea and identifies the first step of the process.

Time-order words are used to list the steps in order.

Spatial words are used to make the directions clearer.

To change the lightbulb in the playroom, you must first turn off the light. You will find the switch beside the window. Next, you must remove the old bulb. Standing on a low stool, turn the bulb to the left, or counter clockwise, until the bulb comes out. Place the old bulb inside a box or basket, so it does not roll and break. Then, take the new bulb out of the package. Reach up and carefully screw the bulb into the socket by turning it to the right, or clockwise. Finally, turn on the light switch to see if the new bulb works.

Practice

A. Copy the sentences. Underline the time-order words. Then put the sentences in logical order in a paragraph.

1. To carry a canoe by car, you must first attach a canoe rack to the roof of your car.
2. Finally, use ropes to tie the canoe securely to your car.
3. Then, rest the canoe on the rack.
4. Next, work with a friend to turn the canoe over.
5. As soon as the canoe is upside-down, lift it up.

B. Copy the sentences, filling in the missing spatial words. Then put the sentences in logical order in a paragraph.

6. They reached the finish line ______ the park exit.
7. They tried to avoid the rocks ______ the shoreline.
8. The canoe race started ______ the covered bridge.
9. The racers paddled fast ______ the lake.
10. They slowed down when they saw the danger sign ______ a raft.

C. Grammar Link Use each word or phrase in a sentence. Think about how the word adds organization to ideas in your writing.

11. below
12. to the right
13. ahead
14. finally
15. as soon as

Writing Activity A News Release

Imagine you have just participated in a local canoe race. Write a news release describing the race and the area where you canoed. Use *time-order words* and *spatial words* to organize your news release.

APPLY GRAMMAR: To make your news release more interesting, add strong, accurate adjectives that appeal to the senses.

Better Sentences

Directions

Read the passage. Some sections are underlined. The underlined sections may be one of the following:
- **Incomplete sentences**
- **Run-on sentences**
- **Correctly written sentences that should be combined**
- **Correctly written sentences that do not need to be rewritten**

Choose the best way to write each underlined section. If the underlined section needs no change, choose "No mistake."

Combine sentences that have similar ideas by joining two nouns.

A run-on sentence can be corrected by forming two sentences that can stand alone.

Sample

Lake Travis is a beautiful lake. Boaters enjoy the clear blue water. They also enjoy the peaceful coves. (1) It is also a great place for swimming. There are many restaurants along the banks of the lake it is a fun place for dining. (2)

1 **A** Boaters and they enjoy the clear blue water and the peaceful coves.

B Boaters enjoy the clear blue water, they also enjoy the peaceful coves.

C Boaters enjoy the clear blue water and the peaceful coves.

D No mistake

2 **F** There are many restaurants along the banks of the lake. It is a fun place for dining.

G There are many restaurants. Along the banks of the lake, it is a fun place for dining.

H There are many restaurants along the banks of the lake, it is a fun place for dining.

J No mistake

Test Tip
Read items carefully. If you work too quickly, you may make careless mistakes.

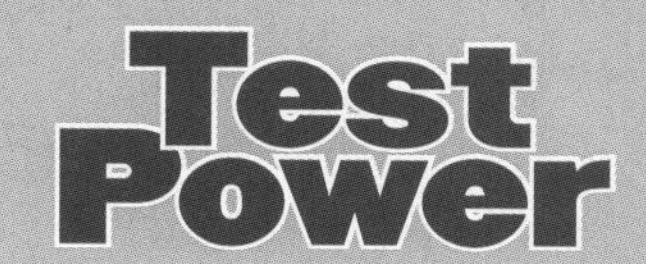

Vocabulary and Comprehension

Directions

Read the passage. Then read each question that follows the passage. Decide which is the best answer to each question. Choose the letter for that answer.

Sample

Raj dialed his home phone number and waited for his mom to answer. "Hi, Mom, it's Raj. I rode my bike to the store. I used my new lock, but now I can't get it open. I wonder if I have the right combination."

His mother said, "Let me check. Where did you leave the information?"

Raj replied, "It's in the top drawer of my dresser."

Raj's mother found the information. After she told Raj the combination, he said, "I know how I can remember it. It's Dad's birthdate!"

If you replace a word with a synonym, the meaning of the sentence will not change.

1 In this passage, found can be replaced with—

A located

B explored

C observed

D remembered

2 What did Raj do first when he realized he had forgotten his combination?

F He looked for it in his dresser.

G He walked home.

H He went to a bike shop.

J He called his mother.

Seeing Like a Writer

What would you write about these pictures? What steps would someone take to make each item in the pictures?

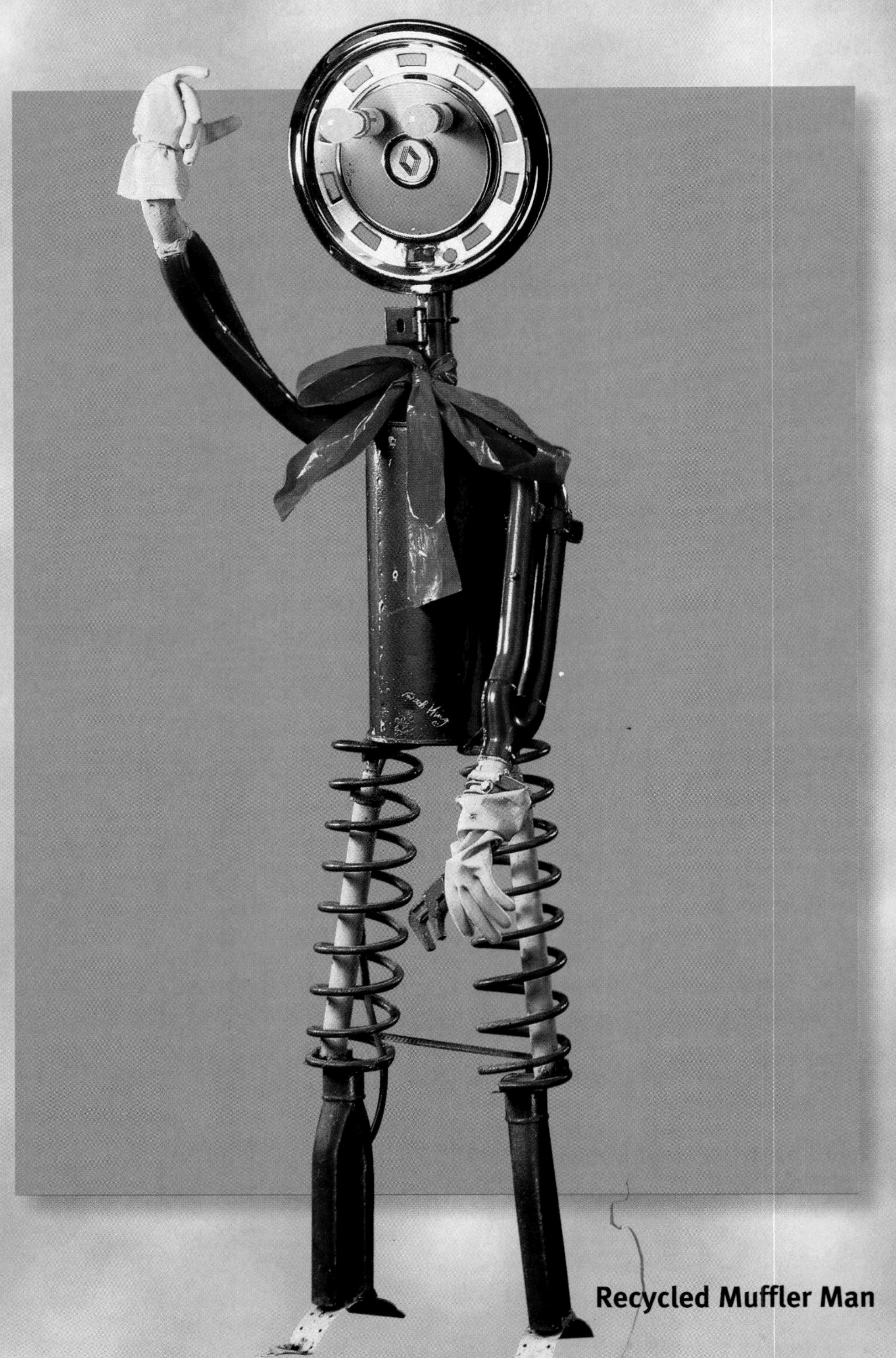

Recycled Muffler Man

Writing from Pictures

1. List adjectives that describe the items in each picture.
2. Make a speech balloon for one of the pictures. In the speech balloon, write what someone in the picture is saying. Use spatial words like *next to, beside, over,* and *near*.
3. What steps would you take to make the items in two of the pictures? Write a paragraph describing how the two processes are alike.

Apply Grammar: Include adjectives in your paragraph to make your writing more interesting and specific. Circle each adjective that you use.

Explanatory Writing

Have you ever read directions for making something? This is an example of explanatory writing. Explanatory writing tells how to complete a particular task step-by-step.

THINK AND WRITE

Purpose

What kinds of things might you describe in an explanatory piece? Why would you describe them? Write your ideas in your journal.

Learning from Writers

Read the following examples of explanatory writing. What process does the writer explain? What words does the writer use to tell you the order in which the steps were completed?

How Can Animals Help People?

Duffy is a dog who is part of a program called Pet Partners. Every week Duffy and other Pet Partners go to hospitals and other places. Their job is to help people who are very sick, sad, or lonely feel better.

How did Duffy get to become a Pet Partner? It wasn't easy. First, Duffy needed to pass many different tests. Testers put food in front of Duffy. They bounced balls in front of him. They even brought in other dogs to distract him. In each case Duffy had to stay still until his trainer told him it was okay to move.

After Duffy passed all his tests, he needed to be trained. During his training Duffy learned how to help people. He learned to be patient with strangers. He learned how to be gentle with young children and very old people. After four months of training, Duffy was ready to be a Pet Partner.

—From a science textbook

Directions to the Bowling Alley

To get to the bowling alley from my school, exit the driveway, and turn right onto Cornell Street. At the stop sign, turn left onto Mitchell Street. Follow Mitchell Street past the knitting shops, and then go three more blocks. You will see a sign for First National Bank. Turn left at the sign, and go past the bank along the gravel driveway. The bowling alley is the big white building on your right. We will be waiting at the side entrance. It is the entrance with a blue light over the door.

–Jeffrey Thomas

Practice and Apply

Thinking Like a Reader

1. What steps must a dog complete to become a Pet Partner?
2. What kinds of information does "Directions to the Bowling Alley" give the reader?

Thinking Like a Writer

3. Why does the author tell about the tests first and Duffy's training second?
4. What words does Jeffrey Thomas use in his directions that tell which way to go?

5. **Reading Across Texts** Think about why each of these models is an example of explanatory writing. Write a sentence telling what each model explains.

Features of Explanatory Writing

DEFINITIONS AND FEATURES

In explanatory writing, the writer informs, or tells, the reader how to do something. The writer describes a process step by step. A good explanation:

- **Informs or explains** how to complete a certain task.
- Gives **step-by-step directions** in a logical order.
- Provides **clear details** that are easy to follow.
- Uses **time-order words** or **spatial words,** such as *under* or *above*, to make the steps clear.

▶ Inform or Explain

Reread "How Can Animals Help People?" on page 304. What does this piece explain? Notice that the author begins the second paragraph by asking a question.

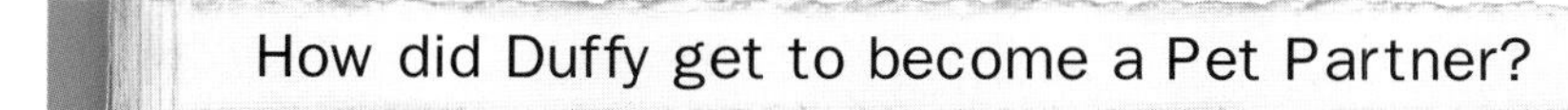

How did Duffy get to become a Pet Partner?

This question tells what the author will explain in the piece. The second and third paragraphs contain information telling how an animal becomes a Pet Partner.

▶ Step-by-Step Directions

Step-by-step directions tell a reader how to complete a task and explain the order of the steps. The sentence below helps the reader understand what Duffy needed to do to become a Pet Partner.

> After Duffy passed all his tests, he needed to be trained.

What did Duffy have to do first to become a Pet Partner?

▶ Clear Details

Clear details make an explanation easy to understand. The author of "How Can Animals Help People?" gives details telling how Duffy was tested.

> Testers put food in front of Duffy. They bounced balls in front of him. They even brought in other dogs to distract him.

How do these details help the reader understand the type of tests Duffy had to take?

▶ Time-Order Words or Spatial Words

Time-order words, such as *next* and *last*, show the sequence of events. Spatial words, such as *behind* and *near*, tell where something is located. These words help make the steps in explanatory writing clear.

> First, Duffy needed to pass many different tests.

What time-order word does the author of "How Can Animals Help People?" use in this sentence?

Practice and Apply

Create a Features Chart

1. List the features of a good example of explanatory writing.
2. Reread "Directions to the Bowling Alley" by Jeffrey Thomas on page 305.
3. Write one example of each feature in Jeffrey's writing.
4. Write why you think Jeffrey's directions are easy to follow.

Features	Examples

Writing PROCESS

Prewrite

In explanatory writing, the writer informs, or tells, the reader how to do something. Writing an explanation can give you a way to tell others how to make something, complete a task, or find a particular place.

Purpose and Audience

The purpose of explanatory writing is to explain something clearly to someone else. Instructions are presented in logical step-by-step order so that readers can easily understand them.

Before you begin writing an explanation, think about your audience. How can you be sure they will understand your explanation? Use words and examples that will be familiar to them.

Audience
Write about how your audience will affect the way you explain directions.

Choose a Topic

Start by **brainstorming** different kinds of information that you could share with someone, such as instructions for making something or directions to a place.

After choosing your topic and audience, **explore ideas** by making a list of elements you will want to include in your explanation.

Directions to My Apartment
Look for apartment buildings
I live in Building D
North on Merrick Road
Right on Planet Road
Look for the school
Turn on the next street
Over the bridge
Four bridges in our town
Turn on June Lane

Organize • Sequence

Explanatory writing must clearly explain a process in a logical, step-by-step order. To plan your instructions, you can use a flowchart. Write a step in each box. How did the writer use her flowchart to organize the information from her list?

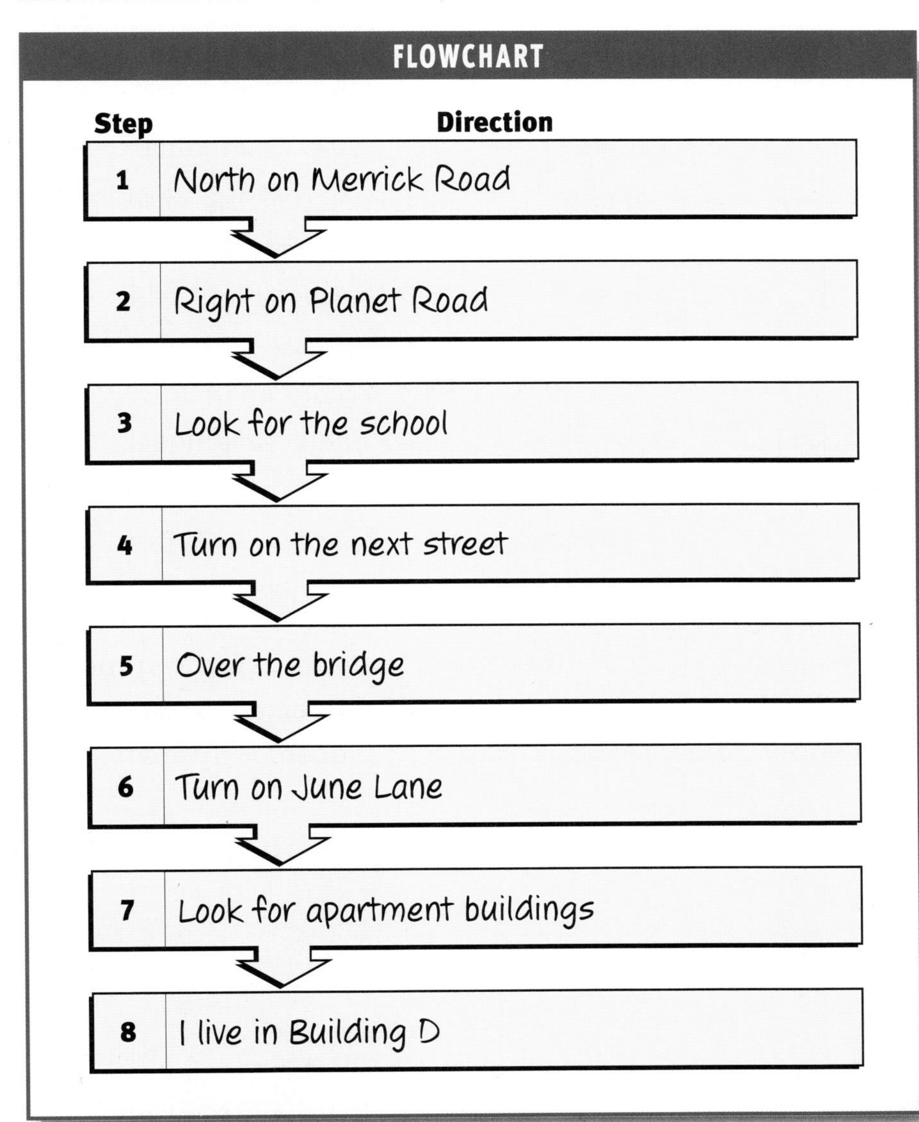

PREWRITE

DRAFT

REVISE

PROOFREAD

PUBLISH

Practice and Apply

Plan Your Own Explanatory Writing

1. Brainstorm a list of things you might explain.

2. Select a topic and list its steps.

3. Think about your purpose and audience.

4. Organize your step-by-step instructions.

Checklist

Prewriting

- Did you choose something to explain?
- Did you think about your purpose and audience?
- Did you make a list of step-by-step instructions that are clear and easy to follow?
- Did you double-check your work to make sure you didn't leave out any important steps?
- Did you decide whether you need to do any research?

Prewrite • Research and Inquiry

▶ Writer's Resources

You may need to do some research to get additional information for your explanatory writing. Make a list of questions. Then decide what resources you need.

What Else Do I Need to Know?	Where Can I Find the Information?
What is the name of the street with the bridge ?	Find a map of the town at the library.
How far down June Lane do I live?	Use the distance scale on the map.
How can I explain how to find Building D?	Find a diagram of the apartment buildings.

▶ Use a Map

To help you write directions, you can refer to a map. A road map shows all the streets in a certain area. It may also show lakes, rivers, parks, and places of interest.

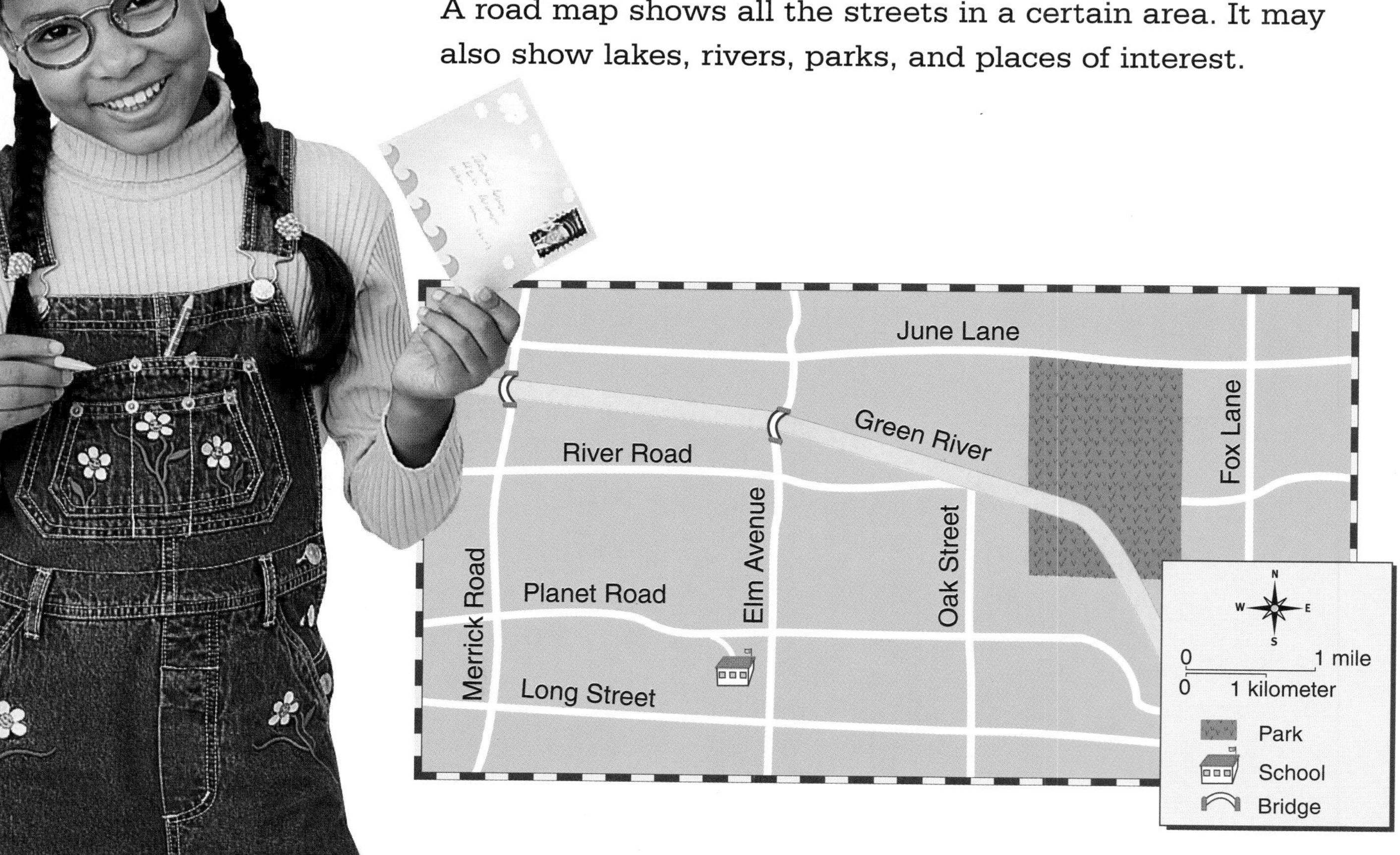

▶ Use a Diagram

A diagram is a drawing that shows how something is arranged or what its parts are. A diagram can be a helpful resource for some explanatory writing. For example, if you were giving directions to your apartment, a diagram of your group of apartment buildings might help you explain exactly how to find your building.

▶ Use Your Research

New information from your research can go into your flowchart. This writer found some important details to add to her directions. What did she add?

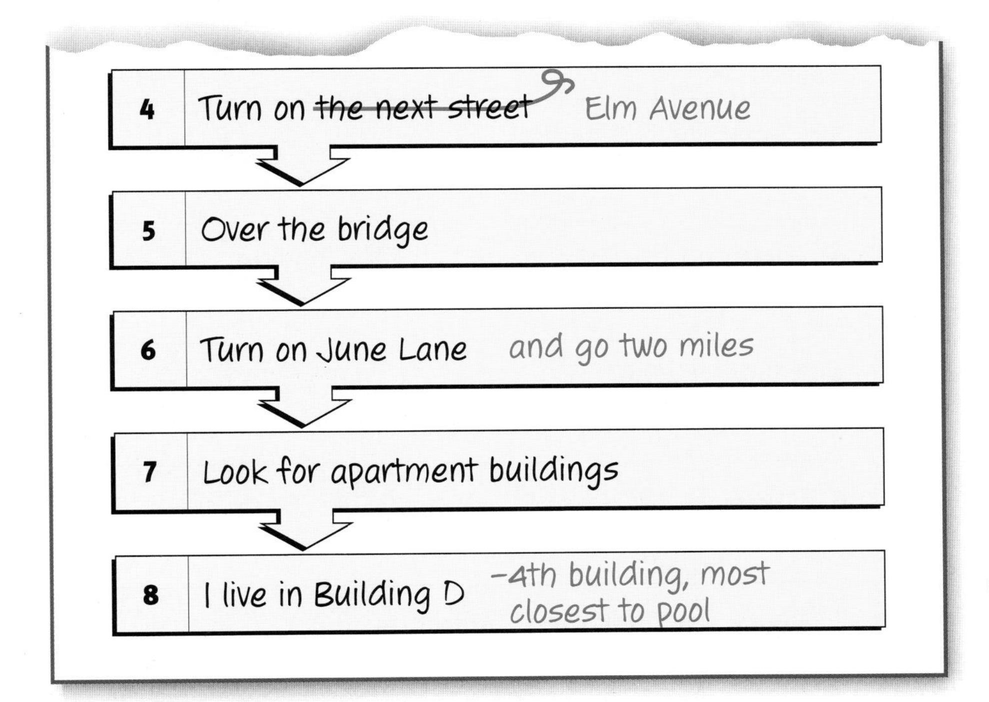

PREWRITE
DRAFT
REVISE
PROOFREAD
PUBLISH

Handbook
page 569

Practice and Apply

Review Your Plan

1. Look at your flowchart.
2. List details you need for your directions.
3. Identify the resources you need to find the missing details.
4. Add new information that you gather to your chart.

Checklist ✓

Research and Inquiry

- Did you make a list of questions or missing details?
- Did you identify some possible resources?
- Did you take notes?

Writing PROCESS

Draft

Before you begin writing your directions, review the chart you made. Think about writing a sentence for each step of your directions. Then group related sentences together to form paragraphs.

Steps are organized in logical time and space order.

One paragraph can tell how to get to my street.

FLOWCHART

Step	Direction
1	North on Merrick Road
2	Right on Planet Road
3	Look for the school
4	Turn on ~~the next street~~ Elm Avenue
5	Over the bridge
6	Turn on June Lane and go two miles
7	Look for apartment buildings
8	I live in Building D -4th building, most closest to pool

One paragraph can tell how to find my apartment.

Checklist

Drafting

- Have you explained how to complete a process or a task?
- Are your steps in logical order?
- Have you given clear details that are easy to follow?
- Have you used time-order words (like *before* and *next*) or spatial words (like *left* and *right*) to help make your directions clearer?

Look at the ways this writer has used the steps in her chart to write a first draft of a letter. She grouped related sentences together in paragraphs. She presented the information in logical step-by-step order and added a short introduction.

DRAFT

129 June Lane

Sayville Maryland 21092

July 12 20__

dear Joanna

I'm so excited you are coming to visit! We can swim in the pool. Take Merrick Road north. Then, turn right on Planet Road. Look for the school building. Turn on Elm Avenue and go over the bridge. Next, turn on June Lane and go too miles. Look for the apartment buildings at the park.

I live in Building D. It's the forth building, the one most closest to the pool. I'll be there!

Your bestest friend

Mariana

Step-by-step directions

Main idea of second paragraph

Supporting details tell how to find Building D.

TECHNOLOGY

If you created a prewriting list or flowchart on your computer, you can copy it into a new document for writing your draft. Rearrange and add to the items or chart to create your draft.

Practice and Apply

Draft Your Own Explanatory Writing

1. Review your prewriting chart.
2. Present step-by-step instructions.
3. Organize the instructions into paragraphs.
4. Add details that make your instructions clear and easy to follow.

Writing PROCESS

Revise

Elaborate

One way to improve your writing is to elaborate. When you elaborate, you add important steps or details that might be missing from your writing. When you revise your explanatory writing, you may need to add or take out details.

The writer added important information that will help make it easier for the reader to follow directions.

> to the traffic light
> Take Merrick Road north^.

The writer added details to describe what the reader will see.

> red brick
> Look for the^apartment buildings at the park.

Word Choice

When you are writing, it is important to choose just the right words for your topic and audience.

Spatial words are helpful for giving directions to a place. These words tell where places are located in relation to one another. The writer added the words *right* and *across from* to help make the directions clearer.

> right
> Next, turn^on June Lane and go too miles. Look for
> red brick across from
> the^apartment buildings^~~at~~ the park.

SPATIAL WORDS

right
left
near
far
east
west
north
south
next to
in front of
close to
behind
across from
around

Better Paragraphs

As you revise your draft, check your paragraphs to make sure each one has a main idea. Do the details in the paragraph support the main idea?

Sometimes writers make the mistake of including too much information in one paragraph. If a paragraph contains more than one main idea, you may be able to make your writing clearer by dividing it into two. Make sure each paragraph has a topic sentence.

We'll have a great time.
I'm so excited you are coming to visit! We can
Here are the directions to my apartment.
swim in the pool. Take Merrick Road north.

Handbook
page 576

Practice and Apply

Revise Your Own Explanatory Writing

1. Read your explanatory writing.
2. Add additional steps and details where they are needed.
3. Elaborate by adding time-order or spatial words to some of your sentences.
4. **Grammar** Have you used adjectives in your writing to describe people, places, or things? Have you used the correct forms of comparative adjectives?

TECHNOLOGY

When you begin revising your draft, you can rename your document using the SAVE AS feature on your computer. That way, if you change your mind about any revisions, you can cut and paste text from the original document.

Revise • Peer Conferencing

Take a break from your writing, and give a partner a copy of your original draft to read. Having someone else read your writing can be very helpful. Your partner may have suggestions and ideas that you haven't thought of.

Good step-by-step directions

Can you give more details about the school?

Would a spatial word be helpful here?

129 June Lane
Sayville Maryland 21092
July 12 20__

dear Joanna

I'm so excited you are coming to visit! We can swim in the pool. Take Merrick Road north. Then, turn right on Planet Road. Look for the school building. Turn on Elm Avenue and go over the bridge. Next, turn on June Lane and go too miles. Look for the apartment buildings at the park.

I live in Building D. It's the forth building, the one most closest to the pool. I'll be there!

Your bestest friend
Mariana

Conferencing for the Reader

- Are features of explanatory writing included in your partner's piece?
  - informs or explains
  - step-by-step instructions
  - clear details
  - spatial words
- It's important to tell your partner what you like about the piece as well as giving suggestions on how it can be improved.

When you revise your explanatory writing, you may want to include some of your partner's suggestions. This writer made some changes in her letter based on her partner's comments.

PREWRITE
DRAFT
REVISE
PROOFREAD
PUBLISH

REVISE

129 June Lane

Sayville Maryland 21092

July 12 20__

dear Joanna

I'm so excited you are coming to visit! We'll have a great time. We can swim in the pool. Here are the directions to my apartment. Take Merrick Road north to the traffic light. Then, turn right on Planet Road. Look for the big white school building on the right. Turn left on Elm Avenue and go over the old wooden bridge. Next, turn right on June Lane and go too miles. Look for the red brick apartment buildings across from the park.

I live in Building D. It's the forth building on the left, the one most closest to the pool. I'll be there!

Your bestest friend

Mariana

PRACTICE AND APPLY

Revise Your Own Explanatory Writing

1. Take notes from your partner's comments.
2. Use the notes to help make your draft better.
3. Put in additional information or details where they are needed.

Checklist

Revising

- Does your letter fit your purpose and audience?
- Do you need to add more details to your instructions?
- Are your steps in logical order?
- Have you used time-order or spatial words?
- Have you used your partner's suggestions?

Writing PROCESS

Proofread

After you have revised your writing, you will need to proofread it to find and correct any errors in mechanics, grammar, usage, and spelling.

STRATEGIES FOR PROOFREADING

- **Reread your revised writing several times.** You'll be more likely to catch all your errors.
- **Reread for punctuation.** If you have written a letter, make sure you have used commas correctly.
- **Check carefully for spelling mistakes.** Start with the last word and read backward.
- **Check each sentence for correct capitalization.** Be sure to use capitals for letter greetings and closings, street names, city names, and dates.

TECHNOLOGY

A spell-checker cannot catch words that are used incorrectly, such as homophones. For example, if you write *peace* instead of *piece*, the spell-checker will not point it out. You must also proofread your writing carefully.

REVIEW THE RULES

GRAMMAR

- Add *-er* or *more* to an adjective to compare two people, places, or things. Add *-est* or *most* to compare more than two.
- Use *better* or *worse* to compare two people, places, or things. Use *best* or *worst* to compare more than two.

MECHANICS

- Begin the greeting and closing of a friendly letter with a capital letter.
- Use a comma after the greeting and the closing.
- Use a comma between the names of a city and state.
- Use a comma between the day and year in a date.

Look at the proofreading corrections made on the draft below. What does the symbol ꩜ mean? Why is the writer taking out the word *most* in the last paragraph?

PREWRITE
DRAFT
REVISE
PROOFREAD
PUBLISH

PROOFREAD

129 June Lane

Sayville, Maryland 21092

July 12, 20__

dear Joanna,

We'll have a great time.

I'm so excited you are coming to visit! We can swim in the pool. Here are the directions to my apartment. Take Merrick Road north to the traffic light. Then, turn right on Planet Road. Look for the big white school building on the right. Turn left on Elm Avenue and go over the old wooden bridge. Next, turn right on June Lane and go ~~too~~ two miles. Look for the red brick apartment buildings ~~at~~ across from the park.

I live in Building D. It's the ~~forth~~ fourth building, the one on the left ~~most~~ closest to the pool. I'll be there!

Your ~~bestest~~ best friend,

Mariana

Checklist

Proofreading

- If you wrote a letter, did you put a proper heading on it?
- Did you indent each new paragraph?
- Did you use adjectives correctly?
- Did you use proper punctuation and capitalization?
- Did you check your spelling?

PROOFREADING MARKS

- ¶ new paragraph
- ^ add
- ꩜ take out
- ≡ Make a capital letter.
- / Make a small letter.
- (SP) Check the spelling.
- ⊙ Add a period.

PRACTICE AND APPLY

Proofread Your Own Explanatory Writing

1. Check for correct punctuation and capitalization.
2. Check for correct use of adjectives that compare.
3. Correct spelling mistakes.
4. Make sure you have used the correct letter form.

Publish

Before you publish your explanatory writing, review your work one last time. Using a checklist can be very helpful.

Self-Check Explanatory Writing

- ❑ Did I write in a way that will interest my audience?
- ❑ Was my purpose clear?
- ❑ Did I give my instructions in a logical step-by-step order?
- ❑ Did I present helpful and clear details?
- ❑ Did I use time-order or spatial words to help make my instructions more precise?
- ❑ Did I use the right form if I wrote a letter?
- ❑ Did I spell each word correctly?
- ❑ Did I proofread and correct all punctuation and capitalization errors?

The writer used a checklist to help her review her letter to her friend. Read the letter and discuss it with a small group of classmates. Are the directions in the letter easy to understand and follow? Do you think the letter is ready to be sent? Why or why not?

129 June Lane
Sayville, Maryland 21092
July 12, 20__

Dear Joanna,

I'm so excited you are coming to visit! We'll have a great time. We can swim in the pool.

Here are the directions to my apartment. Take Merrick Road north to the traffic light. Then, turn right on Planet Road. Look for the big white school building on the right. Turn left on Elm Avenue and go over the old wooden bridge. Next, turn right on June Lane and go two miles. Look for the red brick apartment buildings across from the park.

I live in Building D. It's the fourth building on the left, the one closest to the pool. I'll be there!

Your best friend,
Mariana

TECHNOLOGY

As you work on your final copy, make sure to save your document often. Rename it so that you'll know it is the final document.

Practice and Apply

Publish Your Own Explanatory Writing

1. Check your revised draft one more time.
2. Make a neat final copy.
3. Draw a map or diagram to go with your explanation.
4. Place your explanation and visual side-by-side on a large poster board.

LISTENING
SPEAKING
VIEWING
REPRESENTING

Present Your Explanatory Writing

Your presentation will be better if you plan it ahead of time. There are many things you can do to make sure your presentation is a success.

STEP 1

How to Give Your Explanation

Strategies for Speaking As you plan your presentation, remember that your purpose is to give information that explains something. Your audience should be able to follow your instructions.

- Make a numbered list of steps so that you will be sure to present them in order.
- Practice speaking in a loud, clear voice.
- Practice looking at your audience.
- Be prepared to answer questions at the end.

Listening Strategies

- Think about your purpose for listening. What kind of information are you listening for?
- Listen for steps as they are identified. Are they in a logical sequence?
- Listen for details that will help you understand the steps.
- Jot down questions you want to ask later.

Multimedia Ideas

You might want to list the steps you will discuss and display the list on an overhead projector. During your presentation, you can point to each step as you prepare to discuss it.

STEP 2

How to Show Your Explanation

Suggestions for Visuals Make your presentation clearer and more interesting by adding visuals to your explanation.

- A large map or diagram can help your audience follow your explanation as you read it aloud.
- As you give the steps of your instructions, point to them on your visual.
- If your instructions contain special words, relate them to places on your map or diagram.

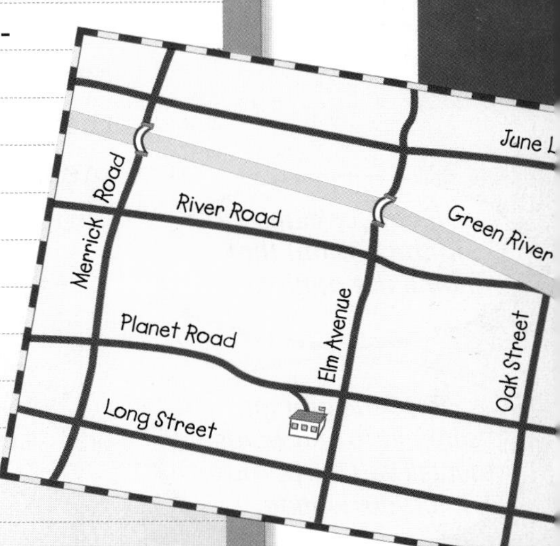

STEP 3

How to Share Your Explanation

Strategies for Rehearsing The more you practice, the more comfortable you will feel on the day of your presentation.

- Ask a friend to listen to your presentation and try to follow your instructions.
- Practice in front of the mirror.
- Practice referring to a visual and then finding your place again in your writing.

Viewing Strategies

- **Look carefully at diagrams, maps, or other visuals a speaker displays.**
- **Visuals may help clarify instructions or directions.**
- **Take note of details on the visual that a speaker may not have time to explain.**

Practice and Apply

Present Your Own Explanatory Writing

1. Read from a clean copy of your writing.
2. Mark places in your writing where you plan to stop to refer to a map or another visual aid.
3. Practice for friends or in front of a mirror.
4. Speak loudly and make eye contact with your audience as you make your presentation.

Writing Tests

On a writing test, you are asked to write a composition in response to a prompt. Remember to read the prompt carefully. Look for key words and phrases that describe the topic of your composition and explain how you should present your ideas.

Look for clues in the prompt that name the audience.

Read the prompt carefully to find words that tell you the purpose of your writing.

This phrase tells you how to organize your ideas.

Prompt

Think about one of your favorite activities. Write a composition in which you tell about this activity and explain how to do it. Be sure to give step-by-step instructions.

How to Read a Prompt

Purpose Read the prompt again. Look for words that tell you the purpose of your writing. The words "explain how to do it" tell you that the purpose of your composition is to inform.

Audience Some prompts name a specific audience for whom you should write. If a prompt does not, think of your teacher as your audience.

Explanatory Writing When you are writing to explain, you tell how to do something by describing the steps in a process. The words "give step-by-step instructions" tell you how to organize your ideas. Use time-order and spatial words to make your instructions easy to follow.

Test Tip

Work at a steady pace so that you complete the test in time.

How to Write to a Prompt

Here are some tips to remember when you are given a prompt in a writing test.

Before Writing **Content/Ideas**	• Think about your purpose. • Keep your audience in mind. • If you are writing to explain, make a list of steps in the process. • Stay focused on the assignment.
During Writing **Organization/ Paragraph Structure**	• Start with a good topic sentence. • In explanatory writing, put your ideas in step-by-step order. • Use time-order and spatial words to make your directions clear. • End with an appropriate conclusion.
After Writing **Grammar/Usage**	• Proofread your work. • Make sure that you have used correct punctuation. • Check that you have used the proper form of adjectives that compare. • Look for spelling errors.

Apply What You Learned

When you read a writing prompt, always look for information about your purpose and audience. Determine the topic and the best way to organize your ideas.

Prompt

Think about something that a person recently showed you how to do.

Write a composition in which you explain how the person taught you to do this activity. Describe each step in the process.

Unit 4 Review

Grammar and Writing Review

pages 262–265

Adjectives and Articles

A. Write each sentence. Then underline the adjectives and circle the articles.

1. We have a wonderful celebration in our happy city.
2. The colorful celebration begins with a loud parade.
3. Talented musicians march in a festive band.
4. Fascinating magicians and clowns follow the band.
5. An entertaining clown makes the little children laugh.

pages 266–267

Adjectives After Linking Verbs

B. Write each sentence. Draw one line under the adjective. Draw two lines under the noun it describes. Circle the linking verb.

6. The parade is entertaining.
7. The horses are sleek.
8. Their manes are braided.
9. The elephants were huge.
10. How many monkeys were brown?

pages 268–269

Proper Adjectives

C. Write each sentence. Capitalize the proper adjectives.

11. A mexican clown performs at the festival.
12. The scottish band plays bagpipes.
13. The indian belly dancers are amazing.
14. A russian musician sings and plays the piano.
15. The german dancers have a fabulous time!

pages 272–275

Adjectives That Compare

D. Write each sentence. Use the correct form of the adjective in parentheses ( ). Some adjectives change their spelling.

16. The music was ______ at the fair than at the rodeo. (loud)

17. The Asian food was ______ than the Greek food. (tasty)

18. The tacos were the ______ food of all. (fine)

19. The corn tortillas were ______ than the flour tortillas. (flat)

20. The stir-fry was the ______ food we tried. (hot)

21. The mangoes were ______ than the oranges. (juicy)

22. The Ferris wheel was ______ than the merry-go-round. (slow)

23. The train was the ______ ride I've ever been on. (fast)

24. The rocket was the ______ ride I saw. (tall)

25. The ticket takers were the ______ workers at the fair. (friendly)

pages 276–279

Comparing with *More* and *Most*, *Good* and *Bad*

E. Write each sentence. Use the correct word or phrase in parentheses.

26. The carnival was ______ than the fair. (more entertaining, most entertaining)

27. The games were the ______ I had ever played. (more difficult, most difficult)

28. The ______ game of all was Shoot the Duck. (more popular, most popular)

29. Toss the Ball was ______ than Hit the Target. (most challenging, more challenging)

30. Jeff played miniature golf ______ than his brother did. (better, best)

31. The chocolate cake was the ______ dessert offered. (better, best)

32. The ______ dessert I tasted was the lemon pie. (worst, worse)

33. Karen was given a prize for wearing the ______ costume to the carnival. (most unusual, more unusual)

34. The storytellers were ______ than the announcers. (more humorous, most humorous)

35. Everyone had a ______ time at this year's carnival. (good, best)

Unit 4 Review

pages 280–281

Combining Sentences: Adjectives

F. Write each pair of sentences as one sentence.

36. The crowd enjoyed the acrobats. The crowd was enthusiastic.

37. The dancing bears were the funniest sight. The dancing bears were black.

38. A clown led the parade. The clown was silly.

39. Puppets danced in the streets. The puppets were huge.

40. The high school band played tunes. The tunes were beautiful.

pages 282–289

Mechanics and Usage: Letter Punctuation

G. Copy the letter. Correct the punctuation as needed.

41–45.

24 South Main Street.
Northfield Minnesota 55057
April 25 2001

Dear Greg

I'm glad you can come to the May Day celebration. I'll meet you at the corner of Main Street and Sixth Avenue at 10:00 A.M.

Your friend
Victor

Unit 4 Review

pages 296–297

Vocabulary: Synonyms and Antonyms

H. Write each sentence. Use a synonym for the underlined word. Then write the sentence again. This time use an antonym for the underlined word.

46. The new house was big.

47. The streets were clean.

48. Beautiful flowers grew in the gardens.

49. The other neighbors were friendly.

50. We liked the quiet community.

pages 298–299

Composition: Organization

I. Write each sentence. Fill in the blank with a spatial word.

51. To get to the parade, turn ______ on Park Street.

52. Travel three blocks and go ______ the bridge.

53. Drive to the end of the street, and park ______ the library.

54. Look for some big trees ______ the sidewalk.

55. I'll be waiting for you ______ the giant oak tree.

pages 308–323

Proofreading an Explanation

J. Write the following paragraphs. Correct mistakes in punctuation, capitalization, grammar, and spelling. There are ten errors.

Last april, my school had a spring parade. Students were divided into teams, and each team made a float for the parade. I was on the spanish teachers team, and we made the bestest float of all.

We started with an simple hay wagon. We made pink yellow and green flowers out of tissue paper. We pushed the flowers through chicken wire to make a wall of flowers. Then we stapled the flower wall on the back of the wagon, we also made huge tissue flowers to go on the sides of the wagon. It was the prettyest float I've ever seen. Decorating it was the highlight of my year.

Project File

ACTIVITY 1 A Humorous Story

Like other kinds of stories, a humorous story must have a beginning, a middle, and an end. But unlike other stories, it should end with an element of surprise or an unexpected twist. Study this humorous story. How do the parts make it funny?

You will need to know the elements of a story when you write your story in the next unit.

Hot Lemonade

by Freddy Goldberg

I'll never forget my last birthday party. Uncle Murray had invited the whole family to dinner at the fanciest restaurant in town.

"We'll have the shrimp appetizer for the table," Uncle Murray told the waiter. Soon, two waiters came and served each of us a bowl of hot water with a slice of lemon. Since I didn't want mine to get cold, I fished out the lemon slice and squeezed it into the bowl. Then I mixed sugar into my drink and savored the hot lemonade.

Then the appetizer came. It was a beautiful mound of peel-your-own shrimp. I was about to dig in when I stopped in embarrassment. The others were dipping their hands into their bowls of water. The water was for washing , not drinking!

Title Is the name of the story.

Beginning Introduces the characters, setting, and the plot.

Dialogue Brings the characters to life.

Middle Develops the plot and tells more about the characters.

Surprise Ending Brings the story to a close with a surprise or unexpected twist.

Write a Humorous Story Think of an event that made you laugh. What made it funny? Now arrange the details into a story. Begin by introducing the characters, the setting, and the plot. Then develop the plot. End the plot with a twist or a surprise ending. Add a title. Look at the model on page 330, and match it with your story.

TIME FOR KIDS

ACTIVITY 2

An Instruction List

The Alaskan square from the museum quilt shows Earth with clean water. What can people do today to make sure we have clean water in the year 2050 and beyond? Use several sources to do research on water conservation.

Letter and List Write a letter to your family that gives a list of instructions for how to keep our water supply clean for future use. In the letter, list at least five easy, practical steps your family members can take.

Extra Practice

Adjectives

A. Write the adjective that describes the underlined noun.

1. Sherlock Holmes was a famous <u>detective</u> in England.
2. He was the hero in many <u>stories</u> written by Sir Arthur Conan Doyle.
3. Holmes solved baffling <u>mysteries</u>.
4. Dr. Watson was Holmes's faithful <u>assistant</u>.
5. Sherlock Holmes always wore a special <u>hat</u>.
6. Readers enjoy the unusual <u>clues</u> in the stories.
7. I have read three <u>stories</u> about Sherlock Holmes.
8. Didn't the detective carry a small <u>diary</u>?
9. He liked to write down interesting <u>facts</u> about a case.
10. Let's read a short <u>book</u> about Sherlock Holmes.

B. Write each sentence. Draw a line under the adjective. Circle the noun it describes.

11. One student will be Sherlock Holmes in the play.
12. We are making a fancy costume for him.
13. Will you sew a checked hat?
14. He has many lines to learn soon.
15. Who will play the evil Dr. Moriarty?
16. Marion tried out for that difficult part.
17. She has a deep voice.
18. The play begins on a dark stage.
19. Then two dogs begin howling at the moon.
20. Dr. Watson is the first character on the stage.

C. Write each sentence. Use an adjective to describe the noun.

21. There are ______ students in the play.
22. Ed and Ramona have sold ______ tickets for the play.
23. A play about Sherlock Holmes will be a ______ success.
24. Does Mr. Rivera have a ______ camera?
25. Come sit in the ______ row with me.

Articles: *a, an, the*

A. Write the article or articles in each sentence.

1. Let's go to the mailbox.
2. I have a feeling that today is my lucky day.
3. Look, you have a letter and a package.
4. Maybe I won an award or a contest!
5. The letter isn't inside an envelope.
6. It doesn't have an address on it.
7. Who would send me a letter in invisible ink?
8. The box is not an ordinary package, either.
9. It has an air hole and a funny smell!
10. Don't look now, but I think the package is moving!

B. Write each sentence. Choose the correct article.

11. Do you think there's (a, an) animal inside this box?
12. I don't think it's (a, an) elephant.
13. Look inside (a, the) air hole.
14. I think I see (a, an) eye, or maybe two.
15. Do you hear (a, an) noise inside?
16. What if it's (a, an) snake?
17. This is (a, an) incredible surprise.
18. Look at (a, the) return address to see who sent it.
19. I've always wanted (a, an) iguana.
20. Will you put your new pet in (a, an) terrarium?

C. Complete each sentence with *a* or *an*. Write each sentence correctly.

21. I went to the library to get ______ book about iguanas.
22. The book said that ______ iguana likes to eat lettuce.
23. Iguanas are vegetarians, so they wouldn't like ______ hamburger.
24. ______ photograph in the book showed iguanas that eat seaweed.
25. They live on ______ island off the coast of Ecuador.

Grammar

Extra Practice

Adjectives After Linking Verbs

A. In each sentence, a noun is underlined. Write the adjective that describes the noun.

1. The street is quiet.
2. The weather is hot.
3. The elm trees are calm today.
4. The library is peaceful.
5. The rooms in the library are cool.
6. The book is heavy.
7. The story is exciting.
8. The chair is comfortable.
9. My voice is loud.
10. The librarian is annoyed.

B. Write each sentence. Draw one line under the adjective. Draw two lines under the noun it describes.

11. My dream was entertaining.
12. The library was crowded.
13. All the books were red.
14. The librarian was happy.
15. The noise was unbelievable.
16. The readers were curious about the books.
17. The chairs were pink.
18. The shelves were messy.
19. His voice was loud.
20. My dream was strange!

C. Write each sentence. Add an adjective to the blank to complete the sentence.

21. I go to the book circle, and I am ______.
22. My friends are ______.
23. The librarian's story is ______.
24. All the listeners are ______.
25. I get an invitation for the next story hour, and I am ______.

Proper Adjectives

A. Write each sentence. Underline the proper adjective. Circle the noun it describes.

1. We are learning about European countries.
2. We imagined flying from an American city.
3. We have already studied the African continent.
4. Our teacher showed us pictures of the English countryside.
5. The Irish coast looks beautiful.
6. We enjoyed a French pastry during our class's "Europe Day."
7. Do you like Italian food?
8. American food is my favorite.
9. Are Canadian meals different from the meals you eat?
10. My aunt likes to cook Swedish meatballs.

B. Write each sentence. Capitalize the proper adjective.

11. My mother loves belgian chocolates.
12. Have you seen pictures of ancient roman ruins?
13. I visited a danish amusement park once.
14. Aunt Thelma made german potato salad for the picnic.
15. I have never tasted any russian dishes.
16. My family often eats chinese food.
17. Have you seen those fast european trains?
18. I would love to ski in the austrian mountains.
19. I would also like to travel on an italian river.
20. We grill polish sausages at our family cookout.

C. Complete each sentence. Use a proper adjective made from the noun in parentheses ( ). Use a dictionary if you need help.

21. Is baseball only an ______ sport? (America)
22. Some ______ students visited our class this year. (Germany)
23. They had already traveled to a ______ city. (France)
24. I have seen the ______ side of Niagara Falls. (Canada)
25. Our class will study ______ countries next. (South America)

Extra Practice

Adjectives That Compare

A. Write the adjective that compares in each sentence.

1. Who is the greatest American inventor?
2. Thomas Alva Edison was smarter than most people.
3. He may have been the smartest inventor ever.
4. He had the quickest mind of American inventors at the time.
5. Schools today are larger than Edison's school.
6. Edison's inventions led to some of the fastest changes in people's lives.
7. Edison was proudest of the gramophone.
8. The gramophone was the earliest record player.
9. Edison recited "Mary Had a Little Lamb" in his loudest voice.
10. His assistant thought it was the oddest thing he had heard.

B. Write each sentence. Choose the correct adjective.

11. Music on the stage sounded (clearer, clearest) than music on a gramophone.
12. Music on the stage sounded (brighter, brightest) of all.
13. Is swing music (older, oldest) than rock and roll?
14. Is folk music (harder, hardest) to play than pop music?
15. Woody Guthrie seemed the (kinder, kindest) of all the folk singers.
16. He wrote songs for the (younger, youngest) of his children.
17. Does a viola play (lower, lowest) notes than a violin?
18. I think low notes are the (louder, loudest) of all.
19. I think a mandolin's sound is (softer, softest) than a guitar's.
20. A violin is (lighter, lightest) to carry than a cello.

C. Use the correct form of the adjective in parentheses ( ).

21. Charlie's electric guitar is ______ than mine. (loud)
22. His voice is the ______ of anyone in the band. (high)
23. Maggie was ______ than I when she began piano lessons. (young)
24. Her piano has the ______ tone I've ever heard. (nice)
25. Is this song ______ than the last one? (long)

Spelling Adjectives That Compare

A. Write each sentence. Underline the adjective that compares. Then write the adjective it was formed from.

1. These trees are larger than the other trees in the woods.
2. Those wildflowers are the prettiest I've ever seen.
3. Those are the biggest leaves in the forest.
4. The wettest part of a woodlands is a swamp.
5. A marsh is saltier than a swamp.
6. The owl is sleepier during the day than at night.
7. The frogs think those insects are tastier than flowers.
8. The air in a swamp is heavier than the air in a meadow.
9. I am happier in a swamp than I am at home.
10. To me, the loveliest places of all are in nature.

B. Write each sentence. Choose the correct adjective.

11. Which swamp is the (bigger, biggest) of all?
12. Some of the (rarer, rarest) frogs live in swamps.
13. Most swamps are (tinier, tiniest) now than before.
14. Great Dismal Swamp is the (larger, largest) swamp I've visited.
15. Bald cypresses grow in (drier, driest) areas than water lilies.
16. I think its mosquitoes are (nastier, nastiest) of all.
17. The lake is (wider, widest) than the canals.
18. Swamp water can be (saltier, saltiest) than regular water.
19. Do some swamps seem (scarier, scariest) than the woods?
20. Fiddlehead ferns have the (prettier, prettiest) leaves of all.

C. Use the correct form of the adjective in parentheses ( ).

21. A drained swamp may be the ______ land of all. (ugly)
22. Someday a lack of water may be our ______ problem. (big)
23. Water from a swamp is the ______ water of all. (tasty)
24. Swamps may be the ______ way to get rid of pollution. (easy)
25. People who pollute are the ______ people I know. (rude)

Grammar

Extra Practice

Comparing with *More* and *Most*

A. Read each adjective. Write the form of the adjective you would use to compare two nouns. Then write the form you would use to compare more than two nouns.

1. foolish
2. nervous
3. amazing
4. interesting
5. frightening
6. talented
7. entertaining
8. delicious
9. exciting
10. impressive

B. Write *more* or *most* to complete each sentence.

11. The Fun House is the ______ enjoyable place in the park.
12. The laughing lady is the ______ hilarious of all.
13. Michelle is ______ curious about her than I am.
14. Doesn't she have the ______ foolish grin on her face?
15. Steep slides are ______ thrilling than rolling barrels.
16. Darryl is ______ frightened than Ginger.
17. The tall mirror is ______ flattering than the short one.
18. This music is ______ annoying than pleasant.
19. The indoor roller coaster was the ______ terrifying of all.
20. Nothing is ______ incredible than that laughing lady.

C. Write each sentence. Use the correct form of the adjective in parentheses ( ).

21. The games at the fair are ______ than the games we play at home. (challenging)
22. What is the ______ amusement park in the world? (famous)
23. This carousel is ______ than any other. (spectacular)
24. Thomas is ______ than Hillary about the rides. (nervous)
25. This fair is the ______ fair we've ever visited. (expensive)

Comparing with *Good* and *Bad*

A. Write the form of the word *good* or *bad* used to compare.

1. I think my city is the best city of all.
2. Our traffic is worse than the traffic in Silver City.
3. Our town has the best parks and swimming pools.
4. I think Chicago's Art Institute is the best museum of all.
5. It has better paintings than the paintings in our museum.
6. Which American city has the worst weather of all?
7. Chicago's snowfall may be worse than the snowfall here.
8. Are the temperatures in the North worse than the temperatures in the South?
9. Devon thinks cold climates are better than warm ones.
10. Cold weather is better than warm weather for skiing.

B. Write each sentence. Choose the correct word.

11. Let's vote on the (better, best) Midwestern city.
12. Do you think Dayton has (worse, worse) weather than St. Louis?
13. I think its river is the (better, best) in the Midwest.
14. Which city has the (worse, worst) traffic of all?
15. I think winter is (worse, worst) in Omaha than in Minneapolis.
16. Is Lake Michigan the (better, best) lake of all for swimming?
17. Is swimming or jogging (better, best) exercise?
18. I think waterskiing is the (better, best) sport of all.
19. Is the pollution in one city (worse, worst) than the pollution in another?
20. Who can say if one city is (better, best) than another?

C. Write the sentence. Use the correct form of the adjective.

21. Neil is a ______ tourist than I am. (good)
22. He thinks that airports are the ______ places of all. (good)
23. These maps are the ______ maps I've seen. (bad)
24. I think driving is the ______ way to travel. (good)
25. Yohji says bus travel is ______ than train travel. (bad)

Extra Practice

Combining Sentences: Adjectives

A. Read each pair of sentences. Write the adjective in the second sentence that could be added to the first sentence.

1. Jason has a computer. The computer is new.
2. Its best feature is the hard drive. The hard drive is fast.
3. His sister downloads games. She chooses funny games.
4. Jason's friends write letters. Their letters are electronic.
5. The screen has colors. The colors are bright.
6. Tanya inserts a game. Her game is new.
7. She enjoys the action. The action is fast.
8. The game includes sound effects. The sound effects are loud.
9. Jason is writing a report. His report seems long.
10. He researches facts on the Internet. He finds interesting facts.

B. Combine each pair of sentences to form one sentence.

11. The computer game had characters. These characters were funny.
12. They swam in a river. The river was deep.
13. There were animals in the river. The animals looked hungry.
14. A hippopotamus was in the river. The animal was fat.
15. The best character wore a hat. His hat was tall.
16. One character carried a suitcase. He carried a large suitcase.
17. I watched the screen. The screen was colorful.
18. Jason played the game. Jason's game was fast-paced.
19. We totaled our score. Our score was high.
20. Tomorrow let's play my game. My game is new.

C. Think of an adjective to complete the second sentence in each pair. Then write one sentence for each pair.

21. Maggie has a computer. Her computer is ______.
22. The computer has a screen. The screen is ______.
23. It can play programs. The programs seem ______.
24. The computer has a printer. It is ______.
25. I don't like the keyboard. The keyboard is ______.

Letter Punctuation

A. Write these letter parts. Add the correct punctuation mark or capital letter.

1. March 3 2003
2. Dear Justin
3. yours truly,
4. Amarillo Texas
5. January 9 2001
6. love, Aunt Ellen
7. september 27, 2002
8. Dear Mr. Tyson
9. Santa Fe New Mexico
10. sincerely yours,

B. Rewrite this letter correctly. Add capital letters and commas where they are needed. There are ten mistakes.

11–20.

17 Forest Avenue
Austin Texas 78746
December 4 2002

dear Dr. Lewis

This month my family will be taking a trip to Tampa Florida. Our stops will include New Orleans Louisiana, and Mobile Alabama. We will return home on January 3 2003.

your friend
Matthew Day

C. Complete each letter part. Use capital letters and commas where needed.

21. ______ friend
22. ______ Texas 78746
23. ______ 8, 2001
24. ______ Uncle Ralph
25. Sincerely ______

Theme **Plan Ahead**

UNIT 5

Pronouns and Story Writing

In this unit you will learn about pronouns. You will also learn how to write a story. A story is a narrative that a writer creates with his or her imagination.

Science Link *Read the beginning of this story about a farmer to find out what problem he needs to solve and what he thinks is the solution.*

Returning from the market one day, Don Emicho was very surprised to find his alfalfa patch in a terrible mess. His little plants were all dug up, strewn about, and nibbled at.

"How strange," he said, deep in thought. "Who could have done this?"

He had to do something before the intruder ate up and destroyed his entire green field of alfalfa. Then he had an idea.

"I know, I know," he smiled, and he started making a trap out of sticks, twigs, and thorns.

from ***The Fox and the Guinea Pig*** by Mary Ann Newman

Thinking Like a Writer

Story In a story, the author describes a setting, telling where the story takes place. Reread the passage.

- What is the setting of this story? How is the setting important to the story?

Pronouns In order to avoid using the same nouns over and over, the author used pronouns in place of some of the nouns.

QUICK WRITE Which pronouns were used here? Which nouns do they replace?

Grammar

Pronouns

RULES

A pronoun is a word that takes the place of one or more nouns.

A pronoun must match the noun it refers to.

Pam is lost. She is lost.

The storm was frightening. It was frightening.

Pronouns can be singular or plural. Singular pronouns take the place of singular nouns. Plural pronouns replace plural nouns or a group of nouns.

Singular Pronouns	I, you, he, she, it, me, him, her
Plural Pronouns	we, you, they, us, them

Pronouns
In your journal, write how pronouns can add variety to your writing.

Guided Practice

Name the pronoun in each sentence.

EXAMPLE: When Pam was thirsty, she sipped some water.
she

1. While Pam was hiking, she met a friend.
2. Paul asked her for help.
3. The bike was broken, and it would not roll.
4. Paul and Pam worked together, and they fixed the bike.
5. "We can go down the trail together," Pam said.
6. "Do you know where the trail ends?" Paul asked.
7. "I have hiked this trail before," Pam replied.
8. Mr. Grinko was waiting for them back at camp.
9. Pam told him about the hike.
10. Paul said, "Pam helped me fix the bike."

REVIEW THE RULES

- A pronoun is a word that replaces one or more nouns. It should always match the noun it refers to.

Grammar

More Practice

A. Write each sentence. Draw a line under each pronoun.

11. As the hikers walked, they saw many kinds of plants.

12. Paul looked at the map when he stopped for a break.

13. "Where should we hike next?" asked Paul.

14. "I like the long trail," said Pam.

15. "Mr.Grinko can lead us to the cabin," said Liz.

B. Write each sentence, using a pronoun to replace the underlined words.

16. Mr. Grinko did not need a map for the hike.

17. Pam, Liz, and Tom walked single file.

18. " Tom, Liz, and I are hungry," said Pam.

19. Pam took the sandwiches out of the backpack.

20. The hikers ate the sandwiches and rested.

Handbook
page 538

C. Spiral Review **Write the paragraph. Underline each noun. Circle each pronoun. Draw an arrow from each pronoun to the noun it stands for.**

21–30. Ms. Cruz works at the Grand Canyon. She guides visitors along a steep trail. It leads to the bottom of the canyon.

Extra Practice, page 410.

Writing Activity A Diary Entry

Write a diary entry telling what you might see if you went to the mountains. Be sure to choose words that help describe what you see.
APPLY GRAMMAR: Include pronouns in your diary entry. Draw a box around each pronoun you use in your diary entry.

Grammar

Subject Pronouns

RULES

A subject pronoun is used as the subject of a sentence. It tells whom or what the sentence is about.

I like the Stars baseball players.

They work hard in every game.

A subject pronoun, like a subject noun, may be singular or plural.

Singular	I, you, he, she, it
Plural	we, you, they

Pronouns

Write how you know when to use a subject pronoun.

Guided Practice

Name the subject pronoun in each sentence.

EXAMPLE: You hit the baseball out of the park. *You*

1. I had trouble hitting the baseball.
2. We have a good coach, Ms. Briggs.
3. She helps our team with plays.
4. I learned to watch the ball carefully.
5. It sometimes comes quickly over home plate.
6. You can watch the game in the park on Saturday.
7. We will play the Bluebirds.
8. They have an excellent record this year.
9. I try to cheer up my friend Manny.
10. He had a sprained arm this year, and couldn't play.

REVIEW THE RULES

- A subject pronoun is used as the subject of a sentence.
- A subject pronoun can be singular or plural.

Grammar

More Practice

A. Write each sentence. Draw a line under the subject pronoun.

11. We will play the Wolves next week.

12. I will substitute for a missing player.

13. She has a broken arm.

14. You can help the coach plan plays against the Wolves.

15. They will have a hard time beating this team!

B. Write each pair of sentences. Complete the second sentence with the correct subject pronoun.

16. Tran and I wait. ______ will bat soon.

17. The Wolves have a run. ______ are ahead.

18. Joanna is at bat. ______ plans her swing.

19. Dad is in the crowd. ______ likes to watch the games.

20. Carla hits the ball. ______ flies over the fence.

Handbook
page 538

C. Spiral Review **Complete each sentence with a subject pronoun, an adjective, or the correct punctuation mark.**

The sun was out. What a (**21.** ______) day it was (**22.** ______) Matt and the rest of the baseball team members were nervous. (**23.** ______) were not used to playing in warm weather. It was always (**24.** ______) and rainy in their town. Matt had an idea. (**25.** ______) poured cold water on his teammates. Now they were ready to play!

Extra Practice, page 411.

Writing Activity A News Broadcast

Write a news broadcast about an athlete. Make certain to include specific details about the athlete's sport.

APPLY GRAMMAR: Include subject pronouns in your broadcast. Underline the subject pronouns.

Grammar

Object Pronouns

RULES

An object pronoun is a pronoun used in the predicate of a sentence.

An object pronoun may be used after an action verb.

Sasha greets her friends. Sasha greets them.

An object pronoun may also be used after a word such as *for*, *at*, *of*, *with*, or *to*.

Lucky looks for Sasha. Lucky looks for her.

Pronouns

In your journal, explain the difference between a subject pronoun and an object pronoun.

An object pronoun may never be used as the subject of a sentence. The following words are object pronouns:

Singular	*me, you, him, her, it*
Plural	*us, you, them*

Guided Practice

Name the object pronoun in each sentence.

EXAMPLE: Mom told us to play outside.
us

1. Lucky always runs away from us.
2. A dog trainer can help you.
3. People can teach a pet to stay near them.
4. Paolo says to Lucky, "Follow me."
5. The boy keeps a treat for her in one pocket.

REVIEW THE RULES

An object pronoun is a pronoun used after an action verb or after a word such as *for*, *at*, *of*, *with*, or *to*.

More Practice

A. Write each sentence. Underline the object pronoun.

6. Frisky will fetch a ball for you.
7. Anita and Sam throw him the ball.
8. The dog brings it back to the children.
9. Animals will do many things for us.
10. Trainers and owners can teach them tricks.

B. Write each sentence with the correct pronoun.

11. Katie called Skipper and threw two sticks for ______. (he, him)
12. The dog returned with ______ in his mouth. (they, them)
13. The dog bounded toward Katie and ______. (I, me)
14. Skipper gave the sticks to ______. (she, her)
15. The day was fun for the dog and ______. (we, us)

C. Spiral Review Write each sentence. Draw a line between the subject and predicate. Underline each noun. Above the noun, write a pronoun that could replace it.

16. Katie washes the dogs often.
17. The dogs are dirty and smelly.
18. Josh finds a brush.
19. The little boy helps Katie.
20. The dogs love the boy.

Extra Practice, page 412.

Writing Activity A Letter

Write a letter to a friend, telling him or her about something you did with a real or imaginary pet. Let your feelings about your pet come through in your writing.

APPLY GRAMMAR: In your letter, include object pronouns. Underline the object pronouns.

Handbook page 538

Grammar

Punctuation in Dialogue

RULES

Dialogue is the exact words spoken by the characters in a story.

Use quotation marks at the beginning and end of a person's exact words. Put the last quotation mark after the end punctuation mark.

Yusef said, "We're excited about our trip."

Begin a speaker's words with a capital letter.

Begin a new paragraph when a new person speaks.

"It's rainy today," complained Luke.

"Let's work a puzzle," answered Kit.

Punctuation in Dialogue

Why is it important to use quotation marks in dialogue? Write your ideas in your journal.

Do not use quotation marks when you do not use a speaker's exact words.

He told us, "I can't go."

He told us that he can't go.

Guided Practice

Write each sentence. Add quotation marks and capital letters.

EXAMPLE: Susan asked, where is the corner puzzle piece?
Susan asked, "Where is the corner puzzle piece?"

1. here is a piece with clouds on it, said Jaime.
2. Luke said, we have almost finished the border.
3. Ms. Herrera asked, are any pieces missing?
4. the puzzle is nearly finished! cried Luke.
5. Jaime asked, where is the last piece?

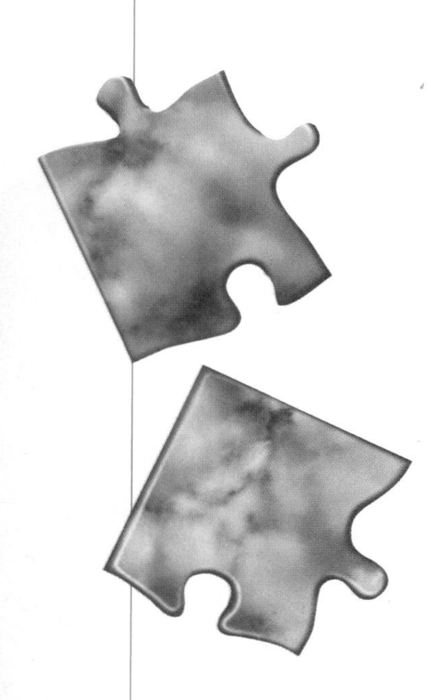

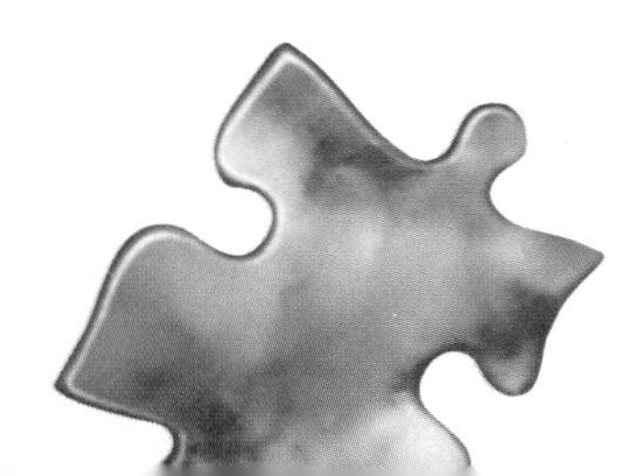

REVIEW THE RULES

- Quotation marks go at the beginning and end of a speaker's exact words.
- A speaker's words begin with a capital letter.
- A new paragraph begins when a new person speaks.

Grammar

More Practice

A. Write each sentence, adding quotation marks around each speaker's exact words.

6. Emily said, I think the puzzle shows a lighthouse.
7. What is that tower? asked Luke.
8. That is the roof of the lighthouse, replied Emily.
9. Does this piece fit in the corner? Kit asked.
10. Emily said, It's the wrong shape.

Handbook page 556

B. Write each sentence. Add quotation marks and capital letters. If a sentence is correct, write *correct* next to it.

11. Yusef said, here is a rebus puzzle I made up.
12. the pictures stand for parts of words, he explained.
13. He asked Maria if she could solve it. Correct
14. She replied, is that a pig or a dog?
15. Yusef said that he would revise the puzzle. Correct

C. Spiral Review **Write the dialogue correctly. Use quotation marks and capital letters. Correct end punctuation and run-on sentences. Begin a new paragraph for each speaker.**

16–25. "We should plan an activity for the next rainy day," says Luke then he turns to Susan. That's a good idea, answers Susan? "could we build a kite?" asks Luke. "We could make crossword puzzles says Emily.

Extra Practice, page 413.

Writing Activity A Conversation

Write a conversation between two friends discussing what they might do on a rainy day. Use different voices for each friend.

APPLY MECHANICS AND USAGE: Include correct dialogue punctuation in your story. Underline words placed inside quotation marks.

Mixed Review

REVIEW THE RULES

- A **pronoun** takes the place of one or more nouns.
- A **subject pronoun** is used as the subject of a sentence.
- An **object pronoun** follows an action verb or words such as *for*, *at*, *of*, *with*, and *to*.
- Use **quotation marks** at the beginning and end of a person's exact words. Put the last quotation mark after the end punctuation.
- Begin a speaker's words with a **capital letter**.
- Begin a **new paragraph** when a new person speaks.

QUICK WRITE

Pronouns

Write a dialogue between two friends. Include at least one subject or object pronoun in each sentence.

Practice

A. Write each sentence or pair of sentences. Use the correct subject or object pronoun in parentheses ( ).

1. My family and (I, me) visited New York City.
2. (We, Us) saw the Empire State Building.
3. New Yorkers ride the subway. (They, Them) also take taxis.
4. My cousins live in New York. I enjoy visiting (they, them).
5. Mom likes Broadway plays. (She, Her) and Dad have seen three this week!
6. Dad likes the parks. He has maps of (they, them).
7. My dad bought pretzels from a stand for (we, us).
8. (He, Him) and my brother had theirs with mustard.
9. Mom took Kevin and (me, I) to the art museum.
10. We bought (her, she) a poster there.

B. Write each sentence. Replace underlined words with the correct pronoun. Add quotation marks and capital letters where needed.

11. Mom said, let's go to Ellis Island.
12. "Ellis Island is where many immigrants arrived," she continued.
13. Grandpa came here with Grandma long ago, Mom told us.
14. "Grandma and Grandpa moved here with their older children," Mom said.
15. Mom was born in the United States, but her brother was not.
16. Life was different for her brother.
17. Now my family and I visit Grandma and Grandpa in New York every year.
18. "New York City holds many memories," Grandma said.
19. I told Grandma and Grandpa, Grandma and Grandpa always make us feel welcome.
20. Now we must say, we'll see you next year.

Handbook
pages 538, 556

C. Challenge Write the dialogue correctly. Replace any incorrect pronouns. Add quotation marks and capital letters where needed.

21–30. Where are we going?" I ask. Mom looks at my brother and I. She says, "we are visiting Grandma and Grandpa." "Do Grandma and Grandpa live on Ellis Island? I ask him. "No," Mom answers. "Them and your uncle live on Staten Island."

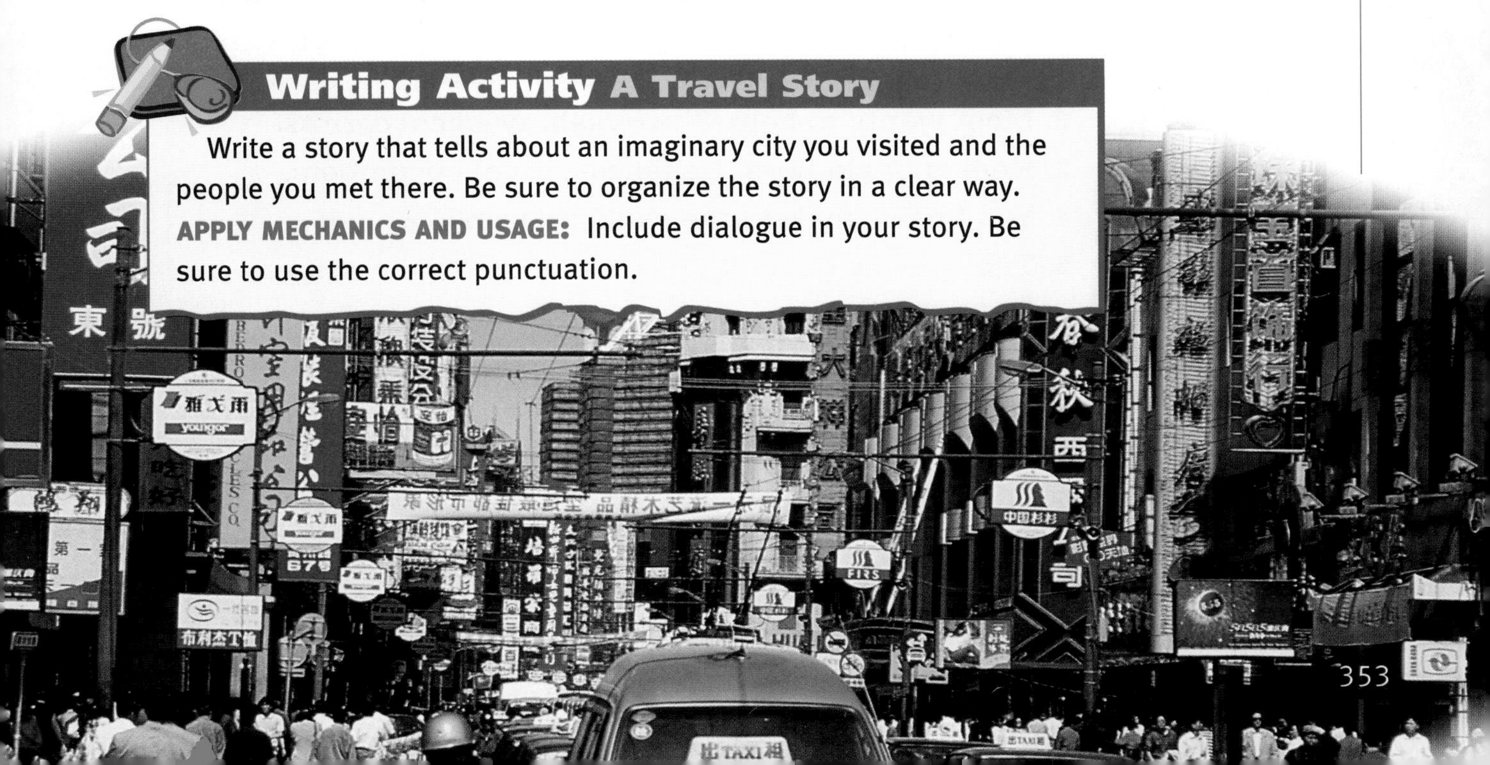

Writing Activity A Travel Story

Write a story that tells about an imaginary city you visited and the people you met there. Be sure to organize the story in a clear way.
APPLY MECHANICS AND USAGE: Include dialogue in your story. Be sure to use the correct punctuation.

Grammar

Pronoun-Verb Agreement

RULES

A present-tense verb must agree with its subject pronoun.

When using the pronouns *he*, *she*, and *it*, add *-s* or *-es* to most action verbs.

She eats a banana.

Do not add *-s* or *-es* to an action verb in the present tense when you use the pronouns *I*, *we*, *you*, and *they*.

We eat a cluster of grapes.

Pronoun-Verb Agreement

How does pronoun-verb agreement help make your writing clear? Write your ideas in your journal.

The subject and verb of a sentence must work together.

Subject	Verb
he, she, it	Add *-s* or *-es* to verb
I, we, you, and *they*	Do not add *-s* or *-es*

Guided Practice

Name the action verb that agrees with the subject pronoun in each sentence.

EXAMPLE: They (want, wants) to make dinner.
want

1. I (wants, want) to make a healthy meal.
2. Mom wants to help. She (wash, washes) carrots.
3. Here is Uncle Ross. He (slices, slice) cucumbers.
4. You (make, makes) the salad dressing.
5. The salad is done. It (look, looks) good!

REVIEW THE RULES

- With the pronoun *he*, *she*, or *it*, add *-s* or *-es* to most present-tense verbs. With *I*, *you*, *we*, or *they*, do not add *-s* or *-es*.

More Practice

A. Write the sentences. Choose the correct verb form.

6. Now we (starts, start) the noodles.
7. They (boil, boils) rapidly.
8. You (mash, mashes) the potatoes.
9. Sue comes to visit. She (watch, watches) us cook.
10. Where is Greg? He (loves, love) noodles.

B. Write each sentence. Write the correct present-tense form of the verb in each blank.

11. I ______ the meal. (serve)
12. It ______ so good! (smell)
13. We ______ for Greg to arrive. (wait)
14. He ______ us on the telephone. (call)
15. "You ______ without me," he says. (start)

C. Spiral Review **Write each sentence. Fix errors in verb forms. Add capital letters where they are needed.**

16. I loves italian spices.
17. they adds flavor to spaghetti sauce.
18. We prepares spaghetti for mr. campbell.
19. He visits us every saturday.
20. You prepares delicious spanish food.

Extra Practice, page 414.

Handbook
page 538

Writing Activity A Cooking Show

Write a scene from a cooking show. Tell your audience how you and your family make your favorite food. Present your ideas in a logical order.

APPLY GRAMMAR: Include sentences with subject pronouns. Be sure to use correct pronoun-verb agreement.

Grammar

Combining Sentences

RULES

You can **combine sentences** with similar ideas by joining two **pronouns**.

You can combine pronouns in the subject.

You and I need to make summer plans.

You can combine pronouns in the predicate.

Did Sue call him or her?

Combining Sentences

When would you want to combine two sentences by joining pronouns? Write your ideas in your journal.

Use the word *and* or *or* to join the pronouns in the subject or the predicate. Remember to use subject pronouns in the subject and object pronouns in the predicate.

She knocked on your door. / *I knocked on your door.* → *She and I knocked on your door.*

The dog will follow you. / *The dog will follow me.* → *The dog will follow you or me.*

Guided Practice

Combine each pair of sentences by joining two pronouns.

EXAMPLE: You are going to the fair. I am going to the fair.
You and I are going to the fair.

1. Did Tom invite you? Did Tom invite him?
2. She canned tomatoes. I canned tomatoes.
3. Did you see Ana? Did you see Felipe?
4. You want to ride the Ferris wheel. I want to ride the Ferris wheel, too.
5. The fair is exciting for you. The fair is exciting for me.

REVIEW THE RULES

- You can combine sentences by joining two subject or object pronouns.

Grammar

More Practice

A. Combine each pair of sentences into one sentence.

6. You groomed the horses. I groomed the horses.
7. Rico helped him. Rico helped me.
8. She brushed the dogs. I brushed the dogs.
9. Does the dog belong to you? Does the dog belong to them?
10. You asked me to clean up. He asked me to clean up.

B. Complete the second sentence with a pronoun. Then combine the two sentences.

11. Ned talks to you. Ned talks to ______.
12. The dogs like him. The dogs like ______.
13. You will wash the car. ______ will wash the car.
14. She will bring rags. ______ will bring rags.
15. Is this note for us? Is this note for ______?

Handbook
pages 529, 538

C. Spiral Review Combine each pair of sentences by forming a compound subject, a compound predicate, or a compound sentence.

16. They watch Yusef at bat. I watch Yusef at bat.
17. Mr. Tanaka stands. Mr. Tanaka cheers.
18. You forgot to watch the ball. I forgot to watch the ball.
19. Kenji steps to the plate. Sally pitches.
20. Kenji runs fast. Kenji reaches first base.

Extra Practice, page 415.

Writing Activity A Description

Write a short poem to describe a way you might stop boredom. Make sure to choose words that tell details.

APPLY GRAMMAR: Include subject and object pronouns. Circle the subject pronouns and draw one line under the object pronouns.

Grammar

Possessive Pronouns

RULES

A possessive pronoun takes the place of one or more possessive nouns.

Some possessive pronouns are used before nouns.

This is Keisha's brush.

This is her brush.

Some possessive pronouns can be used alone.

This brush is Keisha's.

This brush is hers.

Pronouns

When would you use a possessive pronoun? Write your ideas in your journal.

Like a possessive noun, a possessive pronoun tells who or what owns or has something.

Possessive pronouns before nouns		Possessive pronouns that stand alone	
my	its	mine	its
your	our	yours	ours
his	their	his	theirs
her		hers	

Guided Practice

Name the possessive pronoun in each sentence.

EXAMPLE: The children planned their projects.
their

1. Keisha drew the layout of her school.
2. Ted brought his drawing paper to school.
3. "Are these drawing pencils yours?" Ted asked Keisha.
4. "Yes, the pencils are mine," said Keisha.
5. "I brought my markers, too," said Ted.

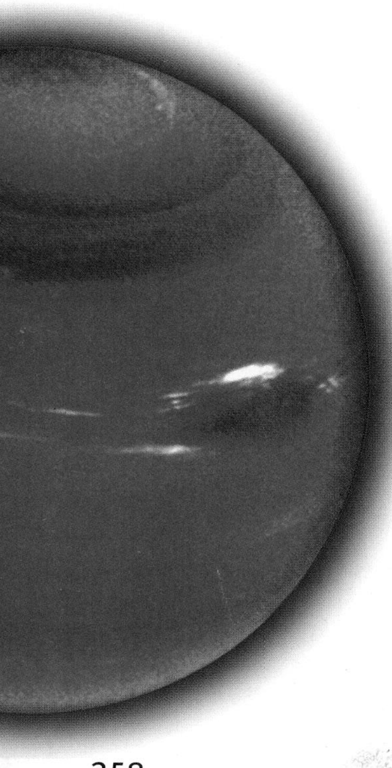

REVIEW THE RULES

- **Possessive pronouns replace possessive nouns.**
- **Some possessive pronouns are used before nouns. Others stand alone.**

More Practice

A. Write each sentence. Underline the possessive pronoun.

6. Keisha and Ted sat at their desks.
7. That bag of art supplies is his.
8. "Will you finish your drawing today?" asked Ted.
9. "Is that green pencil ours?" asked Keisha.
10. Keisha looked through her bag.

B. Write each sentence. Use a possessive pronoun in place of the underlined word or words.

11. That marker is Keisha's.
12. The marker's color is blue.
13. "Now we can finish Ted's and Keisha's artwork," said Ted.
14. "I am finished with Keisha's," said Keisha.
15. Those drawings are Ted's and Keisha's.

C. Spiral Review Write the sentences. Fix errors in possessive nouns, possessive pronouns, and adjective forms.

16. Keisha and Ted display theirs artwork.
17. "Your drawing is more better than mine,"says Keisha.
18. "I think yours is nicer than mine's," answers Ted.
19. Keishas picture shows a spring scene.
20. She drew the most prettiest flowers of all.

Extra Practice, page 416.

Writing Activity A Biography

Write a short biography of an imaginary alien from the planet Op. Make sure your choice of words helps describe the appearance and life of the alien you are writing about.

APPLY GRAMMAR: Include possessive pronouns in your biography. Circle each possessive pronoun that appears in the story.

Handbook
page 539

Grammar

Contractions: Pronouns and Verbs

RULES

A contraction is a shortened form of two words.

An apostrophe (') shows where letters are left out.

A contraction can be formed from a pronoun and a verb.

She is recycling. She's recycling.

THINK AND WRITE

Contractions

How do pronoun-verb contractions differ from possessive pronouns? Write your ideas in your journal.

Do not confuse the contractions *it's*, *they're*, and *you're* with the possessive pronouns *its*, *their*, and *your*.

Contraction	Meaning	Contraction	Meaning
I'm	I am	we're	we are
I've	I have	we've	we have
I'd	I had/would	we'd	we had/would
I'll	I will	you're	you are
he's	he is/has	you've	you have
it's	it is/has	you'll	you will
she'd	she had/would	they're	they are
he'll	he will	they've	they have
she'll	she will	they'll	they will

Guided Practice

Name the contraction that can be formed from the words.

EXAMPLE:

1. you will

2. we would

3. I had

4. I am

5. he has

REVIEW THE RULES

- A contraction can be formed from a pronoun and a verb.
- Do not confuse *it's*, *you're*, and *they're* with *its*, *your*, and *their*.

Grammar

More Practice

A. Write the sentences. Form contractions by combining the underlined words in each sentence.

6. We are learning ways to help Earth.
7. Claire said she would help me collect newspapers.
8. They have recycled their aluminum cans.
9. I will reuse these plastic bags.
10. We have helped Earth in a small way.

B. Write each sentence, using the correct word.

11. Our town has (it's/its) own recycling center.
12. (Their/They're) happy to help Earth.
13. (Your/You're) recycling center will open soon.
14. (Its/It's) fun to go to the recycling center.
15. (You're/Your) helping Earth by recycling.

C. Spiral Review **Write the paragraph. Fix errors in contractions and possessives. Add apostrophes where needed.**

16–20. Don't forget! Its important to recycle. Every week, take you're cans and bottles to the center. The mayors office can provide information. Your doing a great job!

Handbook
pages 538–539, 553

Extra Practice, page 417.

Writing Activity A Fable

Write a fable showing the importance of protecting Earth. Choose colorful words.

APPLY MECHANICS AND USAGE: Include pronoun-verb contractions in your fable. Underline the contractions.

Science Link

Grammar REVIEW

Mixed Review

REVIEW THE RULES

- A present-tense verb must agree with its subject pronoun.
- You can combine sentences with similar ideas by joining pronouns.
- A possessive pronoun shows who or what owns something and takes the place of one or more possessive nouns.
- A contraction is a shortened form of two words, such as a pronoun and a verb.
- Do not confuse the contractions *it's*, *they're*, and *you're* with the possessive pronouns *its*, *their*, and *your*.

Pronouns
Write a short letter to a friend. Use three contractions and three possessive pronouns.

Practice

A. Combine each pair of sentences by joining pronouns with *and* or *or*.

1. Rena wrote to you. Rena wrote to me.
2. You answered the letter. I answered the letter.
3. Her parents invited you. Her parents invited me.
4. She lived on a ranch. They lived on a ranch.
5. She rode horses. I rode horses.
6. There were enough horses for us. There were enough horses for them.
7. Rena's brother helped me. Rena's brother helped her.
8. You went camping. He went camping.
9. You thanked Carlos. I thanked Carlos.
10. They had a great time. We had a great time.

B. Write each sentence. Choose the correct word in parentheses ( ).

11. Ms. Johnson showed me (her/hers) horses.

12. She (send/sends) a postcard to Carlotta once a week.

13. Which horse is (your/yours)?

14. That horse is (my/mine) favorite one.

15. I (put/puts) the blanket on the horse's back.

16. (Its/It's) mane is long and silky.

17. The men are saddling (their/they're) horses.

18. (Their/They're) riding a long distance.

19. (We're/We'd) having a wonderful time.

20. (Its/It's) fun to visit a ranch.

C. Challenge Write the paragraph. Correct errors in possessive pronouns and contractions.

21–30. Jessica's family is taking a trip. Their sending e-mails to they're friends. Its fun to communicate by e-mail. Shell tell me about hers vacation. Id like to dream about mine's. Tell me where your going on you're vacation. Youll have a good time.

Grammar REVIEW

Handbook pages 538–539, 553

Writing Activity A Postcard

Create a postcard about a state you'd like to visit. On one side, draw a picture of something special about the state. On the other, write about what you would like to see there. Be sure to write in the "I" voice.

APPLY MECHANICS AND USAGE: Include an underlined pronoun-verb contraction in your postcard.

Social Studies Link

Common Errors with Pronouns

As a writer, you need to pay special attention to how you use different kinds of pronouns. Using the wrong kind of pronoun is a mistake that many writers make from time to time. This chart gives examples of errors to look for and shows how each can be corrected.

Common Errors	Examples	Corrected Sentences
Using an object pronoun as the subject of a sentence	Lauren and me went to the museum today.	Lauren and I went to the museum today.
Using a subject pronoun in the predicate of a sentence	Pedro came with Lauren and I.	Pedro came with Lauren and me.
Confusing contractions and possessive pronouns	We learned about China and it's rulers of long ago.	We learned about China and its rulers of long ago.

Pronouns

How can you tell when to use subject pronouns and object pronouns? Write your answer in your journal.

REVIEW THE RULES

PRONOUNS

- Use a subject pronoun (*I*, *you*, *he*, *she*, *it*, *we*, *they*) as the subject of a sentence.
- Use an object pronoun (*me*, *you*, *him*, *her*, *it*, *us*, *them*) after an action verb or after words such as *for*, *at*, *of*, *with*, or *to*.
- An apostrophe shows where one or more letters have been left out of a contraction of a pronoun and a verb. Possessive pronouns do not have apostrophes.

Practice

A. Write each sentence. Use the pronoun in parentheses ( ) that completes the sentence correctly.

1. The Chinese emperor's clay warriors amaze Lauren and (I, me).
2. The life-size soldiers were buried with (he, him).
3. (He, him) and his workers placed more than 8,000 figures in the pit.
4. Each statue has a different expression on (its, it's) face.
5. Lauren and (I, me) stare at the figures.

B. Write each sentence. Use a pronoun in place of the underlined words.

6. Pedro and Lauren look at the soldiers.
7. The soldiers and the horses are in the case.
8. The statue's hair looks braided.
9. "The emperor amazes Sarah," says Sarah.
10. We think about the statues and the emperor.

Handbook
pages 538–539

C. Write each sentence. Correct errors in subject, object, and possessive pronouns.

11. The museum planned the tour for my class and I.
12. Sally and me listened carefully to the guide.
13. The museum's displays and it's models were fascinating.
14. The tour gave our teacher and we a good understanding of China's culture.
15. Pedro and me want to visit China one day.

Grammar Troubleshooter, pages 518–519.

Writing Activity A Story

Imagine that you have traveled to a particular place and time in the past. Write a story telling about your experiences. Use precise words in your story.

APPLY GRAMMAR: Be sure to use subject pronouns and object pronouns correctly in your story. Do not include apostrophes in possessive pronouns.

Mechanics and Spelling

Directions

Read the passage and decide which type of mistake, if any, appears in each underlined section. Choose the letter for your answer. If there is no error, choose "No mistake."

Be sure that proper nouns are always capitalized.

When a one-syllable word ends in a vowel and a consonant, double the consonant before adding an ending that begins with a vowel.

Make sure a contraction has an apostrophe in the correct place.

Sample

Joy wanted to play basketball with <u>her brother, vernon, but he</u> (1) said she was too small. He went outside to join his friends at the neighborhood basketball court. In the middle of the game, someone ran <u>onto the court, grabed the ball</u> (2), and raced for the basket. It was a perfect shot! The boys were impressed. Vernon, however, was the most impressed. <u>He hadn't known that his little sister</u> (3) was a basketball star!

1 **A** Spelling
B Capitalization
C Punctuation
D No mistake

2 **F** Spelling
G Capitalization
H Punctuation
J No mistake

3 **A** Spelling
B Capitalization
C Punctuation
D No mistake

Test Tip
Be sure to select only one answer choice for each item.

Grammar and Usage

Directions

Read the passage and choose the word or group of words that belongs in each space. Choose the letter for your answer.

Sample

Spring is a wonderful time of the year. As the days __(1)__ longer, the air __(2)__ warms up. Snow and ice melt, and warmer weather moves in. The buds on the trees begin to appear. Flowers, like snowdrops and crocuses, pop up. The birds __(3)__ happily in the trees. Spring brings sights, sounds, and smells that change every day. That is why it is __(4)__ favorite season.

Decide whether an adjective or an adverb belongs here.

Make sure the verb tense fits with the rest of the sentence.

Select the verb that agrees with the subject of the sentence.

Some possessive pronouns are used before nouns, but some are used alone.

1 **A** grew
B were growing
C grow
D had grown

2 **F** slower
G slowly
H slow
J slowest

3 **A** sing
B sings
C is singing
D was singing

4 **F** I
G me
H my
J mine

TIME FOR KIDS Writer's Notebook

RESEARCH

RESEARCH

I use the **dictionary** every time I write. Sometimes I have to make sure a word I want to use means what I think it means. Other times, I need to check a word's spelling. The dictionary helps me be a better writer!

COMPOSITION SKILLS

WRITING WELL

Dialogue is conversation between characters in a story. It usually starts and ends with quotation marks. If I listen carefully to the way people talk, I can write dialogue that is natural and believable.

VOCABULARY SKILLS

USING WORDS

"I have a tear in my pants." "I cried a tear." Tear and tear are **homographs**: words that are spelled the same but have different meanings and are pronounced differently. Wait and weight are **homophones**. They are words that sound the same but are spelled differently. What homographs and homophones can you think of?

Read Now!

As you read about the work that emergency workers do, jot down any words that you don't understand and look them up in a dictionary.

TIME FOR KIDS

PHOTO ESSAY

TO THE RESCUE!

Emergency workers rush in to save lives after disaster strikes.

After an earthquake in Taiwan, a man is lifted to safety.

THE RESCUERS

Every day, throughout the world, specially trained men and women rush in to handle disasters on a moment's notice. Dealing with the results of earthquakes, fires, floods, and tornadoes is all in a day's work for these brave and tireless workers.

When disaster strikes, the rescuers get busy. They must leave the comfort of their own homes, often traveling across the world to help others. The rewards are the miracles they pull off. Just one example: In 1999, a 6-year-old boy was saved after being trapped under a pile of concrete for 87 hours!

"It's a lot of work and dedication," says Sonja Heritage, an emergency medical worker who has rescued earthquake victims. "You've got to love it to do it."

LIFE SAVERS: Sonja Heritage and Otto, a rescue dog, on the scene at an earthquake in Taiwan. Dogs are specially trained to sniff out humans who may be buried under piles of rubble.

EARTHQUAKE CLEAN UP: Rescue workers scale a collapsed building to search for signs of survivors.

Cover: Bobby Vip/Reuters; Rescue workers: Tom Szlukovenyi/Reuters; Rescue dog: Susan Walsh/AP

*inter*NET CONNECTION **Go to www.mhschool.com/language-arts for more information on the topic.**

Steve Helber/AP

WATER LIFE: After a flood, a U.S. Navy helicopter carried two people to safety in a special basket.

Torsten Blackwood/AFP

HELPING OUT: International Red Cross workers give out food to hungry people in war-torn East Timor, in Asia. The International Committee of the Red Cross (ICRC) is the oldest rescue group in the world. This organization does not take sides in a conflict. The ICRC helps victims of war, hunger, and disasters throughout the world.

Write Now!

Rescue workers have many stories to tell about people they have helped. Think about a time when someone needed your help and write about what you did to help that person.

Dictionary

You use a **dictionary** to find the meaning of a word. A dictionary also tells you how to spell a word and how to pronounce, or say, it.

- At the top of every dictionary page, you will see two **guide words**. The first guide word tells you the first word on that page. The second guide word tells you the last word.
- **Entry words** are all the words explained in a dictionary. They are listed in dark type in alphabetical order.
- A **pronunciation key** is usually found at the bottom of every other page in a dictionary. It shows you how to read the respelling, or pronunciation, of each entry word.

Example sentences show how the word is used.

Each definition, or meaning, of the word is numbered.

Pronunciation is shown in () and helps you sound out a word. How a word is divided into syllables is also shown.

The part of speech shows if a word is a noun, a verb, an adjective, or an adverb. Each form is correctly spelled.

consul / contemporary

consul A person appointed by a government to live in a foreign city: *A **consul** helps his or her country's citizens and business there.* **con•sul** (kon' səl) *noun, plural* **consuls.**

consult 1. To go to for advice or information: *We **consulted** a map to find out where we were.* 2. To talk together: *My teacher **consulted** with my parents.* **con•sult** (kən sult') *verb,* **consulted, consulting.—consultation** *noun.*

consultant A person who has a lot of expert knowledge of a profession or line of work and whose job is giving advice to others in that profession or line of work. **con•sul•tant** (kən sul' tnt) *noun, plural* **consultants.**

contain 1. To hold: *The jar **contains** candy.* 2. To include as a part of: *Candy **contains** sugar.* 3. To keep back or hold back: *I tried to **contain** my laughter when your chair tipped over.* **con•tain** (kən tān') *verb,* **contained, containing.**

contemporary 1. Belonging to the same time: *Abraham Lincoln and Robert E. Lee were **contemporary** figures.* 2. Modern; up-to-date: ***contemporary** furniture.* **con•tem•po•rar•y** (kən tem´ pə rer´ē) *adjective.*

at; āpe; fär; câre; end; mē; it; īce; pîerce; hot; ōld; sông; fôrk; oil; out; up; ūse; rüle; pu̇ll; tûrn; chin; sing; shop; thin; t͟his; hw in white; zh in treasure. The symbol ə stands for the unstressed vowel sound heard in about, taken, pencil, lemon, and circus.

Practice

A. Write *yes* if you will find the information in a dictionary. Write *no* if you will not.

1. The name and phone number of a doctor

2. The correct spelling of the plural form of a noun

3. How to say a word

4. The meanings of a word

5. The zip code of a city

B. Write the answer to these questions about the dictionary entries on the previous page.

6. Will you find the word *content* before or after this page in the dictionary?

7. What does the word *consult* mean in this sentence? *Consult a dictionary to find the meaning of a word.*

8. How many meanings does the word *contain* have?

9. Is the word *contemporary* a verb, an adverb, or an adjective?

10. How do you spell the past tense of the word *consult*?

C. Find the following words in the dictionary. Then write your own example sentence for each word.

11. above

12. medicine

13. examine

14. treatment

15. healthy

*inter***NET** CONNECTION

Go to: www.mhschool.com/language-arts for more information on the topic.

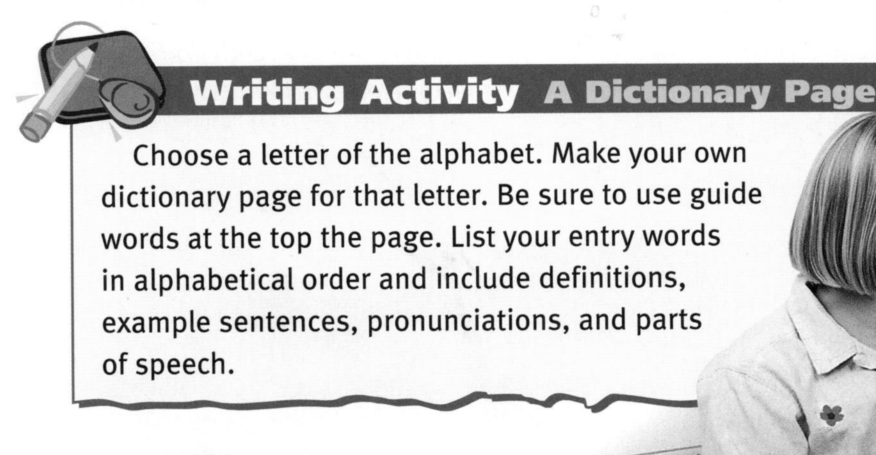

Writing Activity A Dictionary Page

Choose a letter of the alphabet. Make your own dictionary page for that letter. Be sure to use guide words at the top the page. List your entry words in alphabetical order and include definitions, example sentences, pronunciations, and parts of speech.

Build Skills

Vocabulary: Homophones and Homographs

Homophones and Homographs

How can you tell a homophone from a homograph? Write your answer in your journal.

DEFINITION

Homophones are words that sound alike but have different spellings and different meanings. **Homographs** are words that are spelled the same but have different meanings and often have different pronunciations.

Homophones		Homographs	
weak	(not strong)	bear	(large animal)
week	(seven days)	bear	(support; carry)
there	(in that place)	saw	(did see)
they're	(they are)	saw	(cutting tool)
wood	(substance from a tree)	wind	(moving air)
would	(is willing to)	wind	(turn)

Look at the highlighted words in the paragraph below. Which are homophones? Which are homographs?

*As Jake walked by, he **saw** Joan using a **saw**. Joan asked Jake if he **would** help her carry some **wood** into the house. By the time they were done, Jake was tired and **weak**. He felt as if he had been working for a **week**!*

Practice

A. Write each sentence. Underline the two words that are homophones or homographs. Write *homophones* or *homographs* to tell which they are.

1. "You're tired from your chores," said Jake.
2. I can't rest until the rest of the wood is cut.
3. Just then, they saw a bear near Joan's saw.
4. The bear ate eight apples from the tree.
5. We can scare the bear by rattling this can.

B. Write each sentence. Underline the homograph. Then write the correct meaning from the Word Bank.

wind (moving air)	**light (to illuminate)**	**sink (to fall or drop)**
wind (turn)	**light (soft sounding)**	**sink (a basin with drain)**
ride (to travel on)		**wave (motion with hand)**
ride (amusement park device)		**wave (swell on water)**

6. I've always wanted to ride on a horse.
7. The horse can smell other animals in the wind.
8. We watched him wave as he rode away.
9. You can go across that river; horses don't sink!
10. He delighted in the light clomping of the hooves.

C. **Grammar Link** **Write each pair of homophones. Underline the homophone that is a possessive pronoun. Then use both homophones in a sentence.**

11. your you're
12. there their
13. our hour
14. there's theirs
15. its it's

Writing Activity A Story

Write a story about an unusual animal you would like to own. What would you do together? Include homophones and homographs in your story.

APPLY GRAMMAR: Make certain that your verbs agree with any subject pronouns that you use.

Composition: Writing Dialogue

A writer includes dialogue in a story to make the story seem more real. When characters speak in their own words, we understand how they are feeling and what they are like.

GUIDELINES

- **Dialogue is conversation between two or more characters in a story. It tells the exact words the characters say.**
- **Put quotation marks around a character's exact words.**
- **Each time there is a new speaker, begin a new paragraph.**
- **Capitalize the first word in a quotation.**
- **Put the end punctuation inside the quotation.**
- **Always tell who is speaking by using words such as *said Nina* or *he explained*. If the speaker's name comes first, put a comma before the quotation.**

Writing Dialogue

Why is it a good idea to include dialogue in a story? Write your ideas in your journal.

Read this story. Notice how the writer uses dialogue to tell what the characters are thinking, feeling, and doing.

Once there was a seamstress who ran out of thread while making the queen's cloak. "Oh no! The cloak will not be done in time for the parade! I will be sent to the dungeon!" the seamstress cried.

"I can help you," said a tiny voice from the corner of the ceiling.

"Who are you?" asked the seamstress.

A little spider showed herself and began spinning beautiful thread for the seamstress. Now the cloak could be made and all would be well!

Quotation marks appear around the speaker's exact words.

A new paragraph shows there is a new speaker.

The writer shows who is speaking here.

Practice

A. Write each sentence. Underline the dialogue. Circle the name of the person who is speaking.

1. "Good morning, John!" said May the milkmaid.
2. "How do you do, May?" asked John the blacksmith.
3. May said, "I'm going to see the king's goose!"
4. "Has it laid a golden egg?" asked John.
5. "No, John," said May. "It laid a diamond egg!"

B. Rewrite each sentence using dialogue. Add quotation marks, and change the wording and punctuation as needed. Pay attention to the pronouns.

6. John said he wishes his goose would lay a diamond egg.
7. May asked him what he would do with the egg.
8. John said he would use it to buy new tools.
9. May asked John if that is all he would buy.
10. John said he would also buy May some cows.

C. Grammar Link Write each sentence. Correct the dialogue punctuation. Choose the correct pronoun in each sentence.

11. May blushed and said (You, Your) are so kind!
12. John replied (He, I) am not like the king.
13. Here's the goose! said May. What does (she, her) want?
14. (Me, I) am not happy said the goose.
15. They yelled Then come live with (we, us)!

Writing Activity A Conversation

Write a conversation between two people. Be sure to use quotation marks around dialogue, indent each new speaker's words, and tell who is speaking each time. Use different dialogue words to reveal the speaker's feelings.

APPLY GRAMMAR: Be certain that present-tense verbs agree with the subject pronouns in your conversation. Circle each subject pronoun and underline the verb that agrees with it.

Better Sentences

Directions

Read the passage. Some sections are underlined. The underlined sections may be one of the following:

- **Incomplete sentences**
- **Run-on sentences**
- **Correctly written sentences that should be combined**
- **Correctly written sentences that do not need to be rewritten**

Choose the best way to write each underlined section. If the underlined section needs no change, choose "No mistake."

Two sentences with the same predicate can usually be combined.

A comma alone cannot be used to join two sentences.

Sample

Daisy wanted to play in the snow. Juan wanted to play in the snow. **(1)** They put on their coats and ran outside. The two children lay down in the snow, they moved their arms and legs up and down. **(2)** When they got up, they saw that they had made beautiful snow angels!

1 **A** Daisy wanted to play in the snow, and Juan wanted to play in the snow.

B Daisy and Juan wanted to play in the snow.

C Daisy wanted to play in the snow. Juan also.

D No mistake

2 **F** The two children lay down in the snow. They moved their arms and legs up and down.

G The two children lay down in the snow they moved their arms and legs up and down.

H The two children lay down in the snow. And moved their arms and legs up and down.

J No mistake

Test Tip

Read directions two times to make sure that you understand the exercise.

Vocabulary and Comprehension

Directions

Read the passage. Then read each question that follows the passage. Decide which is the best answer to each question. Choose the letter for that answer.

Sample

"Happy birthday, Carla!" said Mr. Lucas. Smiling, he handed his daughter a beautifully wrapped gift.

Carla grinned excitedly as she unwrapped the present. "Oh, Daddy!" she exclaimed. "It's a beautiful dancing doll! How does it work? Will you show me?"

"Of course, I will," said Dad. "Bring it over here."

"I love her already," Carla said as she handed the beautiful dancing doll to her father.

"You need to wind the key," instructed Dad.

Carla wound a small key on the doll's back. The doll began dancing round and round on the floor. "Thanks, Dad!" said Carla. "This is the best gift ever!"

When you define a word, remember that homographs have different meanings.

1 The word *wind* in this story means—

A a breeze

B turn or twist

C breathe

D shake

2 How does Carla feel about her gift?

F She is disappointed.

G She dislikes it.

H She loves it.

J She feels it's useful.

Seeing Like a Writer

Place yourself in one of the pictures. What would you write to describe the time and place of this scene?

Celebración en Los Andes by Gonzalo Endara Crow

Writing from Pictures

1. Write two sentences about each picture. Describe what is happening. Use pronouns to refer to people.
2. Write a story about one of the pictures. Describe a problem a person has and how he or she solves it.
3. Choose two pictures. What would a character in one picture say to a character in the other picture? Write a dialogue.

   Apply Grammar: Use pronouns in your writing. Circle subject pronouns and underline object pronouns.

Story

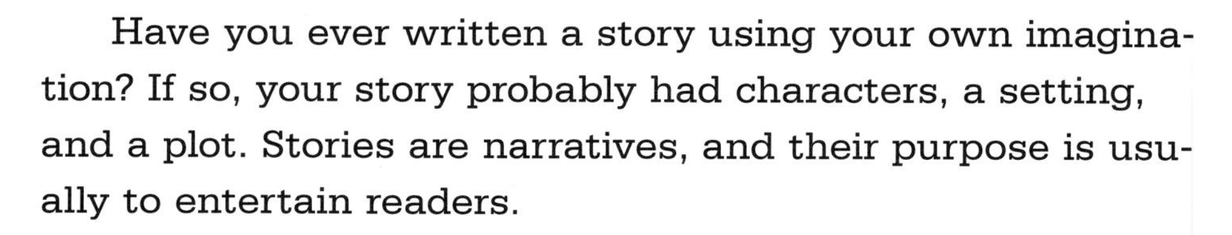

Have you ever written a story using your own imagination? If so, your story probably had characters, a setting, and a plot. Stories are narratives, and their purpose is usually to entertain readers.

Purpose

Why do you think people write stories? Write your response in your journal. Also tell why other people like to read them.

Learning from Writers

Read the following two stories. Who are the main characters? Where do the stories take place? Think about what happens in the stories and how the stories end.

Chandra and the Sick Elephants

Once upon a time a long time ago, a girl named Chandra lived in a small village in India. . . . One morning, the Rajah returned from a walk in the gardens to find Chandra at the gate, staring in at the elephants. "What are you doing here, Elephant Bather?" he asked.

"I worry about the elephants," she said. "I love them all and know them well. Maybe I can help them."

The Rajah thought for a moment. "Go ahead and try," he said. . . .

Chandra approached Misha, the Rajah's favorite elephant. She studied his feet: the nails, pads, the cuticles. She studied his tusks. . . .When Chandra got to the first ear, she discovered a painful-looking infection inside the ear canal. The other ear was the same. So were the ears of the other elephants. Chandra cleaned their ears, sang the elephants a soothing song, and went home.

At dawn the next day, when Chandra returned, the elephants. . . greeted her with joyful trumpeting.

The Rajah was overjoyed. He declared a festival day and invited everyone in the land to the palace.

—David Barry, from *The Rajah's Rice*

A Dream Come True

Happy Martinez always wanted a pony. Where he lived, in the Arizona desert, it seemed as if everyone had a pony.

One day, Happy saw a little pony stuck on the pathway down the canyon. A rock blocked its way, and it couldn't move up or down. Happy inched down the path, speaking quietly to the pony. When he reached the pony, he took off his belt and looped it around the pony's neck.

Happy and the pony walked up the path together. When they reached home, Dad came out to see them.

"Can I keep him?" begged Happy.

"Someone may call about him," said Dad. "If so, you will have to give him back." Weeks went by, and no one called. Dad said that Happy could have the pony.

"I will call him Dream," said Happy, "because he is my dream come true."

–Tommy Ortega

Practice and Apply

Thinking Like a Reader

1. Who are the main characters in "Chandra and the Sick Elephants"?
2. In "A Dream Come True," how does Happy rescue the pony?

Thinking Like a Writer

3. How does David Barry show that the elephants are cured?
4. What word does Tommy Ortega use to describe how Happy asked if he could keep the pony?

5. **Reading Across Texts** Compare the two literature models. Where does information about the setting appear in each story?

Features of a Story

DEFINITIONS AND FEATURES

A story is a narrative that a writer creates from his or her imagination. A good story:

- Has **characters** who are the people in a story.
- Has a **plot** with a problem that is solved at the end.
- Describes a **setting**, telling where and when the story takes place.
- Has an interesting **beginning**, **middle**, and **end**.
- Uses **dialogue words** that show how the characters are speaking.

Characters

Reread "Chandra and the Sick Elephants" on page 382. The actions and thoughts of characters make up a story. What does this sentence tell about Chandra's thoughts?

> "I worry about the elephants," she said. "I love them all and know them well. Maybe I can help them."

Chandra cares about the elephants and wants to aid them. The story is about how she helps the elephants.

Plot

Every story has a plot. The plot involves a problem that needs to be solved. In David Barry's story, the elephants are sick.

> Chandra cleaned their ears, sang the elephants a soothing song, and went home.

How does Chandra solve the problem?

▶ Setting

A story's setting is the time and place in which the action occurs. Details about the setting often help the reader create a picture in his or her mind.

> Once upon a time a long time ago, a girl named Chandra lived in a small village in India.

What is the setting of this story?

▶ Beginning, Middle, and End

The beginning of a story usually introduces the characters, the setting, and a problem. The middle tells the events that result from the problem. The ending solves the problem and concludes the story in a logical way.

> The Rajah was overjoyed. He declared a festival day and invited everyone in the land to the palace.

How does this paragraph end the story logically?

▶ Dialogue Words

Dialogue words show how the characters are speaking and how they feel. What dialogue word does the author use in this sentence?

> "What are you doing here, Elephant Bather?" he asked.

The author uses *asked* to show that the character has asked a question.

Practice and Apply

Create a Story Map

1. Reread "A Dream Come True" on page 383.
2. Draw a story map. List the title of the story, the setting, the characters, and the problem.
3. Then list each event separately.
4. At the bottom, write the solution to the problem.

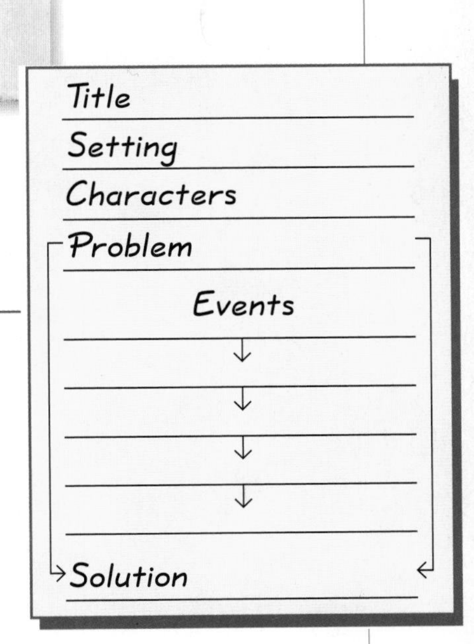

Writing PROCESS

Prewrite

A story is a form of writing that is created from the author's imagination. Writing a story gives you the opportunity to share your creativity and imagination with others.

Purpose and Audience

The purpose of writing a story is to entertain your audience. It is also a way to express your thoughts and ideas through a real or imaginary situation or topic.

Before writing, you need to think about your audience. Who will be reading your story? How will you make your story fun for your audience to read?

Audience

Who might read your story? Write about how you will create characters and events that will capture your reader's attention.

Choose a Topic

Begin by **brainstorming** a list of ideas or situations that might make an interesting plot, or story line. Remember that a good story should include a problem and show how that problem is solved.

After you have chosen the plot for your story, **explore ideas** by listing the events that will take place, as well as ideas for the characters and setting.

Girl and her aunt
Traveling by dog sled on a frozen lake
Saw something moving on the ice
Snowstorm was starting
Man took the rope
Man was holding onto hole in ice
Aunt tied rope to dog sled
Dogs pulled man from lake
Man thanked them
Man gave them bag of gold

Organize • Story Map

A story needs to have a clear beginning, middle, and end so that the audience can understand the events. To plan your story, you can use a story map. How did this writer use her story map to organize all the elements of her story?

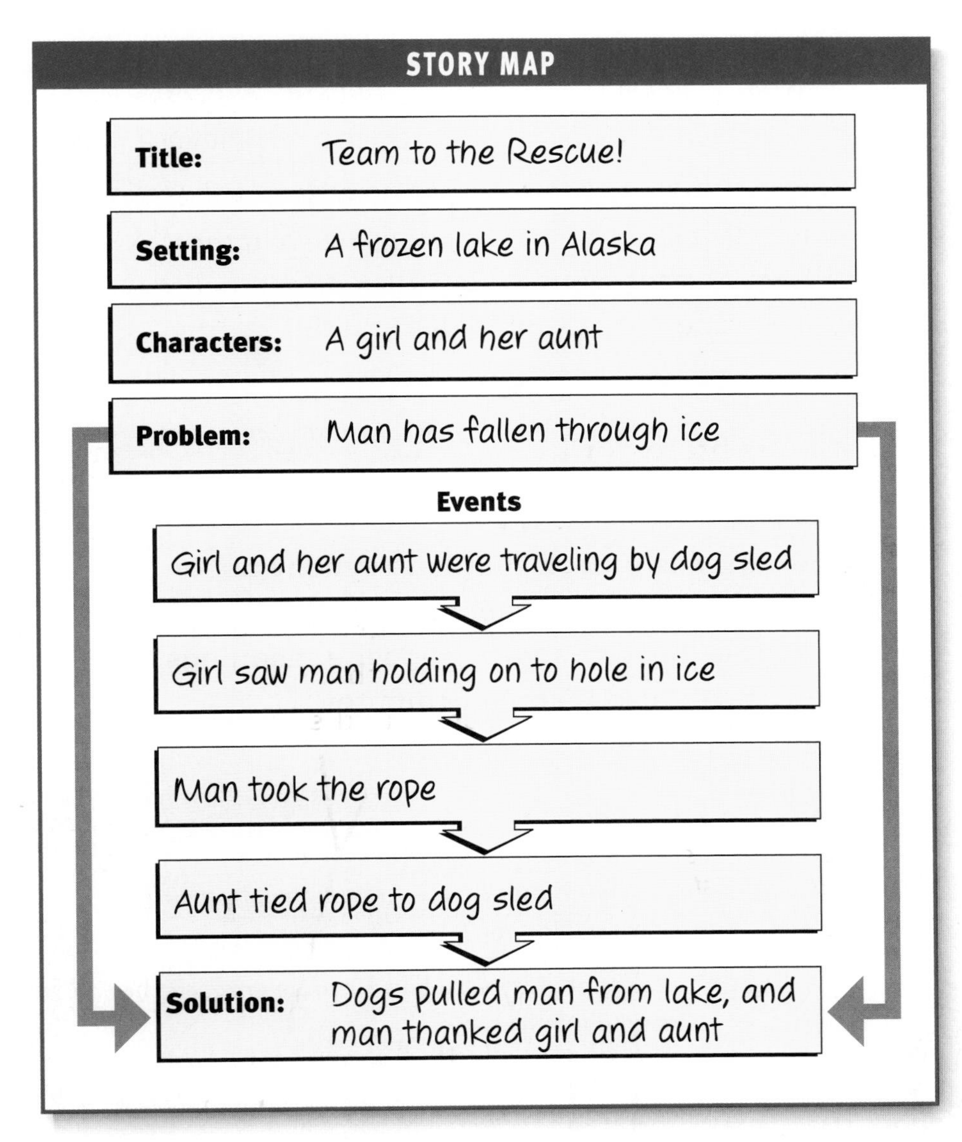

PREWRITE

DRAFT

REVISE

PROOFREAD

PUBLISH

Practice and Apply

Plan Your Own Story

1. Think about your purpose and audience.
2. Brainstorm ideas for the plot, characters, and setting.
3. Choose a plot idea and write more details.
4. Organize events into a beginning, a middle, and an end.

Checklist

Prewriting

- Have you thought about your purpose and audience?
- Have you listed story ideas from your imagination?
- Have you chosen a topic or situation and explored your ideas about it?
- Have you selected an interesting setting and characters?
- Are your ideas organized in a chart?
- Do you need to do any research?

Prewrite • Research and Inquiry

Writer's Resources

You may wish to do research to make your story more entertaining and realistic. Make a list of questions and decide what resources may help you answer them.

What Else Do I Need to Know?	Where Can I Find the Information?
Is there a more precise word for took I can use?	Look up take in a thesaurus.
Can I use the word mushing to mean "traveling by dog sled"?	Look up mush in the dictionary.

Study a Thesaurus

A thesaurus is a book that lists synonyms, or words with the same or similar meanings. It also lists antonyms, or words with opposite meanings. A thesaurus can also be on a computer.

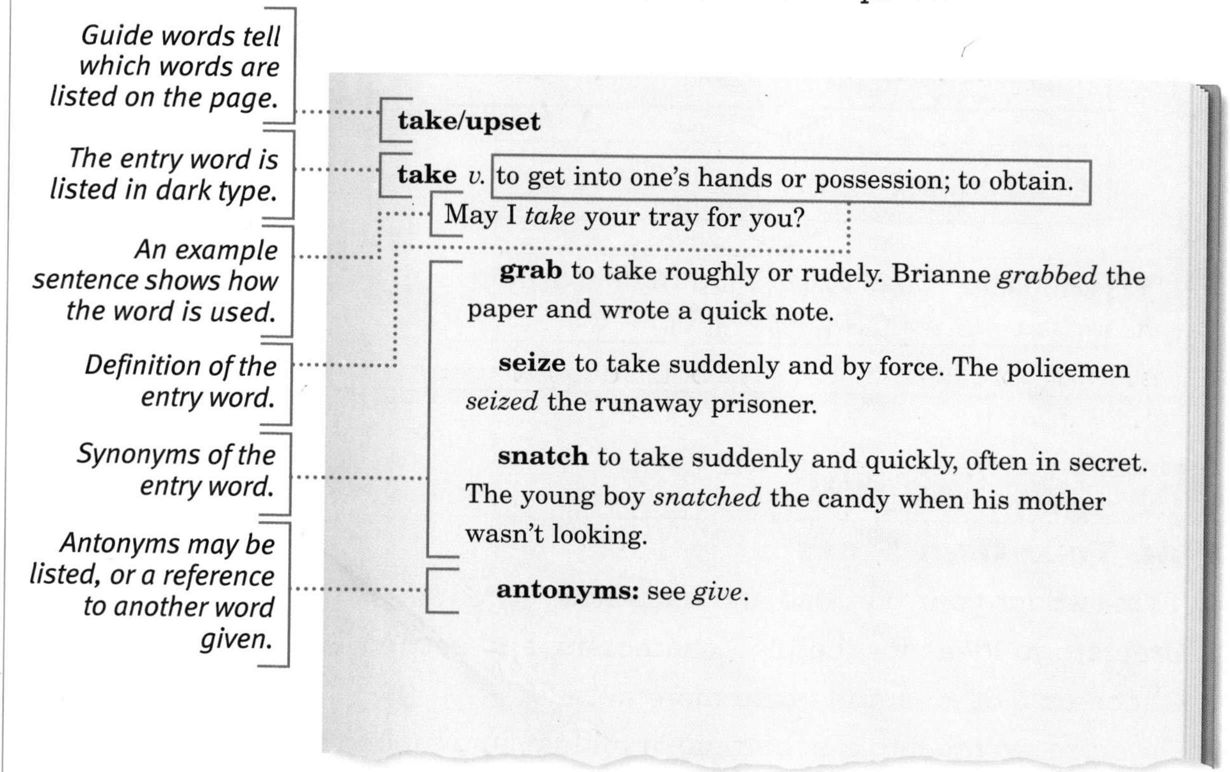

▶ Use a Dictionary

A dictionary lists words in alphabetical order. In each listing, you will find the pronunciation of the word, as well as one or more definitions, example sentences, and parts of speech. You can use a dictionary to make sure you are using words correctly and to check their spelling.

▶ Use Your Research

The new information that you gathered from your research can be added to your story map. How did this writer use information from a dictionary and a thesaurus to change her story map?

PREWRITE
DRAFT
REVISE
PROOFREAD
PUBLISH

Handbook
page 570–571

Checklist

Research and Inquiry

- Did you make a list of questions?
- Did you find the resources you need?
- Did you note all your findings?

Practice and Apply

Review Your Plan

1. Review your story map.
2. List questions you may have about ideas or words in your story.
3. Identify the resources you will need to find answers to your questions.
4. Add the information you gather to your story map.

Writing PROCESS

Draft

Before you begin writing your story, look over the chart you created. Think how you will arrange the parts of the story into paragraphs. Remember to give your story a clear beginning, middle, and end.

STORY MAP

Title: Team to the Rescue!

Setting: A frozen lake in Alaska

Characters: A girl and her aunt

Problem: Man has fallen through ice

Events

Girl and her aunt were ~~traveling by dog sled~~ mushing across a frozen lake

Girl saw man holding on to hole in ice

Man ~~took~~ grabbed the rope

Aunt tied rope to dog sled

Solution: Dogs pulled man from lake, and man thanked girl and aunt

Main idea of first paragraph: characters and setting

Events are organized in sequence. This could contain dialogue.

Conclusion: how the problem is solved

Checklist

Drafting

- Does your story fit your purpose and audience?
- Have you included interesting characters for your story?
- Have you described the setting?
- Does your plot have a clear beginning, middle, and end?
- Does your story include a problem that is solved?

Look at how the writer used ideas from her chart to write a first draft. She added more information about the characters and setting in the first paragraph. She elaborated on the plot by adding details about the events and including dialogue.

DRAFT

Team to the Rescue!

Beth and her Aunt Sue were mushing across a frozen lake. There wasnt much daylight left, and Beth wanted to get back to camp before dark. She was tired. Sue was tired.

Main idea of first paragraph

Supporting details about characters and setting

All of a sudden, Beth saw something moving on the ice. She shouted, pointing ahead. They saw a man holding on to the edge of a hole in the ice.

Main idea of second paragraph: the problem

The man grabbed the rope, and Aunt Sue tied the other end to the sled. Then she said, pull!

The dogs barked and pulled hard. Beth gripped the reins. The team pulled the man free just as the ice split open. "Your safe now, Beth said. "Thank you!" the man said.

Main idea of last paragraph: the solution

TECHNOLOGY

Find out how to adjust line spacing on your computer. It's a good idea to double-space your draft so that you will leave more room to make corrections.

Practice and Apply

Draft Your Own Story

1. Review your story map.
2. Include an imaginative plot and interesting details.
3. Tell more about the characters and setting.
4. Create a clear beginning, middle, and end.

Writing PROCESS

Revise

Elaborate

One way to improve your writing is to elaborate. When you elaborate, you add important ideas and details that might be missing from your writing. When you revise your story, you may want to give more information about the action and the characters to help readers feel as if they are part of the story.

The writer added details to tell the reader more about the setting.

> One cold winter afternoon,
> ^Beth and her Aunt Sue were mushing across a
> in Alaska
> frozen lake^.

The writer added more dialogue to tell a character's exact words.

> "Look, Aunt Sue!"
> ^She shouted, pointing ahead.

Word Choice

When you are writing, be sure to choose words that will help you tell an interesting and vivid story.

In a story, you need to select words that will help readers understand the feelings, thoughts, and reactions of characters when they speak.

> exclaimed gasped
> "Your safe now, Beth ^~~said.~~ "Thank you!" the man ^~~said.~~

DIALOGUE WORDS

- replied
- responded
- cried
- shouted
- whispered
- asked
- gasped
- exclaimed
- begged
- chuckled
- pleaded

Better Sentences

While continuing to revise your draft, review your sentences to make certain they work well together. Read the sentences aloud. Do the ideas in the story flow smoothly from one to another? Do the sentences vary in length and in structure?

Sometimes you can combine two sentences to help the flow and rhythm of your story. Leave out words that repeat.

She was tired.
Sue was tired.
→ She and Sue were tired.

Handbook
page 529

Practice and Apply

Revise Your Own Story

1. Provide specific details that show what the characters do.
2. Use dialogue to make your story characters come alive.
3. Choose dialogue words to show the characters' feelings and thoughts.
4. **Grammar** Combine or change sentences to make them clearer and easier to understand.

TECHNOLOGY

Review your draft for logical order. Do the ideas flow smoothly? If not, try moving paragraphs or sentences around by cutting and pasting text.

Revise • Peer Conferencing

Step back from the story you are writing. Ask a partner to read a copy of your first draft. In exchange, you can read your partner's story. This way, both of you can offer new ideas about each other's work.

Team to the Rescue!

Beth and her Aunt Sue were mushing across a frozen lake. There wasnt much daylight left, and Beth wanted to get back to camp before dark. She was tired. Sue was tired.

> This beginning makes me want to read more!

All of a sudden, Beth saw something moving on the ice. She shouted, pointing ahead. They saw a man holding on to the edge of a hole in the ice.

The man grabbed the rope, and Aunt Sue tied the other end to the sled. Then she said, pull!

> The plot isn't clear here. You need to add more details.

The dogs barked and pulled hard. Beth gripped the reins. The team pulled the man free just as the ice split open. "Your safe now, Beth said. "Thank you!" the man said.

> Can you make the ending more interesting? Maybe you could add more dialogue.

Conferencing for the Reader

- **Are features of a story included in your partner's piece?**
  - **interesting beginning, middle, and end**
  - **characters**
  - **a plot with a problem to be solved**
  - **a setting**
  - **dialogue**
- **Be certain to tell your partner strong points about the piece, as well as what needs some work.**

Review the comments your conferencing partner made about your story. As you revise your story, think about how to address the comments. This writer made some changes based on her partner's ideas.

REVISE

Team to the Rescue!

One cold winter afternoon,
^Beth and her Aunt Sue were mushing across a
in Alaska
frozen lake^. There wasnt much daylight left, and
and
Beth wanted to get back to camp before dark. She^
were
~~was tired~~. Sue^ ~~was~~ tired.

All of a sudden, Beth saw something moving on
"Look, Aunt Sue!" When they got closer,
the ice.^ ~~S~~he shouted, pointing ahead.^ ~~T~~hey saw a
clinging
man ~~holding on~~^ to the edge of a hole in the ice.
Aunt Sue slid a thick rope across the ice.
^The man grabbed the rope, and Aunt Sue tied
cried
the other end to the sled. Then she ~~said~~^, pull!

The dogs barked and pulled hard. Beth gripped
the reins. The team pulled the man free just as the
exclaimed
ice split open. "Your safe now, Beth^ ~~said~~. "Thank you!"
gasped
the man^ ~~said~~. ^"You saved my life!"

PRACTICE AND APPLY

Revise Your Own Story

1. Read your draft aloud or have your partner read it to you. Listen carefully to how it sounds.
2. Take notes from your partner's comments.
3. Use the notes from your peer conference to help make your draft better.

Checklist

Revising

- Does your story suit your purpose and audience?
- Did you use interesting dialogue words?
- Did you use words that provide readers with a clear picture of the setting?
- Did you create a plot with a beginning, a middle, and an end?
- Did you read sentences aloud to see if they are easy to understand?

Writing PROCESS

Proofread

After revising your story, you will need to proofread it to find and correct any errors in spelling, mechanics and usage, or grammar.

STRATEGIES FOR PROOFREADING

- Reread your revised story, looking for one different kind of error at a time. That way, you will be more likely to catch all the errors.
- Check for spelling errors by starting at the bottom of your story and moving up from right to left. This will help you concentrate on spelling rather than on the story itself.
- Check for the correct use of apostrophes and quotation marks. Apostrophes are needed in contractions, and quotation marks in dialogue.

TECHNOLOGY

A spell-checker will not point out words that have been left out of a sentence. It's important to use the spell-checker and read over your work yourself. Read carefully to be sure you do not "see" words that are not there!

REVIEW THE RULES

GRAMMAR

- A possessive pronoun replaces one or more possessive nouns. Be careful not to confuse possessive pronouns with contractions that combine a pronoun and a verb.

MECHANICS

- An apostrophe shows where a letter or letters have been left out of a contraction.
- Use quotation marks at the beginning and end of a person's exact words.
- Begin a speaker's words with a capital letter.
- Start a new paragraph for each new speaker.

Look at the proofreading corrections made on the draft below. What does the symbol # mean? Why does the writer need to start a separate paragraph here?

PREWRITE

DRAFT

REVISE

PROOFREAD

PUBLISH

PROOFREAD

Team to the Rescue!

One cold winter afternoon, Beth and her Aunt Sue were mushing across a frozen lake in Alaska. There wasn't much daylight left, and Beth wanted to get back to camp before dark. She and Sue were tired.

All of a sudden, Beth saw something moving on the ice. "Look, Aunt Sue!" she shouted, pointing ahead. When they got closer, they saw a man clinging to the edge of a hole in the ice. Aunt Sue slid a thick rope across the ice. The man grabbed the rope, and Aunt Sue tied the other end to the sled. Then she cried, "Pull!"

The dogs barked and pulled hard. Beth gripped the reins. The team pulled the man free just as the ice split open. "You're safe now," Beth exclaimed.

"Thank you!" the man gasped. "You saved my life!"

Checklist

Proofreading

- Did you make sure all words are spelled correctly?
- Did you write possessive pronouns and contractions correctly?
- Did you use quotation marks around a speaker's exact words?
- Did you write dialogue correctly?

Practice and Apply

Proofread Your Own Story

1. Correct spelling mistakes.
2. Check to be sure you haven't confused pronouns with contractions.
3. Make sure you have used apostrophes correctly.
4. Include correct punctuation for dialogue.

PROOFREADING MARKS

- # new paragraph
- ^ add
- take out
- ≡ Make a capital letter.
- / Make a small letter.
- (sp) Check the spelling.
- ⊙ Add a period.

Publish

Before publishing your story, review it one last time. A checklist such as the one below will be helpful.

Self-Check Story

- ❑ **Did I consider the purpose for my story?**
- ❑ **Did I think about my audience as I wrote? Will my audience find the story entertaining?**
- ❑ **Did I give details about the characters in my story?**
- ❑ **Did I create a plot with a clear beginning, middle, and end?**
- ❑ **Did I include and describe an interesting setting?**
- ❑ **Did I use dialogue words to vary the characters' responses?**
- ❑ **Did I include dialogue and write it correctly?**
- ❑ **Did I make sure my sentences flowed smoothly? Did I combine sentences when necessary?**
- ❑ **Did I proofread and correct all my errors?**

The writer used the checklist while reviewing her story one last time. Read "Team to the Rescue!" and talk with a partner about the story. Do you think that the story was ready to be published? Why or why not?

PREWRITE
DRAFT
REVISE
PROOFREAD
PUBLISH

Team to the Rescue!

by Jessica Peters

One cold winter afternoon, Beth and her Aunt Sue were mushing across a frozen lake in Alaska. There wasn't much daylight left, and Beth wanted to get back to camp before dark. She and Sue were tired.

All of a sudden, Beth saw something moving on the ice. "Look, Aunt Sue!" she shouted, pointing ahead. When they got closer, they saw a man clinging to the edge of a hole in the ice.

Aunt Sue slid a thick rope across the ice. The man grabbed the rope, and Aunt Sue tied the other end to the sled. Then she cried, "Pull!"

The dogs barked and pulled hard. Beth gripped the reins. The team pulled the man free just as the ice split open. "You're safe now," Beth exclaimed.

"Thank you!" the man gasped. "You saved my life!"

Handwriting

Leave the same amount of space between each pair of words. This helps to make the line easier to read.

Practice and Apply

Publish Your Own Story

1. Check your revised story one more time.
2. Make a neat, final copy.
3. Add illustrations or an appropriate background drawing.

LISTENING
SPEAKING
VIEWING
REPRESENTING

Present Your Story

To present your story in the best way possible, it is good to plan first. There are several things you can do to make sure your presentation is successful.

STEP 1

How to Tell Your Story

Suggestions for Speaking As you plan how to act out your story, remember that your purpose is to entertain the listeners. You will want to present your story so that the audience will be "on the edge of their seats."

- Speak slowly and in a clear voice so that your audience can hear you.
- Change your voice when characters speak.
- Use body movements and gestures to add interest and suspense to your story.

Listening Strategies

- Set a purpose: Are you listening to be informed or entertained?
- Try to picture the characters and events in your mind.
- Listen for details of plot and setting.
- Pay close attention to dialogue spoken by the characters. What do you learn about the characters when you hear them "speak"?
- Let the speaker know you are paying attention by focusing your eyes on her or him.

Multimedia Ideas

You may wish to make a video recording of your presentation. Set up the video camera in an appropriate place before you read and ask a partner or teacher to videotape you reading your story.

STEP 2

How to Show Your Story

Suggestions for Visuals Visuals can make your presentation more entertaining.

- Hang up a large drawing that represents your setting, or display photos or slides of the setting.
- Include your drawings of the characters so that your audience sees them as you do.
- Volunteers can pantomime the story as you read it aloud, or they can read the characters' words.

STEP 3

How to Share Your Story

Strategies for Rehearsing You will feel more comfortable on the day of your presentation if you have given yourself plenty of time to practice.

- Practice in front of a family member or a friend.
- Tape-record yourself telling the story. Review where your reading is strong and where it needs help.
- If classmates are participating in your presentation, help them prepare beforehand.

Practice and Apply

Present Your Own Story

1. Speak slowly and clearly, and refer to your notes.
2. Provide visual aids such as photographs or illustrations.
3. Practice reading your story aloud in front of friends and family members.
4. Present your story, coordinating your spoken words with your visuals.

TIP!

Viewing Strategies

- Sit where you can see any visuals the speaker displays.
- Think about how the visuals connect to the story being told.
- Look carefully at the visuals for details that can add to the story.

Writing Tests

On a writing test, you are required to write a composition in response to a prompt. Remember to read the prompt carefully. Look for key words and phrases that describe the topic of your composition and explain how you should present your ideas.

Are there words in the prompt that name the audience? Look for clues.

Look for words that tell you the purpose of your writing.

Prompt

Imagine that one summer morning a brother and sister step outside to find that everything is covered with snow.

Write a story about what might happen if there were a snowstorm in the summer.

This phrase tells you the setting of your story.

How to Read a Prompt

Purpose Read the prompt again. Look for words that tell you the purpose of the writing. The words "Write a story" and the subject of the story let you know that you are writing to entertain.

Audience A prompt often tells you who your audience is. If it does not, think of your audience as your teacher.

Writing a Story When you write a story, you use your imagination to think of a plot, characters, and a setting. The phrases "a brother and sister" and "a snowstorm in the summer" tell you who your main characters are and what your setting should be.

Test Tip
Leave yourself enough time to check your work.

How to Write to a Prompt

Here are some tips to remember when you are given a prompt on a writing test.

Before Writing **Content/Ideas**	• Think about your purpose. • Keep your audience in mind. • Make a list of your ideas. Then choose the best ones to include in your writing. • Stay focused on your subject.
During Writing **Organization/ Paragraph Structure**	• Give your writing an interesting beginning. • If you are writing a story, check that the events in the plot are in a logical order. • Use details in a story to give a clear picture of the setting and characters. • Use dialogue to bring your characters to life.
After Writing **Grammar/Usage**	• Proofread your work. • Make sure that verbs agree with pronouns. • Use the correct punctuation in dialogue. • Check the spelling of all words.

Apply What You Learned

When you read a prompt on a writing test, always determine your purpose and audience. Think about the best way to organize your ideas.

Prompt

You are taking care of a friend's pet rabbit while she is on vacation. One morning you leave the cage door open, and the rabbit gets out. It takes you the entire day to find him.

Write a story about where the rabbit goes and how you finally get him back.

Unit 5 Review

Grammar and Writing Review

pages 344–345

Pronouns

A. Write each sentence. Underline the pronoun or pronouns.

1. She is Jarod's new dog, Patches.
2. Jarod loves to play with her.
3. He throws a ball for Patches.
4. It flies across the yard.
5. "You can get it!" Jarod calls.

pages 346–347

Subject Pronouns

B. Write each sentence. Use a subject pronoun to replace the underlined words.

6. <u>Betty</u> is going on a hike with her friend.
7. <u>Betty and her friend</u> are very good hikers.
8. <u>The friends</u> will hike to the base of a nearby mountain.
9. <u>The mountain</u> is beautiful.
10. <u>Betty, her friend, and I</u> will take pictures.

pages 348–349

Object Pronouns

C. Write each sentence. Use the correct pronoun in parentheses ( ).

11. Mr. Smith asks ______ to paint a mural. (we, us)
12. Our art class asks ______ many questions about the mural. (he, him)
13. Mr. Smith tells ______ to paint a school scene. (us, we)
14. Then Mr. Smith turns to ______. (I, me)
15. "The walls are waiting. What will you put on ______ ?" Mr. Smith asks. (they, them)
16. I smile but do not tell ______. (he, him)
17. I see Sarah and watch ______. (her, she)
18. "I am painting ______!" she says, pointing to the squirrels outside. (they, them)
19. I turn to the wall and start painting ______. (him, it)
20. "Look, Mr. Smith! I'm painting ______!" I say. (you, we)

pages 350–351

Punctuation in Dialogue

D. Write each sentence. Place quotation marks around the speaker's exact words.

21. Hi, Lisa, says Rick. Look at my new puppy!

22. He is so cute! Can I teach him a trick? asks Lisa.

23. Yes, Rick replies. But he already knows a trick.

24. What trick is that? Lisa asks.

25. He can make food disappear! laughs Rick.

pages 354–355

Pronoun-Verb Agreement

E. Write each sentence. Underline the pronoun. Then choose the verb in parentheses ( ) that agrees with the pronoun.

26. Mom and Dad say they (want, wants) pizza tonight.

27. I (am, are) in the mood for tacos.

28. My sister Ruth says she (crave, craves) Chinese food.

29. It (get, gets) close to dinnertime.

30. We (disagree, disagrees) about our choice of restaurant.

31. I (feel, feels) hungry.

32. Finally, Mom smiles because she (has, have) an idea.

33. "You (have, has) five dollars each," she says.

34. Then we (drive, drives) to the grocery store.

35. Ruth and I select what we (want, wants)!

Unit 5 Review

pages 356–357

Combining Sentences:

F. Combine each pair of sentences to form a single sentence.

36. You ride horses in the summer. I ride horses in the summer.

37. She swims in the summer. He swims in the summer.

38. I play soccer in the fall with her. I play soccer in the fall with him.

39. We wear costumes in the fall. They wear costumes in the fall.

40. We build snowmen in the winter with you. We build snowmen in the winter with them.

41. You garden in the spring. She gardens in the spring.

42. We plant flowers with you. We plant flowers with them.

43. He smells the summer flowers. I smell the summer flowers.

44. You have fun all year. I have fun all year.

45. Everyone is proud of us. Everyone is proud of them.

Possessive Pronouns

pages 358–359

G. Write each sentence. Choose the correct possessive pronoun.

46. Mr. O'Brien takes (his, her) family on a trip.

47. Mrs. O'Brien brings (his, her) camera along.

48. Carl and Dan bring (our, their) cameras, too.

49. "Let me take (your, our) picture now," Carl says to (her, his) parents.

50. "I'm glad you took (our, his) picture," Mr. O'Brien comments.

Contractions: Pronouns and Verbs

pages 360–361

H. Write the sentences. Write a contraction for the words in parentheses ( ). Circle any possessive pronouns.

51. (We are) going to visit our friends in the country.

52. (They are) excited to show us their farm.

53. When we get there, (I am) happy to see my friend.

54. "Your farm is amazing! (You are) so lucky to live here!" I say.

55. "(It is) a great place to live," our friends agree.

Unit 5 Review

pages 374–375

Vocabulary: Homophones and Homographs

I. Write each sentence. Underline the words that look or sound alike. Next to each sentence, write whether the words are homophones or homographs.

56. They're on their way to see a concert.

57. "You're going to hear your favorite music," Dan says.

58. "And the ticket fare is very fair!" says Gina.

59. "The show is starting! Let's show our support!" says Dan.

60. The two concert lovers are thrilled to hear the music!

pages 376–377

Composition: Writing Dialogue

J. Rewrite each sentence using dialogue. Add quotation marks, and change the wording and punctuation as needed.

61. Jacob asked me what movie I wanted to see.

62. I said that I really didn't care this time.

63. Jacob said he wanted to see the new monster movie.

64. I told him I was afraid that movie would be too scary.

65. Jacob agreed and suggested we see the basketball movie.

pages 386–401

Proofreading a Story

K. Write the following paragraphs. Correct the nine mistakes in punctuation, capitalization, grammar, and spelling.

One morning I woke up and came downstairs for brekfast as usual. But when I got to the kitchen, I new something was wrong. My mother and little sister had turned into rabbits! Mom brought me a bowl of carrots. Sue kept wiggling her nose. What were I going to do? I decided to call my uncle. "Hello," I said. Something strange is going on at my house.

Uncle Harry responded, "Sniff! Sniff!"

"Oh, no," I screamed. Uncle Harry is a rabbit, too."

I decided I better go look at myself in the bathroom mirror. I was walking toward the bathroom when I herd my alarm go off. I realized they had all been a Dream!

Project File

ACTIVITY 1 A Research Report

A research report focuses on a subject and gives factual details about it. Facts should come from more than one resource. A research report should include all the features shown below.

You will need to know how a research report is written before you make your own.

The Mighty Mount Everest
by Theo McCauley

Title Tells what the report is about.

Mount Everest is the tallest mountain in the world. At 29,028 feet, it is taller than any other mountain on Earth. Because of its incredible height, people have always wanted to scale it.

Introduction Tells the subject and the main idea of the report.

Mount Everest, which stands on the border between the countries of Nepal and Tibet, is part of the Himalaya Mountains. Teams from England started climbing it in 1852, but for many years no one could reach the top. More than a century later, Edmund Hillary from New Zealand and Tenzing Norgay from Nepal finally reached the mountain's highest point on May 29, 1953.

Body Gives facts and details from different sources.

Since then, people have tried to climb Mount Everest almost every year. For those looking for adventure, it is a big challenge—maybe the biggest challenge on Earth.

Conclusion Brings the report to a close by summarizing important points.

Write a Research Report Is there a mountain or a forest near your home? What do you know about this place? What would you like to find out? Explore a place that interests you by gathering information and writing a research report. Your school librarian can help you look for facts. Look at the model on page 408 to make sure you make a good research report.

ACTIVITY 2

A Realistic Story

Rescue workers like Sonja Heritage travel around the world to help others during a natural disaster. Choose a recent natural disaster, such as a famous earthquake or flood, and do research to find out about the event.

To the Rescue! Write a story about an imaginary rescue mission that took place during the event you researched. Include in your story a rescue worker, a rescued victim, and realistic descriptions of the setting and event based on your research. Draw an illustration to help readers envision your story.

Extra Practice

Pronouns

A. Write each sentence. Draw a line under the pronouns.

1. Matt was on vacation and he went to stay in the country.
2. He will stay with Mr. and Mrs. Wilson for two weeks.
3. The Wilsons own a farm, and it is very large.
4. Matt thought he would have a terrific time.
5. Matt was pleased that the Wilsons showed him around the farm.
6. Matt met the neighbors, and they were very friendly.
7. One girl's name is Joanna, and she is nine years old.
8. The boy is Matt's age, and he is called Andrew.
9. "I am happy to meet you," said Matt.
10. They walked to the barn to feed the animals.

B. Write each sentence. Replace the underlined words with the correct pronouns.

11. Joanna proudly showed Matt her horse.
12. Andrew asked Matt about horses.
13. Andrew and Joanna carried hay to the livestock.
14. Joanna showed the boys the horses' stalls.
15. "I wish my family and I had a horse at home," said Matt.
16. "Please come and ride anytime with Joanna and me," said Andrew.
17. Matt realized there was a lot to do in the country.
18. He knew he would love the farm.
19. The boys both learned to ride that summer.
20. Matt became great friends with Joanna and Andrew.

C. Write each pair of sentences. Circle the pronoun. Draw one line under the noun or nouns the pronoun refers to.

21. The Wilsons have a garden. They grow many vegetables.
22. Matt tasted fresh corn. He announced it was delicious.
23. A rabbit had found the lettuce. It had nibbled the leaves.
24. Matt told Mr. and Mrs. Wilson, "We could build a fence."
25. The fence will keep a rabbit out. It will protect the garden.

Subject Pronouns

A. Write the subject pronoun in each sentence.

1. I take dance lessons with my friend Kate.
2. We have a great dance teacher named Mr. Jackson.
3. He is a famous tap dancer.
4. Kate and I met Mr. Jackson's sister, Mary.
5. She is a famous tap dancer, too.
6. Sometimes they dance as a team.
7. We love watching Mr. Jackson and Mary tap!
8. You should come see them, too.
9. Kate and I cannot dance that well.
10. We will have to practice.

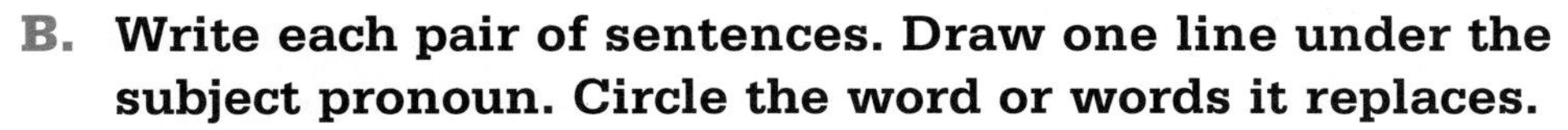

B. Write each pair of sentences. Draw one line under the subject pronoun. Circle the word or words it replaces.

11. Tony dances with Kate. He is a good partner.
12. Kate and I stretch. We are ready to perform.
13. Mr. Jackson starts the show. He tells about the dancers.
14. The dance looks great. It is going to surprise Mr. Jackson.
15. Mr. Jackson is pleased. He cheers and pats us on the back.
16. "Tony, keep practicing. You will be ready soon," said Mr. Jackson.
17. Kate and I practice for a week. We look very good.
18. The dancers and I are ready to perform. We tell our parents about the show.
19. Our parents are excited. They cannot wait to see the dance.
20. The performance goes smoothly. It is a success.

C. Write each pair of sentences. Complete the second sentence with the correct subject pronoun.

21. Kate is nervous. ______ needs my comfort.
22. Kate and I listen. ______ hear Mr. Jackson talking.
23. Mr. Jackson starts the show. ______ tells about the dancers.
24. Our parents sit in the front row. ______ all smile.
25. The dance is finally done. ______ was a lot of fun.

Grammar

Extra Practice

Object Pronouns

A. Write the object pronoun in each sentence.

1. Leah handed me an interesting rock.
2. The rock had black and gold specks in it.
3. Leah asked me if I noticed what the specks were.
4. I told her that I had to find out.
5. Our teacher can explain the specks to us.
6. The specks are minerals, and a volcano formed them.
7. I will show you a chart of how rocks form.
8. The chart shows me that volcanic rocks cool quickly or slowly.
9. Rocks that cool quickly have tiny crystals in them.
10. Rocks that cool slowly have large crystals easily seen by us.

B. Rewrite each sentence, replacing the underlined word or words with an object pronoun.

11. Leah and I asked Jake to go rock hunting.
12. We looked carefully for the rocks in a nearby field.
13. Jake showed a piece of granite to Leah and me.
14. Leah pointed to the crystals.
15. I showed Jake a bumpy round rock.
16. Jake cracked the rock open for Leah.
17. The inside of the rock looked like diamonds to Jake and me.
18. The rock fascinates Jake.
19. I showed Leah another interesting stone.
20. This stone had an imprint of a leaf on the stone.

C. Write the sentences. Complete each sentence with the correct pronoun.

21. Leah showed (me, I) the rock under the magnifying glass.
22. I pointed out the fine crystals to Leah and (he, him).
23. My dad asked (she, her) if he could see the crystals.
24. Leah allowed (he, him) to look at the rock.
25. My dad told (we, us) that he found our rock fascinating.

Punctuation in Dialogue

A. Write each sentence. Draw one line under the part of each sentence that is a quotation.

1. "It rains a lot in Portland, Oregon," says Sally.
2. "Rain helps all the roses grow," says Tom.
3. "That is why it is called the City of Roses!" exclaims Sally.
4. Tom says, "It snows a lot on Mt. Hood."
5. "I can see Mt. Hood from the Rose Gardens," points out Sally.
6. "We can also see the Willamette River," says Tom.
7. "Let's count the bridges on the river," suggests Sally.
8. Tom counts out loud: "One, two, three, four...."
9. "I count six bridges," says Sally.
10. "I wish I knew what they were called," says Tom.

B. Write each sentence correctly. Add quotation marks around each speaker's exact words.

11. Where is the main library? asked Sally.
12. Tom answered, It is in downtown Portland.
13. What an old building that is! said Sally.
14. My great-grandmother was born on this street, said Tom.
15. Portland must be an old city, remarked Sally.
16. Tom said, Many people first came here in wagons.
17. The bridges were not here then, said Sally.
18. I forgot, Tom cried. We need to find the bridges' names.
19. Sally replied, Let's look for a book on bridges in the library.
20. This book says the Fremont Bridge is the tallest one, said Tom.

C. Write each sentence correctly. Add quotation marks and capital letters.

21. Sally says, the red one is called the Broadway Bridge.
22. the one with the train track is the Steel Bridge, says Tom.
23. Sally asks, what is the bridge in the middle called?
24. Tom answers, that one is the Burnside Bridge.
25. portland has more bridges than raindrops! exclaims Sally.

Grammar

Extra Practice

Pronoun-Verb Agreement

A. Write each sentence or pair of sentences. Draw one line under the subject pronoun. Draw a circle around the verb that agrees with it.

1. I start to write a story.
2. It begins with a female wolf.
3. She lives in the distant mountains.
4. Her pups are tired. They sleep in a cave.
5. One pup wakes up. He yawns.
6. A blackbird is chirping. It sits in a tree.
7. A rabbit looks up suddenly. It runs into a hole.
8. Three deer are grazing. They eat the tender grass.
9. The pup is soon lost. He searches for the trail home.
10. The sky fills with heavy clouds. It becomes dark.

B. Write each sentence. Choose the correct verb.

11. The moon is full, and it (shine, shines) in the sky.
12. I (write, writes) more about the cub.
13. He (finds, find) a path in the woods.
14. It (lead, leads) to a meadow.
15. The pup sees a wolf. She (howls, howl) at the moon.
16. He comes closer. They (watches, watch) each other.
17. "You (is, are) not my mom!" says the pup.
18. "But I know her. She (is, am) on that cliff," says the wolf.
19. "She (searches, search) for you," adds the wolf.
20. The pup howls to his mom. She (run, runs) to get him.

C. Write each sentence. Write the correct present-tense form of the verb in parentheses ( ).

21. "I ______ you are okay!" says the mother wolf. (see)
22. "I ______ to go home," says the pup. (want)
23. The wolf and her pup thank the other wolf. Then they ______ home. (return)
24. The pup sees his sisters. He _____ about his adventure. (tell)
25. I ______ the story with a happy ending. (finish)

Combining Sentences

A. Underline the pronouns in each sentence. Circle the word that connects them.

1. You and I want to make puppets.
2. She and he want to use clay for the heads.
3. She or I will bring the clay.
4. Ms. Arroyo, the art teacher, talks to you and him.
5. You and he ask Ms. Arroyo for clay and fabric.
6. Other students ask her or me to share our art supplies.
7. Ms. Arroyo gives us and them beads and feathers.
8. You and they make puppets from the supplies.
9. He and I create a dragon puppet.
10. Ms. Arroyo asks you or her to create a play.

B. Write each pair of sentences below as one sentence by combining pronouns.

11. You thought of ideas for the play. I thought of ideas for the play.
12. He chose the puppets. I chose the puppets.
13. Students gave him a name. Students gave her a name.
14. He called this puppet Sir Jack. She called this puppet Sir Jack.
15. She named this puppet Lady Lily. I named this puppet Lady Lily.
16. You said Lady Lily saves Sir Jack. I said Lady Lily saves Sir Jack.
17. Lady Lily amazed us. Lady Lily amazed them.
18. They asked about Sir Jack. I asked about Sir Jack.
19. He would not free Sir Jack. She would not free Sir Jack.
20. Lady Lily recognized him. Lady Lily recognized them.

C. Write each pair of sentences as one sentence by filling in a pronoun in the second sentence, and by combining the pronouns.

21. Ms. Arroyo talked to you. Ms. Arroyo talked to ______.
22. You told her Lady Lily frees Sir Jack. ______ told her Lady Lily frees Sir Jack.
23. Ms. Arroyo told us to begin. Ms. Arroyo told ______ to begin.
24. Ms. Arroyo clapped for her. Ms. Arroyo clapped for ______.
25. You enjoyed this class. ______ enjoyed this class.

Extra Practice

Possessive Pronouns

A. Write the possessive pronoun in each sentence.

1. I take notes for my science report.
2. Pete writes his report about the green heron.
3. Anna, have you chosen a topic for your report yet?
4. I will write mine about the barn owl.
5. Both birds have their own way of hunting.
6. The green heron uses bait to fish for its prey.
7. The barn owl uses its sense of hearing to find prey.
8. I think our reports will be the most interesting of all.
9. The heron picks up a leaf or twig in its beak.
10. He takes his place on a rock overlooking the water.

B. Write each sentence. Choose the correct possessive pronoun in parentheses ( ).

11. As fish swim by, the heron watches (their, theirs) movements.
12. The heron uses (his, their) leaf like a fishing lure.
13. The fish thinks the leaf is (its, mine) next meal.
14. The heron is thinking that the fish will be (his, theirs).
15. The bird quickly grabs the fish and tilts (his, yours) head upward.
16. All herons swallow (their, theirs) meals headfirst.
17. Barn owls catch (their, its) prey at night.
18. (Their, Theirs) faces are cup-shaped with ears near the eyes.
19. The shape of (its, yours) face helps the owl catch the sounds of moving prey.
20. Barn owls hunt rodents in (our, ours) fields.

C. Write each sentence. Use a possessive pronoun in place of the underlined word or words.

21. I have finished <u>my report</u>.
22. Pete says, "These facts will have <u>the students'</u> attention."
23. <u>Our friend Anna's</u> report needs a few more facts.
24. The photographs on the desk are <u>Anna's</u>.
25. Pete will use them in <u>Pete's</u> report.

Contractions: Pronouns and Verbs

A. Write the pronoun-verb contraction in each sentence.

1. We're learning about pollution at school.
2. We've discovered there are many ways to help Earth.
3. I'll carpool with my friends to baseball practice.
4. She's convinced her dad to take the train.
5. I'm going to ride my bike to school.
6. He's careful to place trash in a trash can.
7. They're going to pick up paper and cans by the lake.
8. Lisa and Samuel say that they'll make posters for school.
9. The posters tell others that they're to help clean up the school.
10. I'll start recycling bottles and cans at my house.

B. Write each sentence. Form contractions by combining the pronoun and verb in each sentence.

11. They are recycling cans and bottles at school.
12. We have thought of other ways to recycle.
13. It is a good idea to use old things again.
14. We will have a rummage sale here at the school.
15. Do you think you would have items to donate?
16. She will donate many stuffed animals.
17. He will give away the old games he used to play.
18. They have set up many tables to sell the items.
19. We have made a lot of money selling our unwanted things.
20. They are all things that could have ended up in a landfill.

C. Write each sentence. Choose the correct word to complete each sentence.

21. (Your, You're) helping clean up Earth by reusing items.
22. (Their, They're) happy to donate the money to charity.
23. (Its, It's) good to reduce the amount of trash we make.
24. (Their, They're) going to start recycling paper at school.
25. (You're, Your) invited to help us keep the school clean.

Dodgers
Dodgers 4
Dodgers 3
Dodgers 1
Dodgers 4

UNIT 6

Adverbs, Prepositions, and Expository Writing

In this unit you will learn about adverbs and prepositions. You will also learn about how to write an expository piece. Expository writing gives facts and information about a topic.

Social Studies Link *Read about how baseball and America changed the day Jackie Robinson was asked to join the Brooklyn Dodgers. Robinson broke through the color barrier that had prevented African Americans from playing in the major leagues—a major turning point in our nation's history.*

The general manager of the Brooklyn Dodgers baseball team was a man by the name of Branch Rickey. He was not afraid of change. He wanted to treat the Dodger fans to the best players he could find, regardless of the color of their skin. He thought segregation was unfair and wanted to give everyone, regardless of race or creed, an opportunity to compete equally on ballfields across America.

To do this, the Dodgers needed one special man.

from ***Teammates*** by Peter Golenbock

Thinking Like a Writer

Expository Writing In expository writing, the author presents information about a topic in an organized way.

- Who does the author give information about in this passage? What information does he give?

Adverbs An adverb is a word that tells more about a verb. Many adverbs end with *-ly*

QUICK WRITE Reread the passage. Find the adverb the author used. What verb does it tell more about?

Grammar

Adverbs That Tell *How*

RULES

An adverb is a word that tells more about a verb. Most adverbs are formed by adding *-ly* to an adjective.
Some adverbs tell *how* an action takes place.

Tracy eagerly attends softball practice.

Adverbs can be placed in different positions in a sentence. Many adverbs that tell *how* end in *-ly*.

Tracy ran.
- *Tracy ran quickly to the base.*
- *Tracy slowly ran to the base.*
- *Tracy ran to the base joyfully.*

THINK AND WRITE

Adverbs

Write two questions that can help you identify adverbs.

Guided Practice

Tell which word is the adverb in each sentence. Then identify the verb that it describes.

EXAMPLE: The team played poorly.
adverb: poorly; verb: played

1. The team waited anxiously for the game.
2. Tracy accidentally dropped the ball.
3. The other team's batter hit the ball perfectly.
4. Laura clumsily tripped on her way to third.
5. Pam missed the catch completely.
6. Our opponents cheered wildly.
7. Coach Sherwin calmly spoke to the team.
8. He patted Laura gently on the back.
9. We suddenly realized we could win!
10. We excitedly raced onto the field.

REVIEW THE RULES

- An adverb tells more about a verb.
- Some adverbs tell *how* an action is done.
- Adverbs that tell *how* often end with *-ly*.

Grammar

More Practice

A. Write each sentence. Circle each adverb. Draw a line under the verb that the adverb describes.

11. The player quickly threw the ball.

12. The pitcher's bad throw hit Ann solidly.

13. The runner slid safely into home plate.

14. "You are playing wonderfully, Tracy!" yelled Mom.

15. Tracy easily scored a run.

B. Write each sentence. Complete the sentence with an adverb. Circle the verb that the adverb describes.

16. The coach ______ cheered the players on.

17. Mary's dad ______ shared his bag of peanuts.

18. Laura pitched ______.

19. Tracy swung the bat ______.

20. Pam ______ threw the ball to first base.

C. Spiral Review Write each sentence. Fill in the part of speech.

21. The players cheerfully ______ onto the field. (verb)

22. The pitcher ______ raised her arms. (adverb)

23. ______ tossed the ball in the air. (pronoun)

24. The batter ______ watched the ball. (adverb)

25. The runners ______ in a heap on home plate! (verb)

Extra Practice, page 490.

Handbook page 540

Writing Activity An Article

Write an article about a championship game. Choose words to help you vividly describe the game, the players, and their skills.
APPLY GRAMMAR: Include adverbs to make your writing clearer.

Grammar

Adverbs That Tell *When* or *Where*

RULES

An adverb is a word that tells more about a verb. Some adverbs tell *when* or *where* an action takes place.

The science fair begins tomorrow. (when)

The science fair takes place outside. (where)

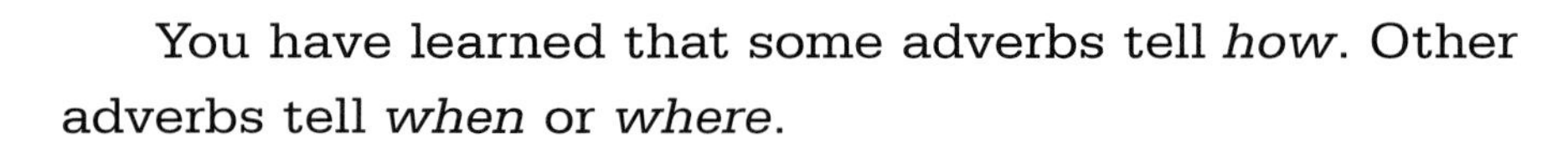

You have learned that some adverbs tell *how*. Other adverbs tell *when* or *where*.

THINK AND WRITE

Adverbs

How can you decide if a word is an adverb? Write your answer in your journal.

When		Where	
first	soon	there	ahead
always	early	outside	around
next	today	up	far
finally	then	here	inside
tomorrow	yesterday	nearby	everywhere

Guided Practice

Name the adverb in each sentence. Tell whether the adverb tells *when* or *where*.

EXAMPLE: Adan looked outside.
outside; tells *where*

1. Adan always liked space.
2. Yesterday he visited the planetarium.
3. Adan walked inside.
4. Adan saw stars everywhere!
5. He soon decided on a science project.

REVIEW THE RULES

- An **adverb** tells more about a verb. Some adverbs tell *when* or *where* an action takes place.

More Practice

A. Write each sentence. Draw a line under the adverb. Then write whether the adverb tells *when* or *where.*

6. Adan started his work early.
7. First, he painted posters with constellations.
8. He scattered stars around.
9. Next, Adan prepared his telescope.
10. He kept his telescope nearby.

B. Write each sentence. Draw a line under the adverb. Then, write whether the adverb tells *how, when,* or *where*.

11. Adan worked excitedly.
12. Finally, he finished his project.
13. Adan quickly arranged his booth.
14. He set up his telescope there.
15. Then, the exhibit was ready.

C. Spiral Review Write each sentence. Fill in the missing part of speech in parentheses.

16. Everyone ______ the science fair. (verb)
17. Adan ______ accepted his award for best booth. (adverb)
18. People looked ______ to see the stars. (adverb)
19. Adan's constellations were ______. (adjective)
20. ______ Adan looked at his ribbon. (adverb)

Extra Practice, page 491.

Writing Activity A Paragraph

Write a paragraph describing a prize-winning project for a science fair. Tell how to set up the display in a logical order.
APPLY GRAMMAR: Use adverbs to make your writing clearer and more interesting. Draw a line under each adverb.

Science Link

Grammar

Handbook page 540

Grammar

Adverbs That Compare

RULES

An adverb can compare two or more actions.

Amy jumped higher than Lauren.

Amy jumped highest of all.

Add *-er* to a short adverb to compare two actions. Add *-est* to compare more than two actions.

Amy ran fast.

She ran faster than her teammate.

She ran fastest of all the women in the race.

Adverbs

How can you tell whether to add *-er* or *-est* to an adverb? Write your ideas in your journal.

Guided Practice

Name the correct form of the adverb in parentheses ( ) that completes each sentence.

EXAMPLE: Amy woke up (earlier, earliest) than Una.
earlier

1. Amy tried (harder, hardest) than her teammate.
2. She crossed the finish line (sooner, soonest) of all the runners.
3. She ran (straighter, straightest) than Ilana.
4. She jumped (higher, highest) of all the runners.
5. Amy came (nearer, nearest) to the record than Una.

REVIEW THE RULES

- Add *-er* to the end of a short adverb to compare two actions.
- Add *-est* to compare more than two actions.

More Practice

A. Write each sentence. Choose the correct adverb.

6. Wilma Rudolph ran (faster, fastest) of all women in 1960.
7. She trained for the Olympics (longer, longest) of all.
8. The 100-meter dash began (earlier, earliest) than the 200-meter dash.
9. The relay race began (later, latest) than the 200-meter dash.
10. Wilma tried (harder, hardest) of all and won all three races!

B. Write each sentence. Use the correct form of the adverb in parentheses ( ).

11. Jesse Owens ran ______ of the runners in 1936. (fast)
12. Owens finished ______ than the German runner did. (soon)
13. The long jump began ______ than the broad jump. (late)
14. Owens jumped ______ of all the athletes. (high)
15. Those games lasted ______ than last year's Olympics. (long)

C. Spiral Review Write the sentences. Fix errors in adjectives and adverbs that compare.

16. Who is the goodest runner today?
17. This runner is friendliest than that one.
18. Nang ran more faster than Tom.
19. Gloria finished soonest than Nang.
20. The winner was happyest of all.

Extra Practice, page 492.

Grammar

Handbook
page 540

Writing Activity An Essay

Write an essay about a contest in which you participated. Describe the contest and tell the results. Give your reader a sense of who you are by using your own voice.

APPLY GRAMMAR: Include adverbs that compare actions. Circle each adverb you use.

Grammar

More Adverbs That Compare

RULES

An adverb can compare two or more actions.

Use *more* or *most* with adverbs that end in *-ly* and with long adverbs.

Nina packed more carefully than Dan.

Jim packed the most skillfully of all.

Use *more* to compare two actions. Use *most* to compare more than two actions. Do not use *more* or *most* with an adverb ending with *-er* or *-est.*

Eric dressed quickly.

Cindy dressed more quickly than Eric.

Alex dressed the most quickly of all.

Adverbs

How can you decide when to use *more* or *most* with an adverb? Write your ideas in your journal.

Guided Practice

Name the correct word to complete each sentence.

EXAMPLE: Tom slept (more, most) soundly than Ned.
more

1. Jim got up (more, most) quickly than Dan did.
2. Dan cooked (more, most) speedily of the campers.
3. Cindy ate (more, most) hungrily than Dan ate.
4. Nina fished (more, most) successfully than Tom did.
5. Alex snored the (more, most) loudly of anyone.
6. Cindy cooked (more, most) willingly than she cleaned.
7. Cindy cleaned up (more, most) cheerfully of all.
8. Jim washed dishes (more, most) slowly than Cindy did.
9. Nina put the food away (most, more) happily than Dan.
10. Dan followed the trail (most, more) easily than Jim could.

REVIEW THE RULES

- The words *more* and *most* are used with long adverbs and adverbs that end in *-ly* to form comparisons.
- Use *more* to compare two actions. Use *most* to compare more than two actions.

More Practice

A. Write each sentence. Choose the correct word to complete the sentence.

11. Alex walked (more, most) comfortably of all in sneakers.

12. Cindy hiked (more, most) slowly than Alex.

13. On the hill, Nina breathed (more, most) easily of all the hikers.

14. Jim breathed (more, most) heavily than Cindy did on the hill.

15. Dan watched the trail (more, most) closely than Alex.

B. Write each sentence. Use the correct form of the adverb in parentheses ( ).

16. Nina hiked ______ than Dan. (briskly)

17. Tom carried supplies ______ of all. (carefully)

18. The rain soaked Jim ______ than it did Cindy. (completely)

19. The storm ended ______ than it had begun. (suddenly)

20. Dan had dressed ______ of all. (warmly)

C. Spiral Review **Write each sentence. Fix errors in adjectives and adverbs that compare. Add commas.**

21–25. Nina Cindy and Alex sat by the fire. Their socks were wettest than their shirts. Alex complained more loudly of the three. He felt most uncomfortable than Nina.

Extra Practice, page 493.

Grammar

Handbook
page 540

Writing Activity Guidelines

Write some guidelines that should be followed by campers or hikers: safety tips, dos and don'ts, and respect for nature.

APPLY GRAMMAR: Include adverbs that compare two or more actions using *more* or *most*. Circle these adverbs.

Science Link

Using *Good* and *Well*

RULES

The word *good* is an adjective. It describes a noun.

> *Mom has a good job.*

The word *well* is usually an adverb. It tells more about a verb.

> *Mom writes well.*

Well is used as an adjective only when it describes a person's health.

> *Mom is well enough to go to work today.*

Adverbs

Write two sentences that can help you remember when to use *good* and *well*.

Use the adjective *good* to describe a noun. It can come before the noun, or it can follow a linking verb.

> *Mom has a good boss.*
>
> *Mom's boss is good.*

Use the adverb *well* to tell more about a verb.

> *Mom works well in her department.*

When *well* refers to health, it describes a noun.

> *Mom was not feeling well yesterday.*

Name the word that correctly completes each sentence.

EXAMPLE: Mom wanted to work with a (good, well) staff.
good

1. My mom is a (good, well) writer.
2. She does her job (good, well).
3. Mom's boss, Ms. Ford, is a (good, well) person.
4. If Mom keeps doing (good, well), she will get a bonus.
5. Ms. Ford is not feeling (good, well) today.

REVIEW THE RULES

- The adjective *good* describes a noun.
- The adverb *well* tells more about a verb. Use *well* as an adjective only to describe someone's health.

More Practice

A. Write each sentence. Choose the correct word to complete the sentence.

6. Every day at work is a (good, well) day.

7. Mom has a (good, well) time at her job.

8. Mom runs her department (good, well).

9. Mom's friend Angie works (good, well) with her.

10. Mom eats a healthful lunch to stay (good, well).

B. Write *good* or *well* to finish each sentence.

11. "Your article is ______," said Ms. Ford.

12. "Are you feeling ______ today?" asked Mom.

13. Mom will get an award for her ______ work.

14. I am learning to write ______.

15. Mom sleeps ______ after a busy day.

C. Spiral Review **Complete each blank with *good, well,* an action verb, or a linking verb.**

At the award ceremony, Mom (**16.** ______) a speech.

"It has been a very (**17.** ______) year," she says. "My boss, Ms. Ford, has taught me (**18.** ______). I (**19.** ______) something new from her every day. I would also like to thank my friend Angie. She (**20.** ______) a great person to work with. Thank you, everyone!"

Extra Practice, page 494.

Handbook
page 580

Writing Activity A Job Description

Write a job description for an interesting job. Organize your ideas to tell the skills needed.

APPLY MECHANICS AND USAGE: Use the words *good* and *well* in your description.

Grammar REVIEW

Mixed Review

REVIEW THE RULES

- An adverb is a word that tells more about a verb.
- An adverb may tell *how, when,* or *where* an action takes place.
- Add -er to short adverbs to compare two actions. Add -est to compare more than two actions.
- Use more with adverbs ending in *-ly* to compare two actions. Use most to compare more than two actions.
- The word *good* is an adjective. The word *well* is an adverb. *Well* is used as an adjective only to describe health.

THINK AND WRITE

Adverbs

Write five sentences about how using adverbs helps you add details to your writing.

Practice

A. Write each sentence. Underline the adverb. Write whether the adverb tells *how*, *when*, or *where*.

1. We waited nearby.
2. I go to the pool early.
3. A woman is paddling gently through the water.
4. May I dive into the pool here?
5. A good swimmer can swim far.
6. My dad swiftly swims laps.
7. I always learn from my dad.
8. Today we take a break and play games.
9. Each swimmer dives quickly into the water.
10. Then the students swim around.

B. Write each sentence. Choose the word that correctly completes the sentence.

11. Rafael swims (more, most) quickly than I do.
12. Tammy dives (higher, highest) of all the students.
13. My sister Jan can swim (good, well).
14. Sissy swims (more, most) swiftly than Ben.
15. The class lasts (longer, longest) than other classes do.
16. Do all the students dive (good, well)?
17. Mr. Chang dives (more, most) beautifully of all.
18. What are the elements of a (good, well) dive?
19. The swimmer started out (faster, fastest) than she finished.
20. Swimming can help you stay (good, well).

C. Challenge Write the following paragraph. Fix errors in the use of *good* and *well*, and other adverb errors.

21–25. It takes practice to learn to swim good. Taking lessons is a well idea. A teacher can help you swim more faster than you could before. You will slide smooth through the water. Swimmers move gracefullyest of all athletes.

Handbook page 540

Writing Activity A Pamphlet

Write a pamphlet about the importance of water safety. Make your pamphlet interesting to your audience.

APPLY GRAMMAR: Use adverbs in your writing. Circle all the adverbs.

Grammar

Negatives

RULES

A negative is a word that means "no." Many negatives contain the word *no* within them.

not *nobody* *nowhere* *none* *no one*

Some negatives include the contraction *-n't*.

can't *don't* *won't* *isn't*

Never use two negatives in one sentence. This is an error called a *double negative*. There is often more than one way to correct a sentence with a double negative. You can take out one negative word, or you can change one of the negative words to a positive word.

Negatives
Write how you can recognize a double negative.

Negative Words		Positive Words	
no	nothing	any	anything
never	nowhere	ever	anywhere
nobody	no one	anybody	anyone

Incorrect: *Julie didn't know nobody at school.*

Correct: *Julie didn't know anybody at school.*
Julie knew nobody at school.

Guided Practice

Name the negative word in each sentence.

EXAMPLE: Julie had never met her new teacher.
never

1. Nobody looked up when Julie walked into the classroom.
2. Julie found nowhere to sit in the classroom.
3. The teacher didn't know Julie was coming today.
4. Julie wished her family hadn't moved to this place.
5. No one in Julie's class seemed very friendly.

REVIEW THE RULES

- A **negative** is a word that means "no."
- Do not use **double negatives**.

Grammar

More Practice

A. Write each sentence. Underline the negative word.

6. Julie hoped she wouldn't have to give a speech.
7. The classroom map didn't show Julie's hometown.
8. No one in Julie's new class had ever been to Oregon.
9. Some of the students had never seen the ocean.
10. Julie thought she would make no new friends.

B. Write each sentence. Choose the correct word.

11. Julie hadn't (ever, never) eaten in the cafeteria.
12. She couldn't find (nowhere, anywhere) to sit.
13. "Don't you have (anyone, no one) to sit with?" asked Lynn.
14. "I don't know (nobody, anybody)," said Julie.
15. Julie (wouldn't, would) never forget Lynn's kindness that day.

Handbook
page 542

C. Spiral Review Write the letter, using correct punctuation and capital letters. Correct double negatives.

16–25.

25 Claremont Road
Redwood City California 94062
Sept 23 2002

dear Ms Tanaka

It wasn't easy starting at a new school. At first I didn't have no friends. Then I met Lynn. I haven't never met a nicer person.

your student
Julie Herrera

Extra Practice, page 495

Writing Activity A Flyer

Write a flyer welcoming new students to your school. Use descriptive language to tell what your school is like.

APPLY GRAMMAR: Include two negatives, and underline them. Make sure you do not use double negatives.

Grammar

Prepositions

RULES

A **preposition** is a word that comes before a noun or pronoun and relates it to another word in the sentence.

The Taylors went to the museum.

We rode home with them.

The following words are common prepositions. Use prepositions to connect a noun or pronoun with another part of the sentence.

Prepositions

about	*at*	*from*	*over*
above	*behind*	*in*	*through*
across	*beside*	*inside*	*to*
after	*by*	*near*	*under*
against	*down*	*of*	*until*
around	*for*	*on*	*with*

People waited | across | the street.

THINK AND WRITE

Prepositions

How are prepositions used in sentences? Write your ideas in your journal.

Guided Practice

Name the preposition in each sentence.

EXAMPLE: The painting was hanging on the wall.
on

1. I visited the museum with my friends.
2. I waited beside them.
3. The line stretched down the block.
4. Finally, we walked through the entrance.
5. The paintings hung near the door.

REVIEW THE RULES

- A preposition comes before a noun or pronoun.
- A preposition relates the noun or pronoun to another word in the sentence.

Grammar

More Practice

A. Write each sentence. Underline the prepositions.

6. Claude Monet was a famous artist from France.
7. Tourists visited his house in the country.
8. They can walk around his beautiful garden.
9. The garden is behind the house.
10. Monet painted pictures of it.

B. Write each sentence. Complete it with a preposition.

11. I am attending a class ______ the museum.
12. I am learning ______ art.
13. We explore the museum ______ the class.
14. You can stand ______ the paintings.
15. The teacher walks ______ us.

Handbook page 543

C. Spiral Review Write the paragraph. Complete each sentence with a preposition, a pronoun, or an article.

Everyone is invited (**16.** ____) the new exhibit. It will present the works (**17.** ____) famous American painters. (**18.** ____) can buy tickets at the museum shop. (**19.** ____) adult ticket costs eight dollars. Children (**20.** ____) ten years old can enter free of charge.

Extra Practice, page 496.

Writing Activity A Poster

Create a poster to tell about an upcoming art exhibit in your city. Make sure the rhythm and flow of your sentences are appealing to your audience.

APPLY GRAMMAR: Use prepositions to give information about the date, time, and location of the show. Underline each preposition.

Art Link

Prepositional Phrases

RULES

A prepositional phrase is a group of words that begins with a preposition and ends with a noun or pronoun.

My Aunt Libby lives in a big red farmhouse.

Aunt Libby often sits under a big oak tree.

A prepositional phrase can be used to add more information to a simple sentence.

My aunt writes poems.

My aunt with the long red hair writes poems.

My aunt with the long red hair writes poems about nature.

Prepositional Phrases

How can you recognize prepositional phrases? Write your ideas in your journal.

Guided Practice

Name the preposition in each sentence. Then name the noun or pronoun that follows it.

EXAMPLE: Life on a farm is busy and fun.
preposition: on; noun: farm

1. Aunt Libby spends her afternoons in the meadow.
2. The deer come to the creek daily.
3. She writes poems about them.
4. The sun sets behind the hills.
5. Aunt Libby walks over the bridge.

REVIEW THE RULES

- A prepositional phrase begins with a preposition and ends with a noun or a pronoun.

More Practice

A. Write each sentence. Circle the preposition. Underline the noun or pronoun that follows it.

6. In the afternoon I visit Aunt Libby.
7. We watch a deer stand alert for danger.
8. This white-tailed deer and her fawns eat at dusk.
9. The mother feeds some young leaves to them.
10. Deer eat many different kinds of plants.

B. Write each sentence. Underline each prepositional phrase. Circle each preposition.

11. My aunt and I walk down the path.
12. I like going to the meadow with her.
13. We see some deer across the creek.
14. We watch the deer play near the giant oak tree.
15. The deer run around the field behind the house.

C. Spiral Review **Write the paragraphs. Underline the prepositional phrases. Fix pronoun errors.**

16–20. Aunt Libby and me will write a poem. I sit on the front porch. Aunt Libby has an idea.

"I will write about you and I!" she says. She begins, "We walked near the deer."

Extra Practice, page 497.

Writing Activity A Scrapbook

Make a scrapbook with words and pictures, showing facts about life in the country. Make your message clear by including many details.

APPLY GRAMMAR: Use prepositional phrases to add information to your scrapbook. Underline each prepositional phrase.

Handbook
page 543

Grammar

Combining Sentences: Complex Sentences

RULES

A complex sentence contains two related ideas joined by a conjunction other than *and*, *but*, or *or*. You can combine two short sentences to form a complex sentence.

Joe is busy. He has a job.

Joe is busy because he has a job.

Joe starts work. The sun rises.

Joe starts work when the sun rises.

Combining Sentences

Write about how you can create a complex sentence out of two simple sentences.

Use these conjunctions, or joining words, to connect the related ideas in complex sentences.

Conjunctions

when	as	as if	although
before	because	as though	if
after	since	where	though
while	until	wherever	unless

Guided Practice

Name a conjunction to connect the two parts of the sentence.

EXAMPLE: Joe works ______ he goes to school.
before

1. Joe works every day ______ he is sick.
2. Joe washes Mr. Ma's car ______ it gets dirty.
3. He cannot deliver papers ______ he gets a bicycle.
4. Joe is happy ______ a neighbor hired him.
5. He feeds the cat ______ the Lees are gone.

REVIEW THE RULES

- A complex sentence contains two related sentences.

More Practice

A. Write each sentence. Choose a word to combine the two parts of the sentence.

6. Joe would mow the lawn ______ it weren't raining.
7. Joe does the weeding ______ it is boring.
8. Joe waters gardens ______ people are on vacation.
9. Joe walks dogs ______ he goes to school.
10. Joe will go ______ he finds a job.

B. Write the complex sentence that can be formed by combining the two shorter sentences with a conjunction.

11. Joe is happy. He has enough money for a bicycle.
12. Joe wanted a red bicycle. He saw the blue one.
13. Dad bought a bike. Joe got his.
14. Joe and Dad go riding. They have time.
15. Joe rides. He will never stop.

Handbook page 541

C. Spiral Review Combine each pair of sentences to form a compound subject, a compound sentence, or a complex sentence.

16. Joe went on a bike trip. His dad went on a bike trip.
17. The day was cloudy. They left anyway.
18. The clouds grew thicker. The rain began.
19. They waited under a tree. The rain stopped.
20. They were happy. They reached the campsite.

Extra Practice, page 498.

Writing Activity An Advice Column

Write an advice column telling people how they can earn money. Make sure to choose words that are clear and precise.

APPLY GRAMMAR: Use complex sentences in your note. Underline the joining words you use.

Grammar

Commas

RULES

A comma is used to show a pause in your writing.

Hello, and welcome to the Grand Canyon!

A comma sets off a person's name when the person is being directly spoken to.

Dad, have you ever seen a rattlesnake?

A comma is used to set off a word that introduces a sentence, such as *yes*, *no*, and *well*.

No, but I heard one under my cabin one night.

Commas

Write how to remember when commas are used in writing sentences.

You may need to use a comma before a name, after a name, or both before and after.

Have you ever been to the desert, Dad?

I wonder, Dad, if there are rattlesnakes here.

Guided Practice

Name the place where a comma is needed in each sentence.

EXAMPLE: Well it certainly is hot.
Well, it certainly is hot.

1. Look at all the sagebrush Mom!
2. Yes the Arizona desert is filled with plant life.
3. Josh did you see the tall cactus?
4. No I was too busy looking at the wide open sky.
5. Thank you Liz for showing me the desert.

REVIEW THE RULES

- Use a comma to set off the name of a person spoken to or a word that introduces a sentence.

More Practice

A. Write each sentence. Use commas where they are needed.

6. Jack let's go camping in the desert.
7. Well it might be cold at night.
8. Maybe we will see coyotes Dad.
9. Have you Christy ever seen a scorpion?
10. No but I have seen plenty of snakes!

B. Write each sentence. Use commas where they are needed. Then write why the comma is needed.

11. Mom do you think it ever snows in Arizona?
12. Yes it snows in Flagstaff during the winter.
13. Look Jack we are coming to a Navajo community.
14. Would you like to learn rug weaving Lynn?
15. Well I would rather learn to make a basket.

C. Spiral Review Write each sentence. Use capital letters and commas correctly.

16. No you do not have to leave phoenix to see coyotes.
17. You can also see jackrabbits wild boars and ravens there.
18. Yes you can see the mountains from the city Jack.
19. Tucson is another interesting city in arizona Lynn.
20. Mom can we go to tucson next?

Extra Practice, page 499.

Grammar

Handbook page 555

Writing Activity A Paragraph

Write a travel schedule for a trip through one area of the United States. Describe what you want to see, visit, and do. Write clear and correct sentences.

APPLY MECHANICS AND USAGE: Include commas when you address the person for whom you are writing the schedule.

Mixed Review

REVIEW THE RULES

- A negative is a word that means "no."
- Avoid double negatives, two negatives in one sentence.
- A preposition comes before a noun or pronoun and relates it to another word in the sentence.
- A prepositional phrase is a group of words that begins with a preposition and ends in a noun or pronoun.
- A complex sentence contains two related ideas joined by a conjunction other than *and, but,* or *or.*
- You can form a complex sentence combining two related sentences with a conjunction such as *when, because,* or *unless.*
- A comma is used to set off the name of a person spoken to or a word that introduces a sentence.

QUICK WRITE

Prepositional Phrases

List five prepositional phrases and use them in sentences.

Practice

A. Write each sentence. Underline the prepositional phrase. Add commas where they are needed.

1. May we go to the movies Mom?
2. Yes I will sit beside you.
3. Do you want a seat in the front row Carol?
4. Well I'd rather sit near the back.
5. Juana let's walk down the aisle.
6. Yes we should go to our seats now.
7. Buy a big snack for us Dad.
8. Do you Sam like movies with monsters?
9. No I prefer movies about real people.
10. Well let's talk after the movie.

B. Write each sentence. Correct the double negatives. Combine the sentence pairs to form complex sentences.

11. I haven't seen no movies since last month.

12. Movies cost a dime. Grandpa was young.

13. I don't never find a seat before the movie begins.

14. I like seeing movies. They first come out.

15. I like adventures. They are so exciting.

16. I like watching the main feature. The previews are finished.

17. A double feature is fun. The weather is bad outside.

18. I don't take no acting lessons now.

19. I will take acting classes next year. Mom says I can't.

20. I don't know nothing as much fun as the movies!

C. Challenge Write the paragraph. Correct the double negatives. Add commas where they are needed. Combine two sentences. Underline the prepositional phrases.

21–30. James you won't never believe this! I was walking down the street. A famous movie star bumped into me. I told her I had never met nobody famous. Well, she pulled a pencil from her purse. Yes she signed her autograph on my notebook!

Grammar REVIEW

Handbook
pages 541–543, 555

Writing Activity A Movie Plot

Retell your favorite movie plot. Be sure that you tell the events and introduce the main characters in a logical order.

APPLY GRAMMAR: Use prepositional phrases to add information to your movie plot.

Common Errors with Adverbs

When you write, it is important to use adverbs correctly. Sometimes, for example, writers make the mistake of using an adjective in place of an adverb. This chart shows errors that writers make at times. As you look at the chart, think about how you should use adverbs in your own writing.

Common Errors	Examples	Corrected Sentences
Using an adjective in place of an adverb	The frogs moved slow across the pond.	The frogs moved slowly across the pond.
Using good *instead of* well	Michael described the frogs good.	Michael described the frogs well.
Using double negatives	Yukiko hasn't never seen a frog.	Yukiko has never seen a frog. Yukiko hasn't ever seen a frog.

Adverbs

How are adjectives and adverbs alike and different? Write your answer in your journal.

REVIEW THE RULES

ADVERBS

- An adverb tells more about a verb. An adjective describes a noun.
- *Good* is an adjective. *Well* is an adverb.
- Correct a double negative by removing one negative word or putting a positive word in its place.
- Remember Many adverbs can be formed by adding *-ly* to an adjective.
- Remember For most adverbs, do not change the spelling of the base word when you add *-ly*.

Practice

A. Write the word in parentheses ( ) that completes the sentence correctly.

1. Do frogs swim and jump (good, well)?
2. Scientists conduct their research (good, well).
3. A (good, well) frog to avoid is the poison dart.
4. The poison protects dart frogs (good, well).
5. A marsh makes a (good, well) home for a frog.

B. Write each sentence. Use the word in parentheses ( ) that completes the sentence correctly.

6. The frogs were not found (nowhere, anywhere).
7. The children looked (careful, carefully) for the frogs.
8. Even scientists searched thoroughly for the frogs, but they couldn't find (none, any).
9. Pollution damaged the pond (quick, quickly).
10. Frogs cannot live (safe, safely) in the pond.

C. Rewrite each sentence correctly.

11. The frogs disappeared sudden from the pond.
12. Wasn't there nothing they could do?
13. The community cleaned up the pond good.
14. People didn't want no more pollution in their town.
15. Frogs and other wildlife returned gradual to the area.

Grammar Troubleshooter, pages 522–523.

Handbook
page 540

Writing Activity A Paragraph

Think of an animal that interests you. Write a paragraph describing how the animal moves, sleeps, eats, and sounds. Make sure that your sentences flow together.

APPLY GRAMMAR: Be sure to use adverbs correctly in your paragraph. Check the spelling of each adverb. Remember that, for most adverbs, you do not change the spelling of the base word when you add *-ly*.

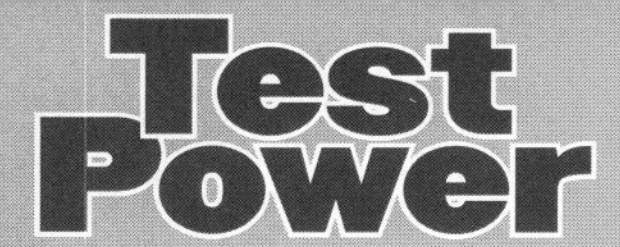

Mechanics and Spelling

Directions

Read the passage and decide which type of mistake, if any, appears in each underlined section. Choose the letter for your answer. If there is no error, choose "No mistake."

Sample

Having a baby sister is a big responsibility. My brother and I help take care of her by giving her a bottle and reading Books to her. We also (1) teach her many things, such as how to eat with a spoon. We beleive that it is our job (2) to help see that she is safe and happy.

My parents my brother and I (3) all work together to look after my sister.

Do not capitalize common nouns.

Remember that i comes before e except after c or when sounded like /ā/.

Use commas to separate words in a series.

1 **A** Spelling
B Capitalization
C Punctuation
D No mistake

2 **F** Spelling
G Capitalization
H Punctuation
J No mistake

3 **A** Spelling
B Capitalization
C Punctuation
D No mistake

Test Tip
Ruling out answers that you know are wrong can help you determine the correct answer.

Grammar and Usage

Directions

Read the passage and choose the word or group of words that belongs in each space. Choose the letter for your answer.

Sample

Ronnie has __(1)__ been to the ocean. Next week he __(2)__ across the country to spend a week at the beach. His friend Amy __(3)__ him sunglasses for his trip. His friend Josh made a kite for __(4)__. He cannot wait to spend a day flying his new kite along miles of sandy beach.

Do not use two negatives in one sentence.

Look for clues in the sentence to decide what verb tense to use.

Irregular verbs have special forms in the past tense.

Use an object pronoun in the predicate of a sentence.

1 **A** not never
B ever
C never
D no ever

2 **F** was traveling
G will travel
H had traveled
J traveled

3 **A** given
B gived
C had gave
D gave

4 **F** him
G he
H his
J they

TIME FOR KIDS Writer's Notebook

RESEARCH

I often ask a librarian at the **library media center** to help me find the right source for the facts I need. Whether it's an encyclopedia that lists topics alphabetically or a CD-ROM on a special subject, the media center is the best place to go to for help.

WRITING WELL

Whether I'm writing an essay that is my opinion or writing a research paper, I use an **outline**. An outline helps me organize my writing. I list every point I want to make. Then I add details that will bring my story to life.

USING WORDS

The Inuit are nomads. They have a nomadic way of life. The word part "ic" is a **suffix**. When I add letters to the end of a word, I can change its meaning. Using suffixes helps me describe better what I want to say. What words with suffixes can you think of?

Read Now!

As you read about Nunavut, think about the main point of each of the three paragraphs. Then write a simple outline of the photo essay.

TIME FOR KIDS

PHOTO ESSAY

CELEBRATING A NEW LAND

Canada's Inuit rule their own territory, Nunavut.

A Land of Their Own

Carlo Allegri/AFP; Cover: Shaun Best/Reuters

Paul Okalik, shown riding on a dog sled, is the youngest leader of any Canadian province or territory. He was 34 when the territory was formed.

Fireworks lit up the Northern night sky just after midnight on April 1, 1999. The fireworks celebrated the birth of Canada's newest territory, Nunavut (NUN-uh-voot). It was the first time in 50 years that Canada had redrawn its map. And it was the first time ever that native people in Canada controlled their own government.

The new territory is home to 21,250 Inuit, Nunavut's native people. *Nunavut* means "our land" in the Inuit's native language.

Nunavut is a region of islands, tundra, and frozen lakes. It was carved out of the Northwest Territories. It is the size of Britain, France, Germany, Italy, and Spain combined. The icy land stretches to the top of the world and includes the north magnetic pole. There are only 28 villages in the territory. The largest has a population of just 4,000. Here's a peek at Nunavut.

Kevin Frayer/Canapress; Caribou photo: Tom Brakefield/Corbis

Piles of stones like this one were used by hunters to mark a trail. Now they are symbols of the new territory. Sometimes the rocks get covered over with snow. That's because winter in Nunavut lasts for nine months.

interNET CONNECTION **Go to** www.mhschool.com/language-arts **for more information on the topic.**

Inuit welcomed their new territory with fireworks.

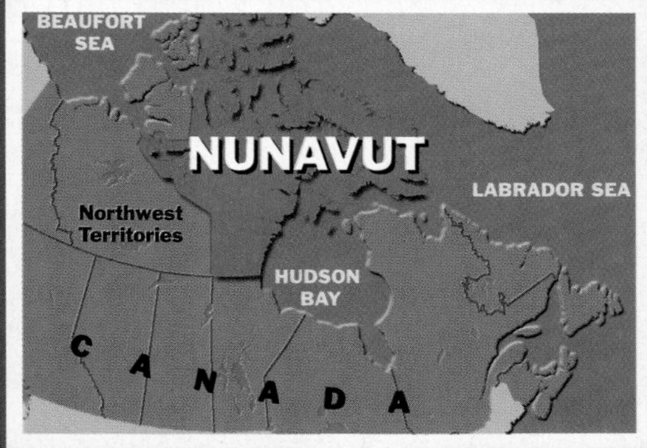

AREA: 733,587 square miles

AREA OF CANADA: 20%

POPULATION: 25,000

INUIT POPULATION: 21,250

CAPITAL: Iqaluit

INDUSTRIES: Fishing, mining, arts and crafts

In Nunavut, there are 30 caribou for every person.

Write Now!

Write a short report about Nunavut using the information from the photo essay and the facts shown above.

Encyclopedia

An **encyclopedia** is a reference book that contains articles on many subjects. Most encyclopedias are made up of a set of books, or volumes. Information is arranged in the volumes alphabetically by subject. The spine of each volume is usually numbered to help you keep the books in order. The spine also has letters or words to tell which part of the alphabet is in that volume. The last volume usually includes an index. The index lists all the articles in the encyclopedia in alphabetical order.

Here is part of a page from an encyclopedia.

Guide words help you locate the article you want.

A pronunciation guide may follow the entry word.

The entry word is the title of the article. If the article is about a person, the entry word is the person's last name.

The author of the encyclopedia article is usually mentioned.

Wilder, Laura Ingalls

WILDER, *WYL duhr,* **LAURA INGALLS,** *IHNG guhlz* (1867-1957), was an American author of books for children. She is best known for her series of nine novels called the "Little House" books. Most of the series is loosely based on her experiences growing up in the Middle West in the 1870s and 1800s. The series has been praised as a vivid literary saga of the American frontier life. The "Little House" stories have a chronological pattern and follow Laura from her childhood wilderness home to her final home with her husband, Almanzo Wilder. The stories show the importance of a closely knit family, and they are filled with humor and tenderness.

Laura Ingalls was born in Pepin, Wis. She lived a rugged pioneer life with her family as they moved from place to place. She described her childhood in the first "Little House" book, *Little House in the Big Woods* (1932). In 1885 she married Almanzo Wilder, who came from an old established family in northern New York. *Farmer Boy* (1933) is the story of his childhood. *These Happy Golden Years* (1943) unites the families with the marriage of Laura and Almanzo.

Jill P. May

Encyclopedias on CD-ROM contain information that is much like print encyclopedias. You search a topic by entering **keywords**. If there is more than one article that deals with the topic, the titles are all listed. By clicking on one title, you can read its contents. The list may also show if there are pictures you can look at to learn more about the topic.

Practice

A. Write your answers to these questions. Use the information on the previous page.

1. In which volume would you look for information about Hans Christian Andersen?
2. Will an article about pioneer life appear before or after an article about photography?
3. Will articles about snow and solar energy appear in the same or different volumes?
4. What keyword would you look for if you wanted to find an article about the life of pioneers in early America?
5. If the guide words at the top of an encyclopedia page are *wildcat* and *wildflower,* will the page contain an article about Laura Ingalls Wilder?

Go to: www.mhschool.com/language-arts **for more information on the topic.**

B. Write which encyclopedia aid will help you find each piece of information.

6. how to say the entry word
7. how to find the entry word on a page
8. what the article is all about
9. the number of the volume that contains the article
10. an alphabetical listing of all the articles in a set of encyclopedias

Writing Activity A Speech

Use an encyclopedia in print or on CD-ROM to get information about an author. Then write a summary about the author. Use the summary to write a speech. Then give the speech about the author to your classmates.

Vocabulary: Suffixes

DEFINITION

A suffix is a word part added to the end of a base word. It changes the meaning of the base word.

play + er = player
care + less = careless
quick + ly = quickly

Suffix	Meaning	Example
-er	person who	baker, builder
-ful	full of	cheerful, careful
-ly	in a certain way	gladly, happily
-less	without	hopeless, painless
-ment	the result of	agreement, settlement
-y	like; full of	thirsty, guilty

THINK AND WRITE

Suffixes
How can knowing the meaning of suffixes help you figure out the meaning of unfamiliar words? Write your ideas in your journal.

Look at the highlighted words in the paragraph below. Find the suffixes. Explain how each suffix changes the meaning of the base word.

When I grow up, I want to be a writer. I could write books, or I could be a reporter for a newspaper. I think it would be great to choose the right words and put sentences together cleverly. What a wonderful accomplishment it would be to write as a career!

Practice

A. Write the sentences. Underline the words with suffixes. They circle the suffixes.

1. My aunt is a gardener and a writer.
2. She writes about how to have a successful garden.
3. Aunt Jane's articles usually appear in Monday's paper.
4. She writes about ways to grow healthy plants.
5. People read her tips with excitement.

B. Choose a word from the Word Bank to replace the words in parentheses. Then write the sentence.

judgment	**merrily**	**worker**
thoughtless	**effortless**	**thankful**
accomplishment	**agreement**	**beautiful**
	careful	

6. Aunt Jane is a hard (person who works).
7. She has a (full of beauty) garden!
8. Everyone admires the (full of care) way she tends to her plants.
9. She makes the work seem (without effort).
10. All are in (state of agreeing) her garden is best.

C. Grammar Link Complete each sentence with an adverb. Circle the suffix.

11. Aunt Jane writes ______ .
12. She works ______ for the city newspaper.
13. Her column appears ______ on Mondays.
14. I would love to write ______ someday.
15. But fame should come ______, not all at once.

Writing Activity A Paragraph

Write about the job you would like to have as an adult. Tell about a person who has inspired your ideas about the future. Use two or three words with suffixes in your writing.

APPLY GRAMMAR: Use at least one prepositional phrase in each sentence of your paragraph.

Composition: Outlining

A writer sometimes uses an outline to organize information by topic before beginning to write. An outline can be written from notes the writer took while reading.

GUIDELINES

- An outline lists the main topics in a report or article. Each main topic can be one paragraph in the report.
- Use a Roman numeral followed by a period before each main topic.
- Each subtopic is a detail that supports or explains the main topic.
- Use a capital letter followed by a period before each subtopic.

THINK AND WRITE

Outlining

How can outlining help you organize your ideas? Write your answer in your journal.

Look at the outline for a report about the California Gold Rush. Notice how the writer has organized the main topics and subtopics.

The California Gold Rush

I. Discovery
  A. Gold at Sutter's Mill in 1848
  B. Spread of Gold Fever
II. The Forty-Niners
  A. Arrival of 40,000 prospectors in 1849
  B. Population growth
  C. Growth of business and agriculture
III. Decline of Gold Fever
  A. In 1851, businesses replace independent miners
  B. Forty-niners become employees
  C. Forty-niners return to previous occupations

A Roman numeral is used for each main topic. Main topics are listed in logical order.

A capital letter is used to list each subtopic. Subtopics provide supporting details and expand the main topic.

Practice

A. Write the outline below. Fill in missing Roman numerals for main topics and capital letters for subtopics.

A Biography of Levi Strauss

I. Who was Levi Strauss?

1. ______ German immigrant

2. ______ Peddler carrying heavy cloth for tents

3. ______ What did Levi Strauss do?

A. Arrived in California, 1853

4. ______ Used cloth to make pants

5. ______ Designed pants we call "Levis"

B. Use the following notes to create an outline for a report about the Sierra Nevada mountain range.

Where is the mountain range located?
Western U.S.
Extends for 400 miles
Mostly in California
What are some special features of the range?
Highest peak is Mt. Whitney
Elevation 6,000 to 12,000 feet
Where can people stay in the range?
Kings Canyon National Park
Sequoia National Park
Yosemite National Park

C. Grammar Link Use the information in the outline you completed for Practice B to write three paragraphs about the Sierra Nevada mountain range. Use at least three prepositional phrases in your writing.

Writing Activity An Outline

Write an outline for a three-paragraph geography report about a specific location. Choose three main topics to cover and then add subtopics that provide details and further information.

APPLY GRAMMAR: Use adverbs in your outline to more clearly describe the details.

Better Sentences

Directions

Read the passage. Some sections are underlined. The underlined sections may be one of the following:

- **Incomplete sentences**
- **Run-on sentences**
- **Correctly written sentences that should be combined**
- **Correctly written sentences that do not need to be rewritten**

Choose the best way to write each underlined section. If the underlined section needs no change, choose "No mistake."

Two sentences can be joined with a comma and and, but, *or* or.

You can often correct a sentence fragment by combining it with a sentence before or after it.

Sample

Rabbits are smart animals, and they are social as well. (1) They are fairly easy to care for. They can be kept in a cage in your house or yard. As long as you take them out for exercise. (2) With the proper care, a rabbit can be a great companion.

1 **A** Rabbits are smart animals. Social as well.

B Rabbits are smart animals they are social as well.

C Rabbits are smart animals, but they are social as well.

D No mistake

2 **F** They can be kept in a cage in your house or yard, you must take them out for exercise.

G They can be kept in a cage in your house or yard as long as you take them out, this is for exercise.

H They can be kept in a cage indoors or outside as long as you take them out for exercise.

J No mistake

Test Tip

Do not spend too much time on one test item. Pace yourself.

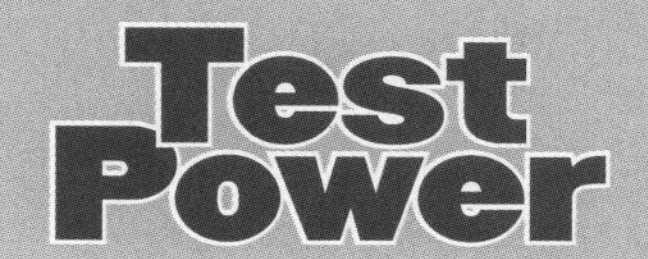

Vocabulary and Comprehension

Directions

Read the passage. Then read each question that follows the passage. Decide which is the best answer to each question. Choose the letter for that answer.

Sample

My neighbor, Angie, is blind. Recently, Angie's parents got her a guide dog named Pepper. A guide dog is a special dog that has been trained to help a blind person live more independently.

Pepper and Angie have grown to be wonderful friends. They are always together, and if Angie leaves the room for a minute, Pepper gets a sad look in his eyes. He is a faithful friend to Angie.

Pepper's trainer said that teaching Pepper to be a guide dog was effortless. Angie and the trainer agree that no dog could be a better companion.

Identifying a base word and suffix can help you define an unfamiliar word.

1 In this passage, the word *effortless* means—

A full of effort

B without effort

C the result of effort

D an effort

2 Which statement does not describe Pepper?

F He is a loyal dog.

G Angie's parents got him for her.

H He helps Angie be more independent.

J He is unfriendly.

Seeing Like a Writer

Imagine that you are a reporter. How can you write about these pictures to share information with others?

Challenging Free Frontiers by Tsing-Fang Chen

Writing from Pictures

1. Write a caption for each picture. Use words that tell how, when, and where the action in each picture takes place.
2. Choose one of the pictures. Look at the details. List as many facts as you can about the picture.
3. Choose two of the pictures. What is similar about the main idea of the pictures? Write a short paragraph. Use the information in the pictures to support your ideas.

   Apply Grammar: Use prepositional phrases as you describe the information in the pictures. Circle each preposition that you use.

Expository Writing

When you create a report or an article that presents information about a topic, you are writing an expository piece. Expository writing presents information about a topic by using facts, details, description, or examples to tell more about the topic.

Learning from Writers

Read the following examples of expository writing. Pay attention to the information the writers provide. How have they used details to develop the main idea of the piece?

Purpose

Why would you want to write an expository piece? Write your ideas in your journal.

People Caused the Problem

When large numbers of people first moved to Florida more than a century ago, the Everglades was thought to be nothing but swampland. No one paid much attention to the beauty of the area or its importance to the wildlife living there. . . .

In the 1920s, engineers straightened rivers. They built thousands of miles of canals and dikes. They hoped to stop flooding and keep water supplies stable for farms and cities. The plan worked.

But the changes also harmed the Everglades. The area shrank in size by half. Much of the fresh water disappeared. And the numbers of birds, alligators, and other animals shrank, too.

"Everything depends on the water," says Sandy Dayhoff, who works for Everglades National Park. "Not only having enough water, but the right amount at the right time." Dayhoff compares the Everglades to a giant bathtub. In the rainy season, the tub is full. In the dry season, it slowly drains. But humans are getting in the way of both parts of this natural cycle.

—From "Saving the Everglades" in *Time for Kids*

Rain Forests

A surprising fact about plants and animals is that half of all species live in rain forests. However, only seven percent of rain forests remain in the world. If all the rain forests are destroyed, then half of all our species of plant and animal life will be, too.

Some of the animals living in rain forests are chimpanzees, toucans, frangipani caterpillars, butterflies, boa constrictors, tree frogs, and mountain gorillas. You can barely find two plants and animals that are alike because each is unique and beautiful in its own way.

Rain forests are our tropical treasures.

–Lisa Sharifi

Practice and Apply

Thinking Like a Reader

1. What is the main idea of "People Caused the Problem"?
2. What information does Lisa Sharifi give about rain forests?

Thinking Like a Writer

3. What type of details does the writer use to support the main idea of "People Caused the Problem"?
4. How does Lisa show that many species live in rain forests?

5. **Reading Across Texts** If the authors of "People Caused the Problem" and "Rain Forests" used the same sources to gather facts, what type of sources might they be? List three possible sources.

Features of Expository Writing

DEFINITIONS AND FEATURES

Expository writing presents information about a topic. Good expository writing:

- Presents a **main idea** and supports it with facts and details.
- Gives **important information** about a topic.
- **Summarizes information** from a variety of different resources.
- **Draws a conclusion** based on the information presented.
- Uses **transition words** to connect ideas.

Main Idea

Reread "People Caused the Problem" on page 462. What is the main idea of the passage?

> But the changes also harmed the Everglades.

Supporting details in the passage explain how the changes people have made to the Florida Everglades have harmed the entire area.

Important Information

Expository writing provides information. This information can tell how, why, or when something happened.

> In the 1920s, engineers straightened rivers. They built thousands of miles of canals and dikes. They hoped to stop flooding and keep water supplies stable for farms and cities. The plan worked.

What information does the author of "People Caused the Problem" give to explain how people changed the Everglades?

▶ Summarizes Information

Writers usually use several resources to gather information about a topic. Then the author summarizes, or sums up, the information.

> Dayhoff compares the Everglades to a giant bathtub. In the rainy season, the tub is full. In the dry season, it slowly drains.

How did the author get the information that is summarized here?

▶ Draws a Conclusion

An author draws conclusions at the end of an expository piece to summarize the main idea and bring the piece to a logical close. Sometimes a conclusion makes a point as well as summarizes the main idea.

> But humans are getting in the way of both parts of this natural cycle.

What conclusion does the author draw?

▶ Transition Words

Transition words help a writer connect ideas. Some transition words and phrases are *however, but, therefore, as a result,* and *finally.*

> But the changes also harmed the Everglades.

What transition word does the author use?

PRACTICE AND APPLY

Create a Features Chart

1. List the features of expository writing.
2. Reread "Rain Forests" by Lisa Sharifi on page 463.
3. Write one example of each feature in Lisa's writing.
4. What facts did you learn from Lisa's piece?

Features	Examples

Prewrite

Expository writing gives facts and information about a topic. You can use expository writing to share ideas about things you have learned through reading and research.

Purpose and Audience

The purpose of expository writing is to explain or inform. In expository writing, you provide details that support your main idea. You use the information you have presented to draw conclusions.

Before you start writing, think about who your audience will be. How can you organize your ideas so that your audience understands them? You also want your facts and information to be clear and complete.

Audience

How does thinking about your audience help you decide what information to include in your writing?

Choose a Topic

Begin by **brainstorming** a list of topics. Start with things you are interested in or topics that you want to learn more about. Use the list to choose a topic that interests you and will interest other people, too.

After choosing a topic, **explore ideas** by listing information that you want to include in your writing.

These are the ideas I want to put in my report.

Dust Bowl
Time period and location
- 1930s
- American prairie

Dust Bowl
How it started
- Early settlers

Dust Bowl
What happened to the people

Dust Bowl
What happened to the land
- Dry soil
- Clouds of dust
- Farms ruined

Organize • Outlining

To help you organize your expository writing, you can use an outline to show the main topics you want to cover and the supporting information that should be included. How did the writer organize his notes in this outline?

OUTLINE

I. Settlers on the prairie

A. Dug up grass

B. Soil became loose

II. Drought in 1930s

A. Dry soil

B. Clouds of dust

C. Area called Dust Bowl

III. Hard years for many people

A. Farms ruined

B. People left homes

Checklist

Prewriting

- Have you thought about your purpose and audience?
- Have you brainstormed topic ideas?
- Have you chosen your topic and listed what you know about it?
- Have you used an outline to organize your ideas?
- What kind of research do you need to do?

PRACTICE AND APPLY

Plan Your Own Expository Writing

1. Think about your purpose and audience.
2. Brainstorm ideas for your topic.
3. Choose a topic and list information to explore.
4. Use an outline to organize the information.

Prewrite • Research and Inquiry

▶ Writer's Resources

You will have to do research to get more information for your expository writing. Begin by making a list of questions. Then decide what resources you need to use to answer your questions.

What Else Do I Need to Know?	Where Can I Find the Information?
What area is called the Dust Bowl?	Look up the Dust Bowl in an encyclopedia.
Why did the soil become loose?	Call a history expert at a college or library.

▶ Use an Encyclopedia

An encyclopedia is a useful source of information for a research report. When you use a CD-ROM encyclopedia, first type in keywords related to your topic. You will then see a list of articles about your subject. Click on the article that you want to read.

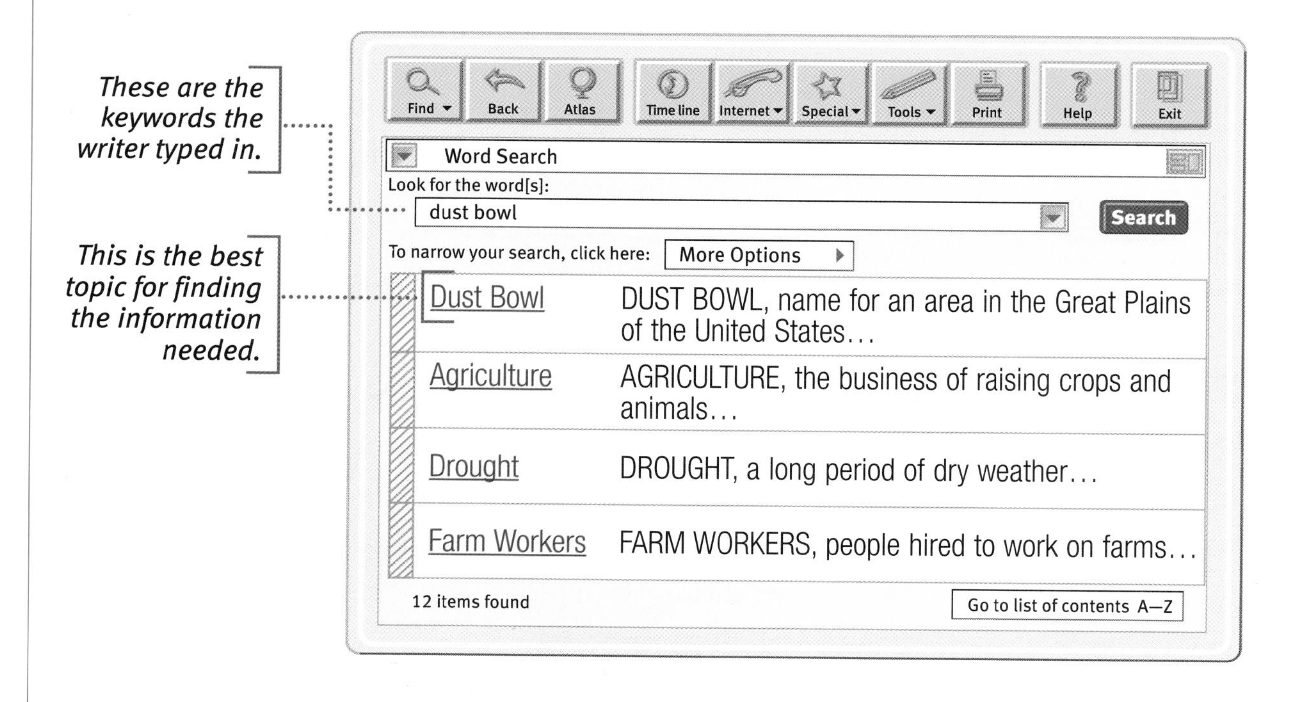

▶ Consult Experts

Experts have detailed knowledge about a subject. They can give you specific information that may be hard to find elsewhere. You can call, write, or e-mail an expert. Remember that experts are busy, so give them time to respond to your questions. Thank them for their help.

▶ Use Your Research

In expository writing, you summarize information from a variety of sources, such as books and magazines. This writer got information from an encyclopedia and an expert. How was this information added to the outline?

I. Settlers on the prairie

A. Dug up grass

B. Soil became loose
because the grass held the soil in place

II. Drought in 1930s

A. Dry soil

B. Clouds of dust

C. Area called Dust Bowl Colorado
New Mexico Kansas Texas Oklahoma

Handbook
page 572

Practice and Apply

Review Your Plan

1. Look at your outline.
2. List the questions you have about your topic.
3. Decide what resources you will use.
4. Add new details and information to your outline.

Checklist ✓

Research and Inquiry

- Did you make a list of questions?
- Did you think of resources you can use to answer your questions?
- Did you write down the facts you found?

Writing PROCESS

Draft

Before you begin your expository writing, look at the outline you made. Think of dividing the information into paragraphs. Each paragraph has a main idea and supporting details.

OUTLINE

I. Settlers on the prairie
  A. Dug up grass
  B. Soil became loose
    because the grass held the soil in place
II. Drought in 1930s
  A. Dry soil
  B. Clouds of dust
  C. Area called Dust Bowl Colorado
    New Mexico Kansas Texas Oklahoma
III. Hard years for many people
  A. Farms ruined
  B. People left homes

Each section of the outline can become one paragraph.

Main idea for second paragraph

Main idea for third paragraph

Checklist

Drafting

- Does your writing fit your purpose and audience?
- Have you given important information about one main topic?
- Have you included facts and details about the topic?
- Have you included information from different sources?
- Does your writing follow your outline?

Look at how the writer used his outline to organize the information in his first draft. He explained the settlers' effect on the land, and then went on to explain what happened when the drought hit.

DRAFT

Hard Times on the Prairie

Many people settled on the Great Plains. They dug up miles of grassland. They did not have no idea that the grass held the soil in place. The soil became loose

In the 1930s, a long drought began. The soil dried out. The wind swept up the dry, loose soil. Parts of Colorado, New Mexico Kansas Texas and Oklahoma became known as the Dust Bowl.

Many farms were ruined. The land had been damaged. thousands of people left there homes. Today many people live in this region. Yes the 1930s where hard years on the American prairie.

Main idea of first paragraph

Main idea of second paragraph

Supporting details tell about the drought.

Main idea of third paragraph

Practice and Apply

Draft Your Own Expository Writing

1. Review your outline.
2. Write about the facts you know and the new information you learned from your research.
3. Put your information in a logical order.

TECHNOLOGY

If you typed an outline on the computer, copy it to use as your draft. Make each item in the outline a complete sentence. Then add and rearrange details.

Writing PROCESS

Revise

Elaborate

One way to improve your writing is to elaborate. When you elaborate, you add details and information that help explain your ideas. When you revise your writing, you may wish to add information that states your ideas more clearly.

The writer added important information to elaborate on a point.

> and planted crops
> They dug up miles of grassland.^

The writer added more details to help the reader understand his information.

> strong prairie
> The^wind swept up the dry, loose soil.

Word Choice

When you are writing, it is important to choose words that will help link ideas that are related.

In expository writing, use transition words and phrases that make one idea flow into another.

> Consequently,
> In the 1930s, a long drought began. ^The soil dried out.

TRANSITION WORDS

and
therefore
as a result
at the same time
when
but
also
thus
for example
before long
however
because
consequently

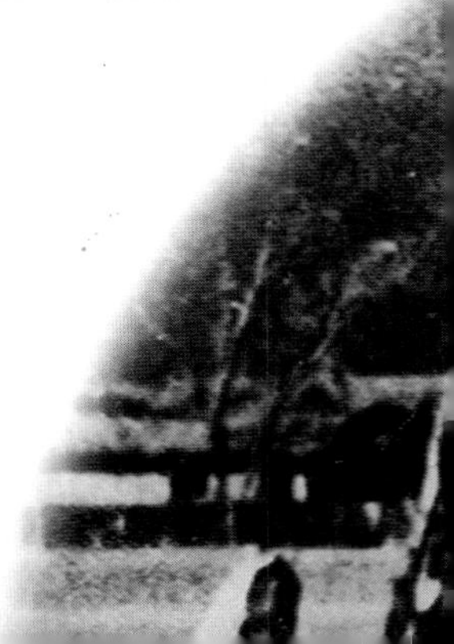

Better Sentences

As you revise your writing, read your paragraphs aloud to see if the information is clear. Do the ideas in your paragraph flow easily from one sentence to the next? Combining sentences can help your ideas flow better.

Sometimes you can combine two short sentences to make one complex sentence that is more interesting.

> Many farms were ruined because the land had been damaged.

Practice and Apply

Revise Your Own Expository Writing

1. Add explanations and descriptions that will help make your meaning clear.
2. Use transition words that will help link ideas in your paragraphs.
3. Put information in a logical order.
4. **Grammar** Should you combine two related sentences to make a complex sentence?

PREWRITE
DRAFT
REVISE
PROOFREAD
PUBLISH

Handbook
page 541

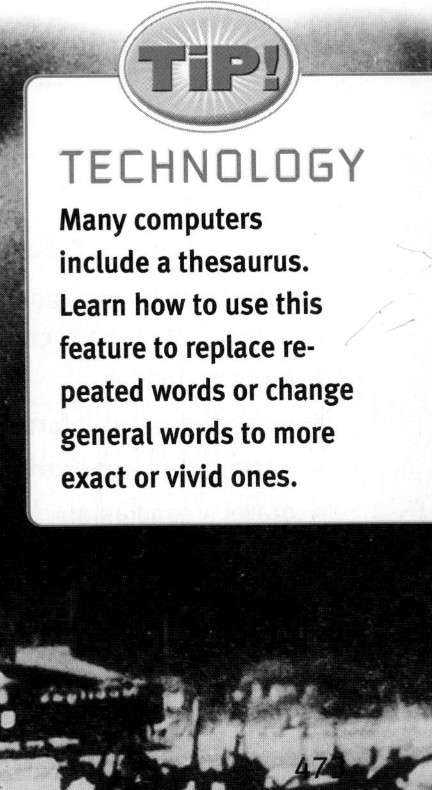

TIP!
TECHNOLOGY
Many computers include a thesaurus. Learn how to use this feature to replace repeated words or change general words to more exact or vivid ones.

Revise • Peer Conferencing

Take a break from writing. Give your partner a chance to read a copy of your first draft and to suggest changes that will make it better.

When did this happen?

You should use a transition word to link these two ideas.

This sentence doesn't fit the main idea of your report.

Hard Times on the Prairie

Many people settled on the Great Plains. They dug up miles of grassland. They did not have no idea that the grass held the soil in place. The soil became loose

In the 1930s, a long drought began. The soil dried out. The wind swept up the dry, loose soil. Parts of Colorado, New Mexico Kansas Texas and Oklahoma became known as the Dust Bowl.

Many farms were ruined. The land had been damaged. thousands of people left there homes. Today many people live in this region. Yes the 1930s where hard years on the American prairie.

Good conclusion!

Conferencing for the Reader

- Are the features of expository writing included in your partner's work?
  - has a main idea
  - gives important information
  - summarizes information
  - draws a conclusion
  - uses transition words
- Make sure to tell your partner what's good about the piece, as well as what needs improvement.

When you revise your expository writing, you can use your partner's comments and suggestions to help you decide what changes need to be made. Look at the changes this writer made after talking to his partner.

REVISE

Hard Times on the Prairie

In the early 1900s,
^Many people settled on the Great Plains. They
and planted crops
dug up miles of grassland^. They did not have no
As a result,
idea that the grass held the soil in place.^The soil
became loose

Consequently,
In the 1930s, a long drought began.^The soil
strong prairie and made huge clouds of dust
dried out. The^wind swept up the dry, loose soil^.
Thus,
^Parts of Colorado, New Mexico Kansas Texas and
Oklahoma became known as the Dust Bowl.

because
Many farms were ruined^The land had been
damaged. thousands of people left there homes.
~~Today many people live in this region~~. Yes the 1930s
where hard years on the American prairie.

Practice and Apply

Revise Your Own Expository Writing

1. Read your draft aloud or have your partner read it to you. Listen carefully to how it sounds.
2. Use notes from your peer conference to fix any problems in your writing.
3. Check that your changes read well.

Checklist

Revising

- Does your expository writing fit your purpose and audience?
- Do you need to elaborate on any of the facts you have included?
- Did you present events in a logical order?
- Did you use transition words to link one idea to the next?
- Do your sentences flow together?

Proofread

After you have revised your expository writing, you will need to proofread it to correct errors in grammar, mechanics and usage, and spelling.

STRATEGIES FOR PROOFREADING

- Reread your revised paper several times. Check for different types of errors each time.
- Check for mistakes in grammar and usage. Avoid double negatives.
- Reread to correct punctuation errors. Be sure to check for commas in a series and after introductory words.
- Check for spelling mistakes. Read your paper from the bottom to the top, word for word, to spot errors more easily.

TECHNOLOGY

It is often easier to catch mistakes on paper than on screen. For proofreading, print out your work, mark the corrections on paper, and then enter the corrections on the computer.

REVIEW THE RULES

GRAMMAR

- A negative is a word that means "no."
- A double negative is an error in which two negatives are used in the same sentence.
- You can correct a double negative by taking out a negative word or changing a negative word to a positive word.

MECHANICS

- Use commas to separate items in a series.
- Use a comma to set off an introductory word.

Look at the proofreading corrections made on the draft shown below. What does the symbol / mean? When does the writer use that symbol?

PROOFREAD

Hard Times on the Prairie

In the early 1900s,
^Many people settled on the Great Plains. They dug up miles of grassland. They did not have ~~no~~ any idea that the grass held the soil in place. As a result, The soil became loose.

In the 1930s, a long drought began. Consequently, The soil dried out. The strong prairie wind swept up the dry, loose soil and made huge clouds of dust. Thus, Parts of Colorado, New Mexico, Kansas, Texas, and Oklahoma became known as the Dust Bowl.

Many farms were ruined because The land had been damaged. thousands of people left ~~there~~ their homes. ~~Today many people live in this region.~~ Yes, the 1930s ~~where~~ were hard years on the American prairie.

PREWRITE

DRAFT

REVISE

PROOFREAD

PUBLISH

Checklist

Proofreading

- Did you spell all the words correctly?
- Did you use commas correctly?
- Did you use capital letters where needed?
- Did you avoid double negatives?

PROOFREADING MARKS

- # new paragraph
- ^ add
- take out
- ≡ Make a capital letter.
- / Make a small letter.
- (SP) Check the spelling.
- ⊙ Add a period.

Practice and Apply

Proofread Your Own Expository Writing

1. Correct spelling mistakes.
2. Check for commas in a series and after introductory words.
3. Check that capital letters are used correctly.
4. Avoid grammar and usage errors, such as double negatives.

Publish

Before you publish your work, review your writing one more time. Use a checklist to help you.

Self-Check Expository Writing

- ❑ Who was my audience? Will my writing be clear to them?
- ❑ What was my purpose for writing? Did I organize my information so that my audience can understand it?
- ❑ Did I add a title?
- ❑ Did I include explanations and facts that support my topic?
- ❑ Did I present the information in a logical order?
- ❑ Did I organize my paragraphs so that the ideas flow smoothly?
- ❑ Did I check for mistakes in grammar?
- ❑ Did I correct all errors in capitalization and punctuation?

The writer used the checklist to look his writing over one last time. Read "Hard Times on the Prairie" and write about it in your journal. Do you think the piece was ready for publishing? Give reasons for your ideas.

Hard Times on the Prairie

by Daniel Harris

In the early 1900s, many people settled on the Great Plains. They dug up miles of grass-land and planted crops. They did not have any idea that the grass held the soil in place. As a result, the soil became loose.

In the 1930s, a long drought began. Consequently, the soil dried out. The strong prairie wind swept up the dry, loose soil and made huge clouds of dust. Thus, parts of Colorado, New Mexico, Kansas, Texas, and Oklahoma became known as the Dust Bowl.

Many farms were ruined because the land had been damaged. Thousands of people left their homes. Yes, the 1930s were hard years on the American prairie.

TIP!

TECHNOLOGY

You may want to add graphics to your document. Learn how to use your computer to insert charts, graphs, or clip-art in your report.

PRACTICE AND APPLY

Publish Your Own Expository Writing

1. Give your revised draft one more careful look.
2. Make a neat final copy.
3. Add maps, charts, photographs, or illustrations to your report.

Present Your Expository Writing

To make a good presentation, you need to plan and practice. Here are some things you can do to make your presentation a success.

STEP 1

How to Give Your Report

Strategies for Speaking As you prepare your report, keep in mind that you are presenting information that might not be familiar to your audience.

- Write each main point on a note card, followed by the details that support it.
- Emphasize the phrases that point out time sequence, reasons, or conclusions.
- Speak loudly and clearly so that everyone can hear you.

Listening Strategies

- **Set a purpose. Are you listening to learn new information, or are you listening to be entertained?**
- **Take notes on the speaker's main ideas.**
- **Listen for details that support the speaker's points.**
- **Save your questions for the end of the presentation.**

Multimedia Ideas

You might want to show slides with your presentation. Be sure that you know how to work the equipment and make a note of when you will change each slide during your presentation.

STEP 2

How to Show Your Report

Suggestions for Visuals Visuals and props can make your presentation more interesting.

- Present maps or diagrams to show your audience where something is.
- Photographs or drawings can help your listeners picture scenes in their heads.
- Props or costumes can bring your ideas to life.

STEP 3

How to Share Your Report

Strategies for Rehearsing The more you practice, the more comfortable you will be when it is time to give your presentation.

- Practice using your props and visuals to be sure they are not distracting.
- Present your report to your family, and ask for suggestions.
- Practice with a partner, and have him or her comment on your presentation.

Viewing Strategies

- **Sit where you can see the speaker and the visuals.**
- **Pay attention to how the visuals support the speaker's ideas.**
- **Note any additional information contained in the visuals.**

Practice and Apply

Present Your Own Expository Writing

1. Write each point you want to make on a separate note card.
2. Prepare maps, photographs, drawings, or props to support your points.
3. Practice your report by presenting it to your family.
4. Present your information clearly, and answer questions.

Writing Tests

On a writing test, you are asked to write a composition in response to a prompt. You must read the prompt carefully so that you will know your topic and understand how to approach it.

Look for words or phrases that tell you the purpose of your writing.

Use a style that suits your audience.

This phrase tells you what kind of information to include in your article.

Prompt

What is the most important information that someone should know about your school?

Write an article for the parents of new students. Tell them about your school. Include facts and details in your article.

How to Read a Prompt

Purpose Read the prompt again. What words tell you your purpose for writing? The words "Write an article" and the topic of the article tell you that your purpose is to inform.

Audience Sometimes a prompt tells you who your audience is. This prompt tells you to write for the parents of new students. If a prompt does not name your audience, write for your teacher.

Expository Writing In expository writing, you present information about a topic. The phrase "Include facts and details" tells you how to support your main idea. Draw a conclusion based on the information you present.

Test Tip

Check that your details support your main idea.

How to Write to a Prompt

Here are some tips to keep in mind when you are given a prompt on a writing test.

Before Writing **Content/Ideas**	• Think about your purpose. • Keep your audience in mind. • Make a list of ideas. • Stay focused on the topic.
During Writing **Organization/ Paragraph Structure**	• Write a good topic sentence. • In expository writing, support your main idea with facts and details. • Use transition words to connect your ideas. • Finish with a strong conclusion.
After Writing **Grammar/Usage**	• Proofread your work. • Use the correct form of adverbs that compare. • Make sure that you have used commas in series and after introductory words. • Look for spelling errors.

Apply

When you read a prompt, look for the purpose and audience. Determine the topic and then plan the best way to organize your ideas.

Prompt

What interesting, important event took place recently?

Write an article for your local paper about an important event that occurred in your community, in your state, or in another country. Include facts and details.

Grammar and Writing Review

pages 420–423

Adverbs

A. Write each sentence. Underline the adverb. Then write whether it tells *how*, *when*, or *where*.

1. The coach arrived early.
2. Lill was at the field since she lived nearby.
3. The girls hurriedly sprinted around the track.
4. It felt a little muggy outside.
5. Wendy kicked the ball hard.
6. Yoko scored a goal first.
7. The coach carefully watched the players.
8. The Rockets desperately needed a win.
9. It began to rain heavily.
10. The teammates quickly packed up their equipment.

pages 424–427

Adverbs That Compare

B. Write each sentence. Choose the correct word in parentheses ( ).

11. My class paints (more, most) skillfully of all the classes at Windridge Elementary.
12. We painted (slower, slowest) today than yesterday.
13. Our teacher praised our work (more, most) frequently than she had on Tuesday.
14. Greg worked (harder, hardest) on the mural than Terrence.
15. Lynn outlined the (more, most) clearly of all the students in the class.
16. Julie drew (more, most) carefully than Briana.
17. Fred started his work (earlier, earliest) than Jeff.
18. The boys in the hall worked (more, most) quietly than the rest of us.
19. Our mural was displayed (longer, longest) than we expected.
20. When it was finished, we all smiled (more, most) happily than we ever had.

Unit 6 Review

pages 428–429

Mechanics and Usage: Using *Good* and *Well*

C. Write each sentence. Choose the word in parentheses ( ) that correctly completes the sentence.

21. Mom had been sick but felt (good, well) enough to go to the show.

22. She and Mark had a (good, well) time at the performance.

23. They could see and hear the actors (good, well).

24. The star of the show sang (good, well).

25. The show got (good, well) reviews in the paper.

pages 432–433

Negatives

D. Write each sentence. Underline the negative word.

26. Lucy had never gotten her hair cut.

27. Nobody had hair as long as Lucy's hair.

28. Lucy was not sure she wanted to get it cut.

29. Lucy didn't like combing out the tangles.

30. She decided that shorter hair wouldn't be as much trouble.

pages 434–435

Prepositions

E. Write each sentence. Circle the preposition.

31. The library is open on Tuesday.

32. Ruth likes going there after school.

33. She sits at the big table and reads.

34. Ruth goes home by six o'clock.

35. The librarian walks Ruth to the bus.

Unit 6 Review

pages 436–437

Prepositional Phrases

F. Write each sentence. Underline the prepositional phrases.

36. The Wilsons went sailing on a boat.

37. They sailed around a group of islands.

38. They floated beside some dolphins.

39. At night, they docked in little harbors.

40. They dove off the boat for a swim.

41. They slept in bunk beds inside the boat.

42. Eric and Jenny looked for big fish.

43. Grandpa told stories about his life as a sailor.

44. Mrs. Wilson taped the stories on a recorder.

45. She is writing about their adventures on the sea.

pages 438–439

Combining Sentences: Complex Sentences

G. Write a complex sentence that can be formed by combining the two shorter sentences with a conjunction.

46. Liz doesn't like cats. They make her sneeze.

47. Liz can tell right away. A cat is nearby.

48. Her eyes water. She goes near a cat.

49. Liz stays away from cats. She doesn't like feeling ill.

50. Liz checks for cats. She enters a room.

pages 440–441

Mechanics and Usage: Commas

H. Write each sentence. Use commas where they are needed.

51. Mom have you ever been to California?

52. Yes I have Jonathan. I lived there as a child.

53. No I haven't been back in more than twenty years.

54. Well I'd like to go with you if you ever return.

55. Sure Jonathan. I'd love to take you.

pages 454–455

Vocabulary: Suffixes

I. Write each sentence. Underline the words that have suffixes.

56. My teacher is a woodworker.

57. He happily carves furniture.

58. He makes wonderful chairs and tables.

59. He shows us how to carve wood safely.

60. We are all very careful with the tools.

pages 456–457

Composition: Outlining

J. Use the following notes to create an outline for a report about Helen Keller.

Who was Helen Keller?
—Born in Alabama in 1880
—Became blind and deaf in childhood illness
—Read by Braille system
—Died in 1968
What did Helen Keller do?
—Overcame severe physical disabilities
—Learned to communicate
—Graduated college with honors
—Gave speeches throughout the world

pages 476–477

Proofreading Expository Writing

K. Write the following paragraph. Correct ten mistakes in punctuation, capitalization, grammar, and spelling.

A endangered animal is any animal that is close to dying out. Some animals is endangered because people hunt them most often than other animals. Other animals are in trouble because they have been forsed to leave there homes. When a tree is cut down or a river is dammed, an animal loses it's home. Furthermore, there are animals that don't have no more food. three species a day on earth become extinct and will not never live on this planet again. Every day, more species move more closer to extinction.

Project File

ACTIVITY 1 A News Article

A news article presents facts and information about a recent or future event. Study the features shown in the following sample, and use them when you write news.

You will need to know the features of a news story to write your own news report.

Red-Tailed Hawk Goes West

TEXAS, June 12 — The Red-Tailed Hawk marching band has been invited to tour the Western states beginning Aug. 15. The band, led by music teacher Albert Chin, will first perform with other bands at the University of Washington. Then they will travel to San Francisco and on to Portland for a final concert at the University of Oregon on Aug. 25.

"This is a really big honor for us," said drum major Artie Russo. "Our band was selected from a group of 25 that competed in this year's Pumpkin Festival. Ours is the only band from the region that was invited."

Band members are now selling T-shirts to help raise the $4500 needed for the trip. These are available in the school office.

Headline *Tells what the article is about and captures the reader's attention.*

Dateline *Tells when and where the article was written.*

Facts *Give information that answers the questions* Who? What? When? Where? *and* Why?

Direct Quotations *Add interesting details to the article and tell the audience more about the topic.*

Write a News Article The Sunday edition of a newspaper often includes several different sections such as travel, books, sports, the arts, and business. These sections make the newspaper more interesting for a variety of readers. Report on a topic that would appear in one of the sections in a Sunday newspaper. Use the model of a news article on page 488 to help you write an article of your own.

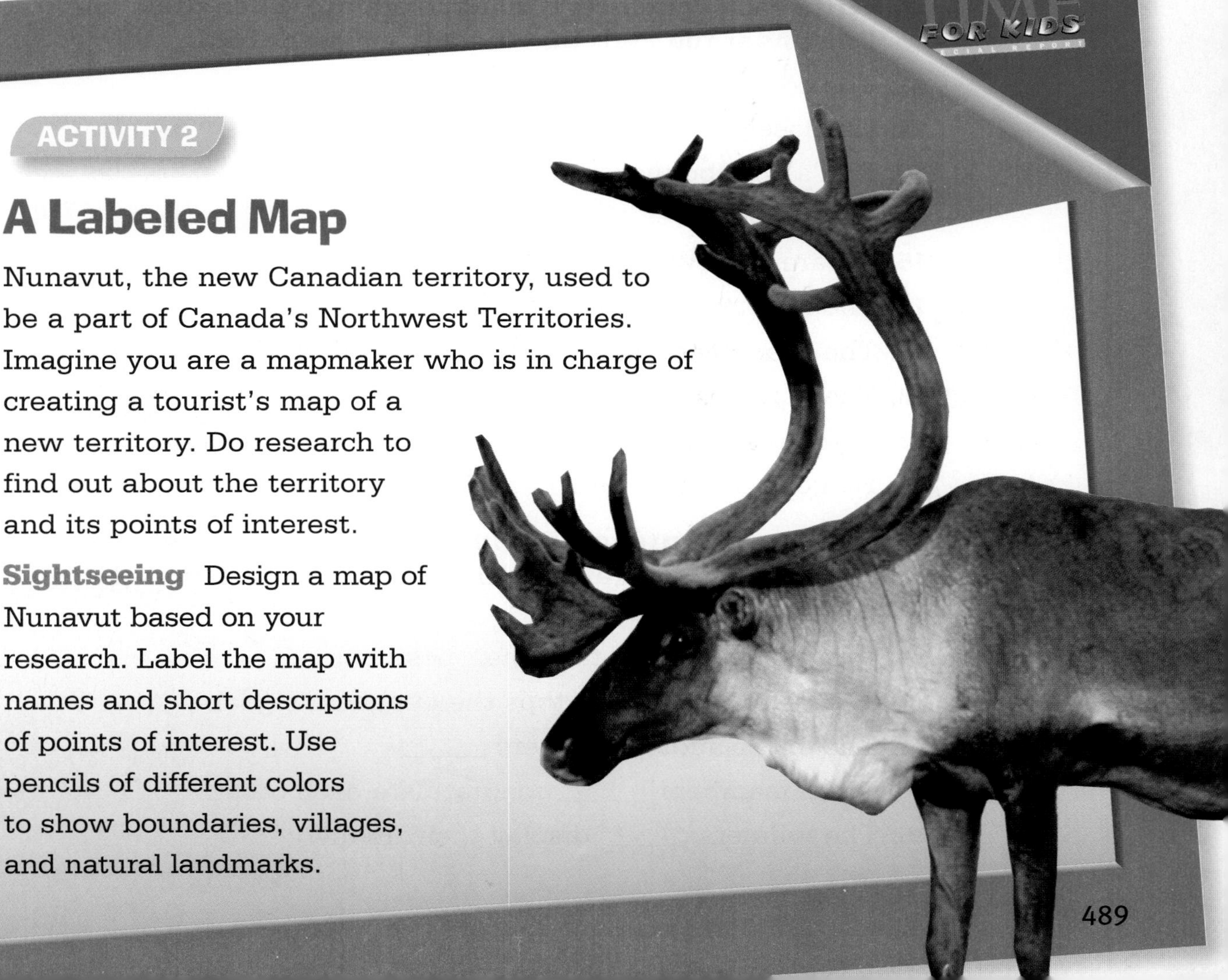

ACTIVITY 2

A Labeled Map

Nunavut, the new Canadian territory, used to be a part of Canada's Northwest Territories. Imagine you are a mapmaker who is in charge of creating a tourist's map of a new territory. Do research to find out about the territory and its points of interest.

Sightseeing Design a map of Nunavut based on your research. Label the map with names and short descriptions of points of interest. Use pencils of different colors to show boundaries, villages, and natural landmarks.

Grammar

Extra Practice

Adverbs That Tell *How*

A. Write each sentence. Circle the adverb that describes each underlined verb.

1. Margie quickly runs onto the soccer field.
2. The coach blows his whistle loudly.
3. The players start slowly down the field.
4. The members of the other team move fast.
5. Ellie fiercely kicks the ball toward the goal.
6. The soccer ball bounces wildly.
7. Rita races swiftly up the field.
8. She carefully aims toward the goal.
9. The goalkeeper barely catches the ball.
10. The girls gladly rest at halftime.

B. Write each sentence. Circle the adverb. Then draw one line under the verb that the adverb describes.

11. The coach stands patiently on the sidelines.
12. He closely watches the teams compete.
13. Rita's shot bounces quickly off the pole.
14. The coach paces slowly on the sidelines.
15. A parent nervously looks at the scoreboard.
16. The spectators clap loudly for their players.
17. The coach nods encouragingly to each player.
18. The players cheer happily with each goal.
19. The goalkeeper gleefully tosses her cap in the air.
20. Win or lose, the coach cheerfully praises his team.

C. Write each sentence. Fill in an adverb to complete the sentence. Then draw one line under the verb that the adverb describes.

21. The players ______ take their positions.
22. The defender ______ stops the opponent's goal.
23. The entire audience cheers ______.
24. Team members ______ congratulate each other.
25. The winners ______ display their trophy.

Adverbs That Tell *When* or *Where*

A. Write each sentence. Draw a line under the adverb. Then write whether the adverb tells *when* or *where*.

1. Ben never misses science class.
2. Ben arrives early to every lecture.
3. Later Rob visits the computer lab.
4. Rob looks everywhere for interesting web sites.
5. Jill always finishes her science homework.
6. Yesterday Jill studied for two hours.
7. The science club meets upstairs.
8. Our club holds a meeting weekly.
9. Rob, Ben, and Jill hurry there.
10. Sometimes Miss Romano comes to our activities.

B. Write each sentence. Draw one line under the adverb. Write whether the adverb describes *how*, *when*, or *where*.

11. The science club hosts a science fair yearly.
12. Students prepare their display early.
13. Students build displays outdoors.
14. Teachers and parents usually help.
15. Ben once won first prize.
16. His displays cleverly use solar power.
17. Ben waits impatiently for the booths to be judged.
18. Finally, the judges announced the winner.
19. Ben proudly accepted the award.
20. He still has his ribbon.

C. Write each sentence. Complete the sentence with an adverb that tells *when* or *where*.

21. Mary ______ has the most interesting booth.
22. She displays her paintings and photographs ______.
23. She designs her booth ______.
24. ______ Mary will be a great artist.
25. She wants to work and live ______.

Grammar

Extra Practice

Adverbs That Compare

A. Write each sentence. Draw one line under the adverb that compares.

1. Our track meet runs longer than any other one.
2. Tina throws a ball faster than Ben can.
3. Lori can run fastest of the three students.
4. Bob jumps higher than Eddy does.
5. Lou jumps highest of all the team members.
6. The Jaguars' team starts sooner than we do.
7. The Tigers came closest of all to defeating us.
8. This year we will work harder than we did before.
9. I always run slowest of all in the 438.
10. The race finished faster than it did last year.

B. Write each sentence. Choose the correct form of the adverb in parentheses ( ).

11. Kara practices (harder, hardest) than I do.
12. Jake always cheers the (louder, loudest) of all.
13. Kim jumps the (higher, highest) of all the team members.
14. Toni sprints (faster, fastest) than Kim does.
15. Judy started (sooner, soonest) than Aileen.
16. Teddy jumped (lower, lowest) than he did in practice.
17. Our team practices (longer, longest) than the other team.
18. Our coach watches (closer, closest) of all the spectators.
19. I had to run (harder, hardest) than my opponent to win.
20. The trip to the state final lasted the (longer, longest) of all.

C. Write each sentence. Write the correct form of the adverb in parentheses.

21. Rick stays ______ than Jake does. (long)
22. Lucy can jump ______ after a warmup than she jumps before. (high)
23. Wes sprinted the ______ on the relay team. (fast)
24. I arrive ______ of all. (early)
25. Our team shouted ______ than the spectators did. (loud)

More Adverbs That Compare

A. Write each sentence. Choose the correct word in parentheses ( ).

1. Alejandro left for camp (most, more) eagerly than Greg.
2. Len packed his things (more, most) rapidly than I did.
3. Gina waited (more, most) patiently of all.
4. Andrea worried (more, most) often about spiders than Julia did.
5. Chuck learned to swim (more, most) quickly of all.
6. Cathie rode (more, most) elegantly than Pam.
7. We found frogs (more, most) frequently in the pond than in the stream.
8. I fell asleep (more, most) slowly than I do at home.
9. Vic learned to name animal tracks (more, most) easily than I.
10. Tasha prepared for hikes (more, most) carefully than we did.

B. Write each sentence. Write *more* or *most* to complete the sentence.

11. The girls cleaned the cabin ______ carefully than the boys did.
12. Robin swam ______ gracefully than Ken.
13. Ed sang the ______ loudly at campfire.
14. Jim ate the ______ rapidly of all.
15. Sandi hiked the ______ swiftly to the top.
16. Our group hiked ______ quietly than the group behind us.
17. The second group stomped ______ eagerly than we did.
18. Dean caught fish ______ quickly than Rosa.
19. Phil learned waterskiing ______ easily than anyone else.
20. Ted left camp ______ suddenly of all.

C. Write each sentence. Use *more* or *most* with the adverb in parentheses ( ).

21. Campers talk ______ of all after "lights out." (loudly)
22. Betsy ate ______ than her friend. (hungrily)
23. Juan cleaned his bunk ______ than Marcos did. (quickly)
24. Kelly packed her things ______ than I did. (slowly)
25. I packed ______ of all. (rapidly)

Extra Practice

Using *Good* and *Well*

A. Write each sentence. Choose *good* or *well* to complete the sentence correctly.

1. Dog training is a (good, well) career.
2. It is helpful to have a dog that behaves (good, well).
3. My dog does not act (good, well) all the time.
4. He is a (good, well) companion for me.
5. Some dog breeds learn new things (good, well).
6. My dog behaves (good, well) around other dogs.
7. He is a (good, well) ball catcher.
8. Many dogs did not do as (good, well) as mine.
9. My dog was not feeling (good, well) yesterday.
10. Today he enjoys (good, well) health.

B. Write each sentence. Use *good* or *well* to complete the sentence correctly.

11. My family has a ______ dog named Otto.
12. My dog listens ______ to commands.
13. Sometimes he does not feel ______.
14. His health is ______ most of the time.
15. Otto performs tricks very ______.
16. When a dog behaves ______, everyone is happy.
17. My dog makes a ______ watchdog.
18. Many scientists think that having a pet keeps us ______.
19. Otto is a ______ companion when I am feeling lonely.
20. I take care of Otto to keep him ______.

C. Write each sentence. Complete the sentence by putting *good* in one blank and *well* in the other.

21. A ______ dog does her tricks ______.
22. You will do ______ to adopt a dog from a ______ shelter.
23. A faithful dog will treat you ______ and be a ______ learner.
24. A dog can be a ______ companion when you are not feeling ______.
25. My dog is my ______ pal, and he listens ______.

Negatives

A. Write *negative* or *not a negative* to tell whether the underlined word is a negative word.

1. Karen had <u>never</u> been to the marsh before.
2. She was <u>not</u> sure what to expect.
3. There seemed to be <u>nothing</u> in the water.
4. No one had <u>shown</u> her what lived in the marsh.
5. <u>Nobody</u> sees the insects at first.
6. The insects were <u>not</u> easy to see.
7. A water bug <u>wouldn't</u> swim any closer.
8. A pond <u>skater</u> doesn't seem to weigh much.
9. The pond skater <u>glides</u> on the water with no effort.
10. Karen <u>didn't</u> know a marsh had so much to see.

B. Write each sentence. Draw a line under the negative word.

11. Karen couldn't believe how a cattail feels.
12. She had never watched a marsh hawk fly before!
13. The marsh hawk glided above us with no effort.
14. The small frogs wouldn't let us get too close.
15. There was a type of frog I had never seen before.
16. None of the insects bothered us that day.
17. It wasn't long before we spotted a mallard duck.
18. He didn't appear to see us.
19. No one moved as we watched the duck float away.
20. Nobody can tell us that a marsh is empty.

C. Write each sentence. Choose the correct word in parentheses ( ).

21. We hadn't seen (any, none) of the catfish.
22. Karen hadn't (ever, never) seen so many wild creatures.
23. She couldn't wait (any, no) longer to tell someone else.
24. No one (wouldn't, would) believe me.
25. We (will, won't) never forget this trip.

Grammar

Extra Practice

Prepositions

A. Write each sentence. Draw a circle around the preposition that comes before the underlined noun or pronoun.

1. Chad enjoys his art class at school.
2. His teacher is a painter of landscapes.
3. The class paints a scene of the river.
4. Chad likes mixing colors with a brush.
5. He set his paints near him.
6. Meg painted a picture of the ocean.
7. Leo painted the tree behind his house.
8. Chad observes carefully around him.
9. The paintings will be in an art show.
10. Meg will share her supplies with them.

B. Write the sentences. Draw one line under the prepositions. There may be more than one preposition in each sentence.

11. Meg and Leo live in an apartment near the hospital.
12. They go to school with Chad.
13. In the summer, Meg lives at the beach.
14. Meg enjoys painting by the water.
15. Leo is interested in wildlife.
16. He paints pictures of plants and animals.
17. Chad likes working with colors.
18. Most students like working under bright lights.
19. The teacher keeps her art books on the desk beside her.
20. She will share them with her students.

C. Write each sentence. Complete the sentence with a preposition that makes sense.

21. Meg is a star artist ______ her art class.
22. Leo creates pictures ______ his supplies.
23. You can see my painting hanging ______ the wall.
24. Chad paints ______the window.
25. I am learning ______ colors.

Prepositional Phrases

A. Write each sentence. Circle the preposition in each underlined prepositional phrase.

1. Liz is spending her summer at her father's house.
2. She is building trails with him.
3. He is a ranger for the Forest Service.
4. The rangers are clearing the brush on the trails.
5. Liz loves to go exploring with them.
6. The rangers lead hikes in the evening.
7. They have spotted herds of wild horses.
8. She loves hearing the coyotes at night.
9. Great horned owls hoot from their nests.
10. Liz feels safe and secure inside her forest cabin.

B. Write each sentence. Draw one line under the preposition. Circle the noun or pronoun that follows the preposition.

11. Many hikers use the trail by the creek.
12. The winding creek leads to a meadow.
13. The people eat their lunch at the top.
14. Liz's dad carried a pack up the trail.
15. The heavy pack had the supplies for them.
16. The hikers chose a place by a waterfall.
17. Liz splashes her hands and feet in the water.
18. The water bubbles around her.
19. After lunch, Liz and Dad hike back down.
20. By that evening, they are very tired.

C. Write each sentence. Draw a line under each prepositional phrase. Draw a second line under the noun or pronoun in the prepositional phrase. Circle the preposition.

21. Liz's father knows many things about the forest.
22. All winter long, he works at the station.
23. He comes home on the weekends.
24. Liz enjoys spending time with her father.
25. She feels as if she learns a lot about nature.

Grammar

Extra Practice

Combining Sentences: Complex Sentences

A. Write the two sentences that have been combined to make each sentence.

1. Miss Joy's class is busy because they have a garden.
2. The students work after school until it gets dark.
3. They water the plants when the sun goes down.
4. They work in pairs to weed since weeding is dull.
5. They set out their seedlings after winter has passed.
6. Sue planted tomatoes because everyone likes them.
7. The children planted squash after Jesse shared her recipe.
8. They check the garden before they go to class.
9. They go to the garden while they study science.
10. You learn a lot when you study plant growth.

B. Write each sentence. Join the two parts with a conjunction.

11. You can study insects ______ you visit a garden.
12. Miss Joy teaches gardening ______ she loves the outdoors.
13. Students can observe wildlife ______ they pick vegetables.
14. Butterflies and bees appear ______ the flowers bloom.
15. Slugs and snails come out ______ the rain falls.
16. Set up a weather station ______ you study climate.
17. You should find out about plants ______ you start seeds.
18. Vegetables are not sold ______ the market is open.
19. Students apply for work ______ school is on vacation.
20. Everyone eats vegetables ______the garden has so many.

C. Write the complex sentence that can be formed by combining the two shorter sentences with conjunctions.

21. Lee gardens at home. She learned about plants.
22. She planted a fruit tree. She had extra space.
23. She eats peaches daily. They are in season.
24. Lee's grandpa helps her. He enjoys gardening, too.
25. Lee makes her garden larger. She runs out of space.

Commas

A. Write each sentence. Circle the introductory word or the name of a person spoken to and the comma or commas.

1. Yes, we drove to California on vacation.
2. No, I didn't get to surf at the beach.
3. Mrs. Johnson, we saw a lot of places in the state.
4. Well, I liked the cable cars in San Francisco.
5. Next time, Dad, I want to take a plane.
6. Yes, we walked across the Golden Gate Bridge.
7. Mom, what was the tallest landmark in San Francisco?
8. What part did you like best, Judy?
9. Well, I have to think about what I liked best.
10. Thomas, my favorite part was the sunny weather.

B. Write each sentence. Add commas where they are needed.

11. Gary we visited Washington, D.C., last November.
12. Yes we took a tour of the White House.
13. No I didn't see the president while I was there.
14. Mom did we tour the Federal Bureau of Investigation?
15. No the building was closed the day we were there.
16. I can't wait for our next trip Dad.
17. Well I know we will have a great time.
18. Yes my sister always keeps a journal on trips.
19. I take pictures and keep notes Mrs. Johnson.
20. Yes it is fun to read about the trip later.

C. Write the sentences. Add commas where they belong. Then write the rule you followed to add the comma.

21. Well here we are in Washington, D.C.
22. Mom the weather is sunny and cold.
23. Judy we rode the metro through the city.
24. I'll race you up the Washington Monument Mom.
25. Yes that is a great idea!

Cumulative Review

Unit 1 Sentences

A. Write each sentence correctly. Add capital letters, end punctuation, and commas where needed.

1. how do you ride a bicycle
2. please show me how to ride a bike
3. the pedals make the wheels turn, and the brakes make them stop
4. how hard is it to balance on a bike
5. george rides his bike to school, but Linda rides the bus

B. Write each sentence. Draw a line between the complete subject and the complete predicate. Draw one line under each simple subject and two lines under each simple predicate.

6. The track team meets after school.
7. My friends joined the team.
8. The coach stretches and runs laps with the team.
9. The girls and boys on the team jog every day.
10. The fastest runners on the team race to the finish line!

Unit 2 Nouns

A. Write the singular possessive and plural possessive forms of each noun.

11. puppy
12. fox
13. child
14. key
15. teachers

B. Write each proper noun, title, or abbreviation correctly.

16. north dakota
17. the wind in the willows
18. mrs julia ramirez
19. nov 5, 2001
20. uncle pete

Cumulative Review

Unit 3 Verbs

A. Write each sentence. Use the correct form of the verb in parentheses ( ).

21. Many birds (fly, flies) south in the winter.

22. They often (migrate, migrates) thousands of miles.

23. Some birds (returns, return) to the same place each year.

24. In winter, I make sure that my bird feeder (is, are) always full.

25. I know that winter birds (have, has) depended on us for food.

B. Write each sentence. Complete the sentence with the past-tense form of the verb in parentheses ( ).

26. Jack ______ a new sign for his flower shop. (make)

27. He ______ a picture of a beautiful garden. (draw)

28. Under the picture he ______, "Buy Boss Plant Food Today." (write)

29. Jeff ______ the sign and went into the store. (see)

30. He bought some plant food and has ______ it to his mom. (give)

Unit 4 Adjectives

A. Write each sentence. Draw one line under each adjective and two lines under each article. Circle any linking verbs.

31. The sky is clear.

32. Red apples hang on the trees.

33. The leaves are colorful.

34. A jolly scarecrow guards the field.

35. The scarecrow wears an old shirt.

B. Write each sentence. Use the correct form of the adjective in parentheses ( ) to compare.

36. Lee's story is ______ than Ed's story. (funny)

37. Sara wrote the ______ story of all. (good)

38. Joe presented the ______ report in the class. (interesting)

39. Ben's pictures were ______ than Mary's drawings. (big)

40. Kim made up the ______ poem that I have ever read. (long)

Cumulative Review

C. Write each sentence correctly. Add punctuation marks and use capital letters where they are needed.

41. Sam Houston is an american hero.

42. He led the battle that freed Texas from mexican rule.

43. Houston Texas was named after this great man.

44. Sam Houston was born in Lexington Virginia.

45. Houston died in Huntsville Texas on July 26 1863.

D. Combine each pair of sentences to make one sentence.

46. The children visited a zoo. The zoo was interesting.

47. They were invited to pet the animals. The animals were adorable.

48. Rex liked the goat. The goat was big.

49. A bunny curled up next to Joe's foot. The bunny was soft.

50. The animals enjoyed their visitors. The animals were friendly.

Unit 5 Pronouns

A. Write each sentence. Use the correct pronoun in parentheses ( ).

51. It is recess time for (we, us).

52. Joe played tag with (I, me).

53. I tagged (him, he) first.

54. (My, Mine) teacher and Meg turned the rope for some girls.

55. Sally jumped rope after (they, them).

B. Write each sentence. Use the correct word in parentheses ( ).

56. My friends are taking an art class during (they're, their) summer vacation.

57. (It's, Its) located on Seventh Street.

58. Visit the class next time (your, you're) in the neighborhood.

59. They (enjoy, enjoys) learning about art.

60. Next summer, I (want, wants) to take the same class.

C. Write each pair of sentences as one sentence by combining pronouns.

61. He went fishing. I went fishing.

62. Billy's cousins came with him. Billy's cousins came with me.

63. His sisters fished with us. His sisters fished with them.

64. We caught a lot of fish. They caught a lot of fish.

65. She cooked the fish. He cooked the fish.

D. Correct each sentence as you write it. Add punctuation marks and use capital letters where they are needed.

66. Dan asked, "would you help me weed my garden?"

67. He added, It is full of unruly weeds.

68. The leaves look yellow, said Gwen.

69. Dan replied, the plants are not getting enough light.

70. Gwen said, get your tools and let's begin.

Unit 6 Adverbs and Prepositions

A. Write each sentence. Draw a line under the adverb in each sentence. Write whether it tells *how*, *when*, or *where*.

71. The bus arrived early.

72. We walked fast.

73. My dog stayed behind.

74. He quietly whined.

75. I will see him soon.

B. Write each sentence. Complete the sentence with the correct adverb in parentheses ( ).

76. Bill and Gail skate (good, well).

77. Gail can skate (fastest, faster) than Bill.

78. Bill jumps (higher, highest) than Gail.

79. Gail spins (more quickly, most quickly) than Bill.

80. Ryan skates the (more skillfully, most skillfully) of all the students in the class.

Cumulative Review

C. Write each sentence correctly using only one negative.

81. Don't never stop learning new things.

82. You won't learn nothing unless you try.

83. Benjamin Franklin didn't discover nothing in just one try.

84. Don't give up on no ideas before you test them.

85. You can't never tell what might work.

D. Write each sentence. Draw one line under the prepositional phrase. Draw two lines under the preposition.

86. My grandmother lives in Pennsylvania.

87. Grandmother lives with Aunt June.

88. During the summer, it is fun to visit my relatives.

89. I swim in a creek that is behind their house.

90. A black dog sleeps on their porch every afternoon.

E. Write each pair of sentences as a single sentence, using the conjunction in parentheses ( ).

91. We drove carefully. The roads were narrow. (because)

92. The air grew colder. We climbed the mountain. (as)

93. We didn't see snow. We reached the top. (until)

94. We began to feel chilly. We put on our coats. (so)

95. We drove back down. We admired the view. (after)

F. Write each sentence. Add commas where they are needed.

96. Sally do you want to read to us?

97. Yes I would like to read this book.

98. Would you like to hear this story boys and girls?

99. Come here Jeffery and sit with the class.

100. Well we better get started so we won't be late for lunch.

Troubleshooter

Contents

Correcting Sentence Fragments

- A sentence is a group of words that expresses a complete thought.
- A sentence fragment does not express a complete thought.

Problem 1

A sentence fragment that does not have a subject

Sentence Fragment: *Took a trip.*

Who took a trip?

Solution 1

You need to add a subject to the sentence fragment to make it a complete sentence.

Sentence: *My family took a trip.*

Problem 2

A sentence fragment that does not have a predicate

Sentence Fragment: *My little sister and I.*

What about you and your little sister?

Solution 2

You need to add a predicate to the sentence fragment to make it a complete sentence.

Sentence: *My little sister and I hiked up a mountain.*

Problem 3

A sentence fragment that does not have a subject or a predicate

Sentence Fragment: *With the other hikers.*

Who is this about? What did they do?

Solution 3

Add a subject and a predicate to the fragment to make it a complete sentence.

Sentence: *We walked with the other hikers.*

Practice **Rewrite the sentence fragments to make complete sentences.**

1. Went to Colorado last winter.
2. Was so excited.
3. The mountains.
4. The people in the hotel.
5. Had never been to Colorado before.
6. Nervous about skiing on the mountain.
7. The ski instructor.
8. A new friend on the slopes.
9. Learned to ski together.
10. Best time of my life.

For more help, see Sentences on pages 2–7 and Handbook page 526.

Troubleshooter

Correcting Run-on Sentences

- A sentence is a group of words that expresses a complete thought.
- A run-on sentence contains two or more sentences that should stand alone.

Problem 1

Two sentences joined with no punctuation between them

Run-on Sentence: *Mrs. Carlson is a great teacher she knows all about frogs.*

Aren't these two complete thoughts?

Solution 1

Separate the two complete thoughts into two sentences, and add the necessary capitalization and punctuation.

Sentences: *Mrs. Carlson is a great teacher. She knows all about frogs.*

Problem 2

Two sentences joined only by a comma

Run-on Sentence: *Be a good listener, stay on the path next to the pond.*

Aren't these two different thoughts?

Solution 2

Add *and*, *but*, or *or* to connect the two thoughts.

Compound Sentence: *Be a good listener, and stay on the path next to the pond.*

Problem 3

Three or more sentences joined with *and*, *but*, or *or*

Run-on Sentence: *Tadpoles live underwater, and they look like fish, and they breathe through gills.*

Doesn't this sentence include three separate thoughts connected by *and*?

Solution 3

Create more than one sentence by separating ideas and using correct end punctuation. Join two closely related ideas to form a compound sentence.

Separate Sentences: *Tadpoles live underwater. They look like fish, and they breathe through gills.*

Practice **Rewrite these run-on sentences correctly.**

1. We went to the pond, and we searched for signs of life, and my group found the tadpoles first.
2. Tadpoles are one stage in the life cycle of a frog, they live underwater.
3. After a while, tadpoles become frogs, then they live on the land and breathe air.
4. I kept a journal about the tadpoles, and I wrote about their habitat, I did not include any photos of the changes I saw.
5. I am glad our class studied frogs, I learned a lot about them.

For more help, see Combining Sentences on pages 8–9, Correcting Run-on Sentences on pages 24–25, and Handbook page 527.

Confusing Plurals and Possessives

- A plural noun names more than one person, place, or thing. Plural nouns usually end in *s* or *es*.
- A possessive noun shows who or what *has* or *owns* something.
- To form the possessive of most singular nouns, add an apostrophe and an *s* (*'s*).
- To form the possessive of a plural noun that ends in *s*, add an apostrophe ('). To form the possessive of a plural noun not ending in *s*, add an apostrophe and an *s* (*'s*).

Problem 1

Using an apostrophe in a plural noun

Incorrect Plural Form: *The girl's read the book.*

Do the girls have or own anything?

Solution 1

Do not use an apostrophe with a plural noun.

Correct Plural Form: *The girls read the book.*

Problem 2

Leaving out an apostrophe in a singular possessive noun

Incorrect Possessive Form: *The girls mother drove her to the play.*

Doesn't the mother belong to the girl?

Solution 2

Correct a singular possessive noun by adding an apostrophe and an *s* (*'s*).

Correct Possessive Form: *The girl's mother drove her to the play.*

Problem 3

Putting the apostrophe in the wrong place in a plural possessive noun

Incorrect Form: *The childrens' favorite part of the play was the music.*

Where does the apostrophe belong in an irregular plural such as *children*?

Solution 3

To form the possessive of a plural noun not ending in *s*, add an apostrophe and an *s* (*'s*).

Correct Form: *The children's favorite part of the play was the music.*

Practice **Rewrite each sentence correctly. Choose the correct word in parentheses.**

1. The young (actor's, actors) were ready to begin their play.
2. Their (teachers, teacher's) had helped them rehearse.
3. The (characters, characters') costumes were all prepared.
4. The (announcers, announcer's) microphone was plugged in.
5. The (musicians, musicians') instruments were unpacked.
6. The (director's, directors) chair was in the back of the theater.
7. The (props, prop's) were set up on the stage.
8. The (men's, mens') choir was ready to begin the opening song.
9. The (children's, childrens') parents were in the audience.
10. The (curtain's, curtains) slowly opened.

For more help, see Plural Nouns on pages 90–95, Possessive Nouns on pages 102–105 and Handbook pages 530–531.

Lack of Subject-Verb Agreement

- In a sentence, a present-tense verb must be singular if the subject of the sentence is singular.
- The verb must be plural if the subject is plural.

Problem 1

Using a plural verb with a singular subject or a singular verb with a plural subject

No Agreement: *The puppy bark at the cat.*

No Agreement: *The other puppies runs around.*

Do the noun and the verb in each sentence agree?

Solution 1

Add *-s* to most verbs if the subject is singular. Add *-es* to verbs that end in *s*, *ch*, *sh*, *x*, or *z*. Do not add *-s* or *-es* if the subject is plural or if it is *I* or *you*.

Subject-Verb Agreement: *The puppy barks at the cat.*

Subject-Verb Agreement: *The other puppies run around.*

Problem 2

Using a singular verb with a compound subject joined by *and*

No Agreement: *My puppy and my cat dislikes each other.*

What is the subject? Is it singular or plural?

Solution 2

Remember to use a plural verb with a compound subject joined by *and*.

Subject-Verb Agreement: *My puppy and my cat dislike each other.*

Troubleshooter

Problem 3

Using the wrong verb form with a compound subject joined by *or*

No Agreement: *The clerks or the manager provide information about the animals in the pet store.*

What is the subject? Is it singular, plural, or both?

Solution 3

When a compound subject is joined by *or*, the verb agrees with the subject that is closer to it.

Subject-Verb Agreement: *The clerks or the manager provides information about the animals in the pet store.*

Practice **Write each sentence. Use the correct form of the verb in parentheses ( ).**

1. The pets (lives, live) in the pet store until they are sold.
2. Dogs and cats (stay, stays) in separate cages.
3. Baby mice or a parrot (is, are) usually in the window display.
4. Mike or his brothers (visit, visits) the animals each day.
5. The boys and their mother finally (buys, buy) their own pet.

For more help, see Subject-Verb Agreement on pages 174–175 and Handbook page 533.

Incorrect Verb Forms

- To form the past tense of irregular verbs, you do not add *-ed* to the verb.
- The spelling of irregular verbs changes in the past tense.

Problem 1

Using an incorrectly formed irregular verb

Incorrect Verb Form: *My friend Julia rided with me to choir practice.*

Is *rided* the correct past tense of *ride*?

Solution 1

Do not add *-ed* to the end of irregular verbs to change them to the past tense. Use the correct spelling of the verb.

Correct Verb Form: *My friend Julia rode with me to choir practice.*

Problem 2

Using an incorrect irregular verb form for the past tense

Incorrect Verb Form: *Choir practice begun at 4 o'clock.*

What are the verb forms of *begin*? When is each one used?

Solution 2

Many irregular verbs have special forms in the past tense. Make sure that you use the correct form.

Correct Verb Form: *Choir practice began at 4 o'clock.*

Troubleshooter

Problem 3

Using the incorrect irregular verb form with *have*

Incorrect Verb Form: *Our choir has sang "The Star-Spangled Banner."*

What form of *sing* do you use with *have* or *has*?

Solution 3

Many irregular verbs have special forms in the past tense with *have*. Check to be sure you know the correct form to use.

Correct Verb Form: *Our choir has sung "The Star-Spangled Banner."*

Practice **Write each sentence. Use the correct past-tense form of the verb in parentheses ( ).**

1. My choir director has ______ some of her own songs. (write)
2. She ______ us to the state capital to sing. (take)
3. We ______ to Austin in a large tour bus. (drive)
4. Each of us ______ one parent along. (bring)
5. Her songs have ______ to be quite popular. (grow)

For more help, see Irregular Verbs on pages 190–193 and Handbook page 535.

Incorrect Use of Adjectives That Compare

- For short adjectives, add *-er* or *-est* to compare. For long adjectives, use *more* or *most.*
- *Good* and *bad* have special forms when they are used to compare.

Troubleshooter

Problem 1

Using *-er* or *-est* instead of *more* or *most*

Incorrect Form: *Ancient history is the interestingest topic that I have studied.*

How do we make comparisons with a long adjective such as *interesting*?

Solution 1

For long adjectives, use *more* or *most* to compare people, places, or things.

Correct Form: *Ancient history is the most interesting topic that I have studied.*

Problem 2

Using *-er* or *-est* with *more* or *most*

Incorrect Form: *Some very old ruins are more higher than the trees.*

How do we make comparisons with a short adjective such as *high*?

Solution 2

With shorter adjectives, add *-er* or *-est* to compare people, places, or things. Do not use *-er* or *-est* with *more* or *most.*

Correct Form: *Some very old ruins are higher than the trees.*

Problem 3

Using the incorrect form when comparing with *good* or *bad*

Incorrect Form: *Their design may have been the goodest in all of history.*

What are the comparative forms of *good*?

Solution 3

Good and *bad* have special forms when used to compare. Use *better* and *worse* when comparing two people, places, or things. Use *best* and *worst* when comparing more than two people, places, or things.

Correct Form: *Their design may have been the best in all of history.*

Practice **Write the sentences. Use the correct form of each adjective in parentheses ( ).**

1. The rainy season is the (hard) time of all for scientists to dig.
2. It is much (easy) for them to dig in dry dirt than in damp mud.
3. The (bad) days of all are the days when the wind is blowing.
4. After much hard work, scientists occasionally find some of the (amazing) artifacts in the world.
5. I am (curious) about these ancient sites than I am about the buildings of today.

For more help, see Adjectives That Compare on pages 272–279 and Handbook pages 536–537.

Incorrect Use of Pronouns

- A pronoun must match the noun or nouns to which it refers.
- A subject pronoun is used as the subject of a sentence. An object pronoun is used in the predicate part.

Problem 1

Using a pronoun that does not match the noun to which it refers

Pronoun Does Not Match: *The boys fished in a lake. He wore life jackets.*

To which noun does *He* refer?

Solution 1

Singular pronouns take the place of singular nouns. Plural pronouns take the place of plural nouns.

Pronoun Match: *The boys fished in a lake. They wore life jackets.*

Problem 2

Using an object pronoun as a subject

Incorrect Pronoun: *Them caught many fish.*

Is the pronoun *Them* being used in the subject or the predicate part?

Solution 2

A subject pronoun is used in the subject of a sentence. *I*, *you*, *he*, *she*, *it*, *we*, and *they* are all subject pronouns.

Correct Pronoun: *They caught many fish.*

Problem 3

Using a subject pronoun in the predicate part

Incorrect Pronoun: *When his cousins visit, Luke enjoys fishing with they.*

Is *they* a pronoun that should be used in the predicate part of a sentence?

Solution 3

An object pronoun is used after an action verb or after a word such as *for*, *at*, *of*, *with*, or *to*. Object pronouns are usually found in the predicate part of a sentence. *Me*, *you*, *him*, *her*, *it*, *us*, and *them* are object pronouns.

Correct Pronoun: *When his cousins visit, Luke enjoys fishing with them.*

Practice **Write each sentence. Use the correct pronoun in parentheses ( ).**

1. Luke grabs his pole and drops (it, him) in the water.
2. (He, Him) feels a tug on the line and pulls the pole up.
3. "Will (you, I) take my picture?" Luke asks his cousins.
4. The cousins take some pictures of the fish, and then (they, he) let it go.
5. Their parents have always taught (them, they) to release the fish they catch.

For more help, see Pronouns on pages 344–349 and Handbook page 538.

Apostrophes

- An apostrophe is used in a contraction to show where a letter or letters have been left out.
- An apostrophe is not used in a possessive pronoun.

Problem 1

Leaving out the apostrophe in a contraction

Incorrect Contraction: *Shes riding her bicycle.*

Which word in this sentence is a contraction?

Solution 1

A contraction is a shortened form of two words. Use an apostrophe to show where one or more letters have been left out.

Correct Contraction: *She's riding her bicycle.*

Problem 2

Putting an apostrophe in a possessive pronoun

Incorrect Form: *The mountain bike is her's.*

Is there a possessive pronoun in this sentence?

Solution 2

Possessive pronouns take the place of possessive nouns. Possessive pronouns do not contain apostrophes.

Correct Form: *The mountain bike is hers.*

Problem 3

Confusing contractions and possessive pronouns

Incorrect Word: *Its a red bike.*

Does the word *Its* show possession or stand for *It is*?

Solution 3

Do not confuse the contractions *it's*, *you're*, and *they're* with the possessive pronouns *its*, *your*, and *their*.

Correct Word: *It's a red bike.*

Practice **Write each sentence correctly. Use the proper form of contractions and possessive pronouns.**

1. Those yellow bike's belong to Heather and Joan.
2. Bicycling is they're favorite hobby.
3. They know its a great form of exercise.
4. Today, theyll meet at the corner after school.
5. Their planning to take a very long bike ride.

For more help, see Possessive Pronouns on pages 358–359, Contractions on pages 360–361, and Handbook page 539.

Incorrect Use of Adverbs

- An adjective describes a noun. An adverb tells more about a verb.
- Do not use two negatives in a sentence.

Problem 1

Confusing adjectives and adverbs

Incorrect Form: *Mr. Moreno drives the bus slow.*

Is the word *slow* describing a noun or telling more about a verb?

Solution 1

Use adverbs to tell more about verbs. Adverbs provide details about how, when, or where an action takes place.

Correct Form: *Mr. Moreno drives the bus slowly.*

Problem 2

Using *good* instead of *well*

Incorrect Form: *Sharon behaved good on the bus.*

Are we describing Sharon or telling how she behaved?

Solution 2

The word *good* is an adjective. The word *well* is usually an adverb. As an adverb, it describes a verb. The only time that *well* is used as an adjective is when it describes health.

Correct Form: *Sharon behaved well on the bus.*

Troubleshooter

Problem 3

Using double negatives

Incorrect Form: *Nobody never walks to school.*

Are there two negatives in this sentence?

Solution 3

Do not use two negatives in one sentence. To correct a sentence with two negatives, change one of the negatives to a positive.

Correct Form: *Nobody ever walks to school.*

Practice **Look for the error in each sentence. Then write the sentence correctly.**

1. Clara writes well articles for the class newspaper.
2. She researches the topics careful.
3. Clara draws good, too.
4. Before this year, Clara hadn't published none of her work.
5. She wasn't never nervous about sharing her stories and illustrations, though.

For more help, see Adverbs on pages 420–423, *Good* and *Well* on pages 428–429, Negatives on pages 432–433, and Handbook pages 540 and 542.

Commas

- Commas are used to set off a person's name when the person is being spoken to.
- Commas are used with introductory words and words in a series.

Problem 1

Using commas incorrectly

Incorrect: *Have you found fossils in coal sandstone or amber?*

Incorrect: *No I have never found a fossil.*

Incorrect: *Have you found fossils Peter?*

Are three or more items listed? Is an introductory word used? Is a person spoken to?

Solution 1

Use a comma to separate words in a series and to set off introductory words. You also use a comma to set off a person's name when the person is being spoken to directly.

Correct: *Have you found fossils in coal, sandstone, or amber?*

Correct: *No, I have never found a fossil.*

Correct: *Have you found fossils, Peter?*

Practice **Write each sentence. Use commas where needed.**

1. Fossil imprints of bones leaves and footprints were found.
2. Yes that imprint was made in mud.
3. Peter what kind of fossil did you find?
4. Is that bone from a squirrel a chipmunk or a mouse?
5. Well let's go inside and do some research to find out.

For more help, see Commas on pages 440–441 and Handbook pages 554–555.

Handbook

Contents

Grammar and Usage

Build Skills

Writing

RULE 1

pages 2–3

Sentences and Sentence Fragments

- A sentence is a group of words that expresses a complete thought.

  David returned my baseball cards.

- A sentence fragment does not express a complete thought.

  My most valuable baseball cards. *(needs a predicate)*

  Sorted them into piles. *(needs a subject)*

Practice **Write each group of words. Write *sentence* or *fragment* to identify each item. Then rewrite each fragment to make a complete sentence.**

1. A cabin by the lake.
2. Mark likes to swim.
3. The lake is cold this summer.
4. Swam every evening.
5. The blinking lights of fireflies.

RULE 2

pages 4–7

Types of Sentences

- There are four different types of sentences.

Description of Types	Examples
A declarative sentence makes a statement.	*Everyone enjoyed Scott's play at school.*
An interrogative sentence asks a question.	*Did you see it?*
An imperative sentence tells or asks someone to do something.	*Go watch it this afternoon.*
An exclamatory sentence shows strong feeling.	*What a great play it was!*

Practice **Write each sentence. Add the correct punctuation. Then write *declarative*, *interrogative*, *imperative*, or *exclamatory* next to each sentence to tell what kind of sentence it is.**

1. The floor needs to be swept
2. Will you set the table for dinner
3. What a terrific meal this is
4. Please pass the corn
5. Would you like some salad

RULE 3 pages 8–9

Combining Sentences: Compound Sentences

- A conjunction is a word that joins words or groups of words.
- A compound sentence contains two sentences that have been joined by a comma and the conjunction *and*, *or*, or *but*.

Linda made her bed, and then she ate her breakfast.

We could go back home, or we could drive to town.

The chair is comfortable, but I like the sofa better.

Practice **Combine each pair of sentences by using a comma and the conjunction *and*, *but*, or *or*.**

1. Melissa saw a rabbit. It hopped away.
2. Rabbits have long ears. Hares have longer ones.
3. Rabbits eat leafy plants. They also eat fruit.
4. A rabbit's tail is about two inches long. It is covered with soft fur.
5. A frightened rabbit will sit still. It will dash away quickly.

QUICK WRITE **Write an example of each type of sentence. Make two of your sentences compound sentences.**

RULE 4
pages 14–15

Complete Subjects and Complete Predicates

- Every sentence has two important parts, the subject and predicate. The subject part of a sentence tells whom or what the sentence is about. The complete subject is all the words in the subject part.

  The gray storm clouds hung overhead.

- The predicate part of a sentence tells what the subject does or is. The complete predicate is all the words in the predicate part.

  Rain began to fall.

Practice **Write *complete subject* or *complete predicate* to tell which part of the sentence is underlined.**

1. Mrs. Garrison <u>teaches computer skills</u>.
2. <u>My class</u> uses the Internet for research.
3. Trisha and I <u>found some information about robots</u>.
4. The pictures of the robots <u>were very detailed</u>.
5. <u>Some robots</u> look a lot like people.

RULE 5
pages 16–19

Simple Subjects and Simple Predicates

- The simple subject is the main word in the complete subject.

  Some robots look a lot like people.

- The simple predicate is the main word in the complete predicate.

  Other robots look like ordinary machines.

Practice **Write each sentence. Underline the simple subject and draw a circle around the simple predicate.**

1. Certain birds make good pets.
2. Common parakeets are very popular.
3. These handsome birds have a lot of personality.
4. Most canaries sing beautifully.
5. All pets need food, a clean home, and love.

RULE 6

pages 20–23

Combining Sentences: Compound Subjects and Compound Predicates

Rules	Examples
A compound subject contains two or more simple subjects that have the same predicate.	*Margie went skating.* *Jo went skating.* *Margie and Jo went skating.*
A compound predicate contains two or more simple predicates that have the same subject.	*Margie unzipped her jacket.* *Margie removed her jacket.* *Margie unzipped and removed her jacket.*

Practice **Combine sentence pairs by forming a compound subject or a compound predicate.**

1. Kate came to the skating rink. Her brother came to the skating rink.
2. Nathan works at the skating rink. Nathan practices at the skating rink.
3. He relaxes on Friday night. He watches television on Friday night.
4. The skating rink opened at 9:00. The bowling alley opened at 9:00.
5. Frank is sick today. Frank can't come today.

QUICK WRITE **Write a story about yourself and a friend. Use the words *ran, hid, camped,* and *frightened* in your story. If possible, use them in compound predicates.**

Handbook

RULE 1
pages 88–91

Singular and Plural Nouns

- A singular noun names one person, place, or thing.

  Renée bought a beautiful doll.

- A plural noun names more than one person, place, or thing. Add *-s* to form the plural of most nouns. Add *-es* to form the plural of nouns ending in *s*, *x*, *ch*, or *sh*.

  Customers crowded around the boxes of watches.

Practice Write the nouns in each sentence. Write whether each one is singular or plural.

1. The girls made sandwiches for a picnic.
2. Lunch was served under a tree.
3. Two squirrels sat quietly on a branch.

RULE 2
pages 92–95

More Plural Nouns

- Use these rules for plural nouns:

Rules	Examples
If a noun ends in a consonant + *y*, change *y* to *i* and add *-es*.	*babies, countries, berries, skies, puppies*
If a noun ends in a vowel + *y*, add *-s*.	*monkeys, chimneys, holidays, highways, boys*
Some nouns have the same singular and plural forms.	*deer, sheep, moose*
Some nouns have special plural forms.	*men, women, children, teeth, feet*

Practice Write each sentence. Use the plural of each word in parentheses ( ).

1. Don't forget to brush your (tooth).
2. (Baby) love to play with (puppy).
3. The (man) and (woman) returned from work.

RULE 3
pages 96–97

Common and Proper Nouns

- A common noun names any person, place, or thing. A proper noun names a particular person, place, or thing. It always begins with a capital letter.

The professor did some research at the Greene Library.

Practice **Write each sentence correctly. Capitalize the proper nouns. Underline the common nouns.**

1. southwest school is sponsoring a festival.
2. The celebration will be held next tuesday.

RULE 4
pages 102–105

Singular and Plural Possessive Nouns

- A possessive noun is a noun that shows who or what owns or has something. A possessive noun can be singular or plural.

The teacher's book is on the desk. (singular)

The teachers' lounge is down the hall. (plural)

The children's pencils are blue. (plural)

Practice **Rewrite each sentence. Use the possessive form of each underlined phrase.**

1. We put the bats that belong to the boys by the fence.
2. The gloves that belong to the children are in the dugout.

RULE 5
pages 106–107

Combining Sentences: Nouns

- You can combine nouns in a subject.

Mom will have hamburgers. Dad will have hamburgers.

Mom and Dad will have hamburgers.

- You can combine nouns in a predicate.

Jason likes pizza. Jason likes chicken. Jason likes pizza and chicken.

QUICK WRITE Write two sentences. In one sentence, include two nouns in the subject. In the other sentence, include two nouns as an object.

RULE 1

pages 170–171

Action Verbs

- An action verb is a word that expresses action. It tells what the subject does or did.

  The squirrel dropped the acorns.

Practice **Write each sentence. Fill in each blank with an action verb that makes sense.**

1. Robin _____ some cold water.
2. She _____ a mile-long race through the park.
3. She _____ her face with a towel.

RULE 2

pages 172–173

Verb Tenses

- The tense of a verb shows whether the action takes place in the present, past, or future.

Rules	Examples
A present-tense verb shows action that happens now.	*Jackie walks to school every day.*
A past-tense verb shows action that has already happened.	*Jackie walked to school yesterday.*
A future-tense verb shows action that will happen.	*Jackie will walk to school tomorrow.*

Practice **Write each sentence. Underline the verb. Then write *present*, *past*, or *future* to tell the tense of the verb.**

1. We will go to Moss Park next week.
2. Denzel showed me his new kayak.
3. He uses the kayak on the lake at Moss Park.

pages 174–175

Subject-Verb Agreement

- A present-tense verb must agree with the subject of a sentence.

Rules	Examples
Add -*s* to most verbs if the subject is singular.	*My teacher sings wonderful songs.*
Add -*es* to verbs that end in *s*, *ch*, *sh*, *x*, or *z*.	*The boy watches his former voice teacher.*
Do not add -*s* or -*es* if the subject is plural or *I* or *you*.	*They love the new song for the recital.*

Practice Write each sentence. Use the verb in parentheses ( ) that agrees with the underlined subject.

1. The performance (begin, begins) in a few minutes.
2. His two sisters (wish, wishes) Milo luck.

pages 176–177

Spelling Present- and Past-Tense Verbs

- The spellings of some verbs change when -*es* or -*ed* is added.

Rules for verbs ending in:	Examples
a consonant + *y* : change the *y* to *i* and add -*es* or -*ed*.	*The baby cries every night.* *The baby cried last night.*
one vowel and one consonant: double the final consonant before adding -*ed*.	*The CD stopped before the last song.*
e: drop the *e* before adding -*ed*.	*Jen invited her friends.*

Practice Write each sentence. Use the correct tense of the verb in parentheses ( ). The tense is shown after the sentence.

1. Ernesto (clap) after the performance. *past*
2. His aunt (reply) with a smile. *present*

QUICK WRITE Write a sentence about a dog. Use the present tense. Then write the same sentence in the past and future. Now change *dog* to *some dogs*.

Handbook

RULE 5
pages 182–183

Main Verbs and Helping Verbs

- The main verb in a sentence tells what the subject does or is.
- The helping verb helps the main verb show an action or make a statement.

Our town is having a Memorial Day parade.

Practice **Underline the main verb in each sentence. Circle the helping verb.**

1. My brother is going to be in a parade.
2. He and his friends will carry flags and banners.
3. They are celebrating the beginning of summer.

RULE 6
pages 184–185

Helping Verbs

- The helping verbs *has, have,* and *had* can be used with a past-tense verb to show an action that has already happened.

Subject	Present Tense	Past Tense
Singular: *he, dog*	has	had
Plural: *we, friends*	have	had

Practice **Write each sentence. Use the correct form of the helping verb in parentheses ( ).**

1. Marcia (has, have) gone to the grocery store.
2. She (have, has) collected a lot of coupons.
3. The store (have, had) taken all of her coupons.

RULE 7 pages 186–189

Linking Verbs

- A linking verb links the subject of a sentence to a noun or adjective in the predicate. A linking verb does not express action.

Dr. Baker is a great dentist.

Some Linking Verbs

am is are was were

Practice **Write each sentence. Underline the verb. Write *linking* or *action* to tell what kind of verb it is.**

1. My dad is a very good gardener.
2. He designs landscapes for homes and offices.
3. Dad was happy about this job.

RULE 8 pages 190–193

Irregular Verbs

- An *irregular verb* is a verb that does not add *-ed* to form the past tense. The spelling of the verb changes to form the past tense.

Marco and Tom run every morning.

Marco and Tom ran yesterday after school.

Marco and Tom have run in races.

Practice **Write each sentence. Use the correct past-tense form of the verb in parentheses ( ).**

1. Ted and I have ______ a new science project. (begin)
2. We planted beans and watched them as they ______. (grow)
3. We ______ a report about our observations. (write)
4. Ted has ______ pictures to go with our report. (draw)
5. I ______ photographs of our beans each week. (take)

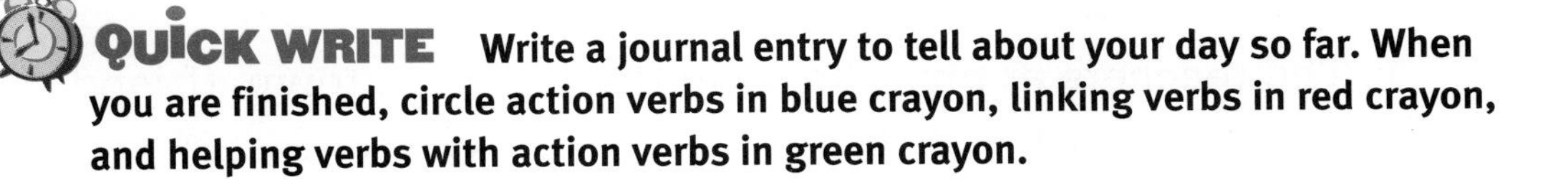

QUICK WRITE **Write a journal entry to tell about your day so far. When you are finished, circle action verbs in blue crayon, linking verbs in red crayon, and helping verbs with action verbs in green crayon.**

RULE 1

pages 262–263

Adjectives

- An adjective is a word that describes a noun.

  I have a smart dog.

- Adjectives can tell what kind or how many.

  I have two brothers.

- When an adjective comes after the noun it describes, the noun and adjective are connected by a linking verb.

  The dog is smart.

Practice **Write each sentence. Draw a line under the adjective and circle the noun it describes. Name the linking verb when there is one.**

1. My backyard is small.
2. The trees are green.
3. Mom planted a beautiful garden.

RULE 2

pages 272–275

Adjectives That Compare

- Use these spelling rules for adjectives that compare:

If an Adjective:	Then	Examples
Ends in a consonant and *y*	Change the *y* to *i*; add *-er* or *-est*	*happy* → *happier* or *happiest*
Ends in *e*	Drop the *e*; add *-er* or *-est*	*safe* → *safer* or *safest*
Has a single vowel before a final consonant	Double the final consonant; add *-er* or *-est*	*big* → *bigger* or *biggest*

Practice **Write each sentence. Write the correct form of the adjective in parentheses ( ).**

1. The teachers at my school are the ______ in town. (friendly)
2. Our new lunchroom is ______ than the gym. (pretty)
3. The fifth-grade class is ______ than our class. (large)

pages 276–279

Comparing: *More* and *Most*, *Good* and *Bad*

- Use more, better, and worse to compare two people, places, or things.

  Amy had more points than Carl.

  Amy had better scores than her sister.

  Jeff was worse at checkers than Cathy.

- Use most, best, and worst to compare more than two people, places, or things.

  Amy had the most points on her team.

  Her team had the best scores in the tournament.

  The visiting team had the worst scores.

Practice **Write each sentence. Choose the correct word in parentheses ( ) to complete each sentence.**

1. Connie is the (better, best) speller in her class.
2. She practices (more, most) hours than anyone else.
3. Calvin is the (worse, worst) speller in the class.

pages 280–281

Combining Sentences: Adjectives

- You can sometimes combine sentences by adding an adjective to one sentence.

  Sam cut the flowers. The flowers were fragrant.

  Sam cut the fragrant flowers.

Practice **Write each pair of sentences as one sentence.**

1. Cheri painted a picture. The picture was colorful.
2. Cheri uses pastels. The pastels are soft.
3. Cheri helped to paint a mural. The mural was huge.

QUICK WRITE **Write a paragraph describing your favorite season. Use at least seven adjectives in the paragraph.**

Handbook

RULE 1
pages 344–349

Pronouns

- A pronoun is a word that takes the place of one or more nouns. The pronoun must match the noun to which it refers.

  Curt plays basketball. He plays with his friends.

- A subject pronoun is used as the subject of a sentence. It tells whom or what the sentence is about.

  He plays basketball after school.

- An object pronoun is used in the predicate of a sentence, often after an action verb.

  Sasha watches him sink the basket.

- An object pronoun may be used after *for*, *at*, *of*, *with*, or *to*.

  Megan gave the ball to him.

Practice **Write each sentence. Use pronouns to replace the underlined nouns.**

1. Carol, Mike, and I like volleyball.
2. Carol plays with Mom.
3. Mike and Carol serve the ball.
4. I hit the ball to Tom, Paige, and Lauren.
5. Tom spikes the ball over the net.

RULE 2
pages 354–355

Pronoun-Verb Agreement

- A present-tense verb must agree with its subject pronoun.

Pronoun	Present-Tense Verb	Examples
he, she, it	Add *-s* or *-es*	*He runs fast.* *She watches the race.*
I, we, you, they	Do not add *-s* or *-es*	*I run fast, too.* *You run the fastest.*

Practice **Write each sentence. Complete the sentence with the correct present-tense verb.**

1. He ______ to cook. (love)
2. She ______ homemade bread. (bake)
3. They ______ banana bread. (prefer)
4. We ______ the process from beginning to end. (watch)
5. As the loaf bakes, it ______ delicious. (smell)

RULE 3

pages 358–359

Possessive Pronouns

- **A possessive pronoun takes the place of one or more possessive nouns.**

  This is Paula's bicycle. This is her bicycle.

- **Some possessive pronouns are used before nouns. Some can be used alone.**

  That is my bicycle. That bicycle is mine.

Practice **Write each sentence. Use a possessive pronoun in place of the underlined word or words.**

1. Those are <u>Trish's</u> school supplies.
2. <u>Laura's</u> markers have dried out.
3. <u>Leah and Lindsay's</u> crayons are brand new.
4. <u>The art studio's</u> door was closed.
5. Bob said, "<u>Bob's</u> supplies need to be replaced, too."
6. "We could sell <u>the class's</u> homemade crafts," said Ann.
7. "I think students will buy <u>Jane's</u> painted rocks," said Jane.
8. "Manuel, we all love <u>Manuel's</u> paintings," said Abby.
9. "Let's work on <u>the school's</u> craft sale now!" said Maisie.
10. Maisie and Jane talked about <u>Maisie and Jane's</u> craft ideas.

QUICK WRITE **Write a story about your classroom. Use at least five pronouns in the story.**

RULE 1

pages 420–423

Adverbs That Tell *How, When,* or *Where*

- An adverb is a word that tells more about a verb. Adverbs often tell how, when, or where.

  Sally tiptoed quietly across the room. (how)

  Later, she looked under the sofa. (when)

  She searched everywhere for her kitten. (where)

Practice Write each sentence. Circle each adverb. Draw a line under the verb that each adverb describes.

1. Yesterday, we visited some friends.
2. Sara smiled cheerfully.
3. Chad reached carefully for the bars.

RULE 2

pages 424–427

Adverbs That Compare

- Adverbs can be used to compare two or more actions. Add *-er* or use *more* to compare two actions. Add *-est* or use *most* to compare more than two actions.

Use	When
-er	Comparing two actions: *Sharon reads faster than her brother.*
-est	Comparing three or more actions: *Sharon reads the fastest of all the children in her class.*
more or *most*	Forming comparisons with longer adverbs and adverbs that end in *-ly*: *Carmen reads more quickly than Sharon.*

Practice Write each sentence. Choose a word from the parentheses ( ) to finish each sentence.

1. The crocuses bloomed ______ than expected. (earlier, earliest)
2. The blossoms withered ______ than we had hoped. (sooner, soonest)
3. We tended the roses ______ carefully of all. (more, most)

pages 438–439

Combining Sentences: Complex Sentences

- A complex sentence contains two related ideas joined by a conjunction other than *and, but,* or *or.*

  Fred likes candy because it is sweet.

- Many complex sentences contain conjunctions that tell *where, why, when, how,* or *under what conditions.*

  Fred always brushes his teeth after he eats candy.

- Some conjunctions are listed in the chart below.

Where	When	Why	How
where	when	as	as
wherever	before	because	as if
	after	since	as though
	while		even though
	since		although
	until		

Practice **Write a complex sentence that can be formed by combining the two shorter sentences with a conjunction.**

1. My dog sits in his doghouse. He doesn't like the rain.
2. He runs out excitedly. The rain stops.
3. He jumps in the puddles. I can stop him.
4. He splashes around. I grab him by the collar.
5. I dry him with a towel. I don't want him to catch cold.
6. He lies still. I brush him.
7. I bring him inside. He can get warm.
8. He loves the fireplace. It warms him.
9. I take him outside. He is good and dry.
10. I love my dog. He is a little wild sometimes.

QUICK WRITE **Think about your favorite activity at school. Write a letter to convince a classmate to join you in that activity. Use at least one complex sentence in your letter. Circle the conjunction you use.**

Handbook

RULE 1

pages 432–433

Negatives and Negative Contractions

- A negative is a word that means "no." Many negatives contain the word *no* within them.

  No one wanted to clean out the attic.

- Some negatives use the contraction *-n't*, which is short for *not*.

  I did not want to clean it, either.

  I didn't want to clean it, either.

Practice Write each sentence. Underline the negative word in each one.

1. Didn't Grandma clean the attic before?
2. No valuables were stored in the attic.
3. The attic was filled with nothing but junk.
4. The broom was nowhere to be found.
5. None of us wanted to do the job.

RULE 2

pages 432–433

Double Negatives

- Do not use two negatives in one sentence.

  Nobody had (ever, never) cleaned the attic.

  I didn't think (no, any) other task could be so dreadful.

Practice Write each sentence. Choose the correct word in parentheses ( ) to finish the sentence.

1. Don't you have (no, any) dust mops?
2. Brandon hadn't (ever, never) used a vacuum before.
3. You don't know (anybody, nobody) who cleans like Dad.
4. I hope we won't (never, ever) have to clean the attic again.
5. We didn't think (anything, nothing) could be so dirty.

RULE 1
pages 434–435

Prepositions

- A preposition comes before a noun or pronoun.
- A preposition shows how the noun or pronoun is linked to another word in the sentence.

A large wooden dresser sat in the corner.

I found a cute hat behind the dresser.

Practice: Write each sentence. Circle the preposition.

1. Grandpa's army uniform was in the trunk.
2. The pictures were tied with a ribbon.
3. Mom's wedding dress was draped over a hanger.
4. Dad found his old baseball glove near the window.
5. What do you think we found behind the door?

RULE 2
pages 436–437

Prepositional Phrases

- A prepositional phrase is a group of words that begins with a preposition and ends with a noun or pronoun.

With everyone's help, we finished cleaning the attic.

Everyone felt good about it.

Practice Write each sentence. Underline the prepositional phrases. Write an *N* above the noun in each prepositional phrase. Write a *P* above each preposition.

1. Behind the door stood an old African drum.
2. A spider had built a huge web in one corner.
3. Our time in the attic flew by.
4. We finished cleaning the attic at noon.
5. We all walked down the stairs together.

QUICK WRITE Write five sentences showing the correct use of negatives. Search reading materials to make a list of common prepositions.

Titles and Names

- Some titles are abbreviations, or shortened forms of a words. Other titles, like *Ms.* and *Mrs.*, don't have longer forms. An initial is the first letter of a name. Titles and initials are capitalized and are followed by a period.

Title	Abbreviation	Title	Abbreviation
Mister	Mr.	Senator	Sen.
Doctor	Dr.	Governor	Gov.

Name	Initials	Name	Initials
James Peter	J. P.	Carol Jean	C. J.

Internet Addresses

- Use abbreviations at the end of Internet addresses.

commercial	.com	educational	.edu
organization	.org	network	.net

Practice **Rewrite each sentence. Change each word or group of words in parentheses ( ) to an abbreviation or initials.**

1. Our class sent an e-mail to (Mary Jane) Stein at www.nature.(network).
2. We asked if (Doctor) Hernandez, a zoologist, could tell us about our state bird.
3. Ms. Stein told us to write to the doctor at www.hstate.(educational).
4. Dr. Hernandez told us to call the office of (Senator) Jones for more information about animals in our state.
5. Our teacher, (Mister) Lee, helped us make the call.

Time

- Use abbreviations to indicate time before noon and after noon. These abbreviations are capitalized with periods after each letter.

Abbreviation	Meaning
8:00 A.M.	8:00 ante meridiem (before noon)
8:00 P.M.	8:00 post meridiem (after noon)

Days and Months

- In informal writing, use abbreviations of the days of the week and the months of the year. These abbreviations begin with a capital letter and end with a period.

Day	Abbreviation	Month	Abbreviation
Monday	Mon.	January	Jan.
Tuesday	Tues.	February	Feb.
Wednesday	Wed.	March	Mar.
Thursday	Thurs.	April	Apr.
Friday	Fri.	May	May
Saturday	Sat.	June	June
Sunday	Sun.	July	July
		August	Aug.
		September	Sept.
		October	Oct.
		November	Nov.
		December	Dec.

Addresses

- Address abbreviations are capitalized and followed by a period.

Avenue	Ave.	Drive	Dr.
Street	St.	Lane	Ln.
Boulevard	Blvd.	Post Office	P. O.

States

- **United States Postal Service** abbreviations for the names of states consist of two capital letters. No period follows these abbreviations.

State	Abbreviation	State	Abbreviation
Alabama	AL	Montana	MT
Alaska	AK	Nebraska	NE
Arizona	AZ	Nevada	NV
Arkansas	AR	New Hampshire	NH
California	CA	New Jersey	NJ
Colorado	CO	New Mexico	NM
Connecticut	CT	New York	NY
Delaware	DE	North Carolina	NC
Florida	FL	North Dakota	ND
Georgia	GA	Ohio	OH
Hawaii	HI	Oklahoma	OK
Idaho	ID	Oregon	OR
Illinois	IL	Pennsylvania	PA
Indiana	IN	Rhode Island	RI
Iowa	IA	South Carolina	SC
Kansas	KS	South Dakota	SD
Kentucky	KY	Tennessee	TN
Louisiana	LA	Texas	TX
Maine	ME	Utah	UT
Maryland	MD	Vermont	VT
Massachusetts	MA	Virginia	VA
Michigan	MI	Washington	WA
Minnesota	MN	West Virginia	WV
Mississippi	MS	Wisconsin	WI
Missouri	MO	Wyoming	WY

Practice **Rewrite each city and state. Use an abbreviation for the name of the state.**

1. El Paso, Texas
2. Portland, Maine
3. Seattle, Washington
4. Highland Park, Illinois
5. Tampa, Florida

First Words in Sentences

- Capitalize the first word of a sentence.

  We gathered paints and paintbrushes.

- Capitalize the first word of a direct quotation. Do not capitalize the second part of an interrupted quotation.

  Dan cried, "Please stop the presses!"

  "I am leaving," Jan declared, "as soon as I can."

- When the second part of a quotation is a new sentence, put a period after the interrupting expression and capitalize the first word of the new sentence.

  "I know that song," said Lisa. "We learned it last week."

Letter Greetings and Closings

- Capitalize all important words in the greeting of a letter.

  Dear Sirs: *Dear Friends and Family,*

- Capitalize the first word in the closing of a letter.

  Sincerely, *Yours truly,*

Practice Rewrite each sentence correctly. Use capital letters where needed.

1. my family is painting T-shirts for the summer block party.
2. "let's ask the neighbors to donate supplies," says Mom.
3. we began the letter with the words *Dear neighbors*.
4. the letter asked each family to donate plain T-shirts.
5. We used the closing *your neighbors*.

Proper Nouns: Names and Titles of People

- Capitalize the names of people and the initials that stand for their names.

  James Robert Perry *J. R. Perry*

- Capitalize titles or abbreviations of titles when they come before or after the names of people.

  Mr. James Perry, Jr. *General J. R. Perry* *Dr. Ellen Mahoney*

- Capitalize words that show family relationships when used as titles or as substitutes for a person's name.

  Then Dad and Grandma Ellen cooked dinner.

- Do not capitalize words that show family relationships when they are preceded by a possessive noun or pronoun.

  Diane's grandmother is a good cook. Her dad is a good cook, too.

- Capitalize the pronoun *I*.

  Can I help cook dinner?

Practice **Rewrite each sentence correctly. Use capital letters where needed.**

1. dad, mom, and i made Thanksgiving dinner this year.
2. Our friend james e. jones was joining us for dinner.
3. My dad and i cooked the yams.
4. Mother helped grandma ellen make stuffing.
5. Our guest dr. carl eng brought dessert.

Proper Nouns: Names of Places

- Capitalize the names of cities, states, countries, and continents. Do not capitalize articles or prepositions that are part of the name.

  City — *Lake of the Woods*
  State — *Wisconsin*
  Country — *United States of America*
  Continent — *North America*

- Capitalize the names of bodies of water and geographical features.

  Mississippi River *Mojave Desert* *Niagara Falls*

- Capitalize the names of sections of the country.

  the South *the Pacific Northwest*

- Do not capitalize compass points when they just show direction.

  New York is east of Cleveland.

- Capitalize the names of streets and highways.

  Elm Street *Stevenson Expressway*

- Capitalize the names of buildings, bridges, and monuments.

  Empire State Building *Mackinaw Bridge*
  Washington Monument

- Capitalize the names of stars and planets.

  The closest star to our planet is Proxima Centauri.
  The planet closest to the sun is Mercury.

- Capitalize *Earth* when it refers to the planet. Do not capitalize *earth* when preceded by *the*. Do not capitalize *sun* or *moon*.

  One moon revolves around Earth.
  The earth revolves around the sun.

Practice **Rewrite each sentence correctly. Use capital letters where needed.**

1. Our class went to chicago, illinois to visit the adler planetarium.
2. The bus drove along the kennedy expressway until it reached lake shore drive.
3. We looked at lake michigan, and we went inside to learn about earth.

Other Proper Nouns and Adjectives

- Capitalize the names of schools, clubs, and businesses.

  Washington Elementary School

  Junior Scientist Club

  Greenfield's Grocery
- Capitalize the names of historic events, periods of time, and documents.

  Battle of Bunker Hill

  Declaration of Independence
- Capitalize the days of the week, months of the year, and holidays. Do not capitalize the names of the seasons.

  We started school on Tuesday, September 1.

  Our first vacation is on Labor Day.
- Capitalize abbreviations.

  Dr. *Ave.* *Mon.* *Apr.*
- Capitalize the names of ethnic groups, nationalities, and languages.

  The French won the war. *I speak Japanese.*
- Capitalize proper adjectives that are formed from the names of ethnic groups and nationalities.

  Italian bread *Egyptian cotton*
- Capitalize the first word of each main topic and subtopic in an outline.

  I. Products and exports

  A. Natural resources

  B. Manufactured goods

Practice **Rewrite each sentence correctly. Use capital letters where needed.**

1. Our school, grant elementary, is having a cultural festival.
2. The creative cooking club is serving foods from around the world.
3. One class is presenting poems in other languages, such as spanish, chinese, and russian.
4. Jenna says that the french poem is lovely.
5. The festival will be held on tuesday, the ninth of october.

Titles of Works

- Capitalize the first, the last, and all important words in the title of a book, play, short story, poem, film, article, newspaper, magazine, TV series, chapter of a book, or song.

  I can't wait to read *Where the Red Fern Grows.*

  Did you see *Bye, Bye, Birdie* at the community theater?

  A clever short story is "The Gift of the Magi."

  My favorite poem by Silverstein is "Captain Hook."

  You should read "Saving the Alligators" in this month's *Animals Monthly.*

  My dad reads *The New York Times.*

  Did you watch *The Sports Front* last night?

  Chapter one of that book is titled "The Long Night."

  I sang "The Star-Spangled Banner" before the big game.

Practice **Rewrite each sentence correctly. Correctly capitalize titles of works.**

1. Our school's Media Club read *matilda* last month.
2. The first chapter is titled "the reader of books."
3. This week, our club will go to see *the nutcracker.*
4. Next week, we will read a play titled *harry's horrible house.*
5. I like when our leader shows films, such as *honey, I shrunk the kids.*
6. Our club members sang "america, the beautiful" at the assembly.
7. The song made them think of the short story "open fields."
8. Our club has been featured in *the daily herald.*
9. The article was titled "kids and communication."
10. Maybe we'll be featured in *media monthly* someday.

End Punctuation

- Use end punctuation at the end of a sentence.
- A period ends a declarative sentence. A declarative sentence makes a statement.

  I have a cold.

- A period ends an imperative sentence. An imperative sentence makes a command or a request.

  Keep yourself warm.

- A question mark ends an interrogative sentence. An interrogative sentence asks a question.

  When will the medicine start to work?

- An exclamation mark ends an exclamatory sentence. An exclamatory sentence expresses strong emotion.

  I finally feel better!

Periods

- Use a period at the end of an abbreviation.

  Dr. *St.* *Tues.* *Jan.*

- Use a period in abbreviations for time.

  2:00 A.M. *2:00 P.M.*

- Use a period after initials.

  P. J. Chamberlain

- Use a period after numbers and letters in an outline.

  I. Margaret Mead
  A. Famous anthropologist
  B. Summary of her work

Colons

- Use a colon to separate the hour and the minute when you write the time of day.

  12:45 *1:15* *6:30*

- Use a colon after the greeting of a business letter.

  Dear Sirs: *Dear Mr. Franklin:*

Apostrophes

- Use an apostrophe and an *s* ('s) to form the possessive of a singular noun.

  Jason's book *my mom's bike* *the car's horn*

- Use an apostrophe and an *s* ('s) to form the possessive of a plural noun that does not end in *s*.

  children's books *men's shoes* *geese's feathers*

- Use an apostrophe alone to form the possessive of a plural noun that ends in *s*.

  ladies' purses *donkeys' brays* *lilies' scent*

- Use an apostrophe in a contraction to show where a letter or letters are missing.

  we + are = we're *he + is = he's* *would + not = wouldn't*

- Do not use an apostrophe in a possessive pronoun.

  its good points *their friends* *your idea*

Practice **Write each sentence. Insert punctuation where needed.**

1. I went to visit Dr Goldstein
2. At 900 AM, the nurse called my name.
3. "JR Hines," she said.
4. Shes a very helpful nurse.
5. Where is the doctors office located

Commas

- Use a comma between the name of the city and state in an address.

  Boston, Massachusetts

- Use a comma after the name of a state or a country when it is used with the name of a city in a sentence.

  We visited San Francisco, California, on our vacation.

- Use a comma between the day and year in a date.

  April 20, 2002 *July 4, 1776*

- Use a comma before and after the year when it is used with both the month and the day in a sentence. Do not use a comma if only the month and the year are given.

  June 4, 2000, is our last day of school.

  Next year, we begin school in September 2001.

- Use a comma after the greeting in a friendly letter and after the closing in all letters.

  Dear Tyler, *Sincerely,*

Practice **Rewrite the following parts of a friendly letter. Place commas where needed.**

124 Grant Road

1. Ithaca NY 14851
2. September 4 2001
3. Dear Ben
4. On September 30 2001 I will be visiting your town.
5. Sincerely

   Daryl

Commas

- Use a comma after introductory words or phrases in a sentence.

  Yes, I enjoy science class.

- Use a comma with nouns in a direct address.

  Greta, please pass the mustard.

- Use a comma to set off a direct quotation.

  "Is this," she asked, "the bottle you wanted?"

  "That's the one," I replied.

- Use commas to separate three or more items in a series.

  Our flag is red, white, and blue.

  I need paper, scissors, and tape.

- Use a comma before *and, but,* or *or* when it joins simple sentences to form a compound sentence.

  My mother can drive us, or we can take the bus.

Practice **Rewrite each sentence. Add commas where needed.**

1. Kelly is that you and Nina opening the door?
2. Yes it's the two of us.
3. Well I'm glad you're here.
4. Nina have you seen my painting?
5. No but I'd like to see it.
6. Your colors are bright vivid and beautiful.
7. You know Tamika I think it's wonderful.
8. I agree and many people will think so, too.
9. "You should be a painter" my dad said.
10. "I think" I replied "you're right!"

Quotation Marks

- Use **quotation marks** before and after the exact words that a speaker says.

  "Someday I'd like to be a firefighter," said Paul.

  "Someday," said Paul, "I'd like to be a firefighter."

- Use a **comma** or **commas** to separate a phrase, such as *he said,* from the quotation itself. Place the comma outside the opening quotation marks but inside the closing quotation marks.

  Veronica asked, "What would you like to be?"

  "When I get older," replied Adam, "I'd like to be a graphic designer."

- Place a **period** inside closing quotation marks.

  Pam added, "I'd like to be a chef."

- Place a **question mark** or an **exclamation mark** inside the quotation marks when it is part of the quotation.

  "What career do you want?" asked Maria.

  "I want to be president, of course!" shouted Lily.

- Use **quotation marks** around the title of a short story, song, short poem, magazine or newspaper article, and chapter of a book.

  "Jack and the Beanstalk" *"Little Miss Muffet"*

  "Yankee Doodle Dandy" *"A Mysterious Visitor"*

Practice **Rewrite each sentence correctly. Add punctuation where needed.**

1. Are you ready for Career Day asked Mrs. Lee.
2. I want to learn about careers in science said Isabel.
3. Will we asked Kevin learn about law enforcement?
4. I want to write articles, such as Tornado Watchers.
5. Hector would prefer writing stories, such as Monsters of the Deep.

Italics (Underlining)

- Use italics or underlining to indicate the title of a book, film, television series, play, magazine, or newspaper.

Pippi Longstocking	Pippi Longstocking
The Wizard of Oz	The Wizard of Oz
Reading Rainbow	Reading Rainbow
Fiddler on the Roof	Fiddler on the Roof
Sports Illustrated	Sports Illustrated
The New York Times	The New York Times

Practice **Rewrite each sentence correctly. Underline titles where needed.**

1. The last play I saw was titled Oklahoma.
2. Before the play, we watched Zoom on television.
3. The kids on Zoom were talking about the book Sheila, the Great.
4. Then they talked about a movie titled Flubber.
5. I read a review of that film in The Chicago Tribune.

Sentence Structure: Diagramming Guide

A **sentence diagram** uses lines to show how the words in a sentence go together. A diagram always begins with the most important words in the sentence. For now, you will learn how to diagram only some of the words in a sentence.

RULE 1 pages 14–19

Simple Subjects and Simple Predicates

- A sentence diagram puts the simple subject and the simple predicate on a straight line called a base line. An up-and-down line separates the simple subject from the simple predicate.

Lions roared.

Lions | roared

Three brown monkeys chattered loudly in the tree.

monkeys | chattered

In the sentence above, *monkeys* is the simple subject and *chattered* is the simple predicate.

Practice **Make a sentence diagram of the simple subject and the simple predicate in each sentence.**

1. One elephant rests.
2. Seals bark excitedly.
3. Some small zebras play.
4. Two green parrots squawk noisily.
5. The tan and brown lion paces hungrily.
6. Other cats howl for their dinner.
7. The zookeeper brings fresh meat.
8. I hold a camera.
9. Kevin quickly snaps a picture.
10. The larger animals sleep outside in the sun.

Compound Subjects

- A sentence with a compound subject has two or more simple subjects. Each of the subjects is placed on a separate line in the sentence diagram. The word *and*, *or*, or *but* is written on a dotted up-and-down line that connects the simple subjects.

Florida and Hawaii have tropical climates.

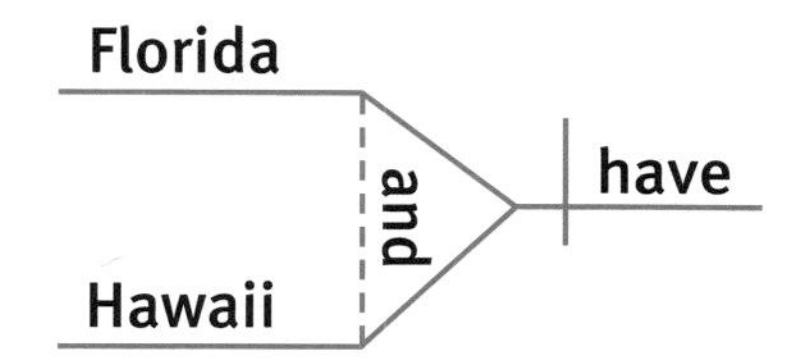

- There may be more than two simple subjects in some compound subjects. Notice how this subject is diagrammed.

Texas, Georgia, and Florida have humid summers.

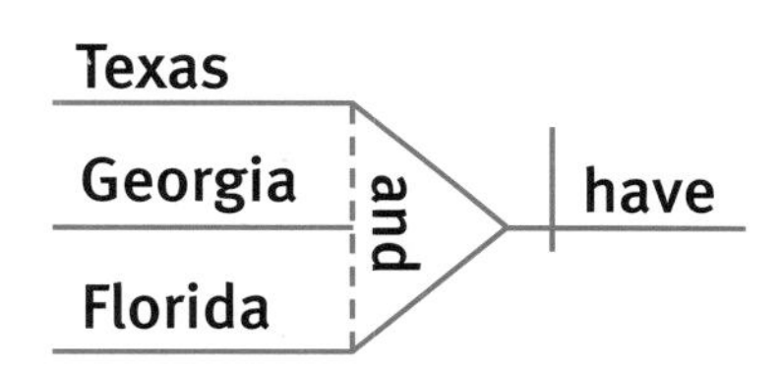

Practice **Diagram each sentence. Be sure you show each important part of the compound subject.**

1. Brianna and Jessica study different climates.
2. Montana, Alaska, and Minnesota have chilly winters.
3. Summer and fall are hot in Texas.
4. Ice or snow comes early in Vermont.
5. Thunderstorms and tornadoes hit the Midwest.
6. Nicholas and Mr. Gomez watch a weather station.
7. Rain, sleet, or hail damaged crops in Iowa.
8. My aunt and my uncle photograph tornadoes.
9. High winds and heavy rain flooded the coast.
10. Freeport and Galveston lost power.

RULE 3
pages 22–23

Compound Predicates

- A sentence with a compound predicate contains two or more simple predicates that have the same subject. Each of the predicates is placed on a separate line in the sentence diagram. The word *and*, *but*, or *or* is written on a dotted up-and-down line that connects the simple predicates.

The students wrote and directed a video.

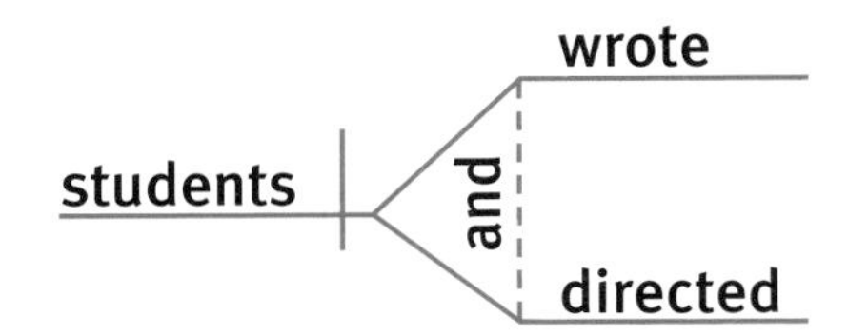

- There may be more than two simple predicates in some compound predicates. Notice how this predicate is diagrammed.

They read, rehearsed, and performed their parts.

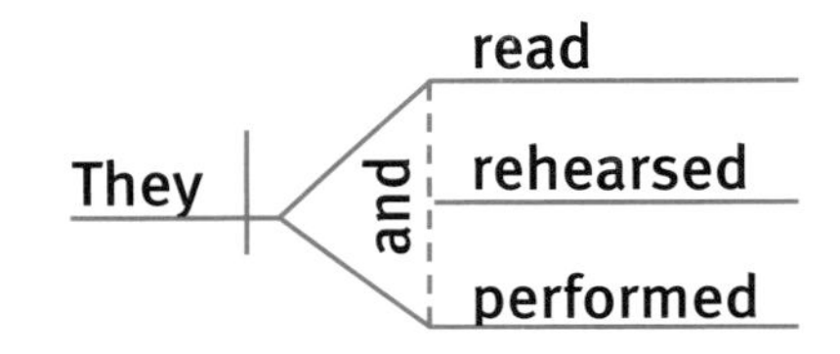

Practice **Diagram each sentence. Be sure you show each important part of the compound predicate.**

1. Students talked, planned, and practiced.
2. Teachers listened and helped.
3. Sarah designed and sewed her costume.
4. Thomas built and painted a set.
5. He made or borrowed props, too.
6. Ms. Stewart read and approved the script.
7. Ben filmed and edited the video.
8. Parents bought or baked refreshments.
9. The audience clapped, stomped, and cheered at the end.
10. People loved or hated the show.

Adjectives

- Adjectives are diagrammed on a line that slants below the words they describe.

Golden sunshine warmed the earth.

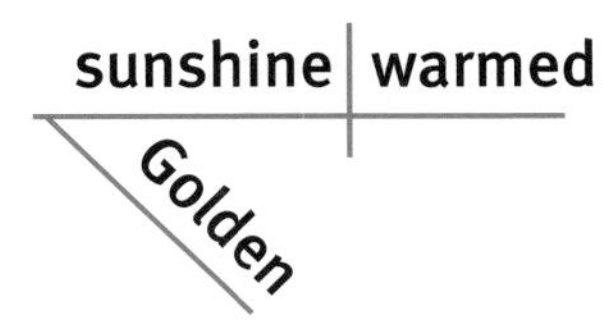

- Sometimes more than one adjective may describe the same noun.

The bright yellow roses smell sweet.

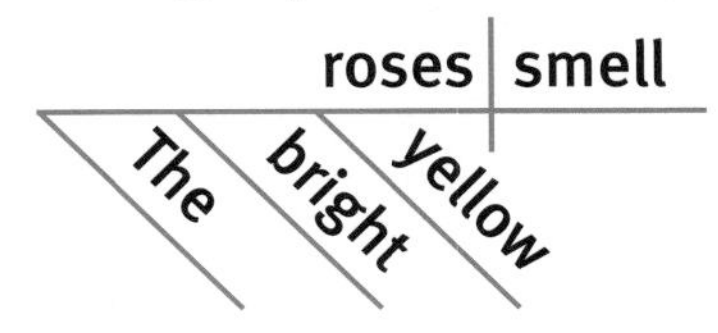

- Remember that *a*, *an*, and *the* are adjectives, too.

Practice **Diagram each sentence. Show the simple subject, the simple predicate, and all the adjectives.**

1. Gentle rain falls.
2. Tiny seedlings sprout.
3. Twelve sunflowers grow.
4. Big, striped butterflies fly merrily.
5. A green grasshopper hops away.
6. One slow snail creeps slowly.
7. The noisy bluejays look for worms.
8. Many spotted ladybugs eat aphids.
9. Hot red peppers ripen quickly.
10. The small garden loves summer!

Handbook

RULE 5
pages 410–411

Adverbs

- Adverbs can describe verbs. In a diagram, an adverb is placed on a slanted line below the verb.

The boys talked excitedly about the art contest.

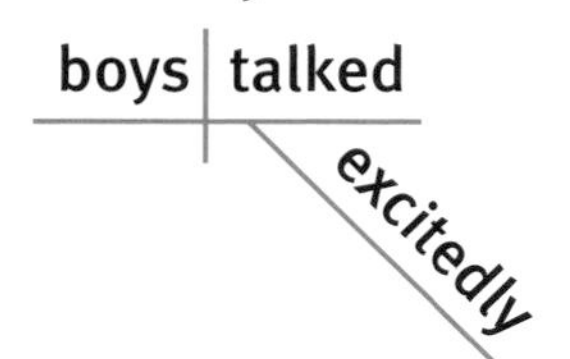

- Remember that an adverb may appear anywhere in a sentence. It does not always follow the verb.

Everyone entered the room quietly.

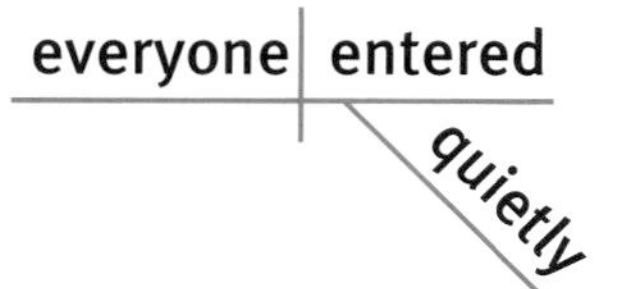

Practice Diagram each sentence. Show the simple subject, the simple predicate, and all the adverbs.

1. The teachers clearly explained the contest rules.
2. Jessica expertly mixed the paints.
3. Kevin measured the water exactly.
4. One student quickly sketched figures.
5. Trista applied the paint smoothly.
6. Sean patiently dripped paint on his canvas.
7. The paintings dried slowly.
8. Next, each contestant cleaned his or her brushes.
9. The judges considered each painting carefully.
10. Jessica received her ribbon happily.

RULE 6
pages 8–9

Compound Sentences

- A compound sentence has two sentences connected by *or*, *and*, or *but*. Each sentence is diagrammed. The connecting word is written on a line between the two sentences. Dotted lines connect this word to each sentence.

The driver ate, and the crew talked quietly.

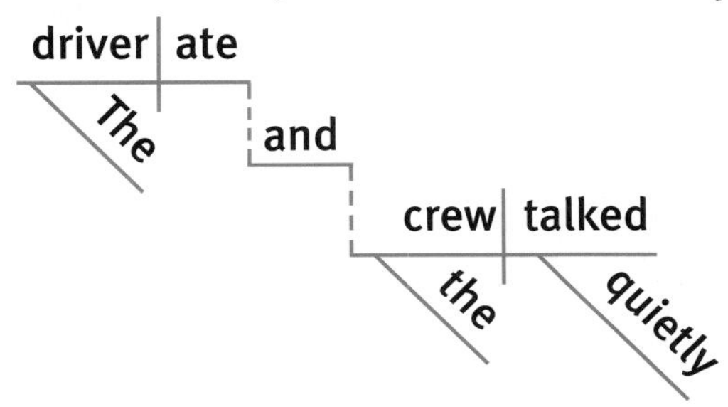

Practice **Diagram these compound sentences. Be sure to include both sentences and the connecting word in the diagram. Show simple subjects, simple predicates, adjectives, and adverbs.**

1. The engines race loudly, but the drivers wait.
2. People listen, or they talk.
3. Jenna sits down, but Charlie stands up.
4. Ronnie drives, and Andrew coaches.
5. The race begins suddenly, and the ten drivers go.
6. Most cars speed, but one racer stalls.
7. The red light flashes, and all the drivers stop.
8. The green car leaves, and the race continues.
9. Mr. Ramos watches eagerly, but his son plays.
10. One driver wins, and the crowd cheers wildly.

Note-Taking and Summarizing

DEFINITIONS AND FEATURES

- When taking notes, write the important facts. Be sure to use your own words instead of the author's.
- If you take notes from a book, write the title and author.
- Summarize your notes to be sure that you understand what you read. Include only the most important ideas.

Topic ······ Settling of the United States

1607—British landed in Jamestown
South—grew crops: cotton and indigo
North—timber, furs, and fishing
Short phrases that summarize important facts

Book: A New Country
Author: Mark Douglas Page: 18
The source of the facts

Practice **Take notes on the following article, listing five facts on a sheet of paper. Then write a summary using your notes and your own words. Give your summary a title.**

Fort Worth, Texas The north central Texas city of Fort Worth is located on the banks of the Trinity River, which flows into Galveston Bay. The city was founded in 1849 by Major Ripley Arnold. It was named for General William Worth, the commander of the Texas army. The city began as a small outpost to protect settlers moving west and has grown into a city with a population of nearly 500,000.

Go to www.mhschool.com/language-arts for more information on the topic.

Parts of a Book

DEFINITIONS AND FEATURES

- The copyright page gives the name of the book, the author, the illustrator, the publisher, and the place of publication.
- The table of contents lists chapters or units and gives the page numbers on which they begin.
- The index lists topics and subtopics in alphabetical order. Use the index to find specific information in the book.

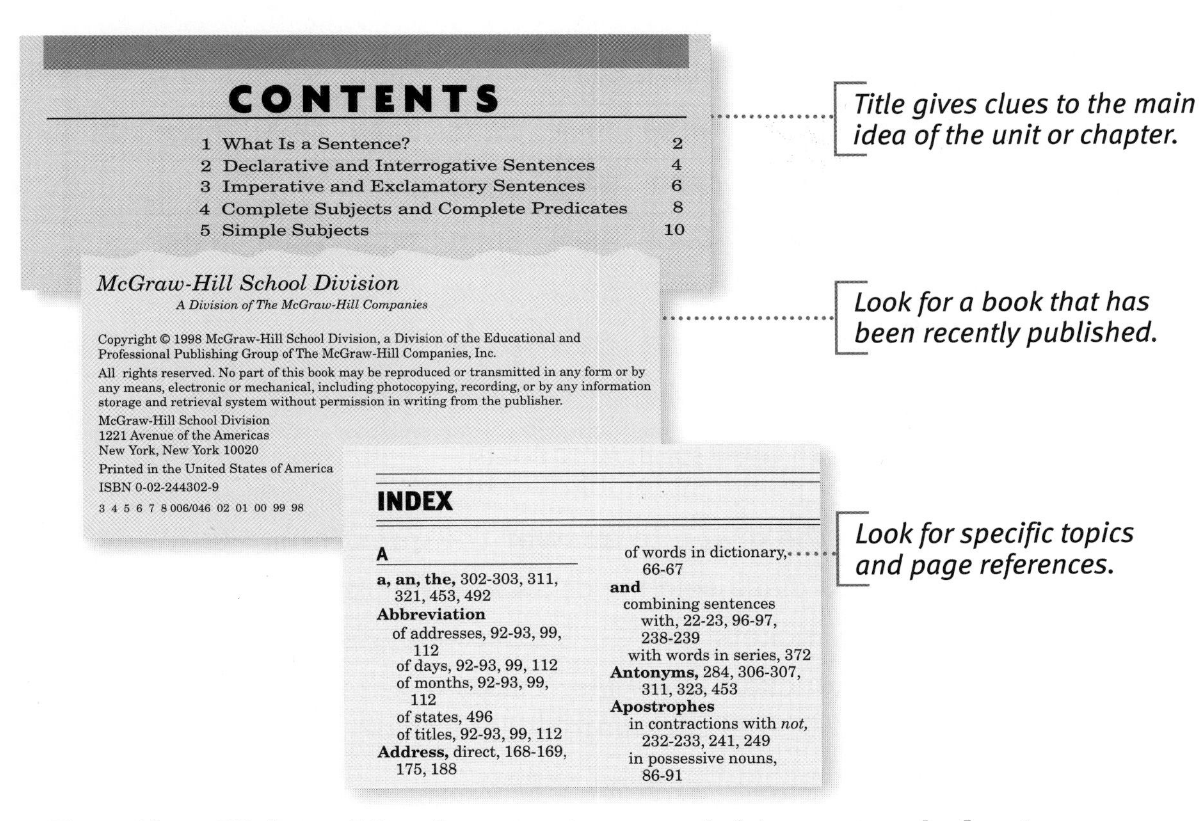

CONTENTS

1 What Is a Sentence? 2
2 Declarative and Interrogative Sentences 4
3 Imperative and Exclamatory Sentences 6
4 Complete Subjects and Complete Predicates 8
5 Simple Subjects 10

McGraw-Hill School Division
A Division of The McGraw-Hill Companies

Copyright © 1998 McGraw-Hill School Division, a Division of the Educational and Professional Publishing Group of The McGraw-Hill Companies, Inc.
All rights reserved. No part of this book may be reproduced or transmitted in any form or by any means, electronic or mechanical, including photocopying, recording, or by any information storage and retrieval system without permission in writing from the publisher.
McGraw-Hill School Division
1221 Avenue of the Americas
New York, New York 10020
Printed in the United States of America
ISBN 0-02-244302-9
3 4 5 6 7 8 006/046 02 01 00 99 98

INDEX

A
a, an, the, 302-303, 311, 321, 453, 492
Abbreviation
of addresses, 92-93, 99, 112
of days, 92-93, 99, 112
of months, 92-93, 99, 112
of states, 496
of titles, 92-93, 99, 112
Address, direct, 168-169, 175, 188
of words in dictionary, 66-67
and
combining sentences with, 22-23, 96-97, 238-239
with words in series, 372
Antonyms, 284, 306-307, 311, 323, 453
Apostrophes
in contractions with *not,* 232-233, 241, 249
in possessive nouns, 86-91

Practice **Write *table of contents, copyright page,* or *index* to tell where in a book you can find this information.**

1. The date the book was published
2. The first page of chapter two
3. The publisher of the book
4. The subject of chapter three
5. Information about mountains in a country.

Go to www.mhschool.com/language-arts for more information on the topic.

Graphs

DEFINITIONS AND FEATURES

- A **graph** is used to show information about numbers. Graphs help readers **compare** information.
- A graph's **title** tells what information can be found on the graph.
- **Labels** give specific information about what is on the graph.
- Different **types of graphs** are used for different purposes.

Graphs help you compare amounts in an easier way.

The title tells you what the graph is about.

Talent Show Tickets Sold

Class	Tickets Sold
Mrs. Ruiz	▬ ▬ ▬ ▬ ▬ ▬ ▪
Ms. Monaco	▬ ▬ ▬
Mr. Smith	▬ ▬ ▬ ▬ ▬ ▬
Ms. Turley	▬ ▬ ▬ ▬ ▬
Mr. Ward	▬ ▬ ▬ ▬ ▬ ▬
Mrs. Brant	▬ ▬ ▬ ▬ ▬ ▪

Key: Each ▬ stands for 10 tickets.

Practice **Use the graph to answer the questions.**

1. Mr. Smith's class sold twice as many tickets as which class?
2. How many tickets did Ms. Monaco's class sell?
3. How many tickets does Ms. Turley's class have to sell to equal the number Mr. Ward's class sold?
4. Which class sold the most tickets?
5. Which class sold the same number of tickets as Mr. Ward's class?

Go to www.mhschool.com/language-arts for more information on the topic.

Library and Media Sources

DEFINITIONS AND FEATURES

- A library or media center includes a variety of materials and resources that are arranged in different sections.
- Fiction books are arranged alphabetically by authors' last names. Nonfiction books are arranged by subject.
- Reference books include books for research, such as dictionaries, encyclopedias, atlases, and almanacs.
- Media resources are non-print materials that you can use to find information, such as CD-ROMs, videotapes, and audiotapes.
- Magazines and newspapers are in a library's Periodicals section.

Nonfiction books are arranged on the shelf by call number.

This is fiction. Fiction books are arranged on the shelf by the authors' last names.

You would find this dictionary in the reference section.

Practice **Write whether each book could be found in the fiction, nonfiction, or reference section of the library.**

1. *The Story of Jackie Robinson* is a biography of Jackie Robinson.
2. *The Complete Encyclopedia of Gardening* is a four-volume set.
3. *Basics of Bowling* explains how to keep score in bowling.
4. *Fred the Diamond Dog* is the story of a dog who plays baseball.
5. *Sports for Kids* is a book with facts and diagrams.

Go to www.mhschool.com/language-arts for more information on the topic.

Periodicals

DEFINITIONS AND FEATURES

- A periodical is a magazine that is printed at regular times, such as every week or every month.
- Periodicals provide up-to-date information about various topics.
- The *Readers' Guide to Periodical Literature* is a set of books or an electronic database that lists articles published in magazines.
- The *Readers' Guide* lists articles by topics and by author. A *Readers' Guide* entry tells you the magazine, issue, and page numbers of an article.

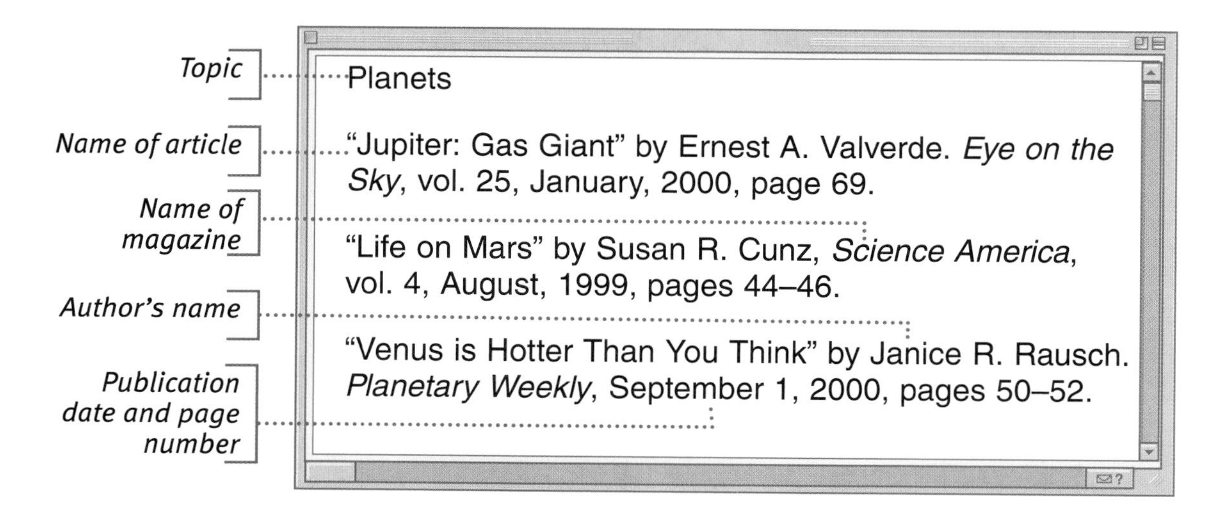

Practice **Look at the entries from the *Readers' Guide* to answer the following questions.**

1. How many magazines include articles about planets?
2. Which magazine has an article titled "Venus is Hotter Than You Think"?
3. Which article is in the magazine *Eye on the Sky*?
4. When was the article "Life on Mars" published?
5. On what page is the article "Jupiter: Gas Giant"?

Go to www.mhschool.com/language-arts for more information on the topic.

Maps and Atlases

DEFINITIONS AND FEATURES

- An atlas is a reference book that contains maps.
- Each map in an atlas shows the name and location of cities, rivers, mountains, and other important features of a country.
- You can use the index or table of contents to find a country.
- Use the scale of miles, key, and compass rose to find places.

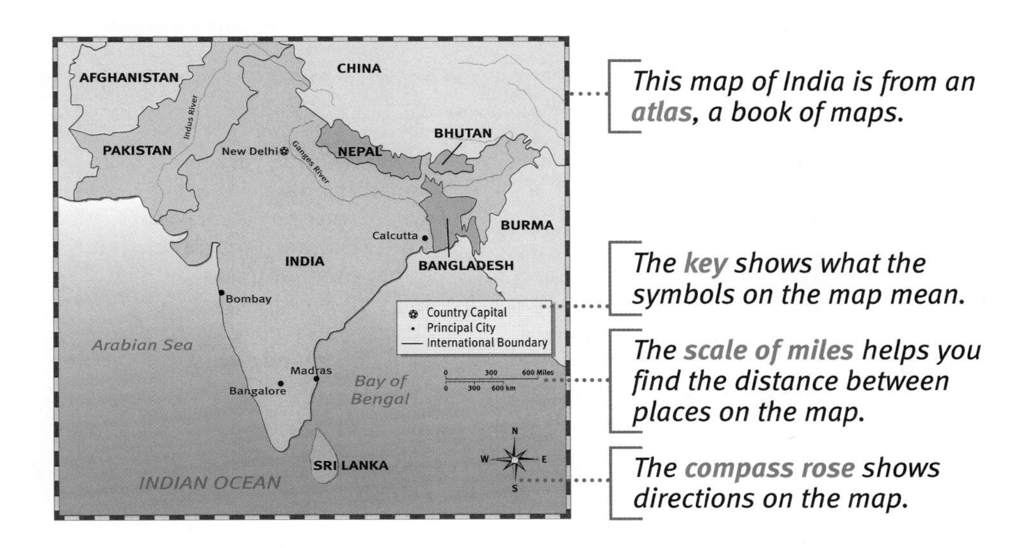

Practice **Use the map to answer the following questions.**

1. Which body of water is west of India?
2. Which country is India's neighbor to the west?
3. Which principal city in India is the farthest west?
4. Which principal city is on India's southeast coast?
5. Which symbol shows that a city is the capital?
6. What is India's capital?
7. In what direction would you travel from India to reach Burma?
8. How can you find out the distance between Bombay and Madras?
9. Is Nepal part of India or a separate country?
10. In what body of water would you find Sri Lanka?

Go to www.mhschool.com/language-arts for more information on the topic.

Dictionary

DEFINITIONS AND FEATURES

- A dictionary lists words in alphabetical order.
- The entry words show the spelling and syllables.
- The guide words show the first and last word on the page. Words on the page come between the guide words alphabetically.
- The pronunciation of each word is shown in parentheses.
- The part of speech is shown after the pronunciation.

Practice **Use the dictionary entries on this page to answer the questions.**

1. What part of the speech is the word *eager*?
2. How many syllables does the word *eager* have?
3. What part of speech is *each*?
4. How many definitions does *eagle* have?
5. Would the word *early* be in the dictionary before or after this page?

Go to www.mhschool.com/language-arts for more information on the topic.

Thesaurus

DEFINITIONS AND FEATURES

- A **thesaurus** is a reference book that lists words and their **synonyms**, or words of similar meaning. A thesaurus also includes **antonyms**, or words with opposite meanings.
- The word that you look up in a thesaurus is called the **entry word**. Entry words are listed in **alphabetical order**.
- **Guide words** show the first and last entry word on each page.
- Some entries include a **cross-reference** that will guide you to other words with similar or opposite meanings.

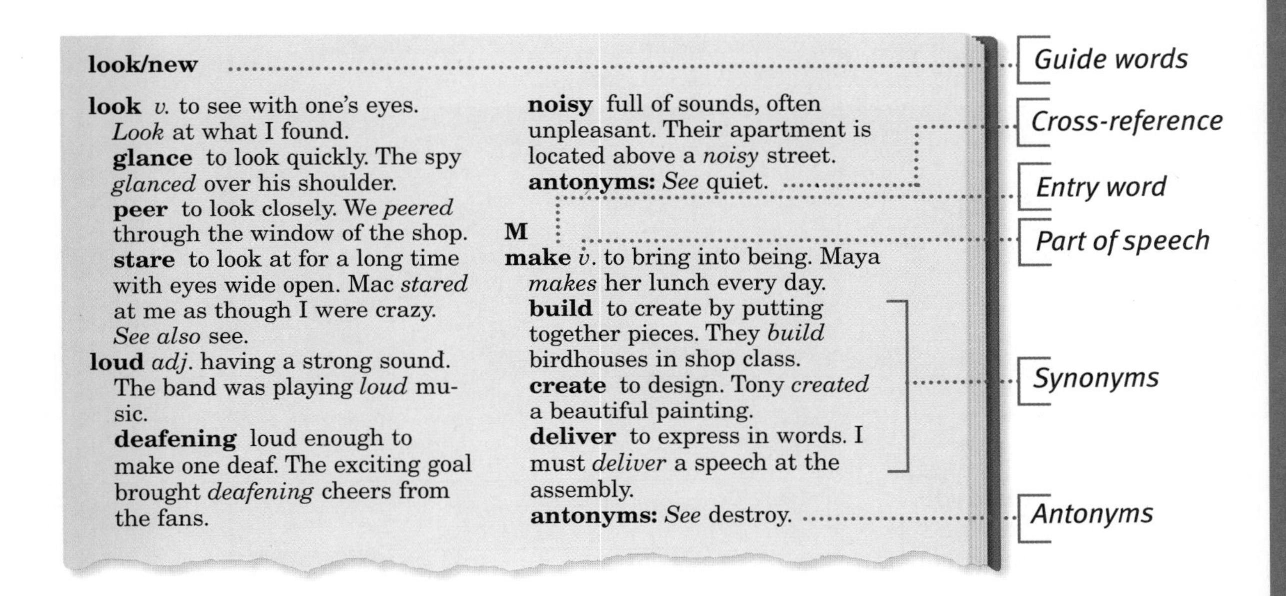

look/new

look *v.* to see with one's eyes. *Look* at what I found.
glance to look quickly. The spy *glanced* over his shoulder.
peer to look closely. We *peered* through the window of the shop.
stare to look at for a long time with eyes wide open. Mac *stared* at me as though I were crazy.
See also see.

loud *adj.* having a strong sound. The band was playing *loud* music.
deafening loud enough to make one deaf. The exciting goal brought *deafening* cheers from the fans.

noisy full of sounds, often unpleasant. Their apartment is located above a *noisy* street.
antonyms: *See* quiet.

M

make *v.* to bring into being. Maya *makes* her lunch every day.
build to create by putting together pieces. They *build* birdhouses in shop class.
create to design. Tony *created* a beautiful painting.
deliver to express in words. I must *deliver* a speech at the assembly.
antonyms: *See* destroy.

Practice **Rewrite each sentence, replacing the underlined word with either a synonym or an antonym. Write *S* for synonym and *A* for antonym.**

1. The principal will make a speech.
2. The shouts of the crowd were loud.
3. We looked at the dog wearing a dress.
4. The soothing music was very loud.
5. Did the children make a sand castle?

Go to www.mhschool.com/language-arts for more information on the topic.

Encyclopedia

DEFINITIONS AND FEATURES

- An encyclopedia is a useful reference tool that contains factual articles about people, places, things, and events.
- Articles are arranged alphabetically by subject in volumes. Each volume is labeled with one or more letters. The label shows the first letter of subjects covered in that volume.
- When searching for information on a person, search by using the last name and then the first name.
- Keywords in CD-ROM encyclopedias can be typed into the search box.

Use this volume to find articles about people, places, things, and events that begin with M.

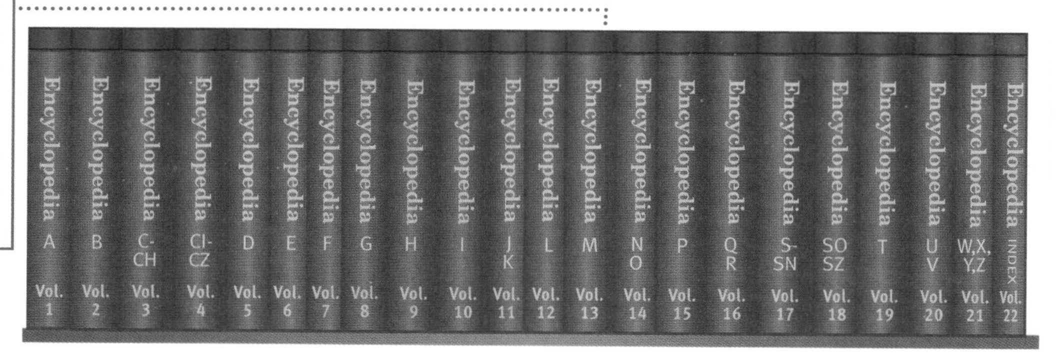

Type in the topic you want to find. Press the ENTER key. An article from the CD-ROM encyclopedia will appear.

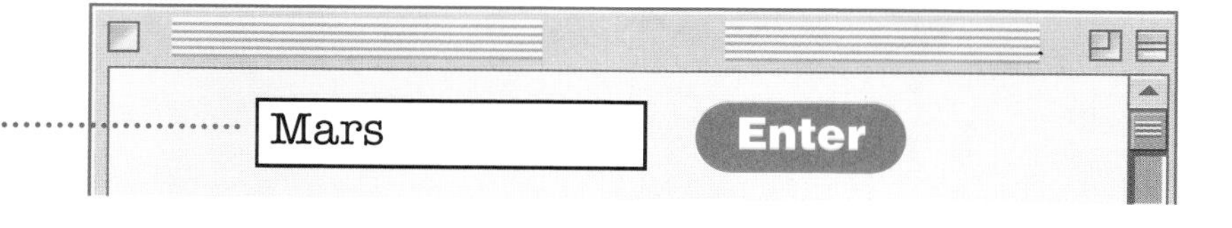

Practice **Write the keyword that you would look up to find information about each subject. Write the volume number in which you could find the information.**

1. how photosynthesis works
2. the history of Mexico
3. the life cycle of the butterfly
4. information about Paul Revere's ride
5. what an aardvark eats

Go to www.mhschool.com/language-arts for more information on the topic.

Choosing Reference Sources for Research

DEFINITIONS AND FEATURES

- Use two or more sources when researching information for a research report.
- You might use sources such as nonfiction books, magazines, videotapes, and interviews with experts.
- Find sources with information about the topic you have selected.

Use two or more resources when researching.

A magazine gives up-to-date information.

An encyclopedia gives general information about topics.

Practice **Read the following topics. Write *book*, *magazine*, *newspaper*, *encyclopedia*, *videotape*, or *interview* to name the best source for information about that topic.**

1. a local astronomer's tips on seeing an eclipse from your town
2. a brief article on Neptune
3. large amounts of in-depth information about Leonardo da Vinci
4. the local weather report for the week
5. instructions for using a telescope

Go to www.mhschool.com/language-arts for more information on the topic.

Handbook

Bibliography

DEFINITIONS AND FEATURES

- A bibliography is a list of all the reference sources you have used to write a report. It may include books, articles, or media resources.
- The bibliography tells your readers where you found your information and provides them with a guide to find out more.
- The bibliography lists the names of the authors, the title of the book or article, the publisher, the place where the book was published, and the date of the book.

BIBLIOGRAPHY

Atlas of the World. New York: Oxon University Press, 1992.

Fowler, Allan. *Save the Rainforests.* Danbury, CT: Children's Press, 1997.

Patent, Dorothy H. and William Muñoz. *Biodiversity.* New York: Clarion, 1996.

Practice Use the sample bibliography to answer these questions.

1. What is a bibliography?
2. Who are the authors of *Biodiversity?*
3. When was *Save the Rainforests* published?
4. Why should a bibliography include the date of the book?
5. Why is it important to include a bibliography at the end of a research report?

Go to www.mhschool.com/language-arts for more information on the topic.

Using the Internet

DEFINITIONS AND FEATURES

- The Internet is a research tool that has current information.
- You can use a search engine to find information about topics. Type in a keyword or phrase about your topic. Some search engines let you type in an entire question.
- On the Internet, you can find daily newspapers and Web sites about special topics.
- At some Web sites, you can send e-mail to experts to ask them questions about topics you are researching.

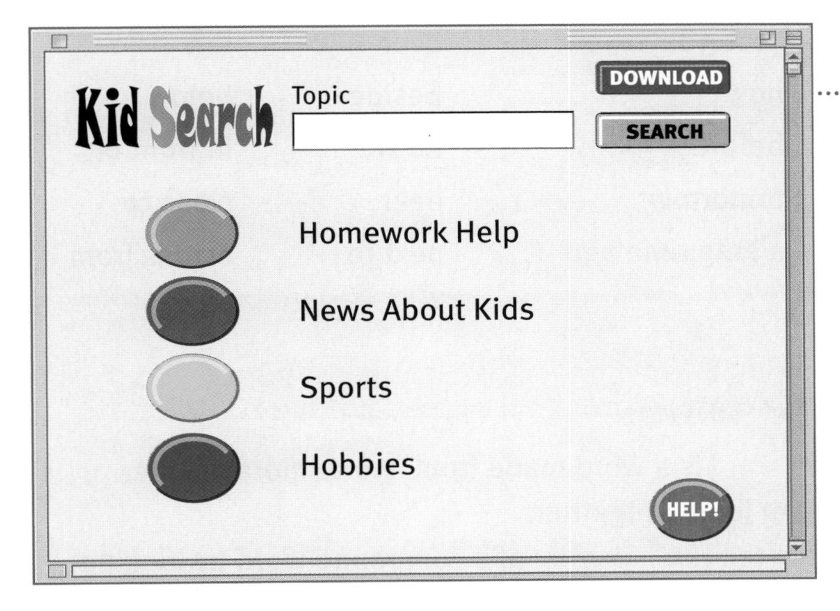

Use a search engine to find articles and Web sites about a topic.

Practice Write the keyword(s) you would use to find the following information with an Internet search engine.

1. You want to find out about Tai Chi.
2. You want to find out who played Luke Skywalker in *The Empire Strikes Back*.
3. You need information about heart disease.
4. You want to find out where the first game of baseball was played.
5. You need information about the human nervous system.

Go to www.mhschool.com/language-arts for more information on the topic.

RULE 1
pages 38–39

Time-Order Words and Spatial Words

- Time-order means the order or sequence in which events occur.
- Use time-order words to make the sequence of events clear.
- Time-order words show how ideas are related to each other and make your writing flow more smoothly.
- Sometimes a group of words works together to tell time order.
- Spatial words tell where something is found or located.
- Spatial words and phrases help make directions clearer.

Time-Order Words and Phrases		Spatial Words and Phrases	
first	finally	inside	on top of
next	this morning	outside	right
then	yesterday	over	left
later	now	beside	below
after	before	above	in front of
last	tomorrow	near	close to
as soon as	a long time ago	next to	across from

RULE 2
pages 122–123

Compound Words

- A compound word is a word made from two or more smaller words that are joined together.
- You can often tell the meaning of a compound word by looking at the two words that make up the compound.
- Many compound words are written as one word (*newspaper*).
- Some compound words are written as two words (*peanut butter, fire engine*).

Two Words	Compound Word	Meaning
door + bell	doorbell	a bell on the door
mail + box	mailbox	a box for mail
board + walk	boardwalk	a footpath made of boards
horse + back	horseback	on the back of a horse
note + book	notebook	a book for making notes

RULE 3
pages 208–209

Prefixes

- A prefix is a word part added to the beginning of a word.
- The word to which a prefix is added is called the root word or base word.
- A prefix changes the meaning of the base word to which it is added.

Prefix	Meaning	Example
re-	again	reappear
dis-	not, opposite of	disorder
un-	not, opposite of	undo
non-	without, opposite of	nonfiction
mis-	badly or wrong	misprint
pre-	before	preschool

RULE 4
pages 296–297

Synonyms and Antonyms

- Synonyms are words that have the same or almost the same meanings.
- Antonyms are words that have opposite meanings.
- A word may have more than one synonym or antonym.

Word	Synonym	Antonym
big	large	small
tidy	neat	messy
fast	quick	slow
happy	glad	sad
angry	mad	calm
tiny	small	large
new	current	old

RULE 5
pages 374–375

Homophones and Homographs

- **Homophones** are words that sound alike but have different spellings and meanings (*two, to, too*).
- You must use **context** to figure out which spelling of a homophone is correct.
- **Homographs** are words that are spelled the same but have different meanings and often have different pronunciations.
- You must use **context** to figure out which meaning of a homograph is correct.

Homophones	Meaning
weak	not strong
week	seven days
there	in that place
their	belonging to them
right	opposite of left
write	to form letters
wood	substance from a tree
would	is willing to

Homographs	Meaning
bear	large animal
bear	support, carry
saw	cutting tool
saw	did see
close	to shut
close	nearby
minute	unit of time
minute	tiny

RULE 6
pages 454–455

Suffixes

- A suffix is a word part added to the end of a word.
- The word to which a suffix is added is called the root word or the base word.
- A suffix changes the meaning of the base word to which it is added.

Suffix	Meaning	Example
-er	person who	teacher
-ful	full of	helpful
-ly	in a certain way	sadly
-less	without	careless
-ment	the result of	agreement
-y	like; full of	thirsty
-able, -ible	able to be	enjoyable, convertible

Problem Words

- The English language includes some confusing words that are often misused. The following charts will help you understand how to use these words properly.

Words	Correct Usage
bad	*Bad* is an adjective. It means "the opposite of good." *He is a* bad *tennis player.*
badly	*Badly* is an adverb. It means "in a bad manner." *The girl behaved* badly *at the concert.*
can	*Can* means "to be able or capable of doing something." *Jeffery* can *play the clarinet.*
may	*May* expresses or asks permission. *You* may *go to the movies on Friday.*
good	*Good* is an adjective that describes something positive. *I read a* good *book last night.*
well	*Well* is usually an adverb. It gives more information about the verb by telling "how." *The author writes* well.
its	*Its* is a possessive pronoun. *Its* has no apostrophe. *Did the dog find* its *bone?*
it's	*It's* is the contraction for "it is." The apostrophe takes the place of the *i* in *is*. It's *seven o'clock.*
lay	*Lay* means "to put something down." Lay *the towels on the shelf.*
lie	*Lie* means "to recline or rest." *My grandmother* lies *down every afternoon.*
learn	*Learn* means "to get knowledge." *The boys* learn *about dinosaurs at the museum.*
teach	*Teach* means "to give knowledge." *The veterinarians* teach *us how to take care of our pets.*

Problem Words

- Some words are easily confused because they sound the same.

Words	Correct Usage
set	*Set* means "to put something down or in a certain place." *He* set *the books on his desk.*
sit	*Sit* means "to be seated." *Please* sit *in the living room.*
their	*Their* is a possessive pronoun meaning "belonging to them." *My neighbors have a treehouse in* their *yard.*
they're	*They're* is a contraction meaning "they are." They're *planning a birthday party for Miguel.*
to	*To* is a direction word meaning "toward." *We walk* to *school together.*
too	*Too* means "also" or "very." *I will eat ice cream,* too. *This math problem is* too *hard.*
whose	*Whose* is an adjective showing possession. *Ted knows* whose *pencil that is.*
who's	*Who's* is the contraction for "who is." The apostrophe takes the place of the *i* in *is.* Who's *going skating next weekend?*
your	*Your* is a possessive pronoun that means "something belongs to you." *This is* your *game.*
you're	*You're* is the contraction for "you are." You're *going to love my new joke.*

Write a story about a real or imaginary pet. Use some problem words in your story. Underline each problem word you use, and check to be sure you have used it correctly.

RULES

- **Silent *e*** When words ***end in silent e***, drop the ***e*** when adding an ending that begins with a vowel. *(rule + ed = ruled)* When adding an ending that begins with a consonant, keep the silent *e*. *(sure + ly = surely)*
- **Spelling with *y*** When a base word ***ends with a consonant followed by y***, change the ***y*** to ***i*** when adding any ending except endings that begin with ***i***. *(try + es = tries; try + ing = trying)*

  When a base word ***ends with a vowel followed by y***, do not change the ***y*** when adding endings. *(donkey + s = donkeys)*
- **Vowel and Final Consonant** When a one-syllable word ***ends in one vowel followed by one consonant***, double the consonant before adding an ending that begins with a vowel. *(fan + ing = fanning)*
- **The letter *q*** is always followed by ***u***. *(quit, quarrel)*
- **Plural: *s* and *es*** Add ***-s*** to most words to form plurals. Add ***-es*** to words ending in *x*, *z*, *s*, *sh*, or *ch*. *(cup + s = cups; class + es = classes)*
- **Plural: *f* and *fe*** To make plurals of words that end with one ***f*** or ***fe***, usually change the ***f*** or ***fe*** to ***v*** and add ***-es***. *(knife + es = knives)*
- ***ie* and *ei* Words** ***i*** comes before ***e*** except after ***c*** or when ***ei*** sounds like */ā/* as in n*ei*ghbor or sl*ei*gh.
- **The /s/ Sound** When ***c*** makes the ***/s/ sound***, it is always followed by ***e***, ***i***, or ***y***. *(place, cider, juicy)*
- **When /j/ is Spelled *g*** ***g*** is always followed by ***e***, ***i***, or ***y***. *(gem, rigid, energy)*
- **The /ch/ Sound** If the ***/ch/*** sound immediately follows a short vowel in a one-syllable word, it is spelled ***tch***. *(latch, snatch)* There are a few exceptions in English: *much*, *such*, *which*, and *rich*.
- **The /f/ Sound** at the end of a word may be spelled ***f***, ***ph***, or ***gh***. *(leaf, graph, rough)*

STRATEGIES

Use these strategies to help you become a better speller.

- **Homophones** Learn common homophones and make sure you have used the correct homophone in your writing. *(They're going to their house. They live over there.)*
- **Rhyming Words** Think of a word you know that has the same spelling pattern as the word you want to spell, such as a rhyming word. *(stew, blew, knew)*
- **Use words that you know** how to spell to help you spell new words. *(blow + sock = block)*
- **Make up clues** to help you remember the spelling. *(u and i build a house; a piece of pie; the principal is your pal)*
- **Related Words** Think of a related word to help you spell a word with a silent letter or a hard-to-hear sound. *(sign-signal; relative-related)*
- **Syllables** Divide the word into syllables. *(par a chute)*
- **Prefixes and Suffixes** Learn to spell prefixes and suffixes you often use in writing.
- **Word Chunks** Look for word chunks or smaller words that help you remember the spelling of the word. *(hippopotamus = hippo pot am us)*
- **Change the way you say the word** to yourself to help with the spelling. *(knife = /k nīf/; beauty = /bē ū tē/)*
- **Visualizing** Think of the times you may have seen the word in reading, on signs, or in a textbook. Try to remember how it looked. Write the word in different ways. Which one looks correct? *(~~atick~~, ~~atik~~, attic)*
- **Personal Word List** Keep an alphabetical Personal Word List in your Spelling Journal. Write words you often have trouble spelling.
- **Dictionary** Become familiar with the dictionary and use it often.

Easily Confused Words

- Some words are easily confused because they are spelled similarly or because they sound alike. These words have different definitions, so you need to be sure you use the correct one.

abroad aboard	all together altogether	breath breathe	ever every	of off	trail trial
accuse excuse	angel angle	cloth clothe	expect suspect	picture pitcher	use used
advice advise	any more anymore	costume custom	farther further	quiet quite	weather whether
affect effect	any way anyway	dairy diary	lay lie	recent resent	were where
all ready already	bean been	desert dessert	loose lose	though through	your you're

Frequently Misspelled Words

- For many writers, some words are difficult to spell. You can use this list to check your spelling.

a lot	busy	finally	knew	our	too
address	buy	first	know	outside	took
again	caught	found	library	people	trouble
against	children	friend	maybe	probably	until
all right	country	front	might	really	upon
already	cousin	guess	minute	school	usually
always	different	happened	morning	since	vacation
answer	doesn't	heard	myself	something	watch
beautiful	dollar	hospital	nickel	sometimes	we're
because	done	house	none	stopped	when
before	enough	hundred	off	straight	whole
believe	especially	I'm	often	stuff	woman
bought	every	instead	once	swimming	women
break	except	interesting	opened	there's	
brought	favorite	into	other	tomorrow	

Common Homophones

- Homophones are words that sound the same but have different spellings and meanings. *Whole* and *hole* are homophones.

ad add	boarder border	flour flower	heard herd	oh owe	tail tale
aisle I'll	cheap cheep	forth fourth	hole whole	pail pale	their there they're
allowed aloud	coarse course	groan grown	in inn	pare pear	threw through
ate eight	creak creek	guessed guest	its it's	passed past	wade weighed
bare bear	days daze	hair hare	loan lone	peace piece	wail whale
base bass	dew do	hall haul	made maid	peer pier	way weigh
beat beet	fair fare	heal heel	meat meet	plain plane	weak week
berry bury	flea flee	hear here	missed mist		

Word Study Steps

To be a better speller, follow these steps.

1. Study each letter in the word.
2. Picture the word in your mind.
3. Write the word carefully.
4. Check the spelling of the word.

Handbook

Poem

A **poem** can describe, explain, or tell a story using word pictures and special forms, sounds, and rhythms.

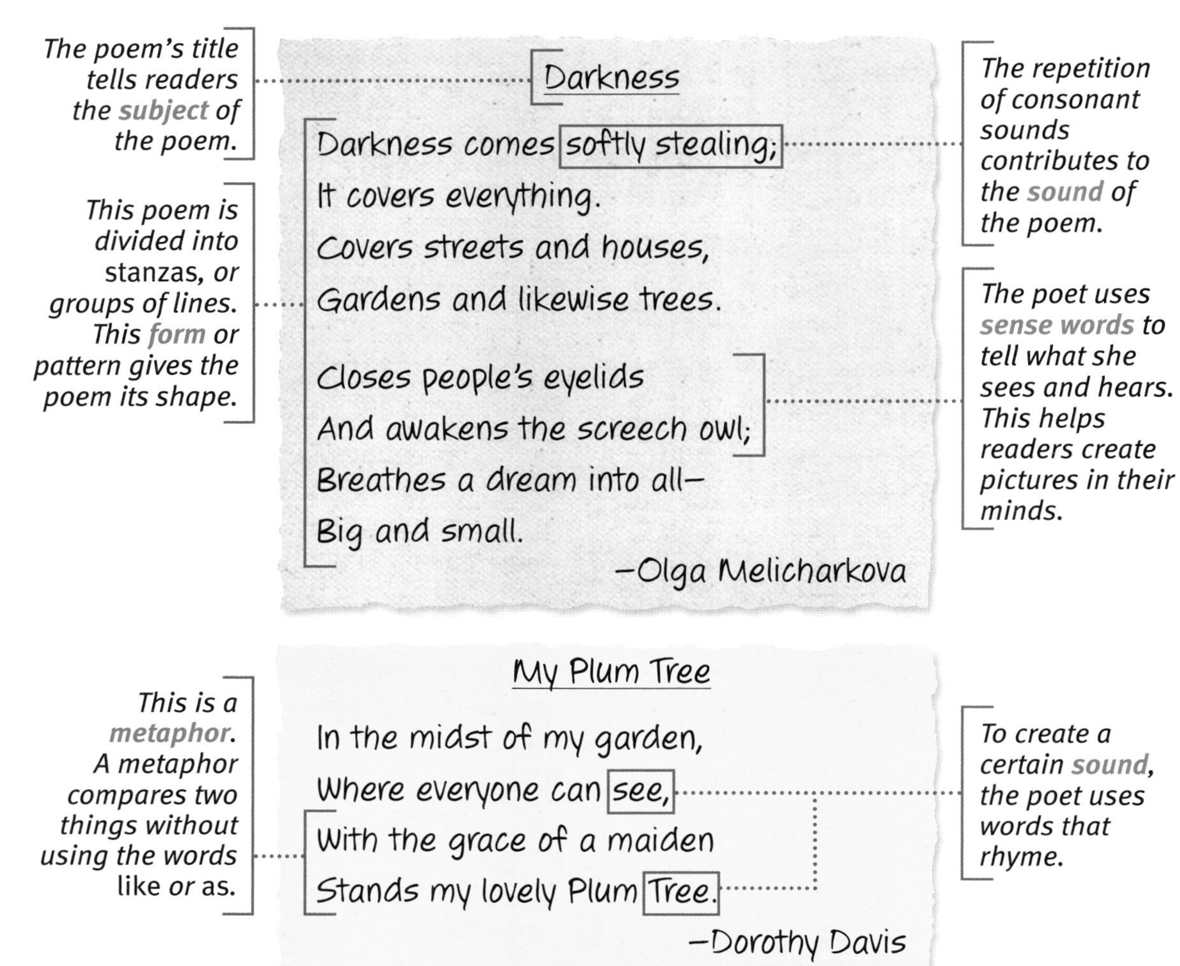

GUIDELINES

- Choose a topic that interests you, such as animals or sports.
- Use similes and metaphors to create vivid word pictures. A simile compares two things by using the words *like* or *as*.
- Decide how you will use sound in your poem.
- Think of a pattern, or form, for your poem.

Practice **Look around you. What would make a good topic for a poem? Choose a topic that interests you. Decide what sense words you could use to describe it. Choose a form for your poem. Will it rhyme? Write your own poem.**

Business Letter

A **business letter** is a letter you write to a company, a businessperson, or someone in the government. Business letters use more formal language than friendly letters. Every business letter has six parts.

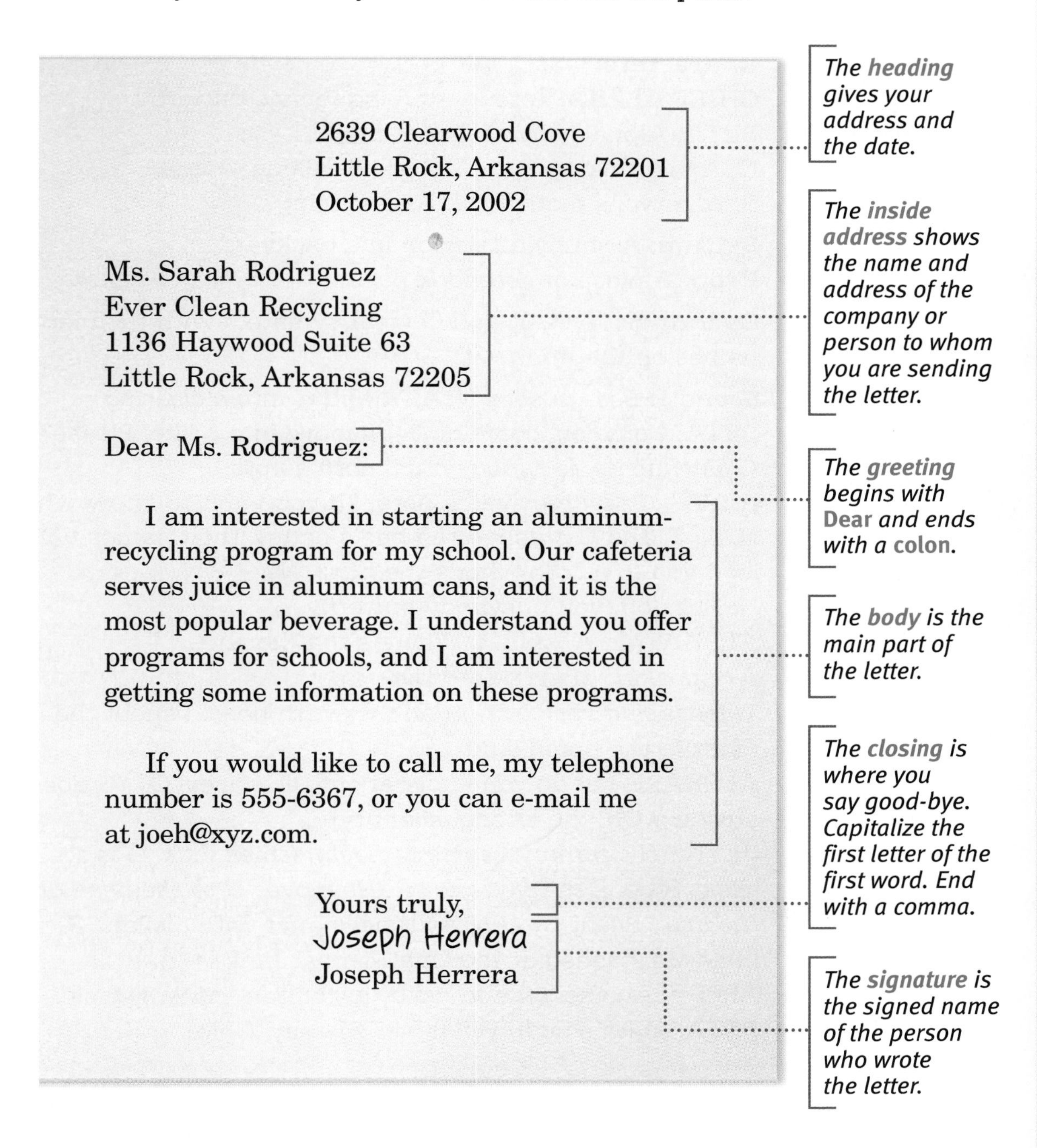

2639 Clearwood Cove
Little Rock, Arkansas 72201
October 17, 2002

Ms. Sarah Rodriguez
Ever Clean Recycling
1136 Haywood Suite 63
Little Rock, Arkansas 72205

Dear Ms. Rodriguez:

I am interested in starting an aluminum-recycling program for my school. Our cafeteria serves juice in aluminum cans, and it is the most popular beverage. I understand you offer programs for schools, and I am interested in getting some information on these programs.

If you would like to call me, my telephone number is 555-6367, or you can e-mail me at joeh@xyz.com.

Yours truly,
Joseph Herrera
Joseph Herrera

Practice **Write a business letter to a local professional, such as a doctor, scientist, or lawyer. Invite him or her to speak to your class about a specific topic.**

Humorous Play

A **humorous play** is a play based on a humorous story. In a play, characters act out parts and speak dialogue.

The play's title should be catchy and interesting.

The list of characters includes a brief description of each one.

The setting describes when and where the action takes place.

Necessary props and costumes should be listed.

Stage directions tell the actors how to move or speak.

Dialogue, or the spoken parts for each character, is included.

The Silent Type

Characters:
CHIEF ALPHA: A tough-talking female butterfly
BETA: Alpha's shy assistant firefly
N: A fast-talking fly A: A slow-talking worm
T: A nervous moth G: A silent slug

Setting: A sunny afternoon in a backyard.
Prop: A piece of notebook paper

Costumes: N, A, T, and G wear sweaters with their letter names on the front.

Scene 1: *Beta pushes N, A, T, and G into a clearing.*
BETA: Come on, come on, let's move into a line. Please? *(They line up as Alpha enters with a note.)*
ALPHA: I just received a note. "If you want to know where N, A, T, and G stashed the bee's honey, their names will lead you to it." So what's the buzz, N?
N: Buzz off, you busybody butterfly.
ALPHA: Mr. A, spill it. Where's that honey?
A: *(speaking slowly)* I—don't—know. Ask T.
T: *(speaking very fast)* I don't fly with bees. I spent the night at the porch light.
ALPHA: What do you know about the honey, G? *(G doesn't answer.)* Oh, the strong, silent type.
BETA: *(His tummy begins to flash.)* Chief, look. G is the silent type. Don't you get it? *(He moves G to the head of the line.)* Silent *G! G-N-A-T* spells *gnat* with a silent *G.* The honey is stashed at the Gnat Zapper Inn!
ALPHA: Another case solved by my brilliant butterfly brain.
BETA: *(with a sigh)* Whatever you say, Chief.

Practice Think of a humorous story that you've heard, or make up your own. Change the story into a play by adding stage directions, scenery, props, and dialogue.

Editorial

An **editorial** is an article that an author writes to express an opinion. Editorials are written mainly to persuade.

<u>Bogged Down</u>

Help! Our mountain bogs are in danger of disappearing forever! Once totaling an area of more than 5,000 acres, North Carolina's mountain bogs have now been reduced to just 500 acres. Unless people become more aware of the importance of protecting these bogs, they will disappear from the face of the earth.

If you would like to help save the natural mountain bogs, there are many things that you ought to do. First, stay on trails when you hike. Your boots can damage and destroy plants that are too small to see. Another choice that you have is to ask your congressperson to pass laws protecting these bogs. If we all work together, we can make sure that these mountain bogs will be around for future generations to enjoy.

State your opinion in a topic sentence.

Include facts and details to support your opinion.

Use opinion words to persuade your audience.

Present your ideas in a logical order.

In the conclusion, summarize facts and restate your opinion.

GUIDELINES

- Think about your audience and your purpose.
- Brainstorm a list of topics that you feel strongly about. Then choose the most interesting or most important topic.
- Do research on your topic to find supporting details.
- Organize your ideas into paragraphs.

Practice **Write an editorial of your own. Choose a topic that interests you. Be sure you state an opinion and back it up with examples and details.**

What Is a Thesaurus?

A **thesaurus** is a reference source you can use to find synonyms, and sometimes antonyms, for many common words. **Synonyms** are words that mean the same or almost the same thing. **Antonyms** are words that have opposite meanings. Use a thesaurus when you are looking for a more interesting or more exact word. Read this sentence:

The sunset was pretty.

If you check the word *pretty* in the thesaurus, you will find these words: *attractive, beautiful,* and *gorgeous*. One of these words will make your sentence more interesting and precise.

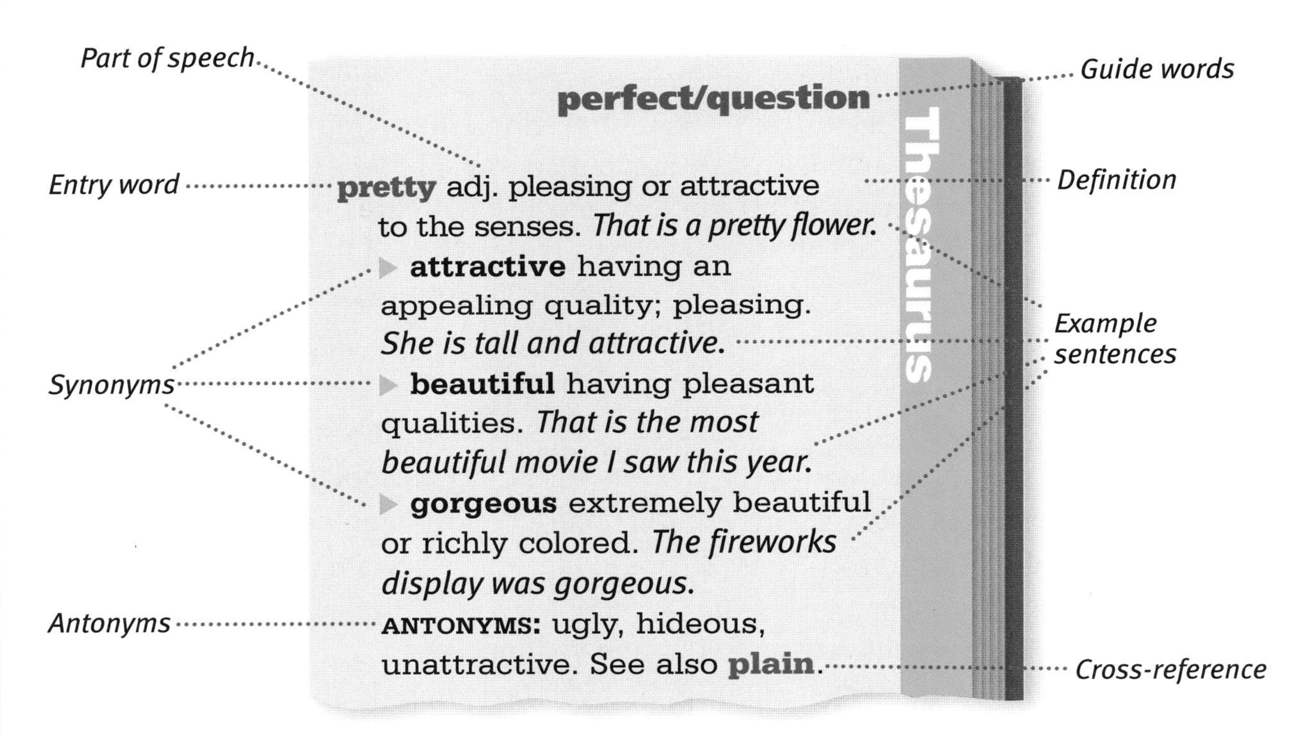

- The guide words at the top of each page show the first and last word on that page.
- The word *pretty* is the entry word.
- The part of speech of each entry is given.
- A definition tells what the entry word and each synonym mean.
- An example sentence helps you to use each entry word and each synonym.
- A cross-reference sends you to additional information.

Practice

A. Answer the questions below by looking up the entry for the word fast.

1. What are the guide words on the page with the entry for *fast*?
2. What part of speech is the word *fast*?
3. What word means the opposite of *fast*?
4. Would an animal be more likely described as rapid or as swift?
5. Write another example sentence for the word *quick*.

DEFINITIONS AND FEATURES

- **Synonyms are words with similar meanings.**
- **There may be different shades of meaning among the synonyms listed within a single entry. For example, an entry for the word *write* might list *scribble* and *input* as synonyms. *Scribble* means "to write quickly or carelessly." *Input* means "to enter information into a computer." You might *scribble* a note on a piece of paper, but you wouldn't *input* a note on a piece of paper. Remember to look at the definitions and example sentences with each word. They will help you figure out whether the synonyms have slightly different meanings.**
- **Near the bottom of some entries you will find a list of antonyms, or words that mean the opposite of the entry word.**
- **In some cases, you will find cross-references. For example, under the entry word *small*, you will find the cross-reference "See *little*." This means that you should look up the word *little*; the word *small* will be listed under *little*.**

B. Use the thesaurus to replace each underlined word with a more exact word.

1. The old plate has a single <u>break</u> on it.
2. The grass was <u>dry</u> because of the heat.
3. <u>New</u> automobiles look different from those that were made 100 years ago.
4. The president will <u>say</u> that the war is over.
5. Our class used microscopes to <u>see</u> tiny animals.

Practice

C. An editorial should use precise, colorful words that will help convince the audience to think a certain way. Rewrite the editorial. Look up each underlined word in the thesaurus. Replace the word with a synonym or antonym that best fits the context of the sentence.

Help the Manatees!

Manatees are big sea animals that live along coasts. Because these gentle animals live in water that is not very deep, they are in danger. Many people answer, "How can we help the manatee?" Here are some things that you can do.

First, be careful if you drive a power boat in shallow water. The boat's propellers can harm manatees. Second, support sanctuaries, or safe places for these animals to live. You can volunteer to help at these sanctuaries, or you can raise money for them. Finally, remember not to throw garbage into the ocean. Manatees can be strangled or poisoned by some of our trash items.

Don't be brave! Do your part to help the manatee. These animals are struggling to survive, but with just a little help, they may be around always.

Practice

D. A letter that uses the same words over and over again is not interesting to read and may not make the right points. Rewrite the letter below. Replace the underlined words with synonyms from the thesaurus.

123 Marine Way
Ocean City, CA 92101
March 15, 2001

Dear Aunt Sandy,

I'm sorry I haven't written in a few weeks. I've been very busy with school. My class is studying the ocean. We are learning a lot of <u>interesting</u> facts about some <u>interesting</u> ocean animals. I wrote a <u>great</u> report about manatees. When I turned it in, my teacher said I had done a <u>great</u> job.

I can't wait to see you next week.

Love,
Roberta

Practice

E. A poem creates a feeling or mood. When you write a poem, you may want to revise it by adding words that are more exact or more descriptive. Rewrite the poem below. Replace the underlined words with synonyms that help create a particular mood or feeling.

The Day

Morning,
<u>beautiful</u>, <u>quiet</u>, <u>bright</u>
walking, doing, slowing, resting,
darkening, <u>disappearing</u>
Night

agree v. to say one is willing. *I agree to clean my room every Saturday.*
▶ **approve** to agree to officially. *The committee will approve the use of music in the cafeteria.*
▶ **consent** to say yes. *I consent to your plan.*
ANTONYMS: refuse, reject, disagree

allow See **let**.

always adv. as long as possible. *I will remember their kindness always.*
▶ **continually** without stop. *My tooth aches continually.*
▶ **forever** for all time. *Ned will be my friend forever.*
ANTONYMS: never, rarely, seldom

angry adj. feeling or showing anger. *Don's remark made me angry.*
▶ **enraged** filled with rage; angry beyond control. *The enraged lion growled loudly.*
▶ **furious** extremely angry. *Marty was furious when he found out I ruined his bike.*

answer v. to give a spoken or written response. *I wonder whether Celia is going to answer my letter.*
▶ **reply** to say in response. *If he insults you, don't reply. Just walk away.*
▶ **respond** to give an answer. *James did not respond to my question.*
ANTONYMS: See **ask.**

ask v. to put a question to. *Let's ask for directions.*
▶ **inquire** to seek information by asking questions. *Please inquire at the desk.*
▶ **question** to try to get information (from someone). *Bill's mother questioned him about where he had been.*
ANTONYMS: See **answer**.

awful adj. causing fear, dread, or awe. *The tree made an awful noise when it fell.*
▶ **dreadful** causing great fear. *I am in shock from the dreadful experience.*
▶ **terrible** causing terror or awe. *Jason received some terrible news.*
ANTONYMS: pleasant, wonderful

battle n. a fierce contest between people or groups. *The football game was a real battle.*
▶ **conflict** a strong disagreement. *The two sides are in a bitter conflict over the issue.*
▶ **struggle** a contest of power or skill. *The struggle between the teams ended in a tie.*

believe v. to think something is true. *Do you believe he is telling the truth?*

▶ **accept** to take as truth. *He hoped she would accept his version of the events.*
▶ **be convinced** to be persuaded. *Lu needs to be convinced that the plan is good.*
ANTONYMS: doubt, reject

big adj. of great size. *Do you have any big boxes?*
▶ **enormous** much greater than the usual size. *There is an enormous spider in the bathtub.*
▶ **huge** extremely big. *That huge man plays football.*
▶ **large** of great size. *Paula seldom has a large lunch.*
ANTONYMS: See **little**.

brave adj. willing to face danger; without fear. *The brave firefighter raced into the burning house.*
▶ **bold** showing courage; fearless. *The bold explorer went where no one else had ever gone.*
▶ **courageous** having courage. *A courageous woman dove into the icy water to save the child.*
▶ **daring** willing to take risks. *The daring princess escaped from the tower.*
ANTONYMS: afraid, fearful

break v. to come apart; to separate into pieces. *These glass animals break easily.*
▶ **crack** to break without fully separating. *I will crack the eggs for the cake.*
▶ **fracture** to break or split a bone. *Juan fractured his ankle and had to leave the game.*
▶ **shatter** to break suddenly into many pieces. *The vase will shatter if you drop it.*

bright adj. filled with light; shining. *Is that light bright enough to read by?*
▶ **brilliant** shining or sparkling with light. *The crown was decorated with brilliant gems.*
▶ **shiny** shining; bright. *Her blue coat has shiny silver buttons.*
ANTONYMS: dark, dull

build v. to put together parts and material. *They built the tree house yesterday.*
▶ **make** to build or prepare. *Andrea made the salad.*
▶ **construct** to put up. *The school was constructed in 1912.*
ANTONYMS: to tear down, wreck, demolish

C

careful adj. done with close attention. *She made a careful check of the electric wires.*
▶ **cautious** using close care. *Sally was cautious when she walked across the narrow bridge.*
▶ **detailed** dealing with all the little parts of something. *The model came with detailed instructions.*
▶ **thorough** leaving nothing out; careful and complete. *Please do a thorough job of cleaning the desk.*
ANTONYMS: careless, sloppy

Thesaurus

cave n. a natural hollow space in a mountain. *Bears sleep in a cave for the winter.*
- **burrow** a hole in the ground made by an animal for shelter. *The rabbits lived in a burrow.*
- **cavern** a large cave, often underground. *We explored a cavern deep in the ground.*

cold adj. having a low temperature. *The desert has hot days and cold nights.*
- **chilly** uncomfortably cool. *The first day was wet and chilly.*
- **icy** very cold. *An icy wind stung our cheeks.*

ANTONYMS: See **hot**.

collect v. to gather or bring (things) together. *Tom collected soda cans to raise money.*
- **assemble** to gather or bring together, especially people. *The mayor assembled the council.*
- **compile** to collect and put together (information), as in a list or report. *Nancy compiled a list of members.*
- **gather** to bring together in one place or group. *Ray gathered all the team members for a photo.*

cook v. to prepare food for eating, using heat. *Dad will cook dinner.*
- **bake** to cook in an oven. *Alice put the cake in the oven to bake.*
- **broil** to cook by exposing to a flame or another source of heat. *Let's broil the hamburgers on the grill.*
- **roast** to cook with little moisture in the oven or over a fire. *Roast the turkey for six hours.*

cry v. to shed tears. *Julian wasn't sure what to do when he heard the baby cry.*
- **sob** to cry with short gasps. *Tina sobbed as she told us what happened.*
- **weep** to show grief, joy, or other strong emotions by crying. *James is happy—he will weep no more.*

ANTONYMS: See **laugh**.

cure v. to bring back to health. *Rest will help cure that strained back.*
- **heal** to make better. *A doctor's job is to heal the sick.*
- **treat** to take care of an illness or injury. *A doctor should treat a high fever.*

ANTONYMS: make ill, harm, hurt, injure, poison

curious adj. eager to learn about something. *I am curious about new inventions.*
- **interested** wanting to find out about something. *Miguel is interested in the habits of whales.*
- **prying** looking or inquiring too closely. *My sister's prying eyes made me uncomfortable as I read the letter.*

D

danger n. a chance of harm or injury. *Fire is a danger to forests.*
▶ **hazard** something that can cause injury. *Bad weather can be a traffic hazard.*
▶ **menace** a person or thing that is a threat. *Careless drivers are a menace.*
▶ **risk** a chance of loss or harm. *Firefighters often place their lives at risk.*
ANTONYM: safety

depend v. to count on. *I can depend on my sister.*
▶ **rely** to trust in. *I will rely on you to be on time.*
▶ **trust** to have confidence in. *You can trust me to walk the dog twice a day.*
ANTONYMS: distrust, doubt

disappear v. to go out of sight. *The jet will soon disappear into the clouds.*
▶ **evaporate** to fade away or end. *Your home run caused the other team's hopes for a win to evaporate.*
▶ **fade** to become fainter and disappear. *We heard the fire engines' sirens fade into the distance.*
▶ **vanish** to go out of sight or existence. *When you use this cleaner, stains will vanish.*
ANTONYMS: appear, reappear, remain

do v. to carry out. *Mrs. Riley will do the job right.*
▶ **execute** to complete; to put into effect. *The soldier executed the orders.*
▶ **perform** to carry out to completion. *The doctor performed the operation.*

dry adj. not wet; free of moisture. *Please bring me a dry towel.*
▶ **arid** dry as a result of having little rainfall. *The Gobi desert is arid.*
▶ **parched** dried out by heat. *It was so hot, my throat was parched.*
ANTONYMS: See **wet**.

easy adj. requiring little mental or physical effort; not difficult. *It is easy to count to ten.*
▶ **facile** not hard to do or achieve. *There is no facile solution to the problem of world hunger.*
▶ **simple** not complicated. *The directions for building the birdhouse were simple.*
ANTONYMS: hard, difficult

employ v. to pay someone to do a job. *Our neighbor will employ Rita to rake the leaves.*
▶ **appoint** to name for a job or an office. *The President can appoint certain judges.*
▶ **engage** to hire. *I will engage a secretary to take notes.*
▶ **hire** to give a job to. *If you hire me, I'll do a good job.*
ANTONYMS: fire, dismiss, let go, discharge

enjoyment n. a happy or pleased feeling. *Baseball gives me much enjoyment.*

▶ **delight** joy. *It is a delight to listen to good music.*

▶ **happiness** gladness. *Matthew got much happiness from the surprise party.*

▶ **pleasure** a satisfied or pleased feeling. *Pleasure can come from a job well done.*

ANTONYMS: dissatisfaction, unhappiness

equal adj. the same in size, amount, or value. *Five pennies are equal to one nickel.*

▶ **even** the same. *At the end of the fifth inning, the score in the game was even.*

▶ **matching** the same or similar, for example in size, color, or shape. *The sisters wore matching hats.*

▶ **similar** almost the same. *The two cars are similar but not exactly alike.*

ANTONYMS: unequal, different

far adj. a long way off; not near. *Steve's house is far from here.*

▶ **distant** extremely far. *Pluto is a distant planet.*

▶ **remote** faraway, in an out-of-the-way place. *We visited a remote village in the jungle.*

ANTONYMS: near, close

fast adj. moving or done with speed. *We rode on a fast train.*

▶ **quick** done in a very short time. *That was a quick game.*

▶ **rapid** with great speed, often in a continuing way. *Jeff kept walking at a rapid pace.*

▶ **swift** moving at great speed, often said of animals or people. *The swift runner flew by us.*

ANTONYM: slow

fear n. a feeling that trouble or danger is near. *He has a fear of heights.*

▶ **fright** a sudden, strong feeling of danger. *Surprising me like that gave me a real fright.*

▶ **scare** a sudden panic. *We jumped out and gave them a scare.*

▶ **terror** a great feeling of danger. *The terror in the movie was caused by dinosaurs.*

ANTONYMS: fearlessness, courage, bravery

frown v. to express anger or sadness with a look on the face. *Mom will frown when she sees the mess our dog made.*

▶ **glare** to give an angry look. *A messy room will make him glare in anger.*

▶ **scowl** to look at in a displeased way. *The barking dog caused Lucy to scowl.*

ANTONYMS: smile, laugh, grin

funny adj. causing laughter. *Delia told us a funny joke.*

▶ **amusing** causing smiles of enjoyment or laughter. *That story was amusing.*

▶ **comical** causing laughter through actions. *The clowns were comical.*

▶ **hilarious** very funny and usually noisy. *That movie was hilarious.*

G

gentle adj. mild and kind; not rough. *Babies need gentle handling.*
▶ **soft** smooth to the touch; not hard or rough. *A soft breeze is blowing across the field.*
▶ **tender** delicate; kind and loving. *When I am sick, I need tender care.*
ANTONYMS: harsh, hard, rough

get v. to go for and return with. *Please get me a sandwich.*
▶ **acquire** to come into possession of through effort. *He acquired a new house.*
▶ **obtain** to get as one's own, often with some difficulty. *Lily worked hard to obtain her job.*

give v. to turn over possession or control of, to make a present of. *I am going to give my mother flowers for her birthday.*
▶ **confer** to give as an honor. *The college will confer a degree upon the guest speaker.*
▶ **contribute** to give in common with others. *We are asking each class to contribute a book to the library.*
▶ **grant** to give in response to a request. *Grant me this favor.*
▶ **present** to give in a formal way. *Mr. Hammond will present the class gift.*
ANTONYMS: See **take**.

good adj. Above average in quality. *This is a good book.*
▶ **excellent** extremely good. *Marie always does excellent work.*
▶ **fair** somewhat good; slightly better than average. *Jeremy did a fair job.*
▶ **fine** of high quality; very good. *She made a fine dinner for the party.*
ANTONYMS: bad, poor

great adj. of unusual quality or ability. *Mark Twain was a great writer.*
▶ **remarkable** having unusual qualities. *That was a remarkable movie.*
▶ **superb** of greater quality than most. *She is a superb singer.*
See also **good**.

guess v. to form an opinion without enough information. *I guess there are six hundred marbles in that jar.*
▶ **estimate** to form an opinion of the value or cost of something. *I estimate that it will cost $50.00 to repair the bike.*
▶ **suppose** to believe that something is possible but not certain. *I suppose Jean will lend you her scarf.*

H

happy adj. having, showing, or bringing pleasure. *Mr. Andersen was happy in his garden.*

▶ **glad** feeling or expressing joy or pleasure. *Tony was glad to visit the museum.*

▶ **joyful** very happy; filled with joy. *A wedding is a joyful occasion.*

▶ **merry** happy and cheerful. *The party was a merry occasion.*

▶ **pleased** satisfied or content. *Harry was pleased with the new coat.*

ANTONYMS: See **sad**.

hard adj. not easy to do or deal with. *Mowing the lawn is hard work.*

▶ **difficult** hard to do; requiring effort. *Steering a ship through a storm is a difficult task.*

▶ **tough** difficult to do, often in a physical sense. *Catching wild horses is a tough job.*

ANTONYM: easy

harm v. to cause someone or something injury or problems. *You can harm a plant by not giving it water.*

▶ **damage** to harm or make less valuable. *You might damage the artwork if you touch it.*

▶ **hurt** to give pain to. *If you fight, you will hurt each other.*

▶ **injure** to hurt. *Rose wears a helmet, so she will not injure herself when she rides her bike.*

ANTONYMS: help, aid, protect, heal

help v. to provide with support; to be of service to. *Will you help me clean this floor?*

▶ **aid** to give help to someone in trouble. *The police aided us in finding the lost children.*

▶ **assist** to help, often in a cooperative way. *Ned assisted his brother in painting the house.*

high adj. located or extending a great distance above the ground. *The bird's nest is on a high branch.*

▶ **tall** having a height greater than average but with a relatively narrow width. *Over the years, the pine trees grew to be very tall.*

▶ **towering** of great or imposing height. *The towering buildings shadowed the people below.*

ANTONYMS: low, short

hot adj. having a high temperature; having much heat. *The oven is hot.*

▶ **fiery** as hot as fire; burning. *The spaceship flew toward the fiery sun.*

▶ **scalding** hot enough to burn, often said of liquids. *A pot of scalding water fell on the floor.*

▶ **scorching** hot enough to cause burning or drying. *The scorching sun blazed down on the weary travelers.*

ANTONYMS: See **cold**.

hurt v. to cause pain or damage. *Did you hurt your knee?*

▶ **harm** to do damage to. *A good rider would never harm a horse.*

▶ **injure** to cause physical damage. *Jon fell and injured his leg.*

important adj. having great value or meaning. *Education is very important.*

▶ **major** chief or most important. *The major reason I jog is to relax.*

▶ **significant** having special value or meaning. *July 4th is a significant day in American history.*

interesting adj. arousing or holding interest or attention. *That was an interesting book.*

▶ **captivating** capturing and holding the attention by beauty or excellence. *Grandpa told us a captivating story about life long ago.*

▶ **fascinating** causing and holding the interest through a special quality or charm. *The snake charmer's act was fascinating.*

ANTONYMS: dull, boring

large See **big**.

laugh v. to make the sounds and facial movements that show amusement. *He laughs at my jokes.*

▶ **chuckle** to laugh softly, especially to oneself. *Carla chuckled when she read my note.*

▶ **giggle** to laugh in a silly, high-pitched, or nervous way. *Jill giggled and turned red.*

▶ **guffaw** to laugh loudly. *Henry guffawed so hard, he had to hold his sides.*

ANTONYMS: See **cry**.

let v. to give permission to. *Mom won't let me go to the game.*

▶ **allow** to grant permission to or for, usually in relation to rules. *The rules do not allow fishing on the beach.*

▶ **permit** to allow (a person) to do something. *He will permit you to use the pool if you ask.*

ANTONYMS: deny, refuse, forbid

like v. to take pleasure in (something); to feel affection for (someone). *I like to go walking in the rain.*

▶ **admire** to have affection and respect for (someone). *Johnny admires his grandfather.*

▶ **enjoy** to take pleasure in (something). *Shelley enjoys music.*

▶ **love** to like (something) a lot; to feel great affection for (someone). *Mary loves to go sailing.*

ANTONYMS: dislike, hate

listen v. to try to hear; pay attention. *Listen when the teacher is speaking.*

▶ **hear** to receive sound through the ears. *Do you hear what I'm saying?*

▶ **heed** to pay careful attention to; listen or mind. *I will*

heed my parents' advice and wear a sweater to the ball game.
ANTONYM: ignore

little adj. small in size; not big. Wanda found a little puppy.
▶ **small** not large. *Wally needs a small box for the gift.*
▶ **tiny** extremely small. *We saw three tiny birds just after they hatched.*
ANTONYMS: See **big**.

look v. to see with one's eyes. *She looked at the moon.*
▶ **glance** to look quickly. *Kenny only glanced at the book.*
▶ **peer** to look closely. *Moe peered at the map to find the town.*
▶ **stare** to look at for a long time with eyes wide open. *Sue was so surprised she just stared at me.*
See also **see**.

loud adj. having a strong sound. *We heard a loud crash overhead.*
▶ **deafening** loud enough to make one deaf. *The dam broke with a deafening roar.*
▶ **noisy** full of sounds, often unpleasant. *The crowd was noisy.*
ANTONYMS: See **quiet**.

love v. to have a strong, warm feeling for. *I love my pets very much.*
▶ **adore** to love greatly. *The children adore their aunt.*
▶ **enjoy** to get joy or pleasure from, be happy with. *I enjoy the company of my sisters.*
ANTONYMS: dislike, hate, loathe, despise

lying v. stretching out. *It is easier to fall asleep lying down than sitting up.*
▶ **reclining** leaning back, lying down. *Jake is reclining on the sofa and reading a book.*
▶ **sprawling** lying or sitting with the body stretched out in an awkward or careless manner. *My dog spent the morning sprawling on the rug with his eyes closed.*
ANTONYMS: standing, sitting

many adj. consisting of a large number. *Dave has many socks.*
▶ **numerous** a great many. *I have asked you numerous times.*
▶ **plenty** (of) enough, or more than enough, suggesting a large number. *We have plenty of plates.*
▶ **several** more than a few but fewer than many. *Keiko has played in several games this season.*
ANTONYM: few

mean adj. lacking in kindness or understanding. *Joe felt bad about being mean to his sister.*
▶ **nasty** resulting from hate. *That was a nasty trick he played on us.*
▶ **selfish** concerned only about oneself. *Kelley is too selfish to care about my feelings.*

▶ **spiteful** filled with ill feelings toward others. *Pat is a spiteful person.*
ANTONYMS: See **nice**.

mild adj. not extreme. *Jackie likes food with a mild taste, but Jon prefers spicy dishes.*
▶ **bland** without any harsh or extreme qualities. *Rice and cottage cheese are bland foods.*
▶ **calm** quiet. *The ocean is calm, and the wind is still.*
▶ **soothing** able to ease irritation. *The cream was soothing on his chapped skin.*
ANTONYMS: rough, wild, fierce, harsh, strong, extreme, spicy

neat adj. clean and orderly. *His clothes always look neat.*
▶ **tidy** neat and clean, often said of a place. *She likes to keep her room tidy.*
▶ **well-groomed** carefully dressed and groomed. *Marvin always looks well-groomed at school.*
ANTONYMS: messy, untidy, sloppy

new adj. having just come into being, use, or possession. *I need to sharpen this new pencil.*
▶ **fresh** seeming new and unaffected by time. *We put fresh flowers in the vase.*
▶ **modern** having to do with the present time; up-to-date. *Modern computers are different from ones used 30 years ago.*
▶ **recent** referring to a time just before the present. *Their recent victory made the team confident.*
ANTONYM: old

nice adj. agreeable or pleasing. *Lynn is a nice person.*
▶ **gentle** mild and kindly in manner. *He is so gentle with the children.*
▶ **kind** gentle and friendly; good-hearted. *Uncle Bob was very kind to send you a gift.*
▶ **pleasant** agreeable; giving pleasure to. *She has a pleasant way of talking.*
▶ **sweet** having or marked by agreeable or pleasing qualities. *He wrote a sweet thank-you note.*
ANTONYMS: See **mean**.

nothing n. not anything. *Ten minus ten leaves nothing.*
▶ **none** no one or not one. *Six people started the problem, but none solved it.*
▶ **zero** nothing. *If none of your answers on the test are correct, your score will be zero.*
ANTONYMS: something, anything, everything, all

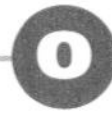

offer v. to present for acceptance or rejection. *If you are hungry, I can offer you a peanut butter sandwich.*
▶ **propose** to put forward a plan. *We propose to write an outline before we do the report.*

▶ **suggest** to mention as a possibility. *I suggest that we leave for home before it gets dark.*

often adv. many times; again and again. *Theo often visits his sister.*

▶ **frequently** happening again and again. *Sarah frequently works late.*

▶ **regularly** happening at fixed times. *Mrs. Day regularly takes the bus.*

ANTONYMS: seldom, rarely

old adj. having lived or existed for a long time. *My grandmother's favorite vase is very old.*

▶ **aged** having grown old. *Minnie helps take care of her aged aunt.*

▶ **ancient** of great age; very old; of times long past. *Dr. Tyrell found an ancient coin.*

ANTONYM: young. See also **new**.

open adj. not having its lid, door, or other covering closed. *It was easy to see the toys in the open toy chest.*

▶ **unclosed** not having its door or other covering shut. *An unclosed box will allow dust to get inside.*

▶ **uncovered** not having the lid or cover on. *Steam rose from the uncovered soup pot cooking on the stove.*

ANTONYMS: closed, shut, covered, locked

perfect adj. without flaw or error in its appearance or nature. *A perfect math test is one with no mistakes.*

▶ **faultless** without error—often describing performance or behavior. *The gymnast performed a faultless routine.*

▶ **flawless** without imperfections such as marks or bumps. *The marble's smooth surface was flawless.*

▶ **ideal** exactly what is hoped for or needed. *Blue is the ideal color for these walls.*

ANTONYMS: imperfect, faulty, flawed, marred

plain adj. not distinguished from others in any way. *The villagers are plain, hard-working people.*

▶ **common** average; not special. *He lives like any common person.*

▶ **ordinary** plain; average; everyday. *It's just an ordinary newspaper.*

ANTONYM: special. See also **unusual**.

pretty adj. pleasing or attractive to the senses. *That is a pretty flower.*

▶ **attractive** having an appealing quality; pleasing. *She is tall and attractive.*

▶ **beautiful** having pleasant qualities. *That is the most beautiful movie I saw this year.*

▶ **gorgeous** extremely beautiful or richly colored. *The fireworks display was gorgeous.*
ANTONYMS: ugly, hideous, unattractive. See also **plain**.

proud adj. having a sense of one's own worth, usually in a positive way. *He was proud of his new baby sister.*
▶ **conceited** having too high an opinion of oneself, in a negative way. *Shelley is too conceited to talk to me.*
▶ **haughty** having or showing much pride in oneself. *He is a haughty football hero.*
ANTONYM: humble

question n. a matter to be talked over. *We discussed the question of sports clubs.*
▶ **issue** a matter to be thought about, not necessarily a problem. *Recycling is an issue that many people have opinions about.*
▶ **problem** a matter needing to be solved. *The meeting will deal with the problem of noise.*
▶ **topic** a subject or matter to be examined. *What is the topic of your speech?*

quiet adj. with little or no noise. *The house was quiet after everyone had gone.*
▶ **calm** free of excitement or strong feeling; quiet. *Remember to be calm during an emergency.*
▶ **peaceful** calm; undisturbed. *The camp is so peaceful early in the morning.*
▶ **silent** completely quiet; without noise. *The band members were silent until the leader raised the baton.*
▶ **still** without sound; silent. *The forest was still.*
ANTONYMS: loud, noisy

reach v. to come to. *We will reach the hotel by sunset.*
▶ **approach** to come near. *The ships slow down as they approach the dock.*
▶ **arrive** to get to or come to. *When you arrive at the museum, wait for me in the front hall.*
▶ **land** to come to the ground or to shore. *The plane should land at the airport soon.*
ANTONYMS: leave, go, depart

ready adj. fit for use or action. *Everything is ready for the party.*
▶ **prepared** ready or fit for a particular purpose. *Jim was prepared for the test.*
▶ **set** ready or prepared to do something. *Willie was all set to go to school.*

really adv. in fact. *What really happened at the store today?*
▶ **actually** in fact; really. *Dan actually got his first job yesterday!*
▶ **indeed** really; truly. *I was indeed waiting for you at the park.*

▸ **truly** in fact; really. *He truly did earn ten dollars.*

right adj. free from error; true. *Every single answer was right.*
▸ **accurate** without errors. *His description was accurate.*
▸ **correct** agreeing with fact or truth. *He found the correct way to solve the puzzle.*
▸ **exact** very accurate; completely correct. *Each math problem has an exact answer.*
ANTONYMS: wrong, mistaken

roar v. to speak or make sounds in a loud, deep voice. *If she hits a home run, the crowd will roar.*
▸ **bellow** to make a loud sound or speak very loudly. *Why does he bellow if I'm standing right here?*
▸ **scream** to make a sudden, sharp, loud cry. *This fake spider made my brother scream.*
▸ **shout** to call loudly. *The announcer had to shout to be heard over the cheering audience.*
▸ **yell** to give a loud cry, or to speak loudly. *I heard him yell, "We won!"*

rude adj. not polite; ill-mannered. *Jack made a rude remark.*
▸ **discourteous** without good manners. *You have no reason to be discourteous to Mr. Braun.*
▸ **impolite** not showing good manners. *They were impolite when they left the party without saying "good-bye."*
ANTONYMS: polite, courteous

run v. to go quickly on foot. *I can run much faster now than I did last year.*
▸ **dash** to go very fast; to run with sudden speed. *Lou dashed to the door when the mailman came with his birthday cards.*
▸ **race** to run very fast; to run in competition with. *The girls raced the boys in the class Olympics.*
▸ **scurry** to move hurriedly. *The puppies scurried to their food dish.*

sad adj. feeling or showing unhappiness or sorrow. *Jake was sad when he lost his dog.*
▸ **downcast** low in spirits; sad. *She was downcast when she did not make the team.*
▸ **miserable** extremely unhappy. *Mary was miserable after her brother left for college.*
ANTONYMS: See **happy**.

same adj. being just like something else in kind, quantity, or degree. *Both pieces of cake are the same size.*
▸ **alike** similar, showing a resemblance. *The twin sisters look alike.*
▸ **equal** the same in size, amount, quality, or value. *She measured equal amounts.*
▸ **identical** the same in every detail. *Our house is identical to the one around the block.*
ANTONYM: different

say v. to make known or express in words. *Mel says that he wants to go home.*

▶ **declare** to make known publicly or formally. *The mayor declared that the town needed more money.*

▶ **pronounce** to say formally or officially that something is so. *The minister pronounced the couple married.*

▶ **speak** to express an idea, or a feeling. *Wendy spoke to us about the new park.*

▶ **state** to express or explain fully in words. *Mr. Combs stated his opinion during the meeting.*

▶ **talk** to express ideas or information; to speak. *Ken talked about his model airplane.*

See also **tell**.

scared adj. afraid; alarmed. *Sheila was scared when she heard a noise.*

▶ **afraid** feeling fear, often in a continuing way or for a long time. *Jerry is afraid of the dark.*

▶ **fearful** filled with fear. *Donna was fearful of the thunder.*

▶ **frightened** scared suddenly or for a short time. *He was frightened when the lights went out.*

▶ **terrified** extremely scared; filled with terror. *Pete was terrified when he heard the screams.*

see v. to receive impressions through the use of the eyes. *She could see the children playing across the street.*

▶ **observe** to notice. *What did you observe during the science experiment?*

▶ **view** to look at, usually for a purpose. *Many people wanted to view the sculpture.*

See also **look**.

shy adj. uncomfortable in the presence of others. *Paula is too shy to speak in front of the class.*

▶ **bashful** easily embarrassed; very shy. *Carl was too bashful to step out from behind the chair.*

▶ **timid** showing a lack of courage; easily frightened. *The timid little boy would not go near the cows.*

ANTONYM: bold

sick adj. having poor health. *Ted was sick in bed all last week.*

▶ **ill** not healthy; sick. *Mark stayed home from school because he was ill.*

▶ **unwell** not feeling well. *Stan has felt unwell for a month.*

ANTONYMS: well, healthy

small See **little**.

smart adj. intelligent; bright; having learned much. *Tommy is a smart boy for his age.*

▶ **clever** mentally sharp; quick-witted. *Some people think that foxes are clever.*

▶ **intelligent** able to learn, understand, and reason. *Shana is an intelligent girl.*

▶ **wise** able to know or judge what is right, good, or true, often describing a person with good sense rather than

one who knows a lot of facts. *The chief was a wise old man.*
ANTONYM: stupid

smile v. to show a smile, in a happy or friendly way. *May Li smiled when she saw the puppy.*
▶ **grin** to smile broadly with real happiness or amusement. *Keith grinned when he saw my costume.*
▶ **smirk** to smile in a silly or self-satisfied way. *Pat smirked at him because she knew the answer.*
ANTONYMS: frown, scowl

strange adj. differing from the usual or the ordinary. *That is a strange little dog.*
▶ **odd** not ordinary. *She has some very odd clothes.*
▶ **weird** strange or odd, in a frightening or mysterious way. *Kids say the weird house is haunted.*
See also **unusual**.

strong adj. having great strength or physical power. *Football players have to be strong.*
▶ **muscular** having well-developed muscles; strong. *Lifting weights has made Neil muscular.*
▶ **powerful** having great strength, influence, or authority. *The governor is a powerful woman.*
ANTONYM: weak

sudden adj. happening quickly and without warning. *The sudden bang from the car's engine made me jump.*
▶ **quick** fast. *The quick movement of the cat's paw surprised the squirrel.*
▶ **startling** surprising; happening without warning. *The outcome of the elections was startling to all of us.*
▶ **unexpected** coming without warning, but not necessarily sudden. *An unexpected storm flooded the streets.*
▶ **unpredicted** not guessed or expected ahead of time. *The team's win had unpredicted results.*

sure adj. firmly believing in something. *Pam is sure that our team will win.*
▶ **certain** free from doubt; very sure. *Russ is certain of his answer.*
▶ **confident** firmly trusting; sure of oneself or of another. *Mac is confident that he will get the job.*
▶ **definite** positive or certain. *It is definite that school is closed on Friday.*
ANTONYMS: doubtful, unsure

surprised adj. feeling sudden wonder. *Joan was surprised when she heard she had won the award.*
▶ **amazed** overwhelmed with wonder or surprise. *I was amazed when the dog did as I asked.*
▶ **astonished** greatly surprised; shocked. *Everyone was astonished when snow fell in June.*

▶ **astounded** greatly surprised; stunned. *Lynn was so astounded that she could not move.*

take v. to get into one's hands or possession; to obtain. *May I take your tray for you?*
▶ **grab** to take roughly or rudely. *Brianne grabbed the paper and wrote a quick note.*
▶ **seize** to take suddenly and by force. *The policemen seized the runaway prisoner.*
▶ **snatch** to take suddenly and quickly, often in secret. *The dog snatched a bone off the table when no one was looking.*
ANTONYMS: See **give**.

talk See **say**.

tell v. to put or express in written or spoken words. *Mandy told us about camp.*
▶ **announce** to state or make known publicly. *Mrs. Grimes announced that she would be leaving.*
▶ **narrate** to tell about events, especially a story. *The camp leader narrated a spooky story.*
▶ **relate** to tell or report events or details. *Paul related the story of how we got lost in the woods.*
See also **say**.

thin adj. not fat. *His father has always been rather thin.*
▶ **lean** with little or no fat but often strong. *A runner must have a lean body.*
▶ **slim** thin, in a good or healthy way. *Dennis has gotten slim since he started exercising.*
ANTONYMS: fat, plump

think v. to have in mind as an opinion or attitude. *Kim thinks we should have a picnic.*
▶ **believe** to accept as true or real. *She believes my story.*
▶ **consider** to regard; to believe. *The coach considers Nick to be his best player.*

unusual adj. not usual, common, or ordinary. *Her eyes are an unusual color.*
▶ **extraordinary** very unusual; beyond the ordinary. *That painting is an extraordinary piece of art.*
▶ **rare** seldom happening, seen, or found. *Bald eagles are rare birds.*
▶ **uncommon** rare or unusual. *Hurricanes are uncommon in this area.*
See also **strange**.
ANTONYMS: common, usual

upset adj. feeling uneasy; distressed. *Tina was upset when no one came to her party.*
▶ **anxious** uneasy about or fearful of what may happen. *The first-graders were anxious on the first day of school.*

▶ **concerned** troubled or worried. *Mom was concerned when my brother was late.*
▶ **worried** uneasy or troubled about something. *Jack was worried that the river would flood.*
ANTONYM: calm

very adv. to a great extent. *The summer day was very hot.*
▶ **considerably** to a large or an important degree. *It will be considerably warmer tomorrow.*
▶ **extremely** greatly or intensely. *The sun overhead is extremely hot.*

walk v. to move or travel on foot. *Ruth walked across the street.*
▶ **march** to walk with regular steps. *The band marched down the street.*
▶ **stride** to walk with long steps, usually with a purpose. *We watched him stride down the hall.*
▶ **strut** to walk in a vain or very proud way. *Joe likes to strut up and down in his new clothes.*

want v. to have a desire or wish for. *Lenny wants lunch.*
▶ **crave** to want badly, often in an uncontrollable way. *Suzanne ran to the store because she craved ice cream.*
▶ **desire** to have a strong wish for. *Molly desired fame and fortune.*
▶ **wish** to have a longing or strong need for. *Gary wished he could have a horse in the city.*
▶ **yearn** to feel a strong and deep desire. *Grandpa yearned for the warm days of summer.*

wet adj. covered or soaked with water or another liquid. *Her hair was wet after the long swim.*
▶ **damp** slightly wet. *Our bathing suits are still damp.*
▶ **moist** slightly wet; damp. *Use a moist cloth to wipe up the dust.*
▶ **sopping** extremely wet; dripping. *Lisa's clothes were sopping after she was caught in the sudden storm.*
ANTONYMS: See **dry**.

whole adj. made up of the entire amount, quantity, or number. *Did you eat that whole pizza?*
▶ **complete** having all its parts. *Is that a complete set of crayons?*
▶ **entire** whole; having all its parts. *The entire class had to stay after school.*
▶ **total** whole, full, or entire, often referring to numbers. *Did you pay the total amount?*

Index

Index

Index

H

Index

Index

ACKNOWLEDGEMENTS

The publisher gratefully acknowledges permission to reprint the following copyrighted material:

"Darkness" by Olga Melicharkova from *Have You Seen A Comet?* Copyright © 1971 by the United States Committee for UNICEF. Published by The John Day Company.

Excerpt from *McGraw-Hill School Dictionary.* Copyright © 1998 McGraw-Hill School Division, a Division of the Educational and Professional Publishing Group of The McGraw-Hill Companies, Inc. Reprinted by permission.

Excerpt from the index of the *McGraw-Hill Science*. Copyright © 2000 McGraw-Hill School Division, a Division of the Educational and Professional Publishing Group of The McGraw-Hill Companies, Inc. Reprinted by permission.

"The Fox and the Guinea Pig" / "El zorro y el cuy" from a traditional folk tale translated by Mary Ann Newman. Copyright © 1997 Macmillan/McGraw-Hill, a Division of the Educational and Professional Publishing Group of The McGraw-Hill Companies, Inc.

"Geography Skills - Using Map Scales" from *Texas: Adventures In Time And Place.* Copyright © 1997 by Macmillan/McGraw-Hill, a Division of the Educational and Professional Publishing Group of The McGraw-Hill Companies. Reprinted by permission.

"How Can Animals Help People?" from *McGraw-Hill Science*. Copyright © 2000 McGraw-Hill School Division, a Division of the Educational and Professional Publishing Group of The McGraw-Hill Companies, Inc. Reprinted by permission.

"The Lost Lake" from *The Lost Lake* by Allen Say. Copyright © 1989 by Allen Say. Reprinted by permission of Houghton Mifflin Company. All rights reserved.

"My Plum Tree" by Dorothy Davis from *Have You Seen A Comet?* Copyright © 1971 by the United States Committee for UNICEF. Published by The John Day Company.

"A Play" from *Childtimes* by Eloise Greenfield and Lessie Jones Little. Copyright © 1979 by Eloise Greenfield and Lessie Jones Little. Published by HarperCollins Children's Books, a division of HarperCollins Publishers.

"A Power-ful Sun!" from *McGraw-Hill Science.* Copyright © 2000 McGraw-Hill School Division, a Division of the Educational and Professional Publishing Group of The McGraw-Hill Companies, Inc. Reprinted by permission.

"The Rajah's Rice" from *The Rajah's Rice* by David Barry. Text Copyright © 1994 by David Barry. Used with permission of W.H. Freeman and Company.

"Seal Journey" from *Seal Journey* by Richard and Jonah Sobol, copyright © 1993 Richard Sobol, text and photographs. Used by permission of Cobblehill Books, an affiliate of Dutton Children's Books, a division of Penguin Putnam Inc.

"Teammates" from *Teammates* by Peter Golenbock, text copyright © 1990 by Golenbock Communications, illustrated by Paul Bacon. Reprinted by permission of Harcourt Brace & Company.

"Whales" from *Whales* by Seymour Simon. Copyright © 1989 by Seymour Simon. Reprinted by permission of HarperCollins Publishers.

"Wilder, Laura Ingalls" from *The World Book Encyclopedia*. Copyright © 2000 by World Book Inc. By permission of the publisher. www.worldbook.com.

Electronic Illustrations

Function Thru Form

Photography

Page 203:

A. Steve Liss for Time for Kids

B. Courtesy Hillside Intermediate School

C. Courtesy Hillside Intermediate School

D. Ann States/SABA for Time for Kids

E. Nina Berman/Sipa

F. The Jackson Citizen Patriot

G. Phillip Greenberg for Time for Kids

H. Lori Cross/Nuckols Farm Elementary School

I. Phillip Greenberg for Time for Kids

J. no credit

K. Richard Harbus

L. MH Photography

M. Mike Mullen/San Gabriel Valley Newspaper/AP

N. Bill Kostroun/AP

O. Brian Diggs/AP

P. Freddi Jacobi

Q. Ann States/SABA for Time for Kids

R. no credit

S. Steve Liss for Time for Kids

Artville: 21, 63, 147, 164, 180, 181, 247, 278, 284, 286, 321, 335, 337, 442, 479.

Christie's Images: 44, Jose Gulio Souza Pinto; 380, Gonzalo Endara Crow.

Colonial Williamsburg Foundation: 365.

Corbis Images: 149, 411, 418-419.

Corbis Sygma: 86-87, Erich Schlegel.

Bob Daemmrich: 89, 99, 110-111, 287, 299, 422, 429, 430, 431.

Denver Photo Library, Western Historic Dept.: 27.

Digital Stock Pro: 92-93, 97, 350, 358, 423.

Fort Lewis College Center of Southwest Studies: 233.

FPG: 7, EJ West; 16-17, Walter Bibikow; 47, Telegraph Colour Library 1997; 122-123, Bruce Byers; 217, Dennie Cody 1995; 224, Kazik Pazovski; 342-343, Jeri Gleiter 1995; 420, Ken Chernus; 472-473, 479, 481.

Richard Hutchings: 3, 88, 107, 215, 251, 255, 285, 437.

The Image Bank: 19, David De Lossy; 90, Carol Kohen; 101, Andrea Pistolesi; 132, Grant V. Faint; 141, Benn Mitchell; 171, Steve Allen; 187, P. Goetgheluck; 190-191, Guido Rossi; 199, Elle Schuster; 267, Sean Justice; 271, Steve Satushek; 279, Florian Franke; 295, Joseph Savant; 296, Kaz Mori; 341, Carolyn Brown; 344-345, James Carmichael; 352-353, Mahaux Photo; 427, David De

(Acknowledgments continued on page 624.)

Lossy; 436-437, Kaz Mori; 441, Chuck Place.

Image Club: 417.

The Image Works: 45, Bob Daemmrich; 303, Stuart Cohen.

Ken Karp Photography: 108,109, 134,138, 142, 146, 148, 220, 222, 228, 232, 234, 308, 310, 316, 320, 386, 389, 394, 398, 400, 469, 474, 478, 480, 486.

Lawrence Migdale: 2-3.

Liason International: 381, Paul S. Howell.

Library of Congress: 478

Monkmeyer: 2; 11, Grantpix; 22, Dollarhide; 96, Menke; 101, Forbert; 141, Gottlieb; 146, Gottlieb; 146-147, Gottlieb; 160, Zimbel; 184, Rue; 185, Rue; 211, Forsyth; 276-277, Goodwin; 280, Conklin; 421, Smith; 430, Renate Hiller; 440, Lanks;

Nebraska State Historical Society: 227, 233.

Photo Researchers: 4, Vera Bradshaw; 5, Renee Lynn; 8, Stephen Dalton; 10, Richard Hutchings; 17, Jeff Greenberg; 23, Carolyn A. McKeone; 37, Joyce Photographics; 57, Mark D. Phillips; 84-085, Ted Kerasate 1987; 92, David M. Grossman; 94, Lawrence Migdale; 95, Blair Seltz; 100, Rainer Berg/Okapia; 103, Tim Davis; 105, Richard Hutchings; 106, Lawrence Migdale; 178, Lawrence Migdale; 183, Rosenfeld Images Ltd./Science Photo Library; 264, Tim Davis; 268, George Holton; 281, Bachman; 297, Renee Lynn; 303, Richard Hutchings; 359, NASA/Science Photo Library; 374, Michael P. Gadamski; 398, Bruce M. Herman; 399, Patrick Vielcanet; 401, Duomo-Vandystadt, Photo by David Madison; 424, Richard R. Hansen; 425, Stephen Dalton; 434, Elaine Nettis; 457, David Weintraub 1993;

Photodisc: 18, 28, 48, 75, 77, 79, 81, 83, 91, 159, 174-175, 175, 182, 184-185, 192, 193, 198, 245, 249, 266, 272, 274, 275, 282, 333, 335, 349, 352, 354, 362-363, 413, 426-427, 428, 432, 433, 438, 491, 493, 495.

PhotoEdit: 15, Myrleen Ferguson; 16, Rudi Von Briel; 29, David Young-Wolff; 41, Mary Kate Denny; 45, Myrleen Ferguson; 62, Myrleen Ferguson; 98, Amy C. Etra; 102, John Neubauer; 104, Richard Hutchings; 122, David Young-Wolff; 129, Myrleen Ferguson; 129, Richard Hutchings; 163, Bill Bachman; 167, Dennis MacDonald; 170, Myrleen Ferguson; 177, Myrleen Ferguson;179, Stephen McBrady; 181, Tony Freeman; 207, Myrleen Ferguson; 209, Michael Newmann; 215, J. Nourok; 253, Felicia Martinez; 262, Michael Newman; 263, Tony Freeman; 263, Tony Freeman; 283, Tony Freeman; 347, Michael Newman; 351, David Young-Wolff; 355, Michael Newman; 373, Jonathan Nourox; 381, Tony Freeman; 439, Michael Newman; 442-443, Spencer Grant; 454, Spencer Grant; 463, David Young-Wolff.

Phototake/P. Arnold: 37.

Science Museum/Science and Society Picture Library: 344.

Stock Boston: 38, Randy Duchaine 89; 39, D.R. Stoecklein 97; 113, John Scheiber; 121, Mug Shots 1995; 125, Roy Morsch; 188, Miro Vintoniuv; 189, Miro Vintoniuv; 208, Carlos Dominquez; 235, Mug Shots 1994; 338, Charles Krebs 89; 307, Ronnie Kaufman 99; 354, Michael Heron; 356, Gordon R. Gainer 1996; 384, Michele Burgess 1994; 461, Miro Vintoniv.

Super Stock: 128, Pieter Brueghel, the elder/Bridgeman Art Library; 302, Calvin Hunt/Lowe Museum U of Miami; 460, Tsing-Fang Chen/Lucia Gallery, NYC.

Tony Stone Images: 219; xvi-1, Schafer & Hill; 9, Art Wolfe; 13, Lorne Resnick; 24, Spike Walker; 25, David Young-Wolff; 65, Stuart Westmorland; 125, John Darling; 168-169, Johnny Johnson; 172, Howard Grey; 173, Kevin Schafer; 186, Charles Sleicher; 190, Art Wolfe; 194, Rohan; 195, Glen Allison; 196-197, Darryl Torckler; 260-261, Frank Oberle; 264-265, Tom Bean; 269, Lori Adamski Peek; 273, Manoj Shah; 315, Peter Cade; 320, Dennis O'Clair; 321, Dennis O'Clair; 346, Lori Adamski Peek; 357, Don Smetzer; 360, Bruce Forster; 361, Gary Yeowell; 363, Kerrick James Photography; 375, Daniel J. Cox; 377, Jim Stamates; 383, Tony Latham; 392-393, Kim Heacox; 398-399, Monica Dalmasso; 401, Art Wolfe; 415, Hawkins/TSI Imaging; 445, Paul Souders; 455, Robert E. Daemmrich; 461, Art Wolfe; 464, David Muench; 497, Daniel J. Cox; 499, Charles Thatcher.

Wilder Lane Home and Museum/Laura Ingalls Wilder-Rose: 453.

Wyoming Division of Cultural Resources: 232-233.

Cover Photo
Mike Moran/Index Stock Imagery

Cover Design and Illustration
Robert Brook Allen

The 6 Trait Writing rubric materials in this work use the Six Trait Writing criteria, as defined by the Northwest Regional Educational Laboratory. For more information, visit its website at www.nwrel.org.